ASCENDANCY AND TRADITION IN ANGLO-IRISH LITERARY HISTORY FROM 1789 TO 1939

ASCENDANCY AND TRADITION

IN ANGLO-IRISH LITERARY HISTORY FROM 1789 TO 1939

W. J. Mc Cormack

CLARENDON PRESS · OXFORD

1985

Oxford University Press, Walton Street, Oxford OX2 6DP

London New York Toronto
Delhi Bombay Calcutta Madras Karachi
Kuala Lumpur Singapore Hong Kong Tokyo
Nairobi Dar es Salaam Cape Town
Melbourne Auckland

and associated companies in
Beirut Berlin Ibadan Mexico City Nicosia

Oxford is a trade mark of Oxford University Press

Published in the United States
by Oxford University Press, New York

British Library Cataloguing in Publication Data

McCormack, W.J.
Ascendancy and traditions in Anglo-Irish
literary history from 1789 to 1939.
1. English literature — Irish authors —
History and criticism
I. Title
820.9'9415   PR8750

ISBN 0 19 812806 1

Set by Grestun Graphics, Abingdon, Oxon
Printed in Great Britain
at the Alden Press, Oxford

For
Seamus Deane

'Here's fine revolution, an we had the trick to see it.'

(*Hamlet*)

'One must have tradition in oneself, to hate it properly'.

(Theodor Adorno)

ACKNOWLEDGEMENTS

Several parts of this book have appeared in print or have been delivered as papers at conferences and seminars, usually in slightly different forms from those incorporated here. 'The Birth of Ascendancy' was read to the 1981 University of Essex conference on the sociology of literature, and is included here by kind permission of the conference committee. My analysis of *The Absentee* had its origins in a seminar paper read in the School of English, University of Leeds in 1978; Professor John O. Mc Cormick of Rutgers University made a number of very useful comments on that early draft. The discussion of James Joyce expands on a paper prepared for the Joyce centenary conference at the University of Leeds — that paper was published in *James Joyce and Modern Literature* (ed. W. J. Mc Cormack and A. J. Stead, published by Routledge and Kegan Paul, 1982). As guest editor of *Crane Bag* Seamus Deane published versions of the two accounts of W. B. Yeats, and I am grateful for his advice and co-operation in shaping and reshaping them.

Much of the material covered by *Ascendancy and Tradition* has, over the years, formed the basis for discussion in my post-graduate seminar in the School of English, University of Leeds. I owe a debt of friendship and support to all the students who have taken part in my weekly airing of these problems and obsessions. Though I recognize the self-defeating quality of such lists, I also want to thank many good friends for their support and encouragement — Christopher Cassin, Neil Cornwell, Declan D'Estelle Roe, David Dickson, Kate Flint, Teri Garvey, Mary King, Sean O'Hagan, Sarah Ward-Perkins, and John Woods. At the appropriate points in my annotations, I acknowledge debts to Professor J. C. Beckett, Arthur Harwood Grayson, Professor R. B. McDowell, and William O'Sullivan for their assistance in matters of detail. The errors which remain are my responsibility and my pretext for further work in the field.

A grant from the Una Ellis-Fermor memorial fund, administered from the University of London, enabled me to travel from Leeds to Ireland during the writing of parts of this book. I am happy to acknowledge this assistance together with vacation grants from the School of English, University of Leeds, provided throughout the years of my teaching there.

W. J. Mc C.

CONTENTS

A NOTE ON SOURCES AND REFERENCES

As the vast majority of the references in this book refer to standard editions of well-known authors, and as manuscripts or other inaccessible material have not been used to any extent, I have decided to dispense with the conventional billboard 'bibliography' — all too often a form of vanity in any case. The first citation of each printed work is accompanied with a full note of publication details, and these references are reflected in the index.

Postcript: While this book was in production, two definitive editions of important texts were published. With reference to Hans Walter Gabler's *Ulysses*, I have taken the opportunity of checking at proof-stage my quotations against this text — James Joyce, *Ulysses: A Critical and Synoptic Edition*, 3 vols (New York, London: Garland, 1984) — while leaving my footnote references as they stood. Thus the reader can easily check the context of my quotation against the more readily available Penguin edition. With reference to Richard Finneran's W. B. Yeats *The Poems: A New Edition* (New York: Macmillan, 1983), I have used this edition for the text of 'The Curse of Cromwell' (see pp. 243–4, where the reasons for this decision will be discernible), but have otherwise referred to the 1963 Macmillan edition still generally available.

Clemson, SC

INTRODUCTION: AGAINST DEFINITIONS

> The last thing one discovers when writing
> a work is what one should put first.
>
> (Blaise Pascal)[1]

The emergence of Anglo-Irish literature lies close to the heart of European romanticism. The Anglo-Irish Renaissance is central to modernist literature in the English language. With these two perspectives in mind I have tried here to describe the functioning of two crucial concepts in my own cultural heritage — the sociological formation of 'Protestant Ascendancy', and the Yeatsian elaboration of an Irish literary 'tradition'.

The task has not been easy. If all the books ever written on the subject were laid end-to-end in a straight line they would on the instant curl into the shape of a question-mark. On the one hand venerable and respectable, on the other a kind of post-war phenomenon not unconnected to Marshall Aid, Anglo-Irish literature slips between the categories to defy definition, indeed perhaps to question the very notion of definition in this area. The bibliography is exhausting and it grows annually, yet the subject is as much obscured as clarified by these additional studies: bright lights cast dark shadows. Every speculative study of Joyce throws Yeats into isolated relief; every close analysis of a poem by Yeats is eloquently silent on the totalities in which the poem may properly be seen; every account of the Abbey Theatre raises unspoken questions about the Renaissance and its coolness towards the novel. In *Ascendancy and Tradition* I have attempted to deal with Yeats and Joyce as mutually defining figures within the totalities which historical as well as literary critical analysis

---

[1] See Blaise Pascal, *Pensées* (London: Dent, 1960), p. 3 (No. 8); I have preferred the translation provided by Philip Thody in his translation of Lucien Goldmann, *The Hidden God: A Study of Tragic Vision in the* Pensées *of Pascal and the Tragedies of Racine* (London: Routledge and Kegan Paul, 1964), p. 6.

depends upon.[2] Yet while committed to a whole view of
Anglo-Irish literature, a view which acknowledges its social
existence, I resist the pressures which would establish the
Anglo-Irish 'thing' as not just a literature but a national
literature — if not indeed a culture or even a civilization.[3]
With such an escalation of dignity comes a concomitant intensity of feeling, feeling often prescribing rules of exclusion —
'Robert Graves (or Samuel Beckett) is not Irish' — or turning
into elegiac celebrations of a dubious past — Yeats as a young
boy in his 'native' Sligo.

   This tendency to become personal about the subject is not
merely a sign of the critic's individual attachment, it is an
indicator of a deeply rooted problem at the centre of the
Anglo-Irish phenomenon. 'The time is coming fast, if it isn't
already here, when the question, "Is So-and-So really an Irish
writer?" will clear a room in seconds.'[4] In this manner did
Derek Mahon commence an assessment of Louis MacNeice
some years ago. The significant feature of this characteristic
self-scrutiny is not Mr Mahon's very proper contempt for the
naïvety of such inquiries, it is the evidently social occasion
on which they arise — clear a room in seconds. For, if Anglo-
Irish literature is a difficult animal to classify, it has also long
been the subject of wondering conversation, anecdote, and
gossip, the locus of an advanced tourism. Here again, the
implications are not simply of innocent vulgarity or the bar-
room availability of a provincial wisdom; in a larger context,

   [2] It may help the reader if I point to the concept of totality as employed by
Georg Lukács in *History and Class Consciousness*, trans. Rodney Livingstone
(London: Merlin Press, 1971), as underpinning much of the argument that follows.
See, in particular, 'Whatever the subject of debate, the dialectical method is
concerned always with the same problem: knowledge of the historical process in
its entirety. This means that "ideological" and "economic" problems lose their
mutual exclusiveness and merge into one another ... The approach of literary
history is the one best suited to the problems of history' (p. 34).
   [3] This escalation is quite explicit in T. R. Henn's writings on Anglo-Irish
literature, which are deeply coloured by the experience of his own family. It is
more surprising to find it at work in F. S. L. Lyons, *Culture and Anarchy in
Ireland 1890–1939* (Oxford: Clarendon Press, 1979), pp. 20, 94, etc. Of course,
this book virtually announces a political programme for Ulster based on the
'cultures' of denominations and quasi-national groups.
   [4] Derek Mahon, 'MacNeice in England and Ireland', in Terence Brown and
Alec Reid (edd.), *Time was Away: The World of Louis MacNeice,* (Dublin:
Dolmen Press, 1974), p. 113.

the argument in favour of an Anglo-Irish civilization leads towards specific attitudes to sectarian violence in Ulster and its place in the politics of the United Kingdom. Like Shakespeare, Yeats is full of quotations, and too many of them have recently been employed as the titles of novels and improving tracts on Irish sociology. Doubtless, a high proportion of these works have dealt with 'the Ulster question', but too often the apt quotation and the beguiling cadence are not employed to do more than confirm a satisfying eccentricity in the topic. Investigating my own cultural heritage (as I suggested at the outset), I have found it more illuminating to see it as part of what Theodor Adorno has termed 'the culture industry' than of Celtic–Anglican civilization. Nor is there summer school but singing monuments of its own magnificence.

The literature itself incorporates much conversation and gossip, the exploits of ward politicians, society belles, 'what the butler Said to a drunken game-keeper In mid-October', the careers of real statesmen, 'strong men, and thieves, and deacons' whose names may be traced in *Who's Who*, Stubb's *Gazette*, or some similar directory.[5] There is an important difference to be drawn between Standish O'Grady and Madame Sosostris as they are rendered in poems by Yeats and Eliot respectively: to declare them both figures of poetic mythology is to impose a blanket term on the unique processes of composition of each poet and, perhaps more damagingly, on the very different social relations within the United Kingdom which locate the work of the two writers. It is not enough simply to remark, as a characteristic of Irish society, that it abounded in 'characters' who required no invention. Such notions take on a different tone if we reflect that it is only with this assimilation into art that O'Grady acquires a degree of coherence. Is not *Toryism and the Tory Democracy* (O'Grady's tract of 1886) effectively read through the prism of 'Beautiful Lofty Things' whereby the significance of that conjuncture of Celticism, contempt for 'the Protestant Ascendancy', and violent rhetoric is refined to 'high nonsensical

⁵ J. M. Synge, 'Preface', in Robin Skelton (ed.), *Collected Works*, vol. i, *Poetry* (London: Oxford University Press, 1962), p. xxxvi.

words'.[6] In the Irish experience, art does not exploit reality; it completes, perhaps concludes it. The dealings between these hypostasized values, art and reality, are prominent and complex in Anglo-Irish literature: each is at times evidently obliged to masquerade as the other. Here indeed is a central problem which lures the scholar-pilgrim towards Sligo — the works he has chosen to read and celebrate, while they are intensely concerned with society and politics, with conversation and rhetoric, are also deeply secretive, arcane, and (in some people's view) wilfully obscure.

The Irish, or the Ulster, experience is a cave-drama of considerable popularity in recent years, but attempts to define it strongly resemble attempts to authenticate it. Professor Denis Donoghue, to whom I shall be indebted continuously in the pages that follow, illustrates in a penetrating exercise in defining this experience the attendant risks. There are two significant moments:

The real trouble in Ireland is that our national experience has been too limited to be true. Since the Plantation of Ulster there has been one story and one story only in Irish feeling: the English, how to get rid of them, or, failing that, to circumvent them, cajole them, twist their tails. Our categories of feeling are therefore flagrantly limited; our history has been at once intense and monotonous. We have had no industrial revolution, no factory acts, no trade union movement: hence the frail basis upon which our Labour Party exists, by contrast with the two major parties which still define themselves in terms of our civil war. A limited history, a correspondingly intimidating mythology, a fractured language, a literature of fits and starts and gestures: no continuity from one age to the next. Irish novelists, the few who survive, feel the anxiety of influence but not the incitement or the challenge of a tradition.[7]

Denis Donoghue's distinctive skills are not engaged here. That is, the historical summary he offers is not really the product of the mind which elaborated his masterly account of Yeats.[8]

[6] W. B. Yeats, 'Beautiful Lofty Things', *Collected Poems* (London: Macmillan, 1963), p. 348. Note that all of Yeats's work — I use the poetry as an example — prior to *The Tower* (1928) was written while he lived in the United Kingdom of Great Britain and Ireland.
[7] Denis Donoghue, 'Being Irish Together', *The Sewanee Review*, vol. 84 (Winter 1976), p. 131.
[8] Denis Donoghue, *Yeats* (Modern Masters Series) n. p.; Fontana, 1971.

The assumptions he makes, however, have a representative status. 'National experience' indiscriminately labels semi-feudalism in pre-plantation Ulster and romantic politics in the nineteenth century, as if the word 'nation' had not changed greatly in the intervening centuries. To argue that Ireland had no industrial revolution, it is necessary to ignore Belfast and the Lagan valley, to go no further. To deny factory laws, you deny Belfast and the statute books of the United Kingdom.[9] The truth is that such a view of Irish history is itself a mythology, not simply because it gets specific facts wrong, but because it reads back into the past the truncated success of bourgeois nationalism in twenty-six counties of Ireland, cavalierly ignoring the historical actuality of the United Kingdom of Great Britain and Ireland in the nineteenth century, and compensating for the 'loss' of Belfast and Ulster by a denial of their previous existence.

The second moment from Professor Donoghue's essay comes near the end of the piece:

It is common to have the experience and miss the meaning . . . it is my impression that Irish writers sense a rift between experience and meaning, but in reverse: the meaning is premature, already inscribed by a mythology they have no choice but to inherit, and the experience is too narrow to be entirely natural and representative.[10]

Here I find the narrowness of the earlier passage entirely enlightened and accepted, and a number of consequences can be noted. The priority of meaning over experience for Irish writing is one way of observing a tendency towards allegory in certain large areas of nineteenth-century fiction. The same proposition might be stated conversely as the tendency towards *abstract* experience in this colonial fiction, a tendency we shall trace in some work by Maria Edgeworth, Sheridan Le Fanu, and — to a lesser extent — Charles Lever.

Ascendancy and Tradition is not intended to rival the various sequential histories and personal guides to Anglo-Irish

---

[9] Some legislation in this area was restricted by region and hence excluded Ireland, but there were specific acts relating to Ireland also. This tendency to legislate for industry on a regional basis was probably more characteristic of the first half of the nineteenth century rather than the years 1850–1921.
[10] 'Being Irish Together', pp. 132–3.

literature recently published.[11] Basically, what follows takes
its bearing from the development of modernism out of the
break-up of the romantic proposition in the nineteenth
century. Nineteenth-century realism lent credence to the
theory of literature as an imitation of reality. The mass of
Irish writing in this period, however, rested upon a confusion
of romantic assumption and naïve reportage. Politics, saturated in such assumptions, took its shape from a concern
with the past: the past, conceived in terms of expropriation,
legitimized a growing obsession with land. Thus, the increasingly bourgeois nature of Irish political activity could
yet be presented as the driving home of ancient rights, the
reassertion of some Gaelic nobility in revenant form. The
novel took the fundamental shape of this view of history and
rendered it fabulous.

Historians have a rather different story to tell, indeed they
have many stories to tell, not all of them reconcilable one
with another. Oliver MacDonagh has indicated a number of
important areas in which early nineteenth-century Ireland
saw the commencement of an experiment in administration
conducted ultimately from Westminster and through Dublin.
In local and municipal government, public order (policing),
and social welfare Ireland was for much of the century at
least formally more advanced than Britain.[12] No doubt the
vision of Ireland as a social laboratory might become as
cloudy as the nationalist stereotype or the fictional convention. But if we add to MacDonagh's argument some consideration of the complex organization of land purchase and the
growth of joint stock company investment later in the
century, we begin to see that Ireland was not metaphysically
different from the West Country or Wolverhampton.[13] If this
sounds like latter-day historical revisionism, we should note

[11]   Roger McHugh and Maurice Harmon, *Short History of Anglo-Irish Litera-
ture from its Origins to the Present Day* (Dublin: Wolfhound Press, 1982); A.
Norman Jeffares, *Anglo-Irish Literature* (London: Macmillan; Dublin: Gill and
Macmillan, 1982); Alan Warner, *A Guide to Anglo-Irish Literature* (New York: St
Martin's Press; Dublin: Gill and Macmillan, 1981).

[12]   Oliver MacDonagh, *Ireland: The Union and its Aftermath.* (London: Allen
and Unwin, 1977), esp. the second chapter, pp. 35-52.

[13]   For Ireland as 'social laboratory' see W. L. Burn, 'Free Trade in Land: An
Aspect of the Irish Question', *Transactions of the Royal Historical Society*, 4th
series, vol. 31; also MacDonagh, op. cit., and Lyons, op. cit., pp. 9-10.

how, in 1837, an anonymous critic seeking to define what Anglo-Irish literature might be, lamented the necessity of Irish participation in the changes determined by the more advanced economy of Britain — and this in the columns of the *Dublin University Magazine*, flagship of that cultural conservatism which nurtured Samuel Ferguson, Isaac Butt, and Sheridan Le Fanu![14] Unionism which resents Union is not simply a demonstration of Irish incorrigibility; it is, as my first chapter aims to demonstrate, a fundamental romantic dichotomy in the political structure of the United Kingdom between 1801 and 1920. Indeed, in the United Kingdom as modified in 1920 by the Government of Ireland Act, the dichotomy persists with a modernist aura of violence and indifference.[15]

If nineteenth-century Ireland is fundamentally relatable to England, and to Britain generally, why is it that in the area of cultural production the relationships are suppressed more often than expressed? The central issue here concerns Ireland's complex role as metropolitan colony within the United Kingdom. In relation to the Empire overseas — the army in India is an instance in point — Ireland was part of the metropolitan 'home country'; in relation to that home *economy* it was in significant ways itself colonial. Much might be written on that issue in political, social, and economic terms; but in a basically cultural context, answers to the question of suppressed relations between Ireland and the rest of the United Kingdom may be gathered under three headings. The first of these is the nationalist mythology of ahistorical uniqueness, a proposition which might have

[14] 'Past and Present State of Literature in Ireland', *The Dublin University Magazine*, vol. 9, No. 52 (March 1837), pp. 365-76. I discuss some aspects of this anonymous article (probably written by Isaac Butt) and its attempt to define Anglo-Irish literature in 'J. Sheridan Le Fanu's "Richard Marston" (1848): The History of an Anglo-Irish Text', in Francis Barker *et al.* (edd.), *1848. The Sociology of Literature* (Chelmsford: University of Essex, 1978), pp. 107-25, esp. pp. 108-11.

[15] In a sense this work relates to southern Ireland rather than to all of Ireland in the period after 1921; in this respect, it postpones the issue of relating partition to cultural production. For the background see Liam de Paor, *Divided Ulster* (Harmondsworth: Penguin, 1970); Michael Farrell, *Northern Ireland: The Orange State* (London: Pluto Press, 1976); Henry Patterson, *Class Conflict and Sectarianism* (Belfast: Blackstaff Press, 1980).

achieved validity if the fate of the Irish language in the past one hundred and fifty years had been other than it was. The second emphasizes the distinctive Catholicism of the Irish population within the British Isles — Daniel Corkery is the chief advocate here — and this sectarian difference can only strain belief if it is also employed to isolate Irish culture from Europe.

A third, more specifically literary answer absorbs these two and effectively sets them up as a mutual cancellation — the third answer may be called Yeatsian tradition. Yet while Yeats's theoretical constructions use the bricks and mortar of literary terminology, they serve to house diverse ideological interests. In rather more *ad hominem* terms, this third answer lies in the extent to which critics of Anglo-Irish literature have derived their historiography from W. B. Yeats. Yeats, of course, was only one of several late nineteenth-century voices who propounded a view of Ireland as more venerable, traditional, and spiritual than degenerate England — though all were perhaps laggard in acknowledging their debt to British exemplars such as Carlyle and Arnold. The proposition that Yeatsian tradition has unacknowledged British debts might be rewritten as a measure of the extent to which Yeats is the concentrated statement — significantly in *literary* terms — of a dominant historiography rooted in both British and Irish aspects of nineteenth-century experience. The Anglo-Irish Renaissance, the Irish genius for words, is not solely a product of native soil.

Of the figures besides Yeats, Standish James O'Grady is taken here to mediate between this Victorian wisdom and the imminent 'Cuchullainoid' mythology of the Renaissance.[16] Beyond anything which might be ascribed to Yeats's influence there lies a further and more pervasive force — the notion that, whatever the stock exchange or the statistics of food production and exports might say, Ireland had a distinctive if not unique social structure, the crowning feature of which was the Protestant Ascendancy. The mysteries of the Protestant

[16] 'A purely fantastic, unmodern, ideal, breezy, springdayish, Cuchullainoid National Theatre' — in a draft of a letter from J. M. Synge to Stephen MacKenna, c.1904; see Ann Saddlemyer (ed.), 'Synge to MacKenna: The Mature Years', *Massachusetts Review*, vol. 5, No. 2 (Winter 1964), pp. 279–95, at p. 281.

Ascendancy, to which J. M. Synge, Lady Gregory, and W. B. Yeats variously adhered, were such that outsiders could do no better than take it on trust. And essential to the viability of this concept was the complementary notion that Ireland had no middle class. In Victorian England, when the aristocracy was adopting bourgeois ways, and the labouring classes were urged to adopt the *mores* (but not the financial expectations) of their betters, this alleged absence of an Irish middle class effectively silenced a comparative study of Irish and British culture. Moreover, while Irish industrialization and urban development should not be written off as nonexistent, it is still true that in Britain middle-class behaviour was increasingly associated with the life of the towns while Ireland saw itself as a rural community with incidental conurbations.

In the second part of Chapter Two, I analyse at length the emergence of the term 'Protestant Ascendancy' in the context of revolutionary alarm in the 1790s. In due course Yeats's use of it to indicate the governing élite in Ireland from the Williamite Settlement (1697) onwards. This is only one anomalous aspect of Protestant Ascendancy, its being back-dated before the moment of its coinage as a phrase to provide an encapsulated history of the eighteenth century *in toto*. There is another, even more striking anomaly between the quasi-aristocratic connotations of the Yeatsian usage and the distinctly mercantile and urban surroundings of the phrase's coinage in the vicinity of the Common Council of Dublin Corporation. Some stages of the evolution of the 1790s neologism into the timeless language of Augustan élitism are provided in the chapter called 'Mid-Century Perspectives': this evolution, though important in itself, is less significant than the negotiation between the sociological formation calling itself 'The Protestant Ascendancy' and the ideological construction of an eighteenth-century hegemony of the same name. From this contradiction, rather than from any mechanical causality in the families of Yeats and Synge and Lady Gregory, derives the modernist, valorized tradition associated with their names.

Joyce stands apart. Or at least, that is the traditional placing of Joyce *vis-à-vis* Yeats and the Protestant Ascendancy. Here,

an attempt is made to relate Joyce's *petit-bourgeois* inheritance to the suppression of middle-class evidences in Irish
Protestantism. Ironically, some attention to the development
of the novel in nineteenth-century Ireland can uncover a
fictional prologue to Joyce's great innovations. For example,
though the absence of a middle class was accepted tacitly on
the western shore of the Irish Sea, in the 1840s (when
Anthony Trollope was as productive of novels set in Ireland
as Sheridan Le Fanu) the author of *The Kellys and the
O'Kellys* (1848) perceived a more recognizably bourgeois
Ireland than any of his Irish contemporaries, Charles Lever
included. Later, it is true that Lever (in such a novel as
Barrington) did attend to the life of the Irish bourgeoisie but
he evidently needed the security of German *biedermeier*
sentiment to feel at ease in his task. Lever, it might be observed in passing, is a proto-modernist at least in his choice
of prolonged exile on the Continent. His novel of 1865,
Luttrell of Arran, provides us with an early instance of the
Irish modernist concern with 'Celtic' primitivism. Whereas
these Irish novelists of the Victorian period — Le Fanu,
Lever, Kickham, Moore, Somerville and Ross — employed
structures in which a polarization between castle and cabin
characterized their reflection of society, extended analyses of
two novels by Maria Edgeworth (who is so much closer in
time to the origins of Protestant Ascendancy ideology) show
how this polarization is shaken with irony, energized more by
desire than achievement.

Irony and desire — these are terms more usually conjoined
in discussion of James Joyce's fiction than in, say, an account
of that neglected novel, *The Absentee.* But the political function of Protestant Ascendancy in the first decades of the
nineteenth century was specifically sectarian — the granting
of priority to a sectarian sociology over and above reformist
administration and incipient democracy. The sectarian
strategy soon articulated rival statements of Irish history
which *together* constituted the romantic reformulation of the
past. In Joyce we discover manifestly one of these histories,
that of the Irish Catholic lower middle classes, urbanized, yet
still traumatized by the devastation of the countryside in
mid-century. The Joyce we discover will be the inheritor of

that disaster, the passing of the Irish language which he is so often thought to have discounted. It is with Joyce that we encounter the ironies of tradition in that he therapeutically enacts in his life's work those repressions which otherwise would have remained repressed, untreated, ascendant. For the violence of a bifurcated history has its sexual as well as political register; and Joyce's *œuvre* (for all the celebrated fissures and discontinuities of his individual texts) offers a vision of an ultimate, if historically postponed wholeness. For this reason, Joyce is the only author here whose work is treated in all its major textual forms.

A contrast between Joyce and Yeats is generally understood: a sustained comparison is less often encountered. If Joyce posits a psychic wholeness (qualified by the historical determinants of his time) Yeats offers Unity of Being. The former lies ostensibly in the future, the latter ostensibly in the past. In the case of Yeats, I offer an approach through the medium of a concept central to the poem 'Nineteen Hundred and Nineteen', the concept of Public Opinion. To this evolution of a concept employed by Yeats in a single poem is added another approach in which the modernist concern with Oedipal conflict conditions the transmission of inherited, 'traditional' Gaelic material, conditions indeed the very fibres of poetic and dramatic form. The drama offers particular advantages for this inquiry — the explicitly multivocal form of expression, the accessible fissures between set and dialogue, setting and allusion, et cetera. Yeatsian tradition ought to lead one to 'The Words upon the Window-Pane', in which the playwright's predilection for cultural heroes made Jonathan Swift manifest through a spiritualist medium in latter-day Dublin. It is doubtless true that 'The Words upon the Window-Pane' draws Yeats's Augustan constructs into play with the filthy modern tide, yet in detailing the *late* eighteenth-century origins of Protestant Ascendancy I find 'Purgatory' to be the more revealing drama. If, as I argue, 'Purgatory' is not only based on what Donald Torchiana has called Yeats's 'theory of the symbolic tragedy of the eighteenth century' but is directly related to that dangerous intersection of modernist aesthetics and totalitarian politics, then an analysis of the play may serve to indicate — however briefly — an area for further inquiry, the place of Protestant Ascendancy ideology in the broader field of European racism.[17]

I take Protestant Ascendancy to be the central cultural assumption of Yeats's meditation on his own inheritance. By it he measured the politics of the Irish Free State; by reference to it, he performed in his *Autobiographies* remarkable transformations of his social experience of the nineteenth century; by celebration of it he brought his own life's work into creative relationship with that of Jonathan Swift, George Berkeley, Oliver Goldsmith, and Edmund Burke. In his exhaustive and valuable study of these relationships, Donald Torchiana has paid tribute to T. R. Henn's account of the Anglo-Irish background in *The Lonely Tower*. Henn, however, is more exegete than critic and nothing better illustrates the debt owed to (or distortion traceable to) Yeats's own reading of history: looking at once at the nineteenth century *in toto* and the early 1920s in isolation, Henn saw that

everywhere the Big House, with its estates surrounding it, was a centre of hospitality, of county life and society, apt to breed a passionate attachment, so that the attempt to save it from burning or bankruptcy became an obsession (in the nineteen twenties and onwards) when that civilization was passing . . . To this society, in the main Protestant, Unionist, and of the 'Ascendancy' in character, the peasantry was linked. The great demesnes had their tenantry, proud, idle, careless, kindly, with a richness of speech and folk-lore that Lady Gregory had been the first to record. The days of *Castle Rackrent* were, in the main, over; the relationship between landlord and tenant varied, but was on the whole a kindly one, and carried a good deal of respect on either side.[18]

---

[17] I use 'racism' to cover all those ideologies which utilize differences of inheritance or belief to create valorized social categories, usually to the end of obliterating or suppressing class interests and conflicts. Nazism is not only the most obvious example but also possesses an articulate intellectual apologetics, for an analysis of which see George L. Mosse, *The Crisis of German Ideology: Intellectual Origins of the Third Reich* (New York: Grosset and Dunlap, 1964; repr. Schocken Books, 1981). For an immediate British context in which the ideology of Irish sectarianism may be read, see Martin Barker, *The New Racism: Conservatives and the Ideology of the Tribe* (London: Junction Books, 1981).

[18] T. R. Henn, *The Lonely Tower: Studies in the Poetry of W. B. Yeats*, 2nd, rev. ed. (London: Methuen, 1965), p. 7.

From the notion of the 'the Big House', Henn is led on to
evoke idyllic social relations in which matters of estate
management, rates of interest, toil itself, do not intrude. It is
true that taxes imposed from Westminster are accorded a
measure of responsibility for the decline of the estates, but
burning and bankruptcy remain magisterially unaccounted
for. The idyll existed before the 1920s, and this is a recurrent
Anglo-Irish complaint — the Golden Age always existed *before* some moveable disaster, before the Union, before the
Famine, before the Encumbered Estates Court, the Land
War, Parnell, the Rising, the Troubles, an accelerating succession of unfortunate falls each one briefly inaugurating
some (retrospectively acknowledged) idyll which is itself
soon dissolved by the next disaster. Ascendancy is the
principal medium by which this fleeting vision of a stable,
pre-lapsarian order is imposed on the insolence of fact and
circumstance. Expanding on the theme of 'Purgatory', Yeats
pointed with approval to Nazi legislation which allowed
(certain, Aryan) families to go on living where their ancestors
had lived — the background to such approval is not exclusively non-Irish.

But the staccato of mere legislated disaster in Ireland was
insufficient for Yeats's imagination; in place of Land Acts
and political demagogues, Yeats saw as the principal barrier
to the past the nineteenth century itself, beyond which lay —
he was to claim — the Irish Augustan age, 'that one Irish
century that escaped from darkness and confusion'.[19] Much
of the material discussed in the succeeding chapters focuses
on that barrier, but here we can note briefly a few details
of Yeats's Augustan age. Having escaped *from* darkness and
confusion, it was necessarily fated to end in, return to, some
such condition, darkness and confusion, the filthy modern
tide — it is important to record this qualification of Yeats's
exemption. The energies of his cyclical history generate a
dual perspective: with reference to the eighteenth century
Goldsmith is not only presented 'deliberately sipping at the
honey-pot of his mind', in 'The Seven Sages' his serene
response to the countryside is also gravely qualified:

---

[19] W. B. Yeats, *Explorations* (New York: Macmillan, 1962), p. 345.

> Oliver Goldsmith sang what he had seen,
> Roads full of beggars, cattle in the fields,
> But never saw the trefoil stained with blood,
> The avenging leaf those fields raised up against it.[20]

This return to violence, breaking down of order into disorder, is the acknowledgement of historical process by which Protestant Ascendancy is born — not among the pastoral beggars — but with avenging leaves and stained trefoils as its symbolic paraphernalia.

Despite this dual function which Goldsmith performs in Yeats's poem, the eighteenth-century figures of Yeats's mythology are too often read simply as heroes. One frequently hears that Swift (or Burke, or Yeats himself) is 'the father of Anglo-Irish literature', though in truth Walter Scott or Goethe may well have an equally valid claim at times to the title. Biological metaphors of this kind have an insidious effect in that they generate notions of a legitimizing family tree which distinguishes the Anglo-Irish writer *from* a larger context instead of locating him *in* it. Swift himself, writing about the Anglo-Scottish Union, drew attention to the absurdities which can arise from a metaphor which has supplanted, instead of moved, reality:

> Henceforward let no stateman dare
> A kingdom to a ship compare;
> Lest he should call our commonweal
> A vessel with a double keel.[21]

Such eighteenth-century sense should be applied drastically to the conceit of stormy love affair or unhappy marriage so often employed of Anglo-Irish relations, from the days of Swift himself to those of Seamus Heaney. Indeed the first step in defining Anglo-Irish literature must be to challenge such dominant metaphors. Once alerted to this unconscious tendency towards organicist assumptions, our critical debate may find it easier to admit that 'the Anglo-Irish writer' is a rhetorical shorthand for written texts which, in turn, stand in positive and potent relation to wider cultural structures.

[20] W. B. Yeats, *Collected Poems*, p. 237.
[21] 'On the Union', in Jonathan Swift, *Poetical Works* (London, 1866), vol. i, p. 68.

In that wider context Tradition is of course a familiar
enough concept. Having denied any crudely causal influence
of the Protestant Ascendancy on Yeatsian tradition, I should
also make it clear that the idea of tradition I associate with
Yeats is not simply that of sanctified continuity. The modernist interest in tradition is self-evidently ironic, and the
complexities of that interest may be traced in figures as
diverse as T. S. Eliot and Martin Heidegger as well as in the
fossil-history of the word's etymology. Hermeneutics, I
should immediately concede, lies well beyond the range of
the present inquiry, which will deal with the issue of tradition
strictly in its Yeatsian form. This is not to suggest that
Yeats's thought on this topic is of merely local interest, nor
to insinuate that it is merely a piece of obfuscating ideology
peddling distortions of an otherwise accessible and unsullied
past. It is a statement of certain continuities — in the nineteenth century crucially — which Yeats elsewhere denied.
And this contradiction between tradition and its material is
a further statement of the disjunction between an Irish local
literature and the European culture into which it cries out
for reinsertion.

We shall have need, therefore, of Eliot's wry comment that
'in English writing we seldom speak of tradition, though we
occasionally apply its name in deploring its absence.'[22] Nowadays, the Anglo-Irish tradition is cited so often that its
existence must be seriously in doubt. However, the notion of
Anglo-Irish literature is given an excessive stability by the
acceptance of tradition as accumulated and accumulating
succession. Just as ascendancy emerges to assert a condition
which is longed for protectively rather than possessed confidently, so (Eliot reminds us) tradition is a negative marker
in many of its citations. If we think spatially about Anglo-
Irish literature as the meeting ground of various directions
and forces — Gaelic culture and Celticism, English romaticism
and revolutionary alarm, bourgeois compensation and subversive allegory — we should consider tradition historically as
the (sometimes contradictory and violent) convergence of
readings, not of texts. Tradition as the convergence of

---

[22] 'Tradition and the Individual Talent', in *Selected Prose of T. S. Eliot,* ed.
Frank Kermode (London: Faber, 1975), p. 37.

readings, tradition as involving a 'Thou' — in Hans-Georg Gadamer's terms — is necessarily an active element in literary history. Less abstractly, my second initial epigraph states the proper corollary of this position.

An introduction should not only introduce to the readers the material which follows, it should also advise them of possible difficulties or surprises lying ahead. In this connection two particular problems will arise in the course of the present argument. First the accepted canon of Anglo-Irish literature will be subjected to new pressures, not only by the attention given to relatively unfamiliar books (*The Absentee*, for example) but by the deliberate fracture of the canonical text as such, a fracture embarked upon to release the covert readings within. For the Anglo-Irish enthusiast, both of these tactics may be uncomfortable, while the reader whose primary interest lies in literary history as a methodology may feel the time and space given to individual texts excessive. The first category of reader will lament the absence of George Moore and J. M. Synge and Samuel Beckett, while deploring the presence of Theodor Adorno, Walter Benjamin, and Georg Lukács. If both parties thought hard about their differences they might find common ground in the striking non-appearance of the great English critics — Leavis, Empson, Williams, and their disciples — who have had so remarkably little to say on the subject of Anglo-Irish literature.

The specifically *literary* history uncovered here can be summarized as romanticism and its transformation into modernism. The specifically *political* element of Anglo-Irish history is the Union and its modification after 1921. These are not hermetically separate. Romanticism adopts Union as symbolic, not so much of its transactions as of its aspirations, its desire; and that desire grows among the fragmented ruins of romanticism itself. Indeed, the symbol itself, with its transcendental, numinous harmony of object and meaning, becomes symbolic of the romantic aspiration. Thus, allegory, which Coleridge declared untenable for the English-speaking world, is particularly significant in the detection of those aspirations and desires in the cultural politics of the United Kingdom of Great Britain and Ireland. Allegory lays bare the absences, distances, and differences which constitute the only ground of desire. To speak of 'desire' in such a large context is not simply to invoke a particular school of continental philosophy, it is to draw attention to the pervasive language of sexuality which underpins conventionally accepted metaphors for Anglo-Irish relations, Anglo-Irish conflict, from Swift's 'Injured Lady' to Heaney's 'Act of Union'. Allegory is not a simple alternative to this violent romanticism: while it stresses division, it is found repeatedly to be a mode through which a series of radically alternative readings of texts suggest themselves. Those readings, of course, will not restrict themselves to the canonical texts *per se*, or even to literature conceived in symbolic terms; they are necessarily historical, uncompleted. And, in its incompleteness, Ireland itself may be found to be a larger arena than its entrenched defenders had realized.

1. ROMANTIC UNION: WORDSWORTH, IRELAND, AND *REFLECTIONS ON THE REVOLUTION IN FRANCE*

> There have been many antirevolutionary
> books written in favour of the Revol-
> ution. Burke has written a revolutionary
> book against the Revolution.
>
> (Novalis)[1]

One of the few generalizations in literary history which stands up to scrutiny is that romanticism is a European rather than an English or a French phenomenon. Given the close association of romanticism and nationalism, it is also a generalization which helps to broaden the basis of literary history from any self-defining local integrity. But if critics and commentators have learned that Goethe can shed light on Scott, and that Chateaubriand is not wholly irrelevant to an interest in Keats, the result has too often been a cosmopolitan indifference to the particular interactions of social and aesthetic concerns in Germany, France, and Britain. In place of the spurious relating of literature to social life which characterized the various national histories, the various literatures are subordinated to a Great Code which excludes all social life. It is not intended here to replace the well-worn legend that Anglo-Irish fiction is about the Big House and Anglo-Irish poetry about 'the discovery of the Gaelic past' with a synchrony in which Maria Edgeworth tangos with De Quincey. The dynamics of literary history do not accept the empirical distinction between concrete detail and abstraction, and text is not regarded as an inviolable sanctuary. If we subject *Reflections on the Revolution in France* to a species of stylistic analysis this is not to deny its political material but rather to extend our concern with that material to aspects which have too often been regarded as secondary. If metaphor is treated as

---

[1] Novalis (F. von Hardenberg), 'Fragmente', *Gesammelte Werke* (Zurich: Buhl, 1945), vol. ii, p. 36.

a form of politics, it goes without saying that the self-contained entity known as Ireland necessarily is reinserted in the complex relations of the romantic age.

Renowned from the outset for its influence in changing opinion, Burke's *Reflections* (1790) came to embody a fixed star in conservative ideology in the nineteenth century. Burke's impact on figures as diverse as Benjamin Disraeli and Alfred Tennyson and Matthew Arnold is but a further indicator of the continuity of that influence which is first measurable in the literary world through the novels of Jane Austen and Walter Scott. Augustan, romantic, Victorian . . . the fixity which Burke came to represent for generations of British thinkers is itself a movement of immediate political and cultural significance. Disraelian imperialism and Arnoldian visions of the Celt are alike indebted to the author of the *Reflections*. And the apparently opposed scales and proportions of these areas of development — global policy, domestic policy, India, and Skibbereen — are already present in the terms of Burke's politics, Burke's aesthetics.

For politics and aesthetics come together in Burke in a conjunction of the most profound significance. There is a line of development between ideas explored by Burke as early as 1756 in his *Philosophical Inquiry into the Origins of our Ideas on the Sublime and the Beautiful* and the famous apostrophe to Marie Antoinette in the *Reflections*. But the biographical line of consistency or development is less pertinent than the extensive links which locate the *Reflections* in the context of Wordsworth's 'Prelude', Coleridge's *On the Constitution of the Church and State*, and Jane Austen's *Mansfield Park*. Nor is this to invoke *influence* as some personal, biographical debt which the poets and novelists owe to the politician — Wordsworth's own employment of the term in such poems as 'Tintern Abbey' and 'Michael' should suggest a more complex relationship — rather it is to point to the intensively literary priorities and preoccupations of the *Reflections* and the mediate access thus afforded us to the politics of fiction and poetry. For a radical such as Paine, of course, Burke's lingering upon the frailties of the Queen's position was an evasion of the real — attention to the plumage and neglect of the dying bird. Yet it is that dichotomy between ornament and use, the illusory and the real, the literary and the political which Burke's work drastically challenges.

From the outset, the *Reflections* attracted attention to its language, and much of the evidence marshalled in James Boulton's *Language of Politics in the Age of Wilkes and Burke* is critical of Burke's use of imagery and metaphor. Doubtless, Burke's style — so conceived — is massively and energetically effective, but it would be mistaken to assume that stricter notions of literary form, and considerations of contemporary literary practice, can be separated from personal style. Polemic, narrative, and metaphor in the *Reflections* contribute to a synthesis which at once enacts and exposes certain preoccupations which run deep in English romanticism and in what we have learned to call Anglo-Irish literature. Indeed, the politics of Burke's sublime and beautiful, as enforced in the epoch of the French Revolution, constitutes one statement — others are available in economic or social terms — of the principles of that essentially fragmentary and separatist 'tradition' of romantic nationalism. Tradition will come to imply, virtually to impose, a unitary concept of continuity and unity, but its romantic origins attest — as does the Irish politics of Union — to the characteristically divided and reciprocal (to go no further) nature of such a movement. One's interest in Anglo-Irish literature, or in the Irish language, or in the velleities of Sean O Faolain, is determined not by some endearing merit dormant in such material but by the necessity of a material history which incorporates Europe and India and America. The Anglo-Irish novel is launched by Maria Edgeworth and we have come to acknowledge that unremarkable truism; what remains crucially to be achieved is the demonstration of that 'fragmentary union' which is Burke's contribution to the aesthetics of Anglo-Irish fiction.

The thrust and tone of Burke's *Reflections* are well known. And yet the important task before us is not economically to summarize the agreed argument of that familiar work but rather to seize upon the distinctions between its past significance and present meaning with especial reference to the trajectory in literary history we call Anglo-Irish literature. In time we shall refer in some detail to the particular narratives and pervasive metaphors of the work, but for the moment a reminder of its ostensible form is needed. The *Reflections* is a letter addressed to a young French gentleman in Paris and written as one continuous sequence of sentences. This specific form is crucial in Burke's tactic of adopting the role of political sage, of the master addressing his pupil.[2] In this of course it shares many characteristics of pamphlet propaganda in the eighteenth century. This has not prevented a recent editor from dividing the text in two 'Parts', the first further divided into ten chapters and the second into five, chapters which are then given titles such as 'A Defense of the French Monarchy and Aristocracy'.[3] What is significant here is not any sacrilegious interference with the seamless text of 1790; on the contrary, we are watching the dissemination of a present-day 'Burke as methodical political scientist' in the context of American public education. Arguments deployed against the introduction of innovative, deliberate government to the detriment of ancient custom are thus rendered serviceable in defence of custom-less *laissez-faire* economics. Burke's 'own' contempt for political theory and abstract argument is theorized in defence of the historical descendants of his enemies. Nor is this instance an isolated one; the application of Burke's ideas to the cause of American conservatism in the age of the Cold War, though happily a temporary phenomenon, has its Victorian precedents. Burke as the founder of the modern Conservative Party is of course an anachronism, and yet Walter Bagehot's *English Constitution* (1865) had, in the words of one sober historian, 'translated the almost mystical celebrations of Burke and Coleridge into inspired commonplaces'.[4] The

[2] Although it is not primarily concerned with the *Reflections* Chris Reid's article 'Language and Practice in Burke's Political Writing', *Literature and History*, vol. 6, (Autumn 1977), pp. 203–18, has been most helpful in developing this discussion.

[3] *Reflections on the Revolution in France*, edited with an introduction by Thomas H. D. Mahoney with an analysis by Oskar Piest (Indianapolis: Bobbs-Merrill, 1955; 13th printing, 1978).

[4] Richard Shannon, *The Crisis of Imperialism 1865–1915* (London: Paladin, 1976), p. 26.

celebrations referred to here were Burke's defence of pre-scription as the fundamental principle of a landed society. And landed property, with its prescriptive rights attached inviolably, forms the central concern of Burke's polemic in the *Reflections*. Nevertheless, as Novalis and others recognized, this was no serene, classic statement of unshakeable truth. It partook of the nervous, innovative, *revolutionary* circumstances into which it intervened.

If we take the broad binary division of the argument into a statement of 'British Tradition' and 'French Enlightenment',[5] we note different narrative strategies within each. The account of British history is present in reverse-chronology; that is, we are taken back from the present occasion and a specific addressee through the adjustments of 1688 and the Glorious Revolution, the vicissitudes of the Great Rebellion, back ultimately to Magna Carta. British constitutional history is thus taken *up* to its original fountain-head where it is emblemized in a statement of historical guarantee. French constitutional history, in contrast, is traced downwards from 'your old states . . . your ancient states' to 'the last generations of your country [which] appeared without much lustre in your eyes'.[6] This contrast in narrative method is entirely at one with Burke's placing of the present generation — 'People will not look forward to posterity, who never look backward to their ancestors.'[7]

Other local instances of specific narrative method could be analysed for their political direction, whether unconscious or otherwise. For example, the introduction of The Reverend Dr Price as stalking-horse is subsequently absorbed in the allusion to The Reverend Hugh Peters, who mocked Charles I and was then executed at the Restoration, a narrative strategy which looks forward fearfully to the fate of those who side with Price and the British friends of the revolution. The resemblance of this device to the tactics of the historical novelist prompts thoughts of other points of comparison.

[5] For the role of these terms in the fifteen innovatory chapter headings introduced by our recent American editor, see Appendix A.

[6] *Reflections on the Revolution in France*, ed. Conor Cruise O'Brien (Harmondsworth: Penguin, 1970), p. 122. All subsequent references to the *Reflections* relate to this edition.

[7] *Reflections*, p. 119.

Like *Waverley*, the *Reflections* advances two rival views of history, and like the Scott novel generally there is both a preference for the organic unity of the past and a recognition of less totally satisfactory circumstances in the present. The device of addressing the *Reflections* to a very young Frenchman produces an emotional force-field not unlike that generated by Scott's unremarkable heroes, who in their ordinariness stimulate in the reader a participating sympathy even in their errors. The difference between Scott and Burke as historical fictionalist is essentially that Scott does not relish the tragic denouement. Burke, in characteristic self-division, reluctantly does relish it.

It was Schopenhauer, Nietzsche's erstwhile master, who suggested that all art aspires to the condition of music. The particular version of romanticism which we find in Burke's historical narratives suggests that all history aspires to the condition of eternity. In the fusion of The Reverends Price (died 1791) and Peters (executed 1660), Burke comments that the two differ 'only in place and time'.[8] Such an aspiration to transcend history is offset constantly in Burke by his awareness of the purely negative terms in which transcendence is available to modern man. The conclusion to that famous passage in the *Reflections* which begins 'Society is indeed a contract' ends with a rhetorically heightened meditation on the consequence of human choice succeeding ordained necessity:

if that which is only submission to necessity should be made the object of choice, the law is broken, nature is disobeyed, and the rebellious are outlawed, cast forth, and exiled, from this world of reason, and order, and peace, and virtue, and fruitful penitence, into the antagonist world of madness, discord, vice, confusion, and unavailing sorrow.[9]

The myth of the Fall is only invoked here at one remove; this world, albeit presented as peaceful and virtuous, is also one of fruitful penitence. The rhetorical emphasis falls upon a more immediate, if officially hypothetical, world of

---

[8] Ibid., p. 158.
[9] Ibid., p. 195; some of his strictly fallacious arguments invoking 'law' are discussed by Herbert J. Muller in *The Uses of the Past: Profiles of Former Societies* (New York: Oxford University Press, 1952), pp. 316 etc.

unavailing sorrow. The world of the Revolution is post-
lapsarian, known and yet unexperienceable except in the
most arithmetical formulae, the most abstract relations. This
sense of cosmic desolation, detectable in different forms in
Wordsworth and Shelley (for whom the political lessons are
also drastically different), also suggests affinities between
Burke and Hegel, Burke and the early Marx, Burke and
Nietzsche. So broadly defined an affinity is perhaps insuf-
ficiently fine to be really useful in argument, and the closer,
localized context of English romanticism now requires
consideration.

What Wordsworth dreaded in Jacobin abstraction and
Jacobin social engineering, Shelley and Blake condemned in
the society defended by Burke — Hanoverian Britain with its
coercive Church and imperial aggression. The consistency of
English romanticism does not lie in any political agreement,
though English romantics of various political views shared
common animosities and sympathies. Dealing in primarily
biographical (and psychological) terms, Thomas McFarland
has located Wordsworth's psyche between the extremes of
severe egotism and a universal benevolence: 'Impelled toward
but at the same time retreating from both isolation and community, Wordsworth came to be as it were suspended in
an emotional force-field between them.'[10] For McFarland,
the resolution of these tensions lay in the poet's increasing
commitment to 'the significant group'; not humanity at large
nor the untrammelled ego, but a significantly intimate and
yet extensive group of individuals earned his loyalty and
emotional commitment. In the solitaries of Wordsworth's
great poems — 'Resolution and Independence', 'Michael',
and of course 'The Prelude' itself — there is more concrete
and accessible evidence of a dialectical process incorporating
solitude and relationship, integrity and integration, in a
constantly renewing and sustaining pattern. If one were to
turn to the case of Shelley and his reputation, then E. T. Webb
and other recent commentators have shown how a comprehensive idealism competed positively with a practical

[10] Thomas McFarland, *Romanticism and the Forms of Ruin: Wordsworth,
Coleridge, and Modalities of Fragmentation* (Princeton: Princeton University
Press, 1981), p. 152.

commitment to specific social projects and political causes.[11] In place of Augustan antithesis, romantic dialectics focused on the objective contradictions of a rapidly developing society experienced in its full European breadth and in the recesses of its common people. The Revolution, and the Grand Alliance against it, made the experience of politics and the experience of war public property.

For comparison with Burke, Wordsworth offers greater scope than Shelley. And the crucially significant group in, his work is not the actual family circle but the 'statesmen' of the Lake District:

> The domestic affections will always be strong amongst men who live in a country not crowded with population, if these men are placed above poverty. But if they are proprietors of small estates, which have descended to them from their ancestors, the power which these affections will acquire amongst such men is inconceivable ... Their little tract of land serves as a kind of permanent rallying point for their domestic feelings, as a tablet upon which they are written which makes them objects of memory in a thousand instances when they would otherwise be forgotten. It is a fountain fitted to the nature of social man from which supplies of affection, as pure as his heart was intended for, are daily drawn.[12]

Less particularly, Burke draws on the same powerful sources of imagery in the *Reflections*, and in defending 'the method of nature in the conduct of the state' — that is, hereditable property — he identifies the state with the home:

> In this choice of inheritance we have given to our frame of polity the image of a relation in blood; binding up the constitution of our country with our dearest domestic ties; adopting our fundamental laws into the bosom of our family affections; keeping inseparable, and cherishing with the warmth of all their combined and mutually reflected charities, our state, our hearths, our sepulchres, and our altars.[13]

Not only does Burke give to the state the emotive connotations of intimate family life, he argues that citizenship and social action have their origin in domestic experience:

[11] See in particular Timothy Webb, *Shelley: a Voice not Understood* (Manchester: Manchester University Press, 1977), pp. 75-98 *et passim*.

[12] *The Letters of William and Dorothy Wordsworth: The Early Years, 1787-1805*, ed. Ernest de Selincourt, rev. Chester L. Shaver Oxford: Clarendon Press, 1967, pp. 314-15; quoted by McFarland, p. 173.

[13] *Reflections*, p. 120.

We begin our public affections in our families. No cold relation is a
zealous citizen. We pass on to our neighbourhoods, and our habitual
provincial connections. These are inns and resting-places. Such divisions
of our country as have been formed by habit, and not by a sudden jerk
of authority, were so many little images of the great country in which
the heart found something which it could fill. The love to the whole is
not extinguished by this subordinate partiality.[14]

There is another, more renowned statement of a similar
sentiment in the *Reflections,* but it is one which requires
attention in the context of its preceding sentences:

Turbulent, discontented men of quality, in proportion as they are
puffed up with personal pride and arrogance, generally despise their
own order. One of the first symptoms of a selfish and mischievous
ambition, is a profligate disregard of a dignity which they partake with
others. To be attached to the subdivision, to love the little platoon we
belong to in society, is the first principle (the germ as it were) of public
affections. It is the first link in the series by which we proceed towards
a love to our country and to mankind. The interests of that portion of
social arrangement is a trust in the hands of all those who compose it;
and as none but bad men would justify it in abuse, none but traitors
would barter it away for their own personal advantage.[15]

The assault on turbulent men of quality is noteworthy, for
it is Burke's version of that repression of egotism which
Wordsworth found it necessary to exercise throughout his
career. In general terms Burke condemns, or at least is
exceedingly wary of, 'separate insulated private men' but the
thrust of the *Reflections* is directed more specifically against
'literary caballers, and intriguing philosophers; with political
theologians and theological politicians'.[16] In short, 'Men of
Letters, fond of distinguishing themselves, are rarely averse to
innovation.'[17] The articulation of caballers or writers is
explicitly contrasted to the silent virtue of a rural image of
society in its organic continuity:

Because half a dozen grasshoppers under a fern make the field ring with
their importunate chink, whilst thousands of great cattle, reposed
beneath the shadow of the British oak, chew the cud and are silent,

---

[14]   Ibid., p. 315.
[15]   Ibid., p. 135.
[16]   Ibid., pp. 91, 93.
[17]   Ibid., p. 211.

pray do not imagine, that those who make the noise are the only inhabitants of the field; that of course, they are many in number; or that,
after all, they are other than the little shrivelled, meagre, hopping,
though loud and troublesome insects of the hour.[18]

Burke does not identify his 'significant group' so clearly as
Wordsworth but the extremes between which he seeks such a
human locus are immediately evident and interconnected. On
the one hand, there are the multitudes who are regimented in
the newly conceived divisions of Jacobin France, or 'a
swinish multitude',[19] a society judged by mathematical
criteria. On the other, there are insulated men. If this looks
like another version of Wordsworthian polarities, we should
note in Burke that insulated men contribute to the establishment of schematic societies, departments, communes, and
cantons. Historically speaking, one should observe that
Wordsworthian fulmination against manufactories and
Burkean denunciations of Jacobinism represent the old antithesis of city and country (*urbs et rus*) in crisis.

In a rather stricter historical sense, the Irish background to
Burke's thought in the 1790s cannot be neglected. Dying in
1797, he did not have to face the decisions of 1799 and 1800
in relation to the proposed Union between Britain and
Ireland. While speculation as to whether he would have been
unionist or anti-unionist is largely pointless in so far as the
altered political circumstances arising between 1797 and
1800 are concerned, the metaphoric implications of union
per se directly relate that issue to Burke's devotion to 'the
little platoon'. The romantic age aspired to wholeness and
unity and yet was characterized by a profound sense of
fragmentary human existences in a disintegrating world. If
we accept that the union between Britain and Ireland was
sought for conscious, specific political reasons, or if we go
beyond this to argue that the union was determined by
economic necessity, we do not invalidate the relevance of the
intense romantic investment in union as a value. Politically,
there was a precedent by which the initiative might be
measured — the union with Scotland in 1707. But the Scottish

---

[18] Ibid., p. 181.
[19] Ibid., p. 173; for some important comments on this phrase see Cruise
O'Brien's annotations, pp. 385-6.

union was generally referred to as resulting from a Treaty of
Union, and the implication was that, in the early eighteenth-
century sense of the word, this was a union between two
nations. This implication of official parity was facilitated
in that a king of Scotland (James VI) had become king
of England (James I), and that the palpable superiority of
England in *realpolitik* was balanced by a Scottish dignity in
the line of succession. The Irish union enjoyed no such
Augustan balance: the means whereby the king of England
was also king of Ireland was memorably warlike, and the
union was (and is) universally referred to as the *Act* of Union,
that is, a parliamentary decision doubly ratified at Westminster and College Green.

As we shall see, the parliament was by the 1790s felt at
least by some to be gravely anomalous, not only in relation
to the middle-class wealth of Ireland but also in relation to
the intrusive power of the London administration. The Irish
government, so to speak, operated independent of the Irish
parliament, and the existence of the Lord-Lieutenant and
Chief Secretary added a further stratum of complexity. If
the real motive behind the union was a need to close the gap
in British defences by drawing Ireland closer to England, then
the uniting of the parliaments (the principal means by which
the Union proper was effected) was singularly beside the
point, for Ireland as symbolized in its parliament and its
military arrangements had never been effectively independent.
If there was a serious intention to reconcile Catholics to the
house of Hanover by means of a union which dissolved the
intransigent Protestant element so active in the Dublin
parliament, then the immediate abandonment of such an
intention in 1801 sabotaged the primary base upon which
a union of palpable social import might have been achieved.
Yet, bearing these unsatisfactory propositions in mind, we
can see that the romantic ideology of wholeness and union is
enacted in the very incompleteness of the union. Leaving
aside the absence of parity between the elements officially
joined in the Act of Union (as they were open to observation
in the preceding century), and passing over the immediate
question of motivation or intention, we find that the administration of Ireland after 1801 was characterized both by

newly created 'union' features — the united parliament, the
united Established Church, and so forth — and by the survival
of pre-union features, the Lord-Lieutenancy, the legal system, etc. Oliver MacDonagh has described these arrangements
as producing 'a curious dualism in Irish government, the effects of which were hardly understood, still less allowed for,
in the nineteenth century'.[20] The Scottish union had preserved
to Scotland a popular Church and a distinctive legal system;
the Irish union perpetuated into an age of increasingly democratic feeling a minority Establishment and a professional élite
in which sectarian pride took consolation. If all this seems
momentarily remote from a discussion of Burke's *Reflections*,
let us recall that the French Revolution was undoubtedly the
active occasion of all Anglo-Irish discussions from 1790
onwards, and that one little platoon to which Burke might
have had to advise loyalty was the 'Junto of jobbers', soon to
announce itself as 'the Protestant Ascendancy'.[21]

Burke's dual concentration on the violent pretensions of
the ascendancy party in Ireland and the innovations of the
Jacobins in France is itself an example of the fragmentation
of the argument for a comprehensive view of things. Protestant Ascendancy is unable to see that Catholics are valuable
allies in the counter-revolutionary struggle; Whigs like Fox
are unable to see that they are the imminent victims of the
revolution they espouse. Burke employs the revolution as a
metaphor ironically imposed upon the ascendancy jobbers,
and the Jacobins are cast in the role of ultra-Protestants, but
the employment of metaphor both draws together and distinguishes the objects cited. From the outset the *Reflections*
was acknowledged as possessing an intimate conjunction of
style and content, as being in effect a literary work. But to
say this is not simply to establish an unproblematic virtue in
the book. James Boulton argues that 'Burke's veneration
for stability, dignity, and a cultural tradition is transmitted
through the image of the noble country-house or castle.'[22]

---

[20] Oliver MacDonagh, *Ireland: The Union and its Aftermath*, rev. ed. (London:
Allen and Unwin, 1977), p. 17.
[21] See below, pp. 87 ff., for Burke's use of these phrases.
[22] James Boulton, *The Language of Politics in the Age of Wilkes and Burke*
(London: Routledge and Kegan Paul, 1963), p. 111.

Success in conveying this to the reader depends not solely on the rigour of the argument or the aptness of the tropes, but on the reader's prior assent to the identification of dignity with country houses. To say that style and content in the *Reflections* are at one is to mark the limitations of the book's potential as well as to measure its drawing of aesthetics and politics into harmony. Once again, the inherent division within the vision of a longed-for wholeness is acknowledged. The apostrophe to the queen in its absence of detail recalls Burke's own judgement in the *Enquiry* (1756) that readers of Homer are impressed by Priam's account of Helen for the very reasons that he does not specify (and so limit) her beauty; the Burkean evocation of a latter-day *reine fatale* is similar:

It is now sixteen or seventeen years since I saw the queen of France, then the dauphiness, at Versailles; and surely never lighted on this orb which she hardly seemed to touch, a more delightful vision. I saw her just above the horizon, decorating and cheering the elevated sphere she just began to move in, — glittering like the morning-star, full of life, and splendour, and joy. Oh! What a revolution! and what an heart must I have, to contemplate without emotion that elevation and that fall! . . . [23]

Surely the most effective analysis of this passage is William Blake's verse paraphrase:

> The Queen of France just touched this globe,
> And the pestilence darted from her robe;
> But our good queen quite grows to the ground,
> And a great many suckers grow all around.[24]

The central metaphor (of elevation) is maintained but, by being stripped of its sonorous repetitions and cast in brutal doggerel, is shown to reveal callous remoteness. Beyond this, of course, the crucial difference between Blake and Burke is

[23] *Reflections*, pp. 169-70; Boulton, op. cit., discusses the apostrophe on pp. 127-33; for Burke on Priam and Helen see *A Philosophical Enquiry into the Origin of our Ideas of the Sublime and the Beautiful*, ed. James T. Boulton (London: Routledge and Kegan Paul, 1958), p. 171.

[24] William Blake, *Poems*, ed. W. H. Stevenson, text by David V. Erdman (London: Longman, 1971), p. 168; for a discussion of Blake's rewritings of Burke see David V. Erdman, *Blake: Prophet against Empire*, rev. ed. (Princeton: Princeton University Press, 1969), pp. xi, 11, 184, 219, 469.

that Blake moves to concentrate on the actuality of a present-tense scene in which meaning is a potential to be drawn out by stylistic emphasis, whereas Burke insinuates a second object of consideration into his evocation of the queen — the effects of time doubly upon her and upon his altered sentiments towards her. If we read elsewhere in the *Reflections* that society becomes 'a partnership not only between those who are living, but between those who are living, those who are dead, and those who are to be born',[25] this 'eternal contract' is in keeping with the mediation of time between the object and subject (so to speak) of the *Reflections*.

Incompleteness, sentiment, the passage of time — the dominant metaphor which draws these concerns together in Burke is *ruination*:

one of the first and most leading principles on which the common-wealth and the laws are consecrated, is lest the temporary possessors and life-renters in it, unmindful of what they have received from their ancestors, or of what is due to their posterity, should act as if they were the entire masters; that they should not think it amongst their rights to cut off the entail, or commit waste on the inheritance, by destroying at their pleasure the whole fabric of their society; hazarding to leave to those who come after them a ruin instead of an habitation . . .[26]

Addressing his young French gentleman, Burke directs the same metaphor towards the same conclusion:

Your constitution, it is true, whilst you were out of possession, suffered waste and dilapidation; but you possessed in some parts the walls, and in all the foundations of a noble and venerable castle. You might have repaired those walls; you might have built on those old foundations.[27]

As James Boulton points out, this use of the great house as an image of the state or of society has a distinguished ancestry including Ben Jonson, Marvell, and Pope. The flourishing house of Jonson's 'To Penshurst' is a model of an orderly society, with the active bountiful garden contributing emblems of human generosity and so forth. In Burke, by way of contrast, the house spatially occupies a large place in his imagery, even when the house itself is ruined or damaged.

---

[25] *Reflections*, pp. 194–5.
[26] Ibid., p. 112.
[27] Ibid., p. 121.

Continuity, expressed through legal concepts such as entail
or prescription, is to be preferred to temporary well-being.
The ruin is a characteristic romantic metaphor in that a form
of incompleteness is reconciled to a form of wholeness,
incompleteness of physical space assimilated to the evidence
of wholeness in time. No doubt Gothic and antiquarian
enthusiasms contribute to the romantic interest in ruins, but
the evidence of the fragmentary text (e.g. 'Kubla Khan', 'The
Prelude', etc.) and of the poets' sense of their own lives as
ruins amid ruins confirms the centrality of the romantic
metaphor.

The legislatures of Britain and France are contrasted
implicitly through this imagery. The National Assembly is
treated simply as that — an assembly of persons speaking as
the nation; the English parliament, however, can be referred
to as 'the two houses', and the sense of a house as a social
entity with its continuous life sanctions the decisions of
parliament.[28] Speaking of British liberty, Burke insists that
'it has its gallery of portraits', and the architectural metaphor
is significant for its insinuation of the ancestral and gener-
ational human material of portraiture as displayed in galleries
of a great house.[29] This device of employing the static architectural metaphor in order to introduce a covert implication
of a (quasi-)dynamic history has other related applications;
having emphasized *'grounds* of hope and fear ... a solid
ground on which any parent could speculate ...', Burke
draws his paragraph up to an explicit topographical trope in
which Jacobin individualism is identified with the process of
architectural ruination:

Barbarism with regard to science and literature, unskilfulness with
regard to arts and manufactures, would infallibly succeed to the want
of a steady education and settled principle; and thus the commonwealth
itself would, in a few generations, crumble away, be disconnected into
the dust and powder of individuality, and at length dispersed to all the
winds of heaven.[30]

'Disconnected into the dust' enacts its sense in the very

[28]   Ibid., p. 102.
[29]   Ibid., p. 121.
[30]   Ibid., pp. 193-4.

tenuousness of its verbal structure, and this harmony of style and content mocks ironically at the ruination of the commonwealth. The young Georg Lukács launched his *Theory of the Novel* (1914-15) from an intense longing for Greek completeness, and declared that 'irony is a negative mysticism to be found in times without a god'; recalling the affinities between the *Reflections* and the emergent form of the historical novel, we note also that, in such circumstances, 'irony is the objectivity of the novel.'[31]

If the great house is a dominant metaphor of the *Reflections*, with the attendant imagery of gardens and grounds and picture-galleries, its recurrent citation is ironic and objective in that Burke uses it primarily as an image of ruination contrasted with a wholeness which historical community may afford:

Is it then true, that the French government was such as to be incapable or undeserving of reform; so that it was of absolute necessity the whole fabric should be at once pulled down, and the area cleared for the erection of a theoretic experimental edifice in its place?[32]

Or again,

The French builders, clearing away as mere rubbish whatever they found, and, like their ornamental gardeners, forming every thing into an exact level, propose to rest the whole local and general legislature on three bases of three different kinds ...[33]

This use of the 'great good place' in contexts where ruination or damage is taking place is one form of paradox which Burke employs; perhaps the most striking instance of it is the single sentence which begins and ends with reversal and oxymoron:

The *fresh ruins* of France, which shock our feelings wherever we can turn our eyes, are not the devastation of civil war; they are the sad but instructive monuments of rash and ignorant counsel in time of *profound peace*.[34] (Emphasis added)

[31] Georg Lukács, *Theory of the Novel*, trans. Anna Bostock (London: Merlin Press, 1971), p. 90.
[32] *Reflections*, p. 230.
[33] Ibid., p. 285.
[34] Ibid., pp. 126-7.

Reflections on the Revolution in France is not so much an Augustan account, or refutation, of the political philosophy and practice of Jacobinism as it is a literary enactment of fundamentally romantic assumptions. In the context of Anglo-Irish literature it is worth noting how its treatment of history occasionally anticipates the devices of the historical novel, and how its sense of history involves the collaboration of a metaphysic of eternity with the psychology of recollection. Metaphor, by means of a related subjectivity, is recurrently ironic. Many of these features of the *Reflections* are echoed in the subsequent sporadic writings on Protestant Ascendancy. The degree of public attention which Ireland earned in the 1790s — and especially from 1798 onwards — ensured that the new romantic mode of expression came to be applied to its political affairs. With the exception of Keats, all the great romantic writers concerned themselves with Irish affairs. One background to this romantic interest in Ireland could be summarized in William Blake's friendship with James Barry, another in Shelley's support for Catholic Emancipation. The first of these links the argument to that band of Irish adventurers — Burke himself, Goldsmith, Sheridan, and so on — who left home to make their way in the larger arena of London and whom Yeats subsequently and selectively declared to be part of an Irish Augustan tradition; the second touches upon one major theme in the nineteenth-century liberal concern with Irish vicissitudes.

This development is part of a broader alteration of relations between Britain and Ireland in the transition from the eighteenth to the nineteenth century. No magical quality resides in the precise date of 1800 or 1801, though the Union clearly marks one major element in this alteration. Using it as an indicator of change, we see that the nominal independence of the pre-Union parliament in Dublin (and, less obviously, of the pre-Union kingdom of Ireland) is absorbed into a united parliament and a united kingdom. We see also, however, that this Union was built on powerful contradictions and dislocations. One index of this contradiction lies in the reports of travellers — whether from Britain or the Continent — who visited Ireland in the late eighteenth century or the early decades of the nineteenth century. No generalized conclusions on this topic could be attempted here, but one or two isolated elements may be briefly noted. In the 1790s, for example, when Ireland was nominally independent, its political affairs were seen as far more thoroughly interwoven with those of Britain than was the case for long periods in the nineteenth century when the official relationship between the islands was one of Union.

In June 1794, William Wordsworth wrote to the bookseller Mathews in London about a projected dissident journal:

> I entirely approve of what you say on the subject of Ireland, and think it very proper that an agent should be appointed in Dublin to disseminate the impression. It would be well if either of you have any friends there, to whom you could write soliciting their recommendation. Indeed it would be very desirable to endeavour to have, in each considerable town of Great Britain and Ireland, a person to introduce the publication into notice ... If you think that by going over to Dublin I could transact any business relative to the publication in a better manner than it could be done by Letter, though I have no friends there I would willingly undertake the voyage, which may be done at any time from this place.[35]

Wordsworth did not make this proposed trip to Ireland, and indeed his encounter with the island did not occur until September 1829, when he stayed with Maria Edgeworth in the course of a five-week tour. Much had changed between 1794 and 1829 — Wordsworth's own political attitudes, the events of 1798 which included *Lyrical Ballads* and the United Irishmen rebellion, Union, the growth of reaction in Britain during the Napoleonic wars, frustration in Ireland at delay in the emancipation of Catholics, an agricultural slump, two Irish Tory prime ministers of the United Kingdom (George Canning and the Duke of Wellington), the rise of Daniel O'Connell.[36] Neither these developments nor the postponement of his own visit prevented Wordsworth from propounding his views on Ireland in the intervening years. It is a measure of the extent to which Ireland was becoming a

---

[35] *The Letters of William and Dorothy Wordsworth: The Early Years*, pp. 126, 128.

[36] George Canning was of course born in London, but, to adapt Wellington's comment on such matters, to be born in a stable does not entail one's being a horse. Canning's family came from Garvagh in County Derry.

topic upon which Englishmen spoke confidently that the contradictions of Union did not inhibit such assertions. The terminology of these assertions is, however, explicitly revealing of the romantic base of this ideological confidence. In the case of Wordsworth, two instances may be significantly related.

Writing to Henry Crabbe Robinson in July 1826, the poet apologized for once again having to abandon plans to visit Ireland. He was, on the other hand, happy to provide advice to intending travellers:

Of Ireland I can say nothing but that every body sees Killarney there are some fine ruins of monasteries, etc not far from Limerick the Vale of the Dargle and the Wicklow Mountains would lie in your way from Killarney to Dublin supposing you to start from Dublin you would go by Limerick and return by the Wicklow country but to one who should leave Wales out the best way of seeing Ireland from London would be to go from London to Bristol and thence to Cork Killarney and Dublin and the Giants Causeway. From Belfast there will no doubt be a Steam Boat to Glasgow . . .[37]

Given that this paragraph is written in his daughter's hand at Wordsworth's dictation, perhaps the breathless lack of punctuation should not be attributed to the poet himself. There is none the less a comprehensive confidence that Ireland is a romantic itinerary, a succession of picturesque scenes with priority given to ruined monasteries. It was just the previous year which had brought Maria Edgeworth and Sir Walter Scott to Killarney for the first time, and the comparison between Maria Edgeworth's attitude to scenery in literature and that evinced by Scott and Wordsworth illustrates the extent to which she retained pre-romantic attitudes generally. This distinction between the romantics' delight in Irish scenery, and the Irish novelist's willingness to rely on handbooks for what descriptions of landscape her novels required, has another dimension. Wordsworth and Scott are primarily looking at a *foreign* landscape, from which the continuous buzz of mundane social activity — boats, hotels, the state of dress of the people — has been

[37] *The Letters of William and Dorothy Wordsworth: The Later Years,* Part I, *1821–1828,* ed. Alan G. Hill, from the 1st ed. of Ernest de Selincourt (Oxford: Clarendon Press, 1978), p. 478.

filtered. We note the irony of this Irish foreignness in the
attitude of two British romantics whose devotion to the
institutions of the United Kingdom of Great Britain and
Ireland was without rival. But we add to it a more intensely
romantic counter-proposition — that the foreignness of Ireland
is related to its pastness, its emblematic depiction in ruination. The ruin, in romantic poetry from Wordsworth's
Grasmere to Holderlin's Patmos, is a metaphor uniting
incompleteness and completeness, the fragmentation of
human domicile and the continuity of memorized landscape.
The 'Gothick ruin' of a Wicklow villa garden, which Maria
Edgeworth focuses upon in *The Absentee*, is for her a superficial imitation of metaphor, romantic longing reduced to
sentimental fabrication.

Maria Edgeworth's travels in France in 1820 offer an
illuminating comparison to Wordsworthian Ireland. As
always, she is concerned to relate the familiar and the unfamiliar, but in comparing French and Irish social occasions
she unwittingly reveals her own tendency to identify the
foreign and the romantic:

In the evening we were at a *fête de village* at La Celle, to which Mme de
Vindé had invited us, as like an Irish *pattern* as possible, allowing for
the difference of dress and manner. The scene was in a beautiful grove
on each side of a romantic road leading through a valley. High wooded
banks: groups of gaily-dressed village belles and beaux seen through the
trees, in a quarry, in the sand-holes, everywhere where there was space
enough to form a quadrille. This grove was planted by Gabrielle
d'Estrées for whom Henry IV built a lodge near it. Fanny and Harriet
danced with two gentlemen who were of our party, and they all danced
on till dew-fall, when the lamps, little glasses full of oil and a wick
suspended to the branches of the trees were lighted, and we returned
to La Celle, where we ate ice and sat in a circle, playing *trouvez mon
ami* — mighty like 'why, when, and where' — and then played loto
till twelve. Rose at six, had coffee, and drove back to Paris in the cool
of the delicious morning.[38]

The most pertinent comment on this passage is that provided
by the editor of Maria Edgeworth's correspondence, in a
footnote — 'Mme. de Genlis . . . speaks of the post-Revolution

[38] *Maria Edgeworth in France and Switzerland: Selections from the Edgeworth
Family Letters*, ed. Christina Colvin (Oxford: Clarendon Press, 1979), p. 187.

changes in *fêtes champêtres*; the gentry no longer danced with the lower classes and their gardens were opened to *cabaretiers* and *traiteurs* etc.'[39] Maria Edgeworth, the foreigner in La Celle, sees a veritable vision of social harmony, dancers in the quarry, Marvellian lamps in the trees; the disenchanted memorialist sees the hired caterer, class tension, 'la morgue des dames de chateaux, qui, dans ces rejouissances, ne vouloient point danser avec les paysans'.[40] This observation of bourgeois encroachment on previous complex distinctions and interactions relies of course on celebration of a past which is less than fully real; as Madame de Genlis expresses it, she works 'pour reparer le temps perdu'.[41] Yet, to the Irish visitor, the evidence of latter-day decline has its own timeless charm.

Wordsworth on Irish landscape and Irish ruination constituted the first instance of the romantic ideology lying behind the confident assertions of English opinion on the subject of Ireland. The second illustrates the extent to which the sectarian tensions excited in the 1790s gave birth to a sociology which continues to colour political debate in Ireland. That Wordsworth's views changed drastically between 1794 and the 1820s is well known, but that fact should not deter us from seeing in the change (and its specific continuities) a more than biographical significance. Writing to Sir Robert Inglis on 11 June 1825, he deplored George Canning's speech on Catholic Relief 'attempting to reconcile us to Papacy, by endeavours to prove that in points of Faith and practice, Protestantism stands pretty much upon a par with it'.[42] If Canning seems to echo a broad inclusive theology, Wordsworth's language follows closely strict formulations:

Were we to abandon the hope of gaining upon the Romanists, we must be prepared to admit the evil of their gaining upon us. Protestant Ascendancy must be renounced, and sooner or later will be substituted Catholic domination — the two religions cannot coexist, in a Country

[39] Ibid., n.1.
[40] Stephanie Félicite, comtesse de Genlis, *Mémoires inédits* (Paris, 1825), vol. v, p. 109.
[41] Ibid., vol. v, p. 107.
[42] *The Letters of William and Dorothy Wordsworth; The Later Years,* Part I, p. 359.

free as our's upon equal terms. For my own part while I condemn as
founded in ignorance, I reprobate as of the most injurious tendency,
every Measure that does not point to the maintenance of Protestant
ascendancy, and to the diffusion of Protestant principles: and this
doctrine I hold not more as a friend to Great Britain, than to Ireland.[43]

Wordsworth (like Coleridge) came to hold views upon the
sanctity of Church and State with which Edmund Burke, in
so many ways their mentor, could not have sympathized.
Yet the differentiation cannot be attributed simply to
galloping reaction on the individual level. The Coleridgean
notion of a 'clerisy', an intellectual class devoted to aims at
once religious and cultural, may certainly be related to the
desire of finding 'a significant group' upon whom the future
of the nation could safely depend, but the conditions upon
which such a proposition relied were not available in Burke's
lifetime. Burke's practical experience as eighteenth-century
parliamentarian qualifies any romantic description of him.
Yet here we find that the consistency of romanticism is what
sceptics must regard as its inconsistency; the divergence of
Wordsworth from Burke on the question of 'the Protestant
religion' is a historical statement of their unanimity. This
romantic contradiction informs much of the subsequent
development of Anglo-Irish literature in the nineteenth
century, and it is entirely in keeping with such dialectical
procedures that Burke's role, Burke's significance, should be
suppressed or denied by the ultimately crowning notion of
an Augustan tradition. Successive stages, or seismic registers,
of that development can be traced in the fiction of Maria
Edgeworth, Sheridan Le Fanu, and Charles Lever; in the
emergence of nineteenth-century Celticism; and climactically,
in the polarized productions of Anglo-Irish modernism whose
terms we can simply call Joyce and Yeats.

  Reflections on the Revolution in France is not advanced
here as a proto-novel upon which Maria Edgeworth subsequently models the real thing. As against such merely
sequential notions of influence in literary history, a more
dynamic alternative must be now developed which, while
immersing itself in the actuality of history, also acknowledges

<hr>

[43] Ibid., pp. 359-60.

the full interaction of reader and text, subject and object. In this sense, consequently, we draw attention to certain novelistic features of the *Reflections*; but the *Reflections,* thus read, is as much influenced by *Castle Rackrent*, the Act of Union, and Yeats's *Collected Poems* as they are influenced by it. To see an unbridgeable distance between the France Burke lamented in the *Reflections* and the Irish Protestant jobbers he mocked in his letters is to travesty their historical and ideological setting. In the words of Thomas McFarland, the modalities of romanticism are fragmentation and longing, ruination and wholeness: the completely romantic poem is, like those *magna opera* upon which Wordsworth and Coleridge so long laboured, incomplete. Among Edmund Burke's writings it may appear futile to search for such a paradigm of the romantic metaphysic — once again the practical demands of a public career would appear to discourage that kind of imitative form. Nevertheless, if we have yet to look at the particular political circumstances in which Burke's letter to his son, Richard, was written — between mid-February and 10 May 1792, in the weeks running up to the publication of a *Collected Works* — we can still take a full measure of *Letter to Richard Burke*.

The letter is indeed unfinished, and was most ostentatiously published as an unfinished text. Bibliographical facsimulation could confirm instantly that the text 'ends' in a series of asterisks, but what is considerably more significant is the fact that, in the five years remaining to him, Burke did not attempt to replace those asterisks. Admittedly, his most dearly beloved son — no biographer can hope to convey the devastation Richard Burke's death in 1794 wreaked upon Burke — was dead within a poignantly shorter time. In turn, this totally unexpected bereavement lends a special poignancy to the 'final' paragraph of *Letter to Richard Burke*: 'All titles terminate in prescription; in which (differently from Time in the fabulous instances) the son devours the father, and the last prescription eats up all the former.'[44] We shall read the *Letter* thoroughly for its scathing analysis of Protestant Ascendancy — 'A word has been lately struck in the

---

[44] 'Letter to Richard Burke', *The Works of Edmund Burke* (London: Bohn, 1855), vol. vi, p. 80.

mint of the Castle of Dublin.' The fiscal metaphor, the
exploitation of commercial idiom, is not limited to the letter
to his son, but is repeatedly employed in the *Reflections*
where the financial system of the Republic is condemned for
its 'continual transmutation of paper into land, and land into
paper':

> By this means the spirit of money-jobbing and speculation goes into
> the mass of the land itself, and incorporates with it. By this kind of
> operation, that species of property becomes (as it were) volatized; it
> assumes an unnatural and monstrous activity . . .[45]

Of course, finance is a central concern of Burke's in his
polemic against republican France, and his use of fiscal
metaphor is apt: it counterbalances in its aptness the irony of
his great-house images of contemporary ruination. In *Letter
to Richard Burke,* the *coinage* 'Protestant Ascendancy' is
ferociously analysed precisely because Burke is aware of the
dangers of its *currency.* In other words, his account of
Protestant Ascendancy is closer to his ironic use of the great
house than to the analysis of republican finance.

Burke's account of Protestant Ascendancy, therefore, is
intimately related to his writings on France, and indeed
Letter to Richard Burke incorporates both formal and tonal
aspects of his romanticism. Its concluding image of prescription, as the son devouring the father, reverses the classical
notion of time (Cronus) swallowing up its children. And this
introduces a motif which will persist in Anglo-Irish literature
from *Castle Rackrent* to 'Purgatory': that is, the symbiosis of
Oedipal conflict and social *mésalliance.* In the former, blood
relationship is both under- and over-valued. In the latter,
class is at once stridently invoked and travestied.

As we approach the modernist period a third element
becomes more prominent — a metaformal self-consciousness
in the work of art by which it expresses its revolt against the
author, its Oedipal assault upon its own creator. That such
themes originate in the romantic period can be confirmed by
reference to areas of literary production other than Ireland.
Burke's condemnation of the volatility, the monstrous

activity of the Revolution is a muted expression of a drastically new element in human consciousness, recognized by the
German poet Novalis:

Most observers of the Revolution, especially the clever and fashionable
ones, have declared it to be a dangerous and contagious disease. They
have gone no further than the symptoms, and have interpreted these as
being in many ways haphazardly confused. Many have regarded it as a
merely local evil, but the most inspired opponents have urged castration
for they have noticed that this alleged illness is nothing other than the
crisis of imminent puberty.[46]

If the Revolution is the onset of adult sexuality, and its
repression drastically symbolized by castration, then the
persistence in Anglo-Irish literature of various forms of sexual
redirection in covert guise — incest, homosexuality, the anti-
Oedipal violence of fathers upon sons — signal larger collocations of cultural, political, and economic interest. Such a
vocabulary does not miraculously begin *ex nihilo* with the
romantic age, but has its earlier, simpler (and ultimately
redundant) manifestation in the Augustan antitheses of the
eighteenth century.

[46] Novalis, loc. cit.

2. EDMUND BURKE AND THE IMAGINATION
OF HISTORY

1. ANGLO-IRISH RELATIONS

> My failing to have a nice ear for vowel
> sounds, and the Anglo-Irish slurred,
> hurried way of speaking, made me take
> the words 'Ireland' and 'island' to be
> synonymous.
>
> (Elizabeth Bowen)[1]

In the eighteenth century Ireland and England were different
from each other. At the end of the nineteenth century they
were different — different from each other and from what
they had been. Moreover, the means and effects of their
alteration were far from identical. Finally, the Irish and the
English differed in how they described and accounted for
these various differences.

Such a cat's cradle of tense parallels could be made more
solid simply by a few references to industrialization, trade,
social infrastructure, education, religious policy. Indeed, the
history of Ireland's relations with England, England's relations with Ireland, is most familiar in the forms of such
extensive differentiation. With a treaty of independence in
1921 the two gave the most concrete institutional recognition to this state of affairs. Yet, at least until 1921, and
arguably afterwards too, there should be added to our model
a higher level of relation in which Ireland and England, so to
speak, concurred, a level at once ideological and effective in
which the two were contained on terms of some extensive
comparability and equity. In the eighteenth century this can
be identified principally as the Monarchy or, more abstractly,
the Protestant Succession: the king of England was also the
king of Ireland. In the nineteenth century, we speak of the
United Kingdom, and the significant alteration is not simply

---

[1] Elizabeth Bowen *Pictures and Conversations* (London: Allen Lane, 1975),
p. 31.

the Union but the emphasis on the kingdom or, more abstractly, the State.

The emergence of the state as a prime initiator in matters of social policy was associated particularly with England, because the organs of political and financial power were located specifically in England. In Ireland the state was indeed active, at times hyperactive, but it was quickly shadowed by a less tangible entity, a concept more romantic than utilitarian, the Nation. To be sure, none of these terms is new: all of them were current in the reign of Elizabeth. But the manner in which they bore upon the realities of life on the two islands marked the difference between the islands in the period under discussion.

The English and the Irish differed as to the differences between them, nor did they agree on the similarities which exacerbated their dispute. This is not to suggest that relations between the two should be approached in a purely descriptive manner. Were I attempting a political account, I should want to deal with the actual forces at work in English and Irish society — and beyond — which produced the situation I have outlined. That is, I should demonstrate that the comparability and equity I have spoken of is radically distinguishable from any formal or moral notions of justice. But as I am to concentrate on a particular manifestation of Anglo-Irish relations in cultural terms, a further economic and political analysis lies beyond my scope. Nevertheless, we begin with history — and for two reasons. First, the great literary movement towards which our inquiry is directed was deeply concerned with the bonds existing between the past and the present. History was seen as a condition in which the present existed — Yeats's Celtic Revival, Joyce's nightmare. The perspective upon the past varied: it was for Yeats one of longing, for Joyce one of resentment and revolt: for both of them it involved a painful recognition of history as a potent form of reality. And second, even the most fleeting attempt at description carries with it implied historical interpretations: no normative account of how things stand is, in this context at least, without its subterranean assumptions of how things might have been.

Prior to the Norman invasion, Ireland had not been unified

in any recognizable form. The Normans who arrived at the end of the twelfth century were never permitted to establish themselves so firmly as to make possible a kingdom rivalling Henry II's England. Over the centuries, the smaller island had never been totally separate from the larger, never totally subdued, nor liberated, nor administered, nor neglected. The Reformation transformed a distinction between Gael and Norman into a schism between Catholic and Protestant, adding to this a new international dimension to Irish affairs through the possibility of a pan-Catholic alliance between Spain and the unreformed Irish (both Gael and Norman). Sometimes English preoccupations with Europe and (later) America allowed certain Irish factions a measure of free manœuvre: at other times, quite other arrangements were required. At all times, it was felt that a sense of anomaly affected relations between the two kingdoms. The charges and recriminations generated by this sense of anomaly are familiar enough: it does not seem to have occurred to either party that a dual kingdom incorporating two islands divided by an extensive and treacherous sea constituted an anomaly within their common tradition of social organization inherited from antiquity: that tradition bespoke territorial consolidation and (with some exceptions or delays) centralization. In 1784, C. T. Greville wrote to the Duke of Rutland, Lord-Lieutenant of Ireland under the Rockingham ministry: 'Ireland is too great to be unconnected with us, and too near us to be dependent on a foreign state, and too little to be independent.'[2] The imaginative shape, or shapelessness, of the observation is at least as significant as its content.

In 1784, of course, the American War of Independence was the recent catalyst. Ireland's exclusively Protestant parliament had two years earlier won a measure of legislative independence from Westminster, in the face of Britain's Atlantic preoccupations. Power in Dublin was still divided between the king's representative (with his secretaries), the administration in Dublin Castle, and the factions of the Irish

---

[2] Historical Manuscripts Commission (henceforth HMC) Rutland MSS, vol. iii, p. 155; for a further and more elaborate example of antithesis in formulating Anglo-Irish relations in this period see a draft letter from the Earl of Buckinghamshire to Edward Tighe, HMC, Lothian MSS, pp. 394-6.

parliament. Since the beginning of the century, when the Williamite wars had intensified the Reformation divisions to an unprecedented level of legislative control, a system had grown up by which the effective running of the king's business was 'undertaken' by a powerful lobby in return for the control of local patronage. The result was that much power rested with a small group who were neither a cabinet nor a civil service: they were the 'undertakers'. And if the system was modified towards the end of the century, it was still the case that both power and authority were vested all but exclusively in the hands of a Protestant élite.

The distressful plight of Irish Catholics under the penal laws has come in for some revisionist analysis in recent years. While a new recognition of the success of many Catholics in business and trade, and the less than absolute application of the law in matters of civil manners and so forth, is timely, it as yet remains undenied that Catholics were excluded from every kind of direct political representation and office. The proportion of the population thus treated is not easily calculated: the question is of course complicated by the exclusion of Protestant dissenters from the establishment. What is of greater urgency for the modern reader of Anglo-Irish relations is a recognition of the balance of population between Britain and Ireland. In 1796 John Keogh complained to Edmund Burke that 'Government appear to forget that the Inhabitants of Ireland are about One third of *all* his majesty's Subjects in Europe.'[3] It would be mistaken to interpret this approximate statistic in the light of a twentieth-century definition of democracy as universal suffrage. Nevertheless, Ireland earned the attention, if not always the respect, of British politicians as a substantial part of the king's realm: that the Irish included a large number who were alienated to some degree by reason of their religion and who had a history of collusion with continental foes did not diminish that attention. It may be said in passing that one of the most important of the altered differences between Britain and

[3] *The Correspondence of Edmund Burke*, ed. Thomas W. Copeland *et al.*, vol. ix, May 1796–July 1797, ed. R. B. McDowell and John A. Woods (Cambridge: Cambridge University Press, 1970), p. 59. On the general issue see K. H. Connell, *The Population of Ireland 1750–1845* (Oxford: Clarendon Press, 1950).

Ireland as from the late eighteenth to the late nineteenth century was the very substantial shift in demographic proportion caused by industrialization in England and famine and emigration in Ireland. The tensions of the late eighteenth century are perhaps more readily collated to Keogh's statement of proportion than to any head-counting within the denominations in Ireland.

Within Ireland the Catholic majority was politically neutralized, though never to the complete security and satisfaction of the more volatile Protestant representatives. In 1792, Burke sought to explain the constitutional adjustments of 1782 by arguing that internal conditions had altered – not numerically, but yet materially – so as to require an alteration of relations between the two kingdoms. Britain, he maintained,

saw that the disposition of the *leading part* of the nation would not permit them to act any longer the part of a *garrison*. She saw that true policy did not require that they ever should have appeared in that character; or if it had done so formerly, the reasons had now ceased to operate. She saw that the Irish of her race were resolved to build their constitution and their politics upon another bottom.[4]

Burke did not always advance so positive an account of 1782. He did, however, stress the peculiar difficulties – of language, as much as anything else – caused by the dual alterations of proportionate interest between England and Ireland and between the social groupings within Ireland. 'The Irish of her race' is one of the more analytical versions of a nomenclature which occurs also as 'Anglo-Irish', 'West Briton', and – in the linguistic arena – 'Hiberno-English'. It has the merit of distinguishing between social function (birth, residence, etc. in Ireland) and ancestry (deriving from English planters, etc.), while at the same time conjoining those elements in a more positive manner than the schismatic hyphen of its principal rivals. When the social world of the Anglo-Irish was finally eclipsed (in the generation of Elizabeth Bowen who has written so beautifully on the subject) it was as if the hyphen, which had always been a signally diminished equation mark,

⁴ 'Letter to Sir Hercules Langrishe', *The Works of Edmund Burke* (London: Bohn, 1855), vol. iii, p. 322.

which had always been a signally diminished equation mark,
became a minus sign, a cancellation.

In the same letter of 1792 to Sir Hercules Langrishe, Burke
employed the 'too much and too little' device of C. T. Greville
to emphasize his point: 'The Protestants of Ireland are not
alone sufficiently the people to form a democracy; and they
are *too numerous* to answer the ends and purposes of *an
aristocracy.*'[5] The internal problem, as Burke presents it,
resembles Greville's in outer form. But 'too great to be
unconnected' and 'too little to be independent' is as near to
tautology as paradox. Furthermore, Greville was speaking of
geographical proximity which, while it may be affected by
changes in strategic alliances and in the technology of war
and trade, is in a sense a stable relation. Burke in contrast is
dealing with classes, and classes are not prescribed bodies of
men and women. It is true, of course, that men and women
sometimes may behave as if class were just as it is here denied
to be. But as class consists of a series of relations in social,
economic, political, and cultural activity, there will be many
individuals involved in more than one 'class' by dint of the
complexity of their social existence. Class conflict, therefore,
does not resemble the warfare of opposing armies, each
dressed in exclusively distinguishing colours. Conflict arises
when the requirement of different sets of relations are
brought antagonistically to bear on an area of social activity
where each claims validity.

It will be clear that the operations of language may be
crucial in deciding how such conflicts develop. *Antithesis*
(offered by Greville in terms of distance and proximity, by
Burke in terms of class roles and forms of government) is
a frequently employed expression of Anglo-Irish relations at
the end of the eighteenth century. Without comment on or
commitment to the substantive arguments embodied in these
pronouncements, we note their characteristic balance of
similarity and dissimilarity, their neo-classical formalism.
However, the substantive arguments are not absolutely
distinguishable from their formalism. Eighteenth-century
rhetoric encouraged the definition of issues in the shape of

[5] Ibid., p. 304.

resolvable antitheses, by the value it found in such formulations of moral choice and aesthetic effect. To see the problem as coherent was to go some way towards its solution. Of course, this last view of Augustan optimism sometimes disguises the deflection of attention away from the crucial (but problematic) issues towards others which have the attraction of being resolvable, even if they are to an extent marginal to the urgent inquiry. (Thomas Gray's Christianity in the Churchyard Elegy is not so much a matter of personal belief as of an acknowledged and conventional system of deflected despair: the irresolvable may be lulled to sleep if rocked on the balanced knees of Antithesis.) The differences between England and Ireland, however, complicated any attempt to apply the antithetical trope to Anglo-Irish relations. By suppressing or neglecting important areas of concurrence, the hostile commentator (from whichever side of the argument) could present the grounds of comparison as too ill-defined to support any resolution — John Keogh's complaint to Burke focuses precisely on this tactic.

In Burke's writings we find a different reaction. Increasingly as the revolutionary decade advances, recurringly whenever he writes of Ireland, Burke is searching for other, additional rhetorical devices by which to convey a deeper sense of the crisis he dreaded. If solutions are necessarily determined by the range and limitation of the language in which the crisis is explored, then for Burke the revolutionary decade called for something more strictly radical in the political language of those who opposed revolution. The values of Augustanism might be conserved but only by a drastic departure from the norms of Augustan optimism. The gathering darkness of Burke's utterances on Ireland in his last years is well known: it should not be held apart from the stylistic experiments of the *Reflections on the Revolution in France.* Burke was rarely guilty of neglecting the concurrences in order to exaggerate the differences: England and Ireland were bound together in the imperial system, this was as firmly held by Burke as his eloquent denunciation of the Irish Undertakers of English policy in Ireland. The underlying unity which he saw at the bottom of Anglo-Irish relations was informed by his acute perception of the internal divisions of Ireland. His formulation of those divisions allows no happy neglect of external realities. Reading the letters of his last seven years we become aware that he all but makes explicit an imminent *tragic* conflict between elements in Irish society which are simultaneously irreconcilable and inseparable. Such a perception of things is no olympian detachment: to it Burke contributes the shape of his own complex origins, the experience of an Irish-born English statesman, of Catholic descent, confronted with the violent purism of revolution. It is convenient to summarize the French Revolution as a contest between Jacobinism and the *ancien régime*: in any such scheme of things, Burke is on the side of the ancients. But he spoke against France as an English whig, one of the party who consolidated the bourgeois liberties of the constitution: in this he has some affinity, however estranged, with the underlying logic of Jacobinism. If this nexus were not sufficiently complicated, we add also that as a child of Irish Catholicism who increasingly responded to appeals from that quarter, he also spoke and wrote as the victim of triumphant English whiggery. That tragic note sounds the end of Burke's Augustanism, and heralds Yeats's distinctive assimilation of Burkean politics to a tragic aesthetic.

It was Oscar Wilde who observed that we have everything in common with the Americans — except language. And if late twentieth-century tourists are still discovering that words do not mean quite the same in Boston (Mass.) and Boston (Lincs.), it is no less true that the language of politics employed in the late eighteenth century by British and Irish alike had its hidden discrepancies. Where this condition bred new terms, or terms peculiar to one side of the debate, the problem was merely one of familiarity. Where the same word acquired diverging meanings, or developed a new meaning disguised as venerable usage, the results were less easy to control. Of course, to speak of words having meanings on some one-to-one basis is undoubtedly to invoke a concept of language now regarded as naïve: this altered perspective on the relationship of language to reality is a further area in which the treachery of an ahistorical, timeless, and universal acceptance of words as fixed should be exposed. Moreover, in time the language of the Anglo-Irish debate is taken up into a growing literature: the relations between so-called ordinary language and literary discourse complicate our approach by positing formal synchronic patterns for analysis and admiration. When Yeats interrogates himself in 'The Man and the Echo'

> Did that play of mine send out
> Certain men the English shot?[6]

he is not inquiring as to his guilt in the matter of James Connolly's death in that he is not attending exclusively to the diachronic patterns of causation and responsibility. He is posing the question — in characteristically dialectical terms — as to how the language of literature relates to life, life here summoned up in the forceful image of death. His theoretical focus, that is, is upon the synthetic nature of literature. If, for a moment, we anticipate the entire extent and conclusion of this present argument, we can note a significant transition: we move from the antithesis of Augustanism to the synthesis of modernism. Neither antithesis nor synthesis is without its contradictions — or rather, Burke abandoned antithesis precisely because it no longer conveyed the full contradiction of the crisis he foresaw. And in Yeats such theoretical inquiries as those of 'The Man and the Echo' usually impinge upon politics with a special and urgent intimacy: it is as if the synthesis were anxious to demonstrate its appetite for 'the real' by publicly displaying the elements it thought to subsume. In due course we shall look closely at major texts by Burke and Yeats with these general features in mind. The intervening years are vital to an understanding of the bonds which draw Yeats and Burke together: divergences of meaning between Yeats's century and Burke's are at least as treacherous as those between Boston (Mass.) and Boston (Lincs.)

Ireland was strategically important in the king's realm: its inhabitants formed a substantial proportion of his European subjects. Its governmental structure resembled that of Britain: with a monarch (always the reigning British king or queen), and a parliament consisting of Lords and Commons.

---

[6] W. B. Yeats, *Collected Poems* (London: Macmillan, 1963), p. 393.

The manner in which the Irish parliament was subordinate
to Westminster and the English privy council need not detain
us here, nor the means by which in the eighteenth century it
became the forum of an exclusively Protestant élite. It is not
the Protestantism of the Irish parliament which distinguished
that body from its English counterpart, but rather the differing denominational allegiances of the parliament and the
population *en masse*. Nevertheless, that lack of concurrence
in belief had its effect on the tone of Irish Protestantism,
which was on the whole theologically lower than the English
Established Church. Pluralism, absenteeism, and the use of
ecclesiastical office as a valued token in the system were
perhaps no less evident in Ireland than in England. Laxity, at
least a marked lack of enthusiasm for enthusiasm, was
certainly to be detected in the Irish Church. Transition to
nineteenth-century conditions altered many aspects of this
image of Irish Protestantism. Extension of the franchise in
the nineteenth century in effect extended the areas of
denominational conflict; and with the Oxford Movement
giving a higher tone to the English Church, and evangelicalism
penetrating the Irish, the isolation of Irish Protestantism grew
on several fronts. Protestant enthusiasm, fired by a new
electoral battle with the Catholic majority in Ireland and by
a renewal of 'Reformation' zeal, became a means towards
political ends, and the legacy of that politicizing of the Irish
Protestant churches remains a volatile element in the politics
of our own period.

The very word 'Protestant' had diverging meanings in the
two islands, soon to be joined in the United Kingdom of
Great Britain and Ireland.[7] For the English, the Reformation
produced two parties — the Anglican (Established) Church
and Protestant dissenters from the Church: for the Irish, the
distinction was more often between the Protestant (Established) Church and various dissenting sects, Presbyterian for
the most part. In the twentieth century, the Irish usage has
become blurred, but the present writer's uncle, living in south
Ulster in the 1950s, used to distinguish (jocularly but with a
recent propriety) between Protestants and Presbyterians.

---

[7] See W. E. H. Lecky, *History of Ireland in the Eighteenth Century* (London,
1898), vol. iv, p. 4n.

Such instances in which Boston (Lincs.) and Boston (Cork) diverge in their use of a word may not seem important. But words combine to form potent and emotive phrases. It is true that in England and Ireland Protestant had its broad and inclusive meaning, and that the concurrence is of broader significance than the divergence. With the arrival of the Hanoverians anxiety about the Protestant Succession was greatly diminished by that dynasty's monotonous reliability in producing male heirs. But towards the end of the century, there emerged a new phrase in Ireland, Protestant Ascendancy, in which the reactions of a revolutionary age were quickly gathered. That now familiar phrase, transparent in its descent to the age of Yeats, is indeed treacherous with altered meanings.

Ascendancy is the central political idea under discussion, Edmund Burke the principal commentator on its emergence in the 1790s. As to the Protestantism of Protestant Ascendancy, two perspectives should be noted at this point. The first is the inclination of some elements in Irish dissent towards deism and to related political notions. These dissenting radicals were distinctively connected with trade, and regarded politics as a matter of commerce rather than theology. The Reverend Edward Hudson, writing to the Earl of Charlemont on 5 July 1799 from Ballymena, County Antrim, described these emerging values as they were affected by the abortive rebellion of the previous year: his letter catches the shifting terminology of these new alignments and reactions:

Things here wear a very different aspect from what they had done for some years past, and indeed, if ever people had reason to be thankful, they of this country have. It is literally a land flowing with gold and silver, which whoever has need not fear the want of milk and honey. Our northerns are not like Dublin tradesmen, who, when trade is good, work one day and drink two. On the contrary, they are working double tides to improve the favourable opportunity. . . The word 'Protestant', which was becoming obsolete in the north, has regained its influence, and all of that description seem drawing closer together. I only wish their affections may not be so entirely to each other as to exclude all others from a share of them. The Orange system has principally contributed to this. I was no friend to the introduction of it into this country, and it has in fact produced the evil I apprehended from it, but, I must confess, it has also produced good which I did not foresee, and which in the then state of the country I did not think could have been produced ... Why, in the name of God, will they not leave us alone at such a time as this? Why interrupt that tide of prosperity which is flowing in upon us? What a stupid question! That very prosperity induces the attempt.[8]

Hudson is a shrewd witness to Protestant attitudes — his promised land of milk and honey is the profit earned by gold and silver. It is unlikely that 'Protestant' was in danger of becoming obsolete in Ulster prior to 1798, though the elements existing within the broader sense of the term were tending towards divergent political objectives. Certainly the aftermath of the abortive rebellion, together with a wartime economic boom, saw a gradual coming together of the reformed denominations, established and dissenting. The imminent Union with Britain, to which Hudson hesitantly refers in concluding his letter, involved promises of emancipation for Catholics to which the dominant Protestant interest objected. The bankers of Dublin, with the Orangemen, constituted a formidable opposition to Union, which only the appropriate arguments of reward and conjured-up papist aggression could overcome.

The second perspective in which the ascendancy of Protestantism should be considered refers to relations with Catholics rather than with fellow-Protestants. Hudson notes the feeling that Catholics are to be excluded from the affections of the converging Protestants 'and all of that description'. This growing antagonism is hardly new in itself — remember 1690, or 1641 for that matter — but there is a distinctive quality contributed to it by the revolutionary state of Europe. Edmund Burke had expressed the situation more trenchantly than Hudson, in a letter to his son:

A very great part of the mischiefs that vex the world arises from words. People soon forget the meaning, but the impression and the passion remain. The word Protestant is the charm that locks up in the dungeon of servitude three millions of your people. It is not amiss to consider this spell of potency, this abracadabra, that is hung about the necks of

[8]   HMC Charlemont MSS, vol. ii, pp. 354-5.

the unhappy, not to heal, but to communicate disease. We sometimes hear of a Protestant *religion*, frequently of a Protestant *interest*. We hear of the latter the most frequently, because it has a positive meaning. The other has none.[9]

Our two perspectives on the Protestantism of Protestant Ascendancy — a convergence of the reformed denominations, and a growing antagonism towards the Catholics — may of course be conflated. Hudson neatly translates the biblical land of milk and honey into the prosperity of his 'northerns': Burke insists that Protestantism is *interest*, not religion. Both are concerned to acknowledge the talismanic quality of such a word as Protestant: what lies between them in simple chronological terms is the rebellion in which Protestant-becoming-radical is defeated, and Catholic-becoming-rebel is exposed and exhibited. Burke did not live to see the rebellion he all but prophesied, and his was a darkly coloured testimony to sectarian feeling in the 1790s. An authenticating mark — and a limitation — of his account of Protestantism as interest is its ferocity; his account of the birth of Protestant Ascendancy is similarly compromised by the multitude of his own engagements in the image he strives to convey. A fuller investigation into the origins of Protestant Ascendancy will follow; for the moment we have noted its readiness on the margins of our argument, readiness to assume to a grander degree the hypnotic powers attributed by Burke to the phrase. From the literature of Yeats's age we know that those powers were exercised and remarkably transformed. It remains to be seen what particular vacuum will be appropriated by the new talisman.

Ireland, like Britain, was monarchy, aristocracy, and democracy; that is, it was ruled by 'kings, lords, and commons'. The theory was clear enough. In January 1792, it was summarized in the Irish parliament: 'Aristocracy . . . reflects lustre on the crown and lends support and effect to democracy while democracy gives vigour and energy to both, and the sovereignty crowns the constitution with dignity and authority . . .'.[10] This has a suitably Whiggish turn to it, for it

---

[9] Burke, *Works,* vol. vi, p. 69.
[10] *Irish Parliamentary Debates* (Dublin, 1792), vol. xii, p. 7.

is the work of Henry Grattan, doyen of Irish parliamentarians between the constitutional adjustment of 1782 and the Union of 1800. Though he is paraphrasing an English minister's definition, Grattan is also adhering to familiar and traditional explanations. Aristocracy is that element under the constitution which descends from the feudal order of nobles whose military service to the crown was rewarded with hereditary distinction. Of, course the British nobility included many who could not trace their titled line further back than a few generations, and the creation of new peerages was by no means restricted to military men. There was nevertheless a consensus of feeling that the British nobility, no matter how it had developed in post-medieval society, still perpetuated the spirit of its origins. The trouble in Ireland was that the prehistory, so to speak, of aristocracy, was entirely different.

The dislocated sense of an aristocracy in eighteenth-century Ireland has several sources. One of these was the disturbed and divisive history of the medieval period, and its survival in modern consciousness. Another, even more immediate in its impact, was the existence on the Continent (and to some extent at home) of a Catholic aristocracy bearing distinctly Irish titles but excluded from Irish political life. Some of these exiles were descendants of Elizabeth I's defeated Irish earls, others were Jacobite relics, the scions of 'Wild Geese' migrants. The twelfth baron Trimleston, petitioning for Catholic rights in 1759, had returned from exile in France, and had inherited his title and estates. This residual Catholic element among the bearers of Irish titles underlined the influx of newly created beneficiaries of recent confiscation and plantation. For those who had access to the Gaelic poetry of Daithi O Bruadair (1650-1694) and Aodhagáin O Rathaille (1670-1728) the superiority of the old aristocracy over the new was a familiar theme. In short, the history of the smaller island had seen the development of an Irish peerage with relations to society as a whole quite distinct from those which had given the English aristocracy its lustre.

There was a crucial extension to the evidence of the Irish aristocracy's dislocation from the ideal — the extensive use of the peerage as a form of political patronage. Within a hundred years its ranks almost doubled. R. B. McDowell neatly encapsulates the British attitude to Irish nobility by recording that

> on one occasion George I was said to have professed himself more ready to grant an Irish peerage than a K.B., adding for good measure that he could make a lord but not a gentleman; and George III, it was rumoured, when he would not permit a Welsh baronet to make an avenue from his house to Saint James's Park, softened the refusal by the offer of an Irish peerage.[11]

Thus, in addition to embodying in hereditary form the divisions of Irish history, the peerage also demonstrated Ireland's accessibility to the English administration in matters of rewards for services rendered. After 1782, the Irish opposition became especially interested in this debasement, as they saw it, of the Irish peerage. In his speech of 19 January 1792 from which we have already quoted, Grattan finally apostrophized the English minister he had paraphrased as

> He who sold the aristocracy and bought the democracy — he who best understands in practice what is this infusion of nobility — He who has infused poison into this aristocratic and this democratic division of power, and has crowned the whole with corruption. He well knows all this as far as Ireland is concerned to be theatric representation, and that the constitution of the country is exactly the reverse of those scenes and farces which are acted on the public stages, of imposture and hypocrisy.[12]

It has been customary to regard this critique by Grattan and his associates of the Irish peerage in terms of Whig liberty. Certainly, the view of Grattan advanced by Yeats in the third section of 'The Tower' owes much to W. E. H. Lecky's consolidation of Grattan's reputation in his *Leaders of Public Opinion in Ireland*:

> I declare
> They shall inherit my pride,
> The pride of people that were
> Bound neither to Cause nor to State,

[11] R. B. McDowell, *Ireland in the Age of Imperialism and Revolution 1760–1801* (Oxford: Clarendon Press, 1979), p. 121.

[12] *Irish Parliamentary Debates*, vol. xii, p. 7.

> Neither to slaves that were spat on,
> Nor to the tyrants that spat,
> The people of Burke and of Grattan
> That gave, though free to refuse. . .[13]

This is a further instance of Yeats's identification of the peasant and the nobleman, for those who shall inherit his pride are 'upstanding men That climb the streams until The fountain leap'. These lines intimately associate the Connemara fisherman and 'a rich man's flowering lawns' where

> Life overflows without ambitious pains:
> And rains down life until the basin spills.[14]

The evocation of Grattan's magnanimity, and the assumed empathy with Burke, are part of Yeats's transformation of history into symbol. In this the poet exploits the long-standing convention that the Irish parliament in its last two decades is referred to as Grattan's Parliament. If the poem is read as presenting in this third section a eulogy of Grattan, then what is suppressed is the impotence of Grattan's style, the isolation of those 'Bound neither to Cause nor to State', the purely oppositional nature of Grattan's condemnation of Irish aristocracy, 'tyrants that spat'. Many commentators evidently wish to read Yeats in this manner, and have no objection to the suppression in that the eulogy satisfies their sentiments. We may do the poet a greater service if we observe the aptness of his choosing as his spiritual forebear one whose style was only painfully related to his active life. Recently, the biographer of 'Speaker' Foster has declared sententious the explanation of Henry Grattan Junior that his father was 'too high to be sold to any Government', and has seen Grattan's refusal to serve in office as 'flamboyant coyness'.[15] There is certainly a discontinuity between the world of rhetorical trope and that of effective power; in Grattan's experience 'unity of being' was remote. John Fitzgibbon, essentially a pragmatist, felt that 'the recollection

[13] W. B. Yeats, *Collected Poems,* pp. 222-3.
[14] Ibid., pp. 166, 225.
[15] A. P. W. Malcomson, *John Foster: The Politics of the Anglo-Irish Ascendancy* (Oxford: Oxford University Press for the Institute of Irish Studies, 1978), pp. 397-8.

of Mr. Grattan's splendid periods is but a slender compensation for poverty and the most absolute dependence on Great Britain.'[16] That was in 1785: Burke's tribute in February 1792 effects a neat balance of Grattan's qualities, though the final clause is revealing:

Grattans speech is a noble performance. He is a great man, eloquent in conception and in Language, and when that is the Case, being on the Right side is of some importance to the perfection of what is done. It is of great consequence to a Country to have men of Talents and Courage in it, though they have no power.[17]

The connection between Grattan's assault on the Irish peerage and his witholding himself from office should not be drawn too definitively in terms of magnanimity. There can be doubt that a public figure, who declines effective power in office, may yet exercise a beneficial influence on the manner in which the state's business is conducted. However, by the purely oppositional nature of Grattan's critique of Irish aristocracy, I do not simply mean that he was thoroughly opposed to its debasement: I mean that his attitude was shaped and informed purely by that which he opposed. He did not so much propose an alternative view of society, simply a selection of better individuals and better motives. According to Grattan's powerful ally George Ponsonby, it was a favourite theme in 1792 'to accuse this side of the House as an aristocracy', and Anthony Malcomson has recently argued that the Ponsonby/Grattan notions of reform were aimed at increasing the representation of landed property rather than at a noble-minded giving though free to refuse.[18] What Grattan certainly feared and resented was the tendency towards 'the monarchy of clerks' by which all Irish interests were subordinated to a civil service directed from London.

Historians are familiar with the low reputation of the Irish peerage in the late eighteenth century. The *cause célèbre* in this regard is of course the Act of Union: to ensure its

---

[16] Quoted Malcomson, p. 364.
[17] Burke, *Correspondence*, vol. vii, p. 83.
[18] Malcomson, pp. 355-7.

passage, the Crown promised sixteen new baronies and fifteen promotions of existing peers to higher ranks of the nobility.[19] In this way, the Union-title so neatly exemplified in Maria Edgeworth's Lord Clonbrony in *The Absentee* came into existence. It can be argued that twentieth-century notions of political morality should not be read back into a context where very different forms of pension and reward were employed — accordingly the Union-titles merely extend the pattern condemned by Grattan in 1792. But there was one crucial distinction between the creation of — say — eighteen new titles for the 1776 elections and the 1800 exercise. It is this, in the eighteenth century patronage was a reward for services rendered and still renderable: in 1800 the Irish parliamentarians rendered themselves incapable of service. This, at least, is an accepted view with much to recommend it: as Oliver MacDonagh has persuasively argued, the fecklessness displayed by Maria Edgeworth's Rackrents in her novel of 1800 is prophetic of nineteenth-century developments in Irish land-ownership.[20] However, the voluntary liquidation of the Irish parliament and the transfer of Irish representation to Westminster should also be seen in the broader context of European romantic nationalism, a creed which supplied new criteria for the embarrassment of the Irish aristocracy. For many reasons, therefore, we hear little of a positive nature about Irish *aristocracy* as such, in the nineteenth century. The term had imploded into a functionless vacuum or was otherwise deprived of any power to impress. The eclipse of one term, however, may make possible the emergence and transformation of another. 'Ascendancy' gradually came to act in Hiberno-English debate many of the roles attributed to aristocracy in England. The means whereby this substitution occurred are not without irony, not without the treachery of altered meaning and forgotten history.

---

[19] See G. C. Bolton, *The Passing of the Irish Act of Union* (London: Oxford University Press, 1966), pp. 205–7.

[20] Oliver MacDonagh, *The Nineteenth Century Novel and Irish Social History* (Dublin: National University of Ireland, [1971]), p. 5.

2.   THE BIRTH OF ASCENDANCY

Ascendancy — shows belief in astrology
(J. M. Synge)[21]

In the matter of Anglo-Irish culture of the late eighteenth century Edmund Burke is an expert witness. That is, he knows too much. An impartial committee of inquiry is readily confused and irritated by the kind of familiarity and intimacy which Burke lends to his testimony. He is unwilling (and, at times, unable) to reduce his experience to the categories of objectivity. His thought runs ahead to the consequences of an argument, or runs back to the origins of a complaint. It is not that he lacks sagacity or a sense of occasion: on the contrary, his public utterances on Ireland roll with the same music as the *Reflections on the Revolution in France.* There is, however, another side to Burke to which the modern reader has access, the private side of the orator as revealed in his voluminous correspondence. From a consideration of both sides of the witness, we can now see that Burke is not only expert witness, but also prosecutor, plaintiff, and accused.

He had been born in 1729, the second son of Richard Burke, a Dublin attorney. The elder Burke had been a Catholic, and his wife (a Miss Nagle) continued to practise her religion privately. Edmund was educated as a Protestant, entered Trinity College Dublin, and subsequently the Middle Temple in London. He married Jane Nugent in 1756, whose father Christopher remained a Catholic and a friend of Samuel Johnson's. Burke's career lay almost entirely in England, first as journalist, writer, and secretary, and — after 1765 — as an MP in the Whig interest. He visited Ireland on a number of occasions, but there is no historical foundation for Yeats's line in 'The Seven Sages':

> *The First.* My great-grandfather spoke to Edmund Burke
> In Grattan's house.[22]

---

[21] Trinity College Dublin (Synge MSS), MS 4373, fo. 22. John Millington Synge's summary of R. C. Trench's brief discussion of the word in *On the Study of Words* (1851); see Trench, *On the Study of Words* [and] *English Past and Present* (London: Dent, 1927), p. 63.

[22] W. B. Yeats, *Collected Poems*, p. 271.

Despite his career in Westminster, Burke remained attached to the country of his birth, championing Irish trade and Catholic emancipation. It is particularly worth noting the coinciding of his campaign against France (commencing in 1790 with the *Reflections*) with his growing commitment to emancipation for Catholics and with his anxiety concerning conditions in Ireland. The ill-fated experiment of appointing Burke's patron, the Earl Fitzwilliam, as Lord-Lieutenant in Ireland (1795) marked a key moment in his relationship with his homeland. From the recall of Fitzwilliam in February 1795 to his own death in July 1797, Burke's letters are dominated by the imminence of death and inescapable conflict in Ireland. In December 1796, he wrote to The Reverend Thomas Hussey, later Catholic bishop of Waterford:

> You state, what has long been but too obvious, that it seems the unfortunate policy of the Hour, to put to the far largest portion of the Kings Subjects in Ireland, the desperate alternative, between a thankless acquiescence under grievous Oppression, or a refuge in Jacobinism with all its horrors and all its crimes. You prefer the former dismal part of the choice. There is no doubt but that you would have reasons if the election of one of these Evils was at all a security against the other. But they are things very alliable and as closely connected as cause and effect. That Jacobinism, which is Speculative in its Origin, and which arises from Wantonness and fullness of bread, may possibly be kept under by firmness and prudence. The very levity of character which produces it may extinguish it; but the Jacobinism which arises from Penury and irritation, from scorned loyalty, and rejected Allegiance, has much deeper roots. They take their nourishment from the bottom of human Nature and the unalterable constitution of things, and not from humour and caprice or the opinions of the Day about privileges and Liberties.[23]

Burke's sense of the inadequacies of antithesis is evident here. 'If the election of one of these Evils was at all a security against the other' is a conditional clause from which Irish Catholics might derive no security whatever. The letter to Hussey is valuable in that it reveals the vigour — not to say, violence — of Burke's feelings, vigour which was more harmoniously arranged in some of his published comments. It also reveals the identification of opposites which gives to

---

[23] Burke, *Correspondence*, vol. ix, p. 162.

his thought a dialectical compaction and concreteness. It is part of his withering irony to dramatize this tragic pact between the upholders of the Protestant Succession in Ireland and the Jacobins of Paris by means of transferring epithets: thus, the Dublin administration becomes 'the Irish Directory' and Napoleon is 'the Zealous Protestant Buonaparte' whose successes are greeted as 'Protestant Victories on the plains of Lombardy'.[24] There is more to this tactic than a juggling of words, a rearrangement of the terms of a trope: the central implication of Burke's account is that the Catholics of Ireland cannot succeed in their legitimate demands against such a combination of hostile foes.

But Burke's scathing use of Protestant as a synonym for Jacobin or Bonapartist should not lead us to assume him a zealous Catholic partisan. In his early writing on the Penal Laws, he was at pains to speak of 'our common Christianity',[25] and in his letter of 1795 to William Smith he commends particular attention to 'the great points in which the leading divisions are agreed'.[26] He was often accused of secret devotion to the sacraments of the Catholic Church, but the motive was generally malicious. Undoubtedly Burke's imagination had a decidedly Christian shape — fortitude and charity are characteristic forms which his advice takes in moments of crisis. But even the distressed letters written after the death of his beloved son, Richard, reveal a philosophical temper within his religious belief. In a public pamphlet he described his grief and his consolation:

> The storm has gone over me; and I lie like one of those old oaks which the late hurricane has scattered about me. I am stripped of all my honours, I am torn up by the roots, and lie prostrate on the earth! There, and prostrate there, I most unfeignedly recognise the Divine justice, and in some degree submit to it.[27]

The gradually emerging repetitions, and the modulated qualification of the last phrase, reveal Burke as peculiarly sensitive to the manner in which language acts upon feeling. If he

[24] Ibid., pp. 162-3. There are many other instances in the correspondence of this period.
[25] 'Tracts on the Popery Laws', Burke, *Works*, vol. vi, p. 30.
[26] 'Letter to William Smith', Ibid., p. 50.
[27] 'A Letter to a Noble Lord', Ibid., vol. v, p. 136.

employs terms like Protestant provocatively, it is not simply because of his Catholic ancestry: the roots of his late assault upon the Irish Directory lie in his lifelong interest in the language of history. When we look to his account of Protestant Ascendancy, we should recall not only his vigour but also his philosophical temper, his long meditation on Irish affairs and his more immediate anxiety.

Burke's view of history was not so much Irish or English but Anglican. He was profoundly appreciative of the *via media* which the Church of England had established, and had no sympathy with papal medievalism or unitarian anarchy. His more extended writings on Irish history reflect this latitudinarian position while striving simultaneously to respond to deteriorating conditions among the religious factions in Ireland. The *Tracts on the Popery Laws* date from 1765 and arise directly from the recent outbreak of sectarian violence which had touched on his own family. The various letters of the 1790s — to Hercules Langrishe, William Smith, and to his son Richard — are no less implicated in the atmosphere of increasing communal tension. One constant principle of his argument is that, whatever Irish Catholics may or may not have done in the reign of Charles I or Elizabeth, the perpetuation of punishment upon succeeding generations is foolishly divisive. Nor is it legislation alone which perpetuates division; the writing of history is itself an intervention into events which might otherwise be more harmoniously shaped. Referring to the works of Clarendon and Temple, he deplores

those miserable performances which go about under the names of Histories of Ireland [and which] do indeed represent those events after this manner: and they would persuade us, contrary to the known order of nature, that indulgence and moderation in governors is the natural incitement in subjects to rebel.[28]

It is Burke's repeated belief that a relaxation of the laws restricting the rights of Catholics would produce a greater integration of the king's Irish subjects into his realms. In the 1765 *Tracts*, however, he juxtaposes to Clarendon and Temple an alternative record:

[28] 'Tracts on the Popery Laws', Ibid., vol. vi, p. 45.

But there is an interior History of Ireland, the genuine voice of its records and monuments, which speaks a very different language from these histories, from Temple and from Clarendon; these restore nature to its just rights, and policy to its proper order.[29]

We detect here the pre-romantic philosopher of the sublime and the beautiful rather than the author of the *Reflections*; monuments and inner histories are the stuff of mid-century antiquarianism. Though the *Tracts* remained unpublished in Burke's lifetime one can see him entering a crucial and timely qualification to this view in the *Letter to Richard Burke* (1792):

The miserable natives of Ireland, who ninety-nine in a hundred are tormented with quite other cares, and are bowed down to labour for the bread of an hour, are not, as gentlemen pretend, plodding with antiquaries for titles of centuries ago to the estates of the great lords and 'squires for whom they labour.[30]

Gentlemen's suspicions of antiquarian research as the latest form of Catholic conspiracy should be considered in the context of a new romantic interest in the past. Sylvester O'Halloran's *General History of Ireland* (1774), Joseph Cooper Walker's *Historical Memoirs of the Irish Bards* (1786), and Charlotte Brooke's *Reliques of Irish Poetry* (1789) are the better-known examples of a movement in historiography to which Burke had made his slight contribution in 1765.[31] The *General History* was to have an influence on Standish O'Grady in the 1870s akin to religious conversion, and in the 1830s the Ordnance Survey discovered that inquiries into local tradition and genealogy produced embarrassing evidence of an 'interior history'.[32] Such consequences did not attend the early antiquarians to any notable extent, though it is noteworthy that the antiquarian O'Halloran in Maria Edgeworth's

[29]   Idem.
[30]   'Letter to Richard Burke', ibid., p. 80.
[31]   For a general discussion of the antiquarian background to Anglo-Irish literature compare Maurice Harmon and Roger McHugh *Short History of Anglo-Irish Literature* (Dublin: Wolfhound Press, 1982), pp. 65-71, and Margaret McCurtain's essay in Robert O'Driscoll (ed.), *The Celtic Consciousness* (Dublin: Dolmen Press, 1982), pp. 371-82.
[32]   For recent comment on this episode see Robert Welch, *Irish Poetry from Moore to Yeats* (Gerrards Cross: Smythe, 1980), pp. 96-103.

The Absentee plays a central role in reconciling past and present, Jacobite and Williamite. What is significant in the 1790s is not so much the achievement of the researchers as the trepidation of the 'gentlemen'. And Burke's timely qualification is in part designed to placate their anxieties.

These anxieties had European as well as local causes. The French Revolution, though welcomed by the Whigs in general, was soon interpreted as having radical implications for British society. Raymond Williams has discussed the manner in which Jane Austen's fiction relates, not to a *settled* landed society, but to a society in which land is either held or sought as a palpable form of security in a time of great social change.[33] Back in 1765 Burke had already recognized the conserving inertia of property, and found the exclusion of Catholics from long leases positively a threat to social stability:

This confinement of landed property to one set of hands, and preventing its free circulation through the community, is a most leading article of ill policy; because it is one of the most capital discouragements to all that industry which may be employed on the last improvement of the soil. . .[34]

By the 1790s the rights of Catholics to hold land had been modified, but the apprehension of Protestants that their monopoly was thereby threatened increased in proportion to the European crisis rather than the local one. Burke is remarkable for the manner in which he sees economic policy, religious bias, and historiography as forming a coherent social and cultural pattern. Those upon whom he was soon to turn his scorn were remarkable for the manner in which they substituted the single concept or slogan of Protestant Ascendancy for the complexity of a society in crisis.

The progress of the French Revolution required of the British government some further reconciliation with the king's Catholic subjects in Ireland. An unsettled Ireland was a dangerous breach in Britain's defences, and since 1782 (and earlier) Ireland had displayed a plethora of discontents.

[33] Raymond Williams, *The City and the Country* (London: Paladin, 1975), pp. 140-5.
[34] 'Tracts on the Popery Laws', Burke, *Works,* vol. vi, p. 43.

Political radicalism among Presbyterians and traditional petitions for restored civil rights from Catholics were further complicated by the spread of violence in the countryside. Protestant Peep O' Day Boys and Catholic Defenders were active from the late 1780s onwards, and the Orange order was born in 1795 as the consequence of accelerating sectarian strife. If the Defenders had some ancestry in the Whiteboy movement of mid-century, and if their name truly reflects some initial emphasis on defensive tactics, the Protestant 'grass roots' organizations represented a new element in Irish unrest. Explicitly sectarian in composition, they approached social and economic matters on the assumption of a supremacy as much mythological as historical. Burke was quite capable of seeing incidents of sectarian prejudice in exaggerated terms, and he may never have fully grasped the implications of the new movement among the Protestant tenantry. In 1792, however, he concentrated most effectively and ironically on the slogan of the hour, Protestant Ascendancy.

It would be foolish to attempt to establish the exact moment at which the phrase was conceived. The elements of the term are, after all, common enough in themselves — even if we make allowances for the slippery meaning of Protestant in Anglo-Irish affairs. Thomas Leland, whose *History of Ireland* escaped Burke's comment in the *Tracts* by appearing in 1773, is said to have been fully aware of the false colouring of his work and to have justified himself by claiming a need to support 'the English ascendancy in Ireland since the reformation'.[35] By this token, ascendancy is the condition enjoyed by those principles or forces which predominate or are in the ascendant in the sense that a planet may be said to be so. Dr Johnson, in his dictionary, illustrates the word by a quotation from Watts which has, for us, an ironical application — 'Custom has some ascendancy over understanding, and what at one time seemed decent, appears disagreeable

[35] See Burke, *Correspondence,* vol. vii, p. 104, n. 9; the phrase quoted, however, derives from Francis Plowden and dates from the early 19th century. For Burke's early encouragement of Leland, and his subsequent disappointment in his *History,* see Walter D. Love, 'Charles O'Conor of Belenagare, and Thomas Leland's "philosophical" history of Ireland', *Irish Historical Studies,* vol. 13 (1962), p. 23.

afterwards.'[36] As a potent collocation, Protestant Ascendancy may be dated with some certainty to the early weeks of 1792, when Hercules Langrishe and others were active in reviving proposals for a generous restoration of civil rights to Irish Catholics. Given the subsequent currency of the phrase, in particular given the manner in which Yeats will deploy it while invoking Edmund Burke as his mentor, a close history of its evolution in 1792 is called for.

By the end of 1791 the British government were resolved on a relaxation of the penal laws in Ireland. The relative independence of the Dublin parliament together with the complexity of any negotiation with the Irish establishment presented a considerable obstacle to their intentions. On 26 December, Henry Dundas, the Home Secretary, wrote both an official and a private letter to the Earl of Westmorland, the Lord-Lieutenant in Dublin Castle. Emphasizing the importance of conceding this reform to achieve harmony between the two kingdoms, Dundas made it plain that Irish Protestant resistance to the king's advisers and their plans would serve only to isolate them from the traditional support they enjoyed in their relations with Westminster. Westmorland replied in some consternation on 11 January 1792, and while he stressed the strength of the 'Protestant gentry', of the 'Protestant interest', and, bluntly, 'Protestant power', there is no sign of the phrase 'Protestant Ascendancy'.[37] More precisely, the word 'ascendancy' is cited only in such a way as to indicate that its imminent collocation with 'Protestant' has as yet no currency. Proposals to enfranchise Catholics, even if limited to elections for county seats, would mean that 'they would gradually gain an ascendancy, and would soon be enabled to make a successful attack on the tithes and established clergy, so odious to themselves and the Presbyterians. . .'.[38] Between 11 and 14 January, Westmorland communicated the gist of Dundas's

[36] Samuel Johnson *A Dictionary of the English Language* (London, 1755), vol. i (2G).
[37] Westmorland to Henry Dundas, 11 January 1792, quoted in Lecky op. cit., vol. iii, p. 45. The two letters of 26 December 1791 are preserved in the State Paper Office, Dublin Castle (Westmorland Corresp., Nos. 27 and 29).
[38] Westmorland to Dundas, 11 January 1792: Lecky, vol. iii, p. 43.

dispatch to 'the principal persons called the Irish cabinet', to John Fitzgibbon (the Lord Chancellor), John Beresford, Charles Agar (the Archbishop of Cashel), Sir John Parnell, the Attorney-General, and the Prime Sergeant:

They all agree in the impracticability of carrying in Parliament either the Point of Arms or Franchise & in the impolicy of attempting it, & they foresee the Ruin of the Protestant Ascendancy of the Peace & Quiet of the Country in success of such a proposal.[39]

This less than articulate letter is the earliest context in which 'the Protestant Ascendancy' has been found. Westmorland's earlier letter, by not using it, suggests that the phrase may have originated in his meeting with Fitzgibbon, Beresford, and the others. (Indeed it is tempting to consider the Lord Chancellor as its possible author, bearing in mind his immediate Catholic forebears.) Within a few days, Major Robert Hobart, the Chief Secretary, in writing to Dundas repeatedly used the phrase to emphasize the strength of resistance to reform: more particularly he insisted that

the connection between England and Ireland rests absolutely upon the Protestant ascendency. Abolish distinctions, and you create a Catholic superiority. If you are to maintain a Protestant Ascendancy, it must be by substituting influence for numbers.[40]

These contexts, whether in Westmorland's correspondence or Hobart's, are, however, private, and do not amount to more than a couple of letters written within less than a week of each other. The day after Hobart wrote to Dundas, Westmorland wrote to the Prime Minister, Pitt, detailing the constitution and social structure of Ireland so frankly as to accept Edmund Burke's term for the situation prior to 1782 as appropriate to conditions ten years later:

---

[39] Westmorland to Dundas, 14 January 1792 (Westmorland Corresp., No. 42). Lecky (vol. iii, p. 41) refers to a meeting of the Irish Privy Council rather than of the Cabinet; for the status and function of the latter at this period, and of the involvement of the Archbishop of Cashel, see Malcomson, *John Foster: The Politics of the Anglo-Irish Ascendancy*, pp. 415-18.

[40] Robert Hobart to Dundas, 17 January 1792, quoted in Lecky, op. cit., vol. iii, p. 51. Hobart is generally acknowledged as being closer to the Protestant party than Westmorland, his superior; during the Union debates he acted with other lesser members of the Cabinet to stimulate Orange reactions. His taking up of the phrase, Protestant Ascendancy, in January 1792 is characteristic.

That frame is a Protestant garrison (in the words of Mr. Burke), in possession of the land, magistracy, and power of the country; holding that property under the tenure of British power and supremacy, and ready at every instant to crush the rising of the conquered. If under various circumstances their generals should go a little refractory, do you lessen your difficulties or facilitate the means of governing, by dissolving their authority and trusting to your popularity and good opinion with the common soldiers of the conquered? Allegory apart, do you conceive England can govern Ireland by the popularity of the government?[41]

And to drive home the point about estates held under British tenure, and as the result of conquest, there was the rising murmur among Protestant landowners, as Westmorland acknowledged, 'the lower Catholics already talk of their ancient family estates.'[42] These confidential exchanges between Dublin and London, in which the phrase Protestant Ascendancy emerges alongside talk of renaissant Catholic claims to land and title, were due to receive a resounding endorsement in the public forum of the Irish parliament meeting on 19 January 1792. And yet it was not parliament, but a lesser assembly, which seized upon the new coinage.

The debate on Langrishe's proposals has already been cited in support of Grattan's position at this time. In reply to Langrishe's notion for a relief bill, the member for County Wexford, George Ogle, declared

for my part, Sir, I ever have maintained, and with my last breath I will maintain the protestant ascendancy: — nor can I think it within the power of human wisdom to do any thing effectual for the Roman Catholics, without endangering that ascendancy in church and state.[43]

It is clear from this, as from Hobart's letter, that the phrase is used as the equivalent to Protestant interest (or to the ascendancy of Protestantism) and not to any specific social 'class' or party. As yet there is no sense of the phrase meaning the Protestant gentry, or indeed the Protestant aristocracy. That such a collective noun should be discerned is

---

[41] Westmorland to William Pitt, 18 January 1792, quoted in Lecky, op. cit., vol. iii, pp. 48-9.

[42] Ibid., p. 48.

[43] *Irish Parliamentary Debates*, vol. xii, p. 24 (19 January 1792).

quickly evident — the same morphosis is occurring to aristocracy in the 1790s. Wolfe Tone, of all people, on 23 July 1792
confides in his journal that 'the Catholics and the Protestant
ascendency are left to fight it out.'[44] At the same time he
records that 'wherever there was a meeting of the Protestant
ascendency, which was the title assumed by that party (and a
very impudent one it was), we took care it should be followed by a meeting of the Catholics . . .'.[45] But before the
collective noun emerged, some definition had to be imposed as
much on the public mind as on the words of the new slogan.

Ogle's phrase and sentiment was to recur throughout the
debate in parliament, but elsewhere in Dublin a more extended definition of its meaning was imminent. On Friday
20 January 1792, the Christmas Assembly of the city Corporation met in the Exhibition House, William Street. The ninth
item of business resulted in a committee's being established
'to prepare an address to his majesty expressive of our
attachment to his majesty's person, family, and government,
and our determination to support the present constitution
both in church and state'. As the committee's efforts have
enshrined one of Anglo-Ireland's most evocative phrases in
our rhetoric, it is only proper to record the participants:
they were the Recorder (Denis George), with six Aldermen
(William Alexander, John Carleton, John Exshaw, Henry
Howison, William James, and Nathaniel Warren), and six
members of the common council (John Giffard, Ambrose
Leet, and Messrs Manders, Powell, Sall, and Twaites.) The
address they prepared reads in full:

To the king's most excellent majesty.
The humble address of the Lord Mayor, Sheriffs, commons, and citi-
zens of the city of Dublin.
May it please your majesty.
We, your majesty's most dutiful and loyal subjects, the Lord Mayor,

[44] *The Autobiography of Theobald Wolfe Tone 1763-1798*, ed. R. Barry
O'Brien (Dublin: Maunsel, 1910), vol. i, p. 108. It is worth noting that, prior to
the excitements generated by the 1792 resolutions, Tone was on very friendly
terms with George Knox, MP, a supporter of Lord Abercorn; from his association
with the Catholic Committee, Tone went on to become the intellectual leader of
the United Irishmen and the founder of the Irish republican tradition, dying by
suicide in 1798.
[45] Ibid., p. 69.

Sheriffs, commons, and citizens of the city of Dublin in common council assembled, beg leave to approach the throne with the most unshaken sentiments of loyalty and affectionate regards for your majesty's person, family, and government.

Sensibly impressed with the value of our excellent constitution both in church and state, as established at the glorious revolution, we feel ourselves peculiarly called upon to stand forward at the present crisis to pray your majesty to preserve the Protestant ascendancy in Ireland inviolate and to assure your majesty that we are firmly resolved to support it free from innovation and are determined most zealously to oppose any attempt to overturn the same, having a firm reliance on the attachment of your majesty and that of your royal progeny to that constitution, which the house of Brunswick was called forth to defend.

In testimony whereof, we have caused the common seal of the said city to be hereonto affixed this 20th day of January, in the year of our Lord, 1792.[46]

This is the first stage of the definition of Protestant Ascendancy, which the Corporation will carry a stage further in September of the same year. The crucial development is the identification of ascendancy with the constitution itself, with the principles of the glorious revolution, rather than simply with 'the Protestant interest' or 'Protestant power'. In due course the Corporation transmitted its address to the king through the offices of the Lord-Lieutenant, and proceeded to convey the same sentiments to the two members sitting for the city constituency. These were Henry Grattan and Lord Henry Fitzgerald, brother to Lord Edward Fitzgerald who was to die six years later while resisting arrest as leader of the United Irishmen rebellion. Grattan and Lord Henry were entreated to 'oppose with all your influence and great abilities any alteration that may tend to shake the security of property in this kingdom or subvert the Protestant ascendancy in our happy constitution'.[47] In addition, the Corporation ordered the publication of its address in the *Dublin Journal* and the *Dublin Evening Post*, and the dispatch of

---

[46]   *Calendar of Ancient Records of Dublin*, ed. Lady Gilbert (Dublin: Dollard, 1909), vol. xiv, pp. 241-2. The *Calendar* only provides the surnames of the committee members, and where possible these have been augmented with Christian names by reference to almanacs etc.

[47]   Ibid., p. 243.

copies to the chief magistrates of the cities and corporate towns in the country.[48]

With the English government keen to accommodate the discontented Catholics, the Irish Opposition in full cry for reform, and the Catholics themselves organized and articulate, the Corporation may well have feared that parliament might have been carried over in the heat of the moment into an extension of Catholic rights damaging to Protestant interests. And whereas parliament was representative principally of land and patronage, the Corporation had a real interest in maintaining the privileges of Irish Protestants as they bore upon commerce and the professions. Langrishe wished to see Catholics free to participate equally in trade and the learned professions, free to bear arms, to intermarry with Protestants, and to vote. 'The Point of Arms' and the franchise were rights which none of Westmorland's advisers could recommend, for the first would have effectively eliminated the convenient state of affairs whereby only government supporters among the lower orders had legal access to firearms, while the second would have soon threatened the permanence of the government itself. 'Mr. Beresford expresses the strongest attachment', Westmorland had reported, '& desires to do whatever his opinion could justify, but could not declare even to support any concession without Ld Waterford's approbation, whose opinions at their last conversation were averse.' As for the Archbishop of Cashel, he 'was unwilling to relax at all, tho he saw no mischief in allowing them admission to Trades & liberty of education, he was averse to admission to the Law & even intermarriage . . .'.[49]

The Corporation of Dublin spoke clearly of 'the security of property', and in the eyes of a hostile newspaper its motives were basely monopolist:

We cannot but admire the *modesty* of the Board of Aldermen, in pretending to address the worthy representatives of the city of Dublin, to support their *alert combination,* in favour of their own authority and consequence: and to keep away any possibility of being brought to share the good things of the *city,* with any of their fellow subjects of

---

[48]   Ibid., pp. 243-44.
[49]   Westmorland to Dundas, 14 January 1792.

a certain description — city leases, city Maces, city monopolies, and contracts are eligible *douceurs*, which the good and loving master G——, with all his tender regards, cannot possibly allow his Catholic friends to be troubled with any share of.[50]

The sly association of the Aldermen with the subversive combinations of working men is part of a deflating metaphor which runs through the *Morning Post's* commentary. In its view what is at stake is not the constitution but material rewards of a municipal monopoly. The *Dublin Chronicle*, reporting the Corporation proceedings, records that 'Messrs Howison, Saul, Powell, Cope, Giffard and some other Members spoke in terms of warm condemnation' of Catholic aspirations.[51] Cope it was who moved that an address be presented, with Bond and Binns objecting. The participation of the common members in the debate underlines its essentially merchant priorities. Giffard, whom the *Morning Post* singled out for ridicule, was an apothecary by trade, who advanced himself by an appointment as surveyor and gauger to the Custom House site when that development was floated under John Beresford's auspices. In 1792, he represented the Apothecary's Guild on the Corporation, and was an intermediary linking the Castle and a spy among the United Irishmen: in 1795 he was dismissed from a post on the *Dublin Journal* and in need of cash from the Lord-Lieutenant if he were to avoid ruin.[52] John Giffard, apothecary, gauger, middleman-spy, and journalist, is significant not because his fellow members of the Corporation may with facility be symbolized in his career, but because his advancement and insecurity together summarize the conditions which called forth 'Protestant Ascendancy'. The phrase is traceable from Dublin Castle to the parliament in College Green, and thence to the Corporation where the involvement of the guild members was prominent. The January initiative did not in itself succeed, and the Chief Secretary wrote to Westmorland that 'all idea of a Catholic game (if ever such was entertained) is at an end, and that the British Government will decidedly

---

[50] *The Morning Post; or Dublin Courant*, 24 January 1792.
[51] *Dublin Chronicle*, 21 January 1792; for the dissent of Bond and Binns see *Dublin Chronicle*, loc. cit., and *Morning Post*, 21 January 1792.
[52] For information etc. on Giffard see Appendix B.

support the Protestant Ascendency.'[53] When Burke came to discuss the emergence of the new phrase he dwelt with a sardonic emphasis on the to-and-fro trading between Corporation and Castle, and on the mentality which characterized Catholic aspirations as a game.

Edmund Burke's involvement in the struggle for Catholic rights was maintained primarily through his son, Richard, who was employed by the Catholic Committee as its agent. Young Burke had come to Dublin on 13 January, and participated in the discussions leading to the parliamentary debate. The House of Commons returned to the issue in February, and in the renewed debate greater attention was given to the meaning of the concept of Protestant Ascendancy. Keen to insist that Irish Protestants should themselves decide the fate of the Catholic question, Richard Sheridan (not the dramatist) advised that

the Roman Catholics of Ireland may now learn that it is to the wisdom and liberality of the Protestants of Ireland they ought to look, and that foreign or ministerial negociation [sic] must be ever suspicious and never successful: every man must agree, that they are entitled to every benefit and advantage compatible with the preservation of the Protestant ascendancy . . .[54]

Grattan's parliament is renowned for its achievement of a limited independence from Westminster, and its critics deplored the unreformed basis of its representation in so far as it placed this independence potentially under the control of the intransigents. Sheridan's speech is not untypical of the prickly Irish Protestant insistence on rights *surpassing* those of the British parliament. Fear of Catholic alliances with French or other external radicals was entirely understandable; fear of negotiations with government ministers is symptomatic of that inwardly directed strategy which was to characterize the culture of the 'Protestant Ascendancy' in the nineteenth century. Sheridan's attitude to Langrishe's renewed proposal was far from dismissive, he thought three of its four proposals 'innocent, perhaps desirable', but he

---

[53] Hobart to Westmorland, 25 January 1792, quoted in Lecky, op. cit., vol. iii, p. 54.
[54] *Irish Parliamentary Debates*, vol. xii, p. 133 (18 February 1792).

proceeded to elaborate his notion of ascendancy in such a way as to transform his reservation into a veto: as he knew that

'Protestant ascendancy' might be used perhaps by some in a very narrow, and by others in a too enlarged sense, he begged leave to submit his idea of Protestant ascendancy to the House: by Protestant ascendancy he meant, a Protestant king, to whom only being Protestant we owed allegiance; a Protestant house of peers, composed of Protestant Lords spiritual in Protestant succession, of Protestant lords temporal, with Protestant inheritance, and a Protestant house of commons, elected and deputed by Protestant constitutents; in short a Protestant legislative, a Protestant judicial, and a Protestant executive, in all and each of their varieties, degrees, and gradations.[55]

If we recall, however, that broadly similar disabilities were maintained in Britain and that the centrality of religious conformism was a self-evident truth in the late eighteenth century, then the resistance of Irish Protestants can be seen as something more than the defence of commercial and social advantage. The real contrast in the argument is not so much between Catholic and Protestant; but between those like Sheridan and Ogle and, shortly, the Corporation of Dublin who expressed loyalty to Protestant*ism* rather than to king or parliament on the one hand, and those on the other hand like Grattan and Burke who acknowledged the primacy of social relations in discussing matters of individual religious belief. If we are here witnessing the public baptism of what W. B. Yeats will later call 'the Protestant Ascendency with its sense of responsibility',[56] we are also witnessing the early exertions of a new force, described by Grattan as Protestant bigotry without religion. This ideology, descending from the intransigents of Grattan's parliament to the generation of Ian Paisley, is necessarily contradictory: asserting the absolute value of Protestantism above all calculations of social amelioration, it nevertheless founds itself upon ascendancy within society, ascendancy in matters of education, trade, property, political participation. To the eighteenth-century

[55] Idem. Sheridan speech is printed at pp. 133-5.
[56] 'Commentary on A Parnellite at Parnell's Funeral', W. B. Yeats, *Variorum Edition of the Poems*, ed. Peter Allt and Russell K. Alspach (New York: Macmillan, 1977; 7th printing), p. 833.

mind, even to the ecclesiastical mind of that period 'Protestant' connoted certain principles in relation to Christian belief. Protestant*ism* was likely to substitute the protest for the belief. It is this which Burke alludes to in the 'Letter to Richard Burke' when he observes sardonically, 'we sometimes hear of a Protestant *religion*, frequently of a Protestant *interest*. We hear of the latter the most frequently, because it has a positive meaning. The other has none.'[57]

Richard Burke's letters to his father in January and February 1792 form one of the most important accounts of the emergence of Protestant Ascendancy. The phrase, as we have seen, occurred in Ogle's speech of 19 January and is expanded in the Corporation's address to the king the following evening. Young Burke, however, does not use the phrase until about 1 March when he dismisses 'the foolish partizans of the protestant ascendancy' and 'the ascendancy gentlemen'.[58] As late as 6 October he is referring to the Protestant Ascendancy as 'a new name which the enemies of the Catholics have adopted'.[59] But before that date his father turned his formidable rhetorical skills to an analysis of what may be very properly called the new coinage. The 'Letter to Richard Burke' may be dated to a period between mid-February and 10 May 1792.[60] Given the concentrated analysis of our phrase, it seems likely that Richard's letter of *c*.1 March stimulated his father's endeavours.

The *Letter to Richard Burke* remains unfinished, and it lacks perhaps the polish of those productions which Burke was able to revise at leisure. Yet leisure was not always the most conducive state in which he worked, and the nervous energy of Burke's focus is complementary to the solemn architectonics of his reflectionary style. Here the object under scrutiny is neither the idealized past nor the conjured distortions of a Jacobin future; it is a distinctively shifting and treacherous present:

[57] 'Letter to Richard Burke', *Works*, vol. vi, p. 69.

[58] Burke, *Correspondence*, vol. vii, pp. 86-9; the letter is addressed to Richard Burke Senior, but is endorsed by Edmund Burke's wife, Jane.

[59] Ibid., pp. 241-2: the letter (pp. 235-46) is to the Earl Fitzwilliam.

[60] See W. B. Todd, *A Bibliography of Edmund Burke*, 2nd. ed. (Godalming, St Paul's Bibliographies, 1982), p. 257.

A word has been lately struck in the mint of the Castle of Dublin; thence it was conveyed to the Tholsel, or city-hall, where, having passed the touch of the corporation, so respectably stamped and vouched, it soon became current in parliament, and was carried back by the Speaker of the House of Commons in great pomp, as an offering of homage from whence it came. The word is *Ascendency.* It is not absolutely new. But the sense in which I have hitherto seen it used was to signify an influence obtained over the minds of some other person by love and reverence, or by superior management and dexterity. It had, therefore, to this its promotion no more than a moral, not a civil or political, use. But I admit it is capable of being so applied; and if the Lord Mayor of Dublin, and the Speaker of the Irish parliament, who recommend the preservation of the Protestant ascendency, mean to employ the word in that sense, that is, if they understand by it the preservation of the influence of that description of gentlemen over the Catholics by means of an authority derived from their wisdom and virtue, and from an opinion they raise in that people of a pious regard and affection for their freedom and happiness, it is impossible not to commend their adoption of so apt a term into the family of politics. It may be truly said to enrich the language. Even if the Lord Mayor and Speaker mean to insinuate that this influence is to be obtained and held by flattering their people, by managing them, by skilfully adapting themselves to the humours and passions of those whom they would govern, he must be a very untoward critic who would cavil even at this use of the word, though such cajoleries would perhaps be more prudently practised than professed. These are all meanings laudable, or at least tolerable. But when we look a little more narrowly, and compare it with the plan to which it owes its present technical application, I find it has strayed far from its original sense. It goes much further than the privilege allowed by Horace. It is more than *parcè detortum.* This Protestant ascendency means nothing less than an influence obtained by virtue, by love, or even by artifice and seduction; full as little an influence derived from the means by which ministers have obtained an influence, which might be called, without straining, an *ascendency* in public assemblies in England, that is, by a liberal distribution of places and pensions, and other graces of government. This last is wide indeed of the signification of the word. New *ascendency* is the old mastership. It is neither more nor less than the resolution of one set of people in Ireland to consider themselves as the sole citizens in the commonwealth; and to keep a dominion over the rest by reducing them to absolute slavery under a military power; and, thus fortified in their power, to divide the public estate, which is the result of general contribution, as a military booty solely amongst themselves.[61]

[61] 'Letter to Richard Burke', *Works*, vol. vi, pp. 64–6.

So far Burke has concentrated solely upon the application of the word ascendancy to the new policy, directed against proposals to grant Catholics civil rights, and he has found disturbing innovations in the usage. His manner is as much hesitant as strategically devious, and his sentences run ahead of the rhythm of his argument. The initial conceit of the phrase as a coinage minted by the public authorities, and then stamped and approved for circulation, is not maintained; instead there follows an involuted recourse to the previous history of ascendancy as a moral term untouched by political or civil usage. This attention to the word as such is then followed by a comparison between ascendancy as it might be achieved by a statesman in the public assemblies of England and the latest Irish usage. 'A liberal distribution' of patronage evidently distinguishes the English practice from the Irish — and here Burke's emphasis must be heard to fall upon *liberal*. With this indirect critique of Irish nepotism, he finally defines new ascendancy as the old mastership.

This is only half of Burke's meditation on the term; he now turns his attention to the Protestant element in Protestant Ascendancy and once again stresses the potency of language as such:

The poor word ascendency, so soft and melodious in its sound, so lenitive and emollient in its first usage, is now employed to cover to the world the most rigid, and perhaps not the most wise, of all plans of policy. The word is large enough in its comprehension. I cannot conceive what mode of oppression in civil life, or what mode of religious persecution, may not come within the methods of preserving an *ascendency*. In plain old English, as they apply it, it signifies *pride and dominion* on the one part of the relation, and on the other *subserviency and contempt* — and it signifies nothing else. The old words are as fit to be set to music as the new; but use has long since affixed to them their true signification, and they sound, as the other will, harshly and odiously to the moral and intelligent ears of mankind.

This ascendency, by being a *Protestant* ascendency, does not better it from the combination of a note or two more in this anti-harmonic scale. If Protestant ascendency means the proscription from citizenship of by far the major part of the people of any country, then Protestant ascendency is a bad thing; and it ought to have no existence. But there is a deeper evil. By the use that is so frequently made of the term, and the policy which is ingrafted on it, the name Protestant becomes nothing more or better than the name of a persecuting faction, with a relation of some sort of theological hostility to others, but without any sort of ascertained tenets of its own, upon the ground of which it persecutes other men; for the patrons of this Protestant ascendency neither do, nor can, by anything positive, define or describe what they mean by the word Protestant. It is defined, as Cowley defines wit, not by what it is, but by what it is not.[62]

Once again we can see Burke wrestling with a novel concept. The direction of his analysis is by now familiar enough. A significant assumption, however, is that the penal laws did not so much *restrict* the rights of Irish Catholics as *exclude* them from citizenship. This emphasis becomes important when Burke develops it in relation to the way in which Protestant Ascendancy will exacerbate 'that worst of all oppressions, the persecution of private society and private manners'.[63] The full title of Maria Edgeworth's *Castle Rackrent*, 'an Hibernian tale taken from the facts, and from the manners of the Irish squires before the year 1782', indicates the extent to which the novelist approaches society through the microcosm of *manners*.

Burke's analysis of the new slogan was written in England, in the form of a letter to his son intended from the outset for publication; although it was prepared for the *Works* of May 1792, the text was unfinished. From this circumstance we can identify a certain urgent irresolution in Burke's thought on the subject. His letters written later in the year substantiate this conclusion by revealing further evidence of his exploratory and yet vigorous interrogation of the phrase. One reason for his difficulty was simply distance from the centre of debate; another was the involuted nature of the debate, generating greater psychic tension in the participants than observers might at first have found reasonable. In the Irish House of Commons, the most extensive and accessible account of Ascendancy came — not surprisingly — from Grattan himself. Richard Burke provided his father with an amusing account of the February debate, juxtaposing the intransigents and Grattan very effectively:

[62]   Ibid., p. 66.
[63]   'Letter to a Peer of Ireland on the Penal Laws', Ibid., vol. iii, p. 287.

Then all the fiery protestants got up and unbottelled their nonsense; when they had exhaust'd themselves they began to be a little ashamed of themselves, and after two or three just and grave lectures from the other side, they intirely changed their tone; It was at last 'our catholic brethren' and the idea of *perpetual* exclusion from the franchise, was generally exploded; tho' when ever any of them argued the point it was upon principles which go to perpetuity and with increasing strength. If the Ponsonbys had not bitch'd the question and played the fool, we should have made a great figure even on the division. Grattan reserved himself to the last and did admirably. Tho' we divided but 25. I *know* from the best authority, that there were 50 in the majority who were with us in their hearts.[64]

Richard did not possess his father's penetrating knowledge of Irish politics and the deviousness of great factions like that of the Ponsonby brothers. The elder Burke, however, fully agreed with his son's estimate of Grattan's performance, and it was on this occasion that he recorded his tribute to Grattan's eloquence and nobility, ending with the telling clause about men of talents and courage who lack power.[65] Though Grattan's reputation has inevitably suffered since the panegyrics of his son were transposed into art by W. B. Yeats, his speech on Protestant Ascendancy shows considerable sensitivity to broader movements in European thought than those of Dublin Corporation or the Catholic Committee.

Grattan's speech begins by summarizing very succinctly the existing laws restricting the rights of Catholics, and proceeds immediately to detail three recent controversies on the subject of political freedom — America, Ireland in 1782, France in 1789 — which underline the urgency and rationality of Catholic appeals. The utter evaporation of the Stuart cause, and the distraction of the papacy in its conflict with France, remove all objects and resources of Catholic disaffection. The Catholic approaches the Protestant applying simply for participation in a society which he fully acknowledges as lawful and without any Jacobite and chimerical rival, 'he desires you to name your own conditions and terms of abjuration, touching any imputed claim on this subject.[66]

[64] Burke, *Correspondence,* vol. vii, pp. 70-1.
[65] Ibid., p. 84.
[66] *Irish Parliamentary Debates,* vol. xii, p. 110.

After this broadly conceived prologue, Grattan then proceeds less predictably into a theological argument augmenting the general philosophical case:

I am well aware in questions of this sort how little religion affects their determination: however, we must not like ardent disputants, in the fury of the controversy forget the subject, nor [with] the zeal of the sectarist, lose all recollection of the Godhead: — it is necessary to remind you, that the Catholics acknowledge the same God, and the same Redeemer, and differ from you only in the forms of his worship and ceremonies of his commemoration; and that however that difference may be erroneous, it is not sufficiently heinous to warrant you in dispensing with the express and prime ordinances of your own religion, which enjoin certain fraternal affection towards all men, and particularly towards fellow christians whom you must allow to be saved, and are commanded to love . . .[67]

This brief homily may have struck the House as platitudinous: certainly none of the Protestant intransigents saw fit to quote theology in defence of their ascendancy. Yet Grattan's assumptions are significant in two respects. First, they are the ground upon which he erects the rhetorical paradox of the intransigents' position according to which Catholics are 'objects to their brethren of perpetual proscription, and objects to our God . . . of perpetual salvation'.[68] The hypothesis is directed into a contradiction in terms, so to speak, illustrating to the Augustan mind of the Irish parliament the moral logic inherent in Catholic relief. The second respect in which Grattan's theological premises are significant is simply that his assumptions will rapidly disappear in the nineteenth century when anti-Catholic evangelicalism will effectively deny the possibility of salvation to the devout and practising papist.

In this regard, Grattan makes explicit assumptions which are shortly to be challenged, thus pointing once again to the transitional nature of the Protestant Ascendancy debate in the 1790s. No doubt, the hardening of attitude among Irish Protestants in the 1820s and after has its parallel on the Catholic side: in the nineteenth century the Irish priesthood

[67] Idem.
[68] Ibid., p. 111.

was less tied by bonds of family or class to the dominant Protestant élite, and was by its training more inclined to speak its mind in terms of *ex ecclesia non salus est*. The exclusivism of nineteenth-century sectarian claims has its secular form also, in the emergence of a romantic nationalism which veered in some instances towards theories of racial purity. Grattan's conclusion to his theological discourse touches upon this emergent interest in racial history, while yet reserving for himself a strictly eighteenth-century perspective: if Christianity does not sanction the proscription of fellow Christians, and if the political climate has dissolved the threat of disaffection, 'we must therefore have recourse to some other law':

we imagine we have found it in our own peculiar situation; that situation we state to be as follows: the Protestants are the few and have the power; the Catholics have not the power and are the numbers: but this is not peculiar to us, but common to all nations — the Asiatics and the Greeks — the Greeks and the Italians — the English and the Saxons — the Saxon, English and Normans, — the vanquished and the vanquisher — they all at last intermingled; the original tribe was in number superior; and yet that superiority never prevented the incorporation, so that this state of our settlement is not peculiar to Ireland, but the ordinary progress of the population and the circulation of the human species, and as it was the trick of Nature, to preserve by intermixture, from dwindling and degeneracy, the animal proportions.[69]

This aspect of Grattan's argument is directed against those provisions of the penal laws which levied penalties in terms of property and personal estate on those who intermarried between the denominations. It implicitly identifies the urge towards marital introversion which was to become such a concern of Irish Protestants later, and sets up a case which Yeats dismisses in his drama of *mésalliance*, 'Purgatory' (1938). Indeed Grattan's concluding words on the subject have — ironically — a Yeatsian ring to them:

In some tribes it might have been otherwise, but they must have died, before they could reach history, a prey to their disputes, or swept off, by the tide of other nations washing them away in their little divisions,

[69] Ibid., p. 112.

and leaving something better on their shore — solitude or a wiser people.[70]

It is only after these impressive preliminaries that Grattan turns to the question of Protestant Ascendancy. Unlike Burke, who fixes upon the newness of the coinage, or at least, of the collocation of words, Grattan acknowledges the existence of the condition now loudly proclaimed as Protestant Ascendancy. In keeping with their very different origins in eighteenth-century Ireland, he does not share Burke's contempt: 'here another principle is advanced, connected indeed with the argument of [peculiar] situation, the Protestant Ascendency — I revere it — I wish for ever to preserve it, but in order to preserve I beg to understand it'.[71] His difficulties here are not those of Burke who is confronted with a novelty in political phraseology. Grattan is sincerely attached to the constitution under which Church and State are Protestant; he merely urges the inclusion of Catholics to the security of this constitution. His difficulty centres on the problems raised when the condition of Protestant Ascendancy is transformed into the touchstone by which all issues are to be resolved. In short, he interrogates the new slogan on three grounds — its ability to attract the Catholic majority to the defence of Ireland in the event of foreign attack; its ability to resist a Union with England, and finally and most immediately:

can it defend itself against a corrupt Minister? — Is the Protestant Ascendancy able to prevent oppressive taxes, controul the misapplication of public money, obtain any of the constitutional bills we have repeatedly proposed, or repeal any of the obnoxious regulations the country had repeatedly lamented?[72]

Answering his own inquiries in the negative, Grattan finds the notion of Protestant Ascendency — if it is to be taken as an active force in political and social life — to be spurious:

there is in this House one man who has more power in Parliament than all the Protestant Ascendancy — I need not tell you, [you] know

---

[70] Idem.
[71] Ibid., p. 113.
[72] Ibid., pp. 113-14.

already, as the Protestant parliament is now composed that which you call the Protestant Ascendancy is a name. We are governed by the *Ascendancy of the Treasury*.[73]

Later, in 1795 when the country was already sliding towards the widespread violence of '98, he summarized the system in Ireland as 'the monarchy of clerks — a government to be carried on by post'.[74] But for the moment, it was a 'Ministerial and an Aristocrate Ascendancy'.[75] 'From all this what do I conclude? — That the Protestant ascendancy in Ireland requires a new strength, and that you must find that strength in adopting a people, in a progressive adoption of the Catholic body . . .'.[76]

The outcome of the February debates was a limited but significant concession to Catholics who were to be admitted now to the professions, to higher education, and who were no longer to suffer penalties on marriage to Protestants. A proposal to admit them to the franchise was, however, defeated, and in a sense the Protestant Ascendancy declined to adopt the Catholic body politically. In Britain, most of the existing penal legislation had been repealed the previous year, and the reconciliation with Catholics which Pitt sought appeared to be well under way. By the end of the year 1792, deteriorating Anglo-French relations brought the issue once again to the foreground of discussion, and once again the notion of Protestant Ascendancy was both flourished and ridiculed by opposing factions.

Once again the Corporation of Dublin was in the vanguard, though the stimulus to their fervour lies close to Richard Burke. In January, prior to the debate on Langrishe's motion, a sub-committee of the Catholic pressure group had drawn up a paper addressed to the people of Ireland; according to the northern radical William Drennan, the paper, though signed by Edward Byrne (a leading Catholic merchant), was 'said to

---

[73]   Ibid., p. 114.
[74]   *The Parliamentary Register* (Dublin, 1795), vol. xv, p. 189. Quoted in Edmund Curtis and R. B. Mc Dowell, *Irish Historical Documents*, 2nd. ed. (London: Methuen, 1977), p. 226.
[75]   *Irish Parliamentary Debates*, vol. xii, p. 114.
[76]   Ibid., p. 116.

be drawn up by young Burke'.[77] In April a 'Circular letter proposing a Roman Catholic Convention' was issued (and apparently printed) under Byrne's name, though it too had been devised by Richard.[78] At a post-assembly of the Corporation held on 11 September, a further publication of Byrne's was considered; it was resolved to publish a letter to 'the protestants of Ireland' affirming the aldermen's loyalty to ascendancy. Having rehearsed the circumstances which led to the Glorious Revolution and which called forth 'severe but necessary restrictive laws' the letter turned to 'the protestant ascendancy, which we have resolved *with our lives and fortunes to maintain*':

And, that no doubt may remain of what we understand by the words 'Protestant Ascendancy,' we have further resolved, that we consider the protestant ascendancy to consist in *A Protestant King of Ireland, A Protestant Parliament, A Protestant Hierarchy, Protestant Electors and Government, The Benches of Justice, The Army and the Revenue. Through all their Branches and Details, Protestant: And this System Supported by a Connection with the Protestant Realm of Britain.*[79]

The final claim of loyalty to Britain passes over in silence the British reforms of 1791, and instead insists that 'the protestants of Ireland would not be compelled by any authority whatever to abandon that political situation which their forefathers won with their swords, and which is therefore their birth-right; or to surrender their religion at the footstool of popery.'

Much of this was relayed by Richard Burke to his father in London in his letters of 6 and 10 October. Burke had already expressed his views on the nature of Protestant Ascendancy — it was the old mastership — but he was now provoked into more fragmentary (though no less telling) definitions in his reply to his son. He refers contemptuously to 'the Jobbing ascendancy' and their policy 'of representing the Country to be disposed to rebellion in order to add to their Jobbs for the

---

[77] *The Drennan Letters 1776–1819* ed. D. A. Chart (Belfast: HMSO, 1931), p. 73. See Todd, op. cit., p. 278.

[78] Todd, op. cit., p. 280.

[79] *Calendar of Ancient Records of Dublin*, vol. xiv, pp. 284–7; and see also Richard Musgrave, *Memoirs of the Different Rebellions in Ireland*, 3rd. ed. (Dublin, 1802), vol. ii, pp. 222–5.

merit of keeping it under'.[80] Grattan visited him in England and reported that 'they who think Like them are in a manner obliged to decline all society' because 'the ascendants are as hot as fire.'[81] The Ascendancy is, ultimately, 'that Junto of Jobbers'.[82] There can be no doubt that it was the intervention of the Dublin Corporation, with its interests in commerce, which prompted Burke's image of Protestant Ascendancy as a word lately struck in the mint. The junto of jobbers embraces more than the Corporation — it touches upon the whole system of patronage by which the Dublin administration governed the country. Burke's later comments on the Protestant Ascendancy have that anguished impatience and abruptness which is characteristic of his last years. Indeed the last paragraph of the *Letter to Richard Burke* in its incompleteness catches his central response to the revolutionary decade in Ireland: 'All titles terminate in prescription; in which (differently from Time in the fabulous instances) the son devours the father, and the last prescription eats up all the former.'[83]

Prejudiced though Burke undoubtedly was on the question, and distraught though he was in his final years, his assessment of Ascendancy carries more conviction than any other. This is partly due to the purely assertive character of the ascendants' own definition and justification, who offer nothing to compare with Grattan's political and theological analysis. William Drennan, in many ways diametrically opposed to Burke politically, concurs with him in seeing the Ascendancy as 'only a few men actuated by the most monopolizing spirit'.[84] Writing from Dublin about April or May of 1793, Drennan records a temporary commercial consequence of the post-assembly resolutions which the ascendants can not have anticipated:

The city appears as quiet as usual, but you meet hosts of manufacturers on the quays begging for relief, and probably there will be parochial meetings for this purpose, who may take this opportunity of expressing

[80] Burke, *Correspondence*, vol. vii, pp. 282, 287.
[81] Ibid., p. 289.
[82] Ibid., p. 290.
[83] 'Letter to Richard Burke', *Works*, vol. vi, p. 80.
[84] *Drennan Letters*, p. 91.

their detestation of a war that has been the cause of such national calamity; but many think that the war has rather accelerated or ripened the evil than been the sole cause of it. They date the origin of the calamity from the period of the Protestant Ascendancy resolutions, in which the Corporation of Dublin was so distinguished . . .[85]

Drennan's economic analysis can be faulted, but he confirms the importance of the Corporation in giving currency to the new slogan, and thus confirms the date of its adoption. If George Ogle and Richard Sheridan vie with the Corporation for the distinction of announcing the birth of Protestant Ascendancy, it is to Edmund Burke that we must look for the most penetrating account of its social origins. By his conceit of the Tholsel and the mint, and by his repeated accusation of jobbery, Burke emphasized the close association of Ascendancy and commercial advantages as enjoyed by a Protestant élite challenged by an emergent Catholic bourgeoisie.

Given the manner by which Protestant Ascendancy became the rallying cry primarily of the landed classes adhering to the Church of Ireland, the Burkean imagery is noteworthy, indeed crucial in revealing the concrete bourgeois motivation of Ascendancy. In time the phrase will enter Yeats's political aesthetics, and in the course of that development its identification with landed property is intensified, despite its origins among the merchant-aldermen and the farmers of patronage. Lord Abercorn in 1792 dismissed 'the silly . . . phrases of Protestant interest and Protestant Ascendancy', though in the commonly accepted definitions of later years he was typical of the Ascendancy position.[86] This transference of the phrase from its commercial-bourgeois origins to a provenance of landed estate should be interpreted specifically in relation to the gradual erosion of landed estate as a political reality during the nineteenth century in Ireland; that is, it should be seen as the propagation of a false sociology. Such a process can be traced equally clearly in relation

---

[85]   Ibid., p. 158. 'Manufacturers' are of course factory employees.
[86]   Quoted in Malcomson, op. cit., p. 355. Malcomson's is the first biography of John Foster, the Speaker of the Irish House of Commons so scorned by Burke in the 'Letter to Richard Burke'; it provides a useful account of the Irish political and parliamentary context in which ascendancy emerged, though it passes over the origins of the slogan with little comment; see pp. 352-3.

to the alleged historical moment of Ascendancy: for Yeats and those who follow him, the flowering of the Protestant Ascendancy was a period (rather imprecisely defined) in the eighteenth century associated broadly with the names of Swift, Berkeley, Goldsmith, Grattan, and Burke. Recovering the evidence of the Dublin Corporation resolutions, we can begin to appreciate the extent to which this historical identification reads back into the reigns of Queen Anne and the first two Georges a condition anxiously asserted in the last revolutionary decade of the century.

There is a third dimension to this transformation of the jobbing ascendants into a cultural tradition, and it is specifically linguistic. The years of the French Revolution saw a significant change in the language of social relations in England — new words were borrowed from France or were imposed by the energy of events in Europe and at home. Aristocracy, meaning government by the best (noblest) citizens, has a long pedigree, but *aristocrat* as meaning an individual who favours such government or is a member of such a governing 'class' is a popular formation of the French Revolution dated by the Oxford Dictionary simply to the year 1789. An almost identical process can be observed in the case of democracy and democrat. At the general level, it is obvious that this development is part of the tendency to define class as the aggregate of numbers of individuals on the basis of birth, status, function or whatever: accordingly, it is impossible to belong to more than one class, and this view can be contrasted with the classic Marxist notion that class is constituted by relations and not by biological individuals. In more local terms, we can see the same process which affected aristocracy and democracy at work within the 1790s notion of ascendancy. George Ogle and Richard Sheridan essentially meant by Protestant Ascendancy a state of society in which all executive, legislative, and judicial office was vested in members of the Established Church. In its September 1792 resolution the Corporation of Dublin follows suit. But it is entirely in keeping with the evolution of aristocracy and aristocrat that the personnel should supersede the principle, and that almost simultaneously ascendancy should be used to identify a social group. Burke defines new ascendancy as the old mastership but, cautious of neologisms, he hesitates to adopt the group terminology: 'the ascendents' is his usual term which, in its absence of sonority, assists him to recognize a 'Junto of Jobbers'.[87]

Throughout the summer Catholic meetings and petitions had been vigorously challenged by Protestant declarations and resolutions. The appearance of this opposition at first gave a check to the plan of the reformers, until the latter obtained a legal opinion in their favour to the effect that their procedure, so long as it was peaceably conducted for the purpose of petitioning, was in no way a violation of the law. It was in this autumn mood of Protestant intransigence that one newspaper sought to typify the ascendancy spirit:

A *Protestant ascendancy* BREWER at Castle Bellingham has unfortunately turned all his ale to vapid by the warmth of his religious zeal, that all his Roman Catholic customers have left off drinking it. In vain does he declare he had no *guile* in signing the manifesto of the *county Louth inquisition* against the devoted Catholics. They have resolved to drink no man's ale, who would swallow all their rights, and have come to a resolution of letting his *tub* stand upon its own bottom. If every little ignorant demogogue was thus spiritedly bereft of support by the people, on whose characters, principles and national rights he presumed to trample, we should have less of vapouring for the ignorance and bigotry of those ascendancy Bashaws who infest society, and bring their little *firkins* of religion to market.[88]

The mocking spirit of this, allied to Burke's more formidable invective, may be difficult to reconcile with the subsequent dignities of the Anglo-Irish Protestant Ascendancy. The Dublin resolutions, personified perhaps a shade unfairly in the wretched figure of John Giffard, *do* relate logically to the sarcasm of the reformers. But the logic is that of a widespread social neurosis, a British and Irish *grande peur*. Ascendancy, by its upward movement from being the synonym of mere interest to being the principle of the constitution itself, facilitated the stimulation of anxiety among Protestants. Yet it took over thirty years to create an electoral context in which the numerical superiority of Catholic voters was fully

[87] Burke, *Correspondence*, vol. vii, p. 290.
[88] *Morning Post*.

effective. Approaching the Catholic Emancipation crisis, Baron Rossmore wrote in August 1827 to Daniel O'Connell reporting the contents of a letter he had sent to George Canning, the Prime Minister, 'pointing at the necessity of tearing up the Ascendancy faction by the roots'.[89] Ascendancy was for some, as late as 1827, the badge of faction, but the manner of its evolution and dissemination was covert. In so far as Hobart reports it to London, it appears to be handed down from above — the Aldermen encouraging the guild representatives to resolve with their lives and fortunes, emphasize this direction. Yet its effect depended on the reception accorded by middle-class Protestants rather than by London or the Irish nobility. Catholics, reformers, and radicals decried the over-heated rhetoric of Giffard and the Castle Bellingham brewer, but their attitude only tends to confirm the ideological nature of the ascendancy appeal. Intending to subvert neither Church nor State, Catholics found it difficult to take the plethora of slogans and accusations as the substance of the debate, whereas it was precisely the substitution of ideology for reality which characterized the 1792 crisis. Only Burke, and Burke only to a limited extent, recognized the importance of acknowledging the reality which this substitution ultimately conferred upon a false sociology. This blend of anxiety, assertion, and deluded rationalism leads naturally into the United Irishman rebellion of 1798, and colours the relations between landlord and tenant in the first third of the nineteenth century. Those two areas constitute the ground upon which Anglo-Irish fiction will grow: the events of 1792 provide a vocabulary and not a theme.

That phrases were at the time flying thick and fast may be judged by a letter which Abercorn received from his supporter George Knox in December 1792, distinguishing finely between Protestant Supremacy and Protestant Ascendancy.[90] We may conclude from these 'hard and soft' options that in the very late eighteenth century there were two notions of Protestant Ascendancy. One simply was the state of affairs

    [89] *The Correspondence of Daniel O'Connell*, ed. Maurice R. O'Connell, vol. iii (1824–8) (Dublin: Irish Manuscripts Commission, 1974), p. 343.
    [90] Quoted in Malcomson, op. cit., p. 352.

as it stood: of this Burke wryly suggested that it 'would be more prudently practiced than professed'; and Grattan added that though he revered it he found it difficult to justify as a political *ne plus ultra*. According to this reading, Protestant Ascendancy did exist prior to 1792 but had not been so named: the naming of it constituted more than the mere identification of a familiar condition, it marked a *need* to go beyond the experience to establish a doctrine. Furthermore, this implicit condition was neither unalterable nor to any high degree admirable — it was the *status quo* diluted with a hint of compromise and a tincture of self-interest. The second notion was, in local terms, an aggressive call to resist the admission of Catholics to citizenship, or it was the doctrine in the name of which such a call was made. The second notion required no extensive proto-history, either implicit or explicit for it was specifically a response to the pressures of the revolutionary age. In broader terms than the local, this second interpretation exemplifies the emergence of an ideology, that is, a false sociology according to which real changes in society are presented in unreal formulations so as to facilitate these changes by deflecting attention towards the chimeras of abstraction. The larger political implications of this development lie beyond a study of specifically literary forms of consciousness, though in the Anglo-Irish instance the two are rarely separable for very long. We have seen how the notion of an aristocracy in Ireland was bedevilled by an acute consciousness of lapses from the ideal. (The acute consciousness is at least as important as any deficiency or delinquency of morals.) Already, in Regency England, there is soon discernible that 'bourgeoisification' of the aristocracy which is often thought to be characteristically Victorian. In Ireland, the pattern differs significantly. A Protestant élite, administering a largely rural society, assumes the identity of the Ascendancy, thereby gradually arrogating to itself the status of a raffish aristocracy and the security of a restricted bourgeoisie from which Catholics will be rebuffed by a flamboyant sectarianism devoid of Christianity. The evangelical fervour of the 1820s and after is an essential part of this process of exclusion and introversion. As for the culture of this stratum of Irish society, so memorably incorporated into poetry by W. B. Yeats, MacNeice saw in it 'nothing but an obsolete bravado, an insidious bonhomie and a way with horses'.[91] The critic who approaches Yeats by way of his attitude to the Protestant Ascendancy of late Victorian and Edwardian times should bear in mind that Yeats, even at his most thoroughly elegiac or celebratory, is always a dramatic intelligence assuming, assisting or creating dramatic tensions and transformation within the material he chooses to employ. That he should find culture where MacNeice finds bravado is not blindness on Yeats's part, but part of a comprehensive poetic strategy: one is more likely to identify imperception in Yeats if one insists on interpreting the poetry simply as celebration or elegy to the neglect of ironic and dramatic tonalities.

The contradictions inherent in this emergent identity, upon which Yeats was later to meditate so actively, were quickly manifested. It was Edmund Burke's view that for many months rebellion in Ireland was deliberately provoked; and when it came in 1798 it proved a terrible demonstration of the passions represented by the new factionalism and the new phraseology of the decade. An anonymous pamphleteer, writing in the wake of the rebellion, traced the sequence of events from the constitutional revision of 1782 down to the massacres at Wexford Bridge:

If an agreement had been made at the Revolution [i.e. in 1782] to select one county in Ireland, for trying an experiment of the effect of *Protestant Ascendancy*, I defy any man to point out a circumstance that has been wanting to make that experiment in the most satisfactory manner in the county of Wexford. Who that knew the county of Wexford, or had ever heard of the Protestant boys of Wexford, could have conceived that the Roman Catholics should have risen there? And yet such is the fact: the rebellion not only broke out there, but was marked with atrocities that disgrace human nature. Does this example encourage us to extend Protestant Ascendancy over the rest of the kingdom?[92]

[91]   Louis MacNeice, *The Poetry of W. B. Yeats* (London: Faber, 1967), 2nd. ed., p. 97.
[92]   *Protestant Ascendancy and Catholic Emancipation Reconciled by a Legislative Union* . . . (London: Wright, 1800), pp. 102-3. Earlier the author had inquired of the Catholics 'will they trust the men, who, in 1792, pledged their lives and fortunes, at their county meetings, to support Protestant Ascendancy . . .?' (p. 94). This echoes the wording of the September resolution by the Corporation of Dublin, and refers to the resulting agitation in the country.

Rebellion in Ireland, at a time of European war, led directly to the Union of Ireland with Great Britain in 1801. But the sequence of events stemming from the 1792 debates, through provocation and rebellion to Union, provided a traumatic incentive to various parties for the adoption of the term, Protestant Ascendancy. For the Protestants, it was the central object of the Glorious Revolution itself, identified increasingly with a pre-Union golden age, but sedulously maintained in a contemporary mythology of castles and cabins. The final selection of 'the Ascendancy', as distinct from some term comparable in its structure to aristocrats/ democrats, is a preference not only for personnel over principle, but it is a preference for an abstraction of class within which the sociology of Ireland may be conjured anew. Burke himself warned his son of the dangers involved in the Catholics adopting the new terminology as a means of demonstrating the moderation of their claims, 'what is it that they got by adopting at all this new Idea of *Protestant* ascendency?'[93] For the Catholics to take up such terms was to render themselves passive before 'this spell of potency, this abracadabra, that is hung about the necks of the unhappy, not to heal but to communicate disease'.[94] Despite these warnings of the insidiously reciprocal effect of an ideological imposition in the language, Protestant Ascendancy is indeed taken up by Irish Catholics as describing at once a degenerate oligarchy and a principle of exclusion from prestige. This manifestly bilateral scheme provided compensation for the renunciations implicit in the Union and in the subsequent modernization of the economy, together with the concomitant cultural trauma.

That Burke recognized the nature of Protestant Ascendancy in its emergence can hardly be doubted. In two observations, more reflective than those of November 1792, he later related the phenomenon to broader perspectives. Indicating a shrewd appreciation of the way in which 'in all ideology men and their circumstances appear upside-down',[95]

---

[93] Burke, *Correspondence,* vol. vii, p. 292.
[94] 'Letter to Richard Burke', *Works,* vol. vi, p. 69.
[95] Karl Marx and Frederick Engels, *The German Ideology* (London: Lawrence and Wishart, 1974), p. 47.

he proffered a bitterly sardonic tribute: 'I think it very possible, that to a degree the Ascendents were sincere. The understanding is soon debauched over to the passions; and our opinions very easily follow our wishes'.[96] It would be mistaken to summarize this dictum as meaning simply that people usually manage to think to their own advantage. Here indeed is a text fit to be borne in mind as we approach Yeats's ultimate drama of passionate ascendancy, 'Purgatory', for Burke's central meaning is the symbolic identity of our faculties, intellectual and sensual. In another observation he provides a further means of relating the particularities of local politics in Ireland to the broader pattern of those expansionist doctrines he opposed in his major campaigns:

I think I can hardly overrate the malignity of the principles of the Protestant ascendency, as they affect Ireland; or of Indianism, as they affect these countries, and as they effect Asia; or of Jacobinism, as they affect all Europe, and the state of human Society itself.[97]

The profligate exploitation which Warren Hastings personifies for Burke, the bourgeois monarchy which the Jacobins ultimately bequeath to Honoré Balzac, and the Protestant Ascendancy which the Dublin Aldermen will contribute to Yeats's problematic aesthetics — all these form part of the social fabric in which the romantic movement traced its devices. It has been customary to see many of these as retrospective — the occasional medievalism of Keats, the Hellenism of Shelley, and the pervasive *recursus* of Wordsworthian memory. And Anglo-Irish literature particularly is accepted as obsessed by the past, dominated by its 'backward look'.[98] Yet no one would question the intensity with which the English romantics were engaged with contemporary experience, were indeed engaged with forming and articulating contemporary experience. It has been the peculiar fate of the Anglo-Irish skein in the romantic tapestry that its concern with the past should be taken as literal, local, and exclusive. The *Dublin University Magazine's* attempt to

---

[96] Burke, *Correspondence,* vol. viii, p. 138.
[97] Burke, *Correspondence,* vol. x, p. 32.
[98] e.g., Frank O'Connor's history *The Backward Look: A Survey of Irish literature* (London: Macmillan, 1967).

diagnose the condition of literature in Ireland in the 1830s reveals the proper balance of this concern with the past (seen as abbreviated and vestigial) and a complementary apprehension of the future as bodied forth in England's more advanced condition. The process by which Yeats ultimately renders that past literature traditional is necessarily linked to the notional separation of Ireland from England; and the tragic price paid for this transformation of the inchoate into the sublime is the extinction or elimination of that Ascendancy through which the processs was sustained. Burke's testimony on the subject of Protestant Ascendancy serves to remind us that our method is literary history, a practical consciousness of the past as produced (in our material) in literature, and not the stratigraphy of events heaped one upon the other in some unchanging diagram. So too his insistence on the affinities of Dublin, Paris, and Bombay should teach us that the childish assumption of Ireland's uniqueness and separateness — Elizabeth Bowen's confusion of Ireland and Island — substitutes geology where one should attend to the intricacies of a colonial culture.

3. CASTLE RACKRENT

certain of our [Dublin] corporate body
talk of *ancestors* as if they had a regular
list of them framed and glazed in the
family mansion, but we request some
of them to point out who their fathers
were — we will not trouble them to go
back farther than merely to tell us
where and when begotten — whether on
a cobler's stall, a butcher's block, or
within the purlieus of Smock-alley —
Qui capit ille facit.

(*Morning Post*, 1792)[1]

1. THE GENESIS OF FICTION

Castle Rackrent (1800) is not the first Irish novel, but with it
the history of Anglo-Irish fiction begins. Diligent though
hardly arcane research will reveal scores of earlier novels
either set in Ireland, written by Irish authors, or (by virtue of
the status of the Dublin book trade) published in Ireland. Yet
that material remains the stuff of a cultural archæology, so
to speak, and it is to Maria Edgeworth that we look for the
reflective qualities of a literary history.

With the exception of Joyce's *œuvre* to which it bears
some resemblance in its ironic totality, no Irish novel has
attracted more attention than *Castle Rackrent*. Of course
it earned (together with the *Tales of Fashionable Life*, 1809,
etc.) its authoress a place in the salons of London during her
occasional descents upon the capital, earned her the respect
of Byron and the friendship of Walter Scott. We will see how
Waverley is strictly indebted to *The Absentee* (1812) rather
than to the formally more adventurous *Castle Rackrent*, and
yet the entire canon of Scott's fiction might legitimately

---

[1] *Morning Post; or, Dublin Courant,* 15 September 1792 [p. 4].

claim a relationship to the little anonymous fiction of 1800. On these grounds Maria Edgeworth gains a place in histories of English literature as one of the lesser women writers of Jane Austen's period. The apparent coincidence of her first novel with the passing of the Act of Union ensures her the attention of Irish commentators. Here, the behaviour of her father in relation to the proposed Union has stimulated interest in his attentive and dutiful daughter. Sincere in his support of the Union initially, Richard Lovell Edgeworth voted against it in the crucial debates of 1799 and 1800. It has been customary to accept this as a good man's refusal to side with bribery, and the Edgeworths saw their conduct in this light. However, the explanation itself requires explanation: the substitution of personal honour for political integrity deserves more comment than simple commendation, and in *The Absentee* Maria Edgeworth's hero will work out some of the consequences of that altered notion of responsibility. The complexity of R. L. Edgeworth's position in relation to the Union had earlier affinities to the historical complexities of *Castle Rackrent* and its *composition*.

The full title is instructive — *Castle Rackrent, an Hibernian Tale: taken from the Facts, and from the Manners of the Irish Squires, before the Year 1782*. Given at length, the title reveals a series of hiatuses, of disjunctions and rhythmic shifts which the short-title *Castle Rackrent* tends to disguise. The architectural unity conveyed in the short title is part of a persistent reading of the novel within an 'Anglo-Irish tradition of "Big House" fiction', according to which tradition is uncomplicated continuity.[2] *Castle Rackrent* advances a focal point at once social and geographical, but 'an Hibernian Tale' implies a narrator (in this case a highly personalized one) who necessarily introduces the possibility of various points of view upon that place. 'Taken from the Facts' ostentatiously assures the reader, but then is rhythmically shaken by 'from the Manners . . .'. Finally, the historical focus of the tale is revealed in 'of the Irish Squires before the Year 1782'. Thus, the immediacy and seeming oneness of *Castle Rackrent* is

    [2] John Cronin, *The Anglo-Irish Novel;* vol. i, *The Nineteenth Century* (Belfast: Appletree Press, 1980), p. 25.

gradually shown to involve a series of qualifications, lapses, and retreats. To readers of the first edition, 1782 promptly called to mind the legislative independence which the Dublin parliament won from Westminster, and the dignity and prosperity associated with Grattan's Parliament. Hence, the novel's full title apparently exempted the contemporary squires of 1800 from the critique issuing through Thady Quirk's narration. But 1782 had also seen the return of R. L. Edgeworth to his Irish estates, and travelling with him on that occasion was his daughter Maria: thus the novel takes the inauguration of her Irish residence as its historical frontier. Does the sub-title therefore act also as an authorial self-exculpation, coyly hidden behind a suspect anonymity?

Such a conspiratorial reading of the title does not allow for the complex interaction of genesis and setting in a work of fiction, especially a work of fiction written anonymously by a woman. The problem is complicated by the timetable of the novel's composition, by the incompleteness of our knowledge of that timetable, and by the structure of the novel itself. *Castle Rackrent* is a historical novel, but its historical aspect does not lie inert in its temporal setting. As with all such fiction, its historical dimension is the dynamic relationship between that setting and the historical moment of its composition: and beyond that, it involves also that relationship in interaction with a historically defined readership. Not all of these aspects can be summoned before the eye on the instant, but a brief chronology may help:

['the events of *Castle Rackrent*']

1782   M. E. returns to Ireland.
          Legislative independence.
1792   (January) The first Protestant Ascendancy debates.
          (September) Energetic Protestant Ascendancy campaign.
          According to one late source, *Castle Rackrent* was written '8 years before it was published', i.e. early in 1792; M. E. out of Ireland for much of the year.
1793-1795   Some time during this period M. E. regaled her aunt Mrs Ruxton with imitations of John Langan's behaviour — the 'original' of Thady Quirk.

1793 (autumn)–1796 The first Part of *Castle Rackrent* written, probably early in the period rather than late.

1795 (4 January) Earl Fitzwilliam arrives in Dublin as Lord-Lieutenant.

(25 February) Fitzwilliam recalled to London.

1795 (autumn)–1798 Second Part written two years after the first — see above.

1796 (January/February) R. L. Edgeworth involved in electioneering in Longford — unsuccessfully.

1798 R. L. Edgeworth elected for St Johnstown, a rotten borough.

(summer) Insurrection in Ulster and Leinster.

(8 September) Invading French army defeated at Ballinamuck, Co. Longford, a few miles from Edgeworthstown.

(October) M. E. preparing to send MS of *Castle Rackrent* to London publishers.

1799 (January) Union proposal defeated in Dublin parliament.

(April) R. L. E. has conversations in Birmingham, which impress him with the advantages for trade resulting from Union.

(late) Glossary for *Castle Rackrent* compiled.

1800 (January) *Castle Rackrent* published anonymously in London by Joseph Johnson, a radical whom M. E. had visited in prison the previous year.

(June) Union bill passed in Dublin parliament.[3]

In time, this chronology can shed a great deal of light on the structure of *Castle Rackrent;* first of all, however, some comment on the political events encapsulated in it is unavoidable.

Of the Protestant Ascendancy debates enough has been said: suffice it to note here that the earliest possible date for the commencement of *Castle Rackrent* is also 1792, though the authoress was admittedly out of Ireland for much

[3] The details of Maria Edgeworth's activities etc. included here are derived from Marilyn Butler, *Maria Edgeworth: A Literary Biography* (Oxford: Clarendon Press, 1972), pp. 126, 174, 181, 190, and esp. 353-6.

of the year. The excitement of Catholic hopes in 1792/3 was revived with the news that the Earl Fitzwilliam was to be appointed Lord-Lieutenant at the beginning of 1795. Fitzwilliam was Burke's patron, a liberal Whig and known adversary of the Dublin Castle junto. His attempts to eliminate the corruption associated with the Beresford faction were curtailed by his recall to London, but a sense of the possible termination of the old ways was strongly felt by Irish liberals. R. L. Edgeworth sought to interest the new Lord-Lieutenant in his telegraph scheme, but the suddenness of Fitzwilliam's fall brought all to naught and underlined the fragility of such enlightened hopes. From 1795 onwards disturbances in the Longford countryside complicated the family's experience of politics. Their distance from ultra-Protestant feeling cut them off from the magistrates and squireens, while the Catholic body lacked political weight and organization. Thus, the by-election of 1796 led R. L. Edgeworth to summarize the influence of money and jobbery in verse:

> Can Poverty from Gold withdraw his hand?
> A Gauger's rod what voter can withstand?[4]

Far from being an upstart liberal opposed by aristocratic power, Edgeworth was a landowner frustrated by the operations of a chicanery with modest, but fully adequate, patronage at its disposal. The gauger, an exciseman or one responsible for hiring men and controlling materials on public works, was symbolic of that area of social pressure where the Orange Order was at that time sending down its roots: John Giffard, of Protestant Ascendancy fame in 1792, was a gauger on the Dublin Custom-house building site. Given these growing pressures and tensions, Edgeworth's election to parliament for a rotten borough is understandable, if not entirely reconcilable with his latter-day reputation. Such ambiguity also characterizes Edgeworth experience in 1798: when the invading French troops came within sight of Edgeworthstown the family was doubly vulnerable — distrusted by the Orange yeomanry, and unaligned to this new radicalism from the Continent. That Maria Edgeworth's family had to flee their

[4] Ibid., p. 120.

home and take refuge in Longford town where they were assailed physically by Protestant militia must colour our reading of the last pages of *Castle Rackrent* with its allusions to the mob in full cry. As for the Union debates, the most important feature is their number and variety — there was no one dramatic moment either of honour or betrayal.

All of these details help us to put in perspective one persistent image of the composition of *Castle Rackrent*. In *The Irish Novelists* Thomas Flanagan has popularized a notion of the relationship between politics and literature in this context which is lamentable both in its factual inaccuracy and theatrical bankruptcy:

> One unambiguous 'no!' to the motion in support of Union was spoken in the harsh, commanding tones of Richard Lovell Edgeworth. At that moment his daughter Maria was sitting at the long table in the crowded Edgeworthstown drawing room, scribbling furiously at the first Irish novel.[5]

Literary history struggles to recover the less dramatic and more extensive links between social co-ordinates which Flanagan isolates in Senate and drawing-room.

The composition of *Castle Rackrent* may have begun as early as 1792 and a completed version (not necessarily the first or the final one) was ready late in 1798. One way to characterize those years refers to the gradually diminished hopes of reform after the limited successes of 1793; another would point to the increasingly subversive methods employed by opponents of the Government from the suppression of the United Irishmen in 1794 onwards. Whether one regards Fitzwilliam as a crusader or an incompetent, the United Irishmen as idealists or incendiaries, the 1790s is a decade intimately characterized as *split*. The hiatus does not occur with the rebellion or the French invasion, or even the Union; it lies more centrally in the network of fears and hopes which tied the Catholic question to the course of the French revolution. Maria Edgeworth's own political experience, as a woman and simply as the daughter of an isolated and (to a

---

[5] Thomas Flanagan, *The Irish Novelists 1800–1850* (New York, London: Columbia University Press, 1959), p. 23.

degree) disorientated liberal, reflected that division as an insight into the history of her class.

It has often been noted that Edgeworth family lore contains anecdotes which may have been models for some of the more extravagant behaviour of the earlier generations of Rackrent. Maria Edgeworth's biographer, Marilyn Butler, simply accepts that 'the Edgeworths of earlier times are beyond question the real models for the four generations of the Rackrent family', and adds that their careers 'could be paralleled in dozens of anecdotes about the Anglo-Irish squirearchy of the seventeenth and eighteenth centuries'. Mrs Butler is certainly right in observing that 'tracing the history of the direct line gives an inadequate idea' of the novelist's borrowings; what is of interest to the literary historian is the bearing upon *form* of the interactions of method and source in the fiction. Here, the biographer leads us to — but does not exploit -- a vital element in the composition of *Castle Rackrent*:

In her grandfather's narrative in the 'Black Book' Maria had an outline which strongly resembled the plot of *Castle Rackrent* — a family saga compounded of debts and prosperous marriages; successive landlords who were selfishly oblivious of their tenants, and yet were strikingly endowed with personal charm, humour, and finally pathos.[6]

Far from confirming any sturdy sense of succession in Maria Edgeworth's exploitation of family history, the presence of a 'black book' of Edgeworth tradition is an indicator of the novelist's nervous reliance on the privacy of a written text as well as on the publicly recognizable narrative skills of a Thady Quirk. The imposition of that short title, *Castle Rackrent*, upon so complex a narrative is an example of the romantic insistence upon a unity which is no more than a (usually degraded) longing for unity. If we note the as yet crudely transcribed material of family history together with the ironies of Thady's narrative, then we have discovered in the backwaters of Anglo-Irish literature a prime example of Walter Benjamin's analysis of romantic symbolism. Illegitimate talk of the symbolic, Benjamin argues, leads to a

[6] Marilyn Butler, op. cit., p. 16.

neglect of a proper discussion of 'content in formal analysis' and of 'form in the aesthetics of content'.[7] Resisting the orthodox pleas to assimilate content and form, we may find in *Castle Rackrent* the origins of an allegorical mode of writing and interpretation which will take us through to the late work of Yeats and Joyce as a characteristic of Anglo-Irish literature.

There is no doubt that *The Black Book of Edgeworthstown*, even in the synthetic edition available to the public, is of compelling relevance to any reading of *Castle Rackrent*. Casually, one reads of Sir John Edgeworth (1638-96) that, having gambled away his wife's most valuable jewels and won them back again 'some time afterwards he was found in a hay yard with a friend, drawing straws out of the hayrick, and betting upon which should be the longest.'[8] Having read the story, Sir Condy's mode of choosing a wife attaches itself to a sequence of such stories. Yet resemblances between the family chronicle and the novel are less significant than silent divergences. *Castle Rackrent* is almost innocent of sectarian allusion, whereas in *The Black Book* the intermarriage of Protestant and Catholic is the marriage of Francis Edgeworth and Jane Tuite sometime around 1590. Their son, John Edgeworth, left his wife and son in their house at Crannelagh 'some days before the fatal 23rd of October, 1641'.[9] In keeping with the long-standing tradition of Papist treachery, rebels suddenly seized the house, humiliated the wife, and made to murder the child: they were prevailed upon to spare the property because 'there was the picture of that pious Catholic, Jane Tuite, painted on the wainscot with her beads and crucifix . . .'.[10] A loyal servant had meantime saved the infant heir by pretending to reserve the privilege of murdering him to himself. Not only are these diverse details of the potency of an image, an illusion in preserving the endangered line of the Edgeworths in Ireland but, the chronicler records:

[7] Walter Benjamin, *The Origins of German Tragic Drama*, trans. John Osborne (London: New Left Books, 1977), p. 160.
[8] *The Black Book of Edgeworthstown and Other Edgeworth Memories 1585-1817*, ed. H. J. Butler and H. E. Butler (London: Faber and Gwyer, 1927), p. 19 (quoting R. L. Edgeworth's *Memoirs*).
[9] Ibid., pp. 11-12.
[10] Ibid., p. 13.

This event was told me ... by an eye-witness of the fact, one Simpson, who was a little foot-boy in Captain Edgeworth's family in 1641, being then eleven years old. He came at my request to my house in 1737. He was then a hundred and seven years old; his understanding and memory seemed perfect, though he was not quite sincere in all his relations. His eyes were very dim, his voice a little hollow, but he was strong and walked from his house to mine, upward of a mile, the day I saw him, and refused to ride. He smelt like new-digged earth.[11]

The value of a narrator, less than ingenuous, in holding together the details of a family's varied generations, was evident to Maria Edgeworth whenever she consulted *The Black Book*. And it is the mode of narrative, the semblance of history together with the discreet silences, which is significant rather than the reportage of betting coups and drinking bouts. Compared to Professor Flanagan's little scenario — and we may call it so — the image of Maria Edgeworth seated at a drawing room table between Simpson and Quirk, looking back to those murderous Jacobites (so to speak) of 1641 and looking forward (so to speak) to the Jacobins of the year of the French, seems plausible.

The issue of sect in *Castle Rackrent* will arise again, but for the moment it is necessary to stress that the novel does not have any one moment of composition like that envisaged above. Yet recalling the prolonged period — perhaps six or more years — during which it was composed, we see also the shifting significance of that saving Catholicism in the family's history. Like the decade of its composition the novel too is split — though it would be rash to argue for any homology between the two. The difference between Part I and Part II — there are no such titles to the sections, the second being headed 'Continuation of the Memoirs of the Rackrent Family: history of Sir Conolly Rackrent', and the first having no comparable heading — the difference between the two lies in the aesthetic significance of their content. The first traces the careers of, successively Sir Patrick (the hardliver), Sir Murtagh (the litigious miser), and Sir Kit (absentee, gambler and 'improver'); the second concentrates on one figure, Sir Condy, and a more complex network of attitudes.

[11] Ibid., pp. 13–14. See also Appendix C.

In moving from the first to the second part of the novel, the reader is moved from the aesthetics of sequence to the less linear and meditative narrative of the fall of the Rackrents. By dividing Sir Condy's career off from the others, the novelist marks the redundancy of that old, sequential notion of history and opts for a mode closer to that of her own age. And here too we finally encounter the real significance of Mrs Butler's observation that the *order* in which Maria Edgeworth read her ancestors' vices into her fiction is irrelevant — she reserves until the climactic second part of the novel all her attention to politics. The romanticization of Sir Condy's eighteenth-century 'origins' is one strategy in which form and content are merged.

From the timetable of *Castle Rackrent's* genesis we know that the history of Sir Conolly Rackrent was written some two years after the earlier chronicle. The details of electioneering suggest that R. L. Edgeworth's experience in 1796 (or again in 1798) was drawn upon, though the most colourful detail — the transportation of a sod of turf upon which oaths might be taken — derives from an earlier generation of Edgeworth lore. The illusory grandeur and scale of the Castle is accompanied in the novel by the exploitation of pretence as a means of reaching truth. Foolishly anxious to know how his companions regard him, Sir Condy feigns death only to discover as he lies shamming death at his own wake that he is held in no high regard. This interpolated 'fiction' on the part of a fictional character underlines the importance of Condy's actual death some pages later. Having sold for cash a jointure upon the lands, Condy resorts to drinking 'with the exciseman and the gauger', and the latter challenges him to drain the drinking horn of his ancestors, the result being brain fever and death after six days. So the sequential chronicle of the Rackrent generations is drawn back upon its earlier episodes, for Sir Patrick — the first of his name — had died in the same manner.

This circling achieves the silent elimination of politics from the novel, for the episode of the elections is not alluded to in Condy's demise. Indeed, election to parliament has already prefigured the death of the Castle; after the family has set up in Dublin, Thady tells us:

There was then a great silence in Castle Rackrent, and I went moping from room to room, hearing the doors clap for want of right locks, and the wind through the broken windows, that the glazier men never would come to mend, and the rain coming through the roof and best ceilings all over the house for want of the slater, whose bill was not paid, besides our having no slates or shingles for that part of the old building which was shingled and burnt when the chimney took fire, and had been open to the weather ever since.[12]

Condy's engagement in politics exposes his castle to this observation, more pointed than, if not categorically different from, the narrator's other revelations. When Sir Condy signs away virtually all of his interest to Thady's son, Jason, the narrative releases a three-stage chorus of popular response which is at once ironically atavistic and indicative of the new politics of the 1790s:

And when I got to the street-door the neighbours' childer, who were playing at marbles there, seeing me in great trouble, left their play . . .

The people in the town, who were the most of them standing at their doors, hearing the childer cry, would know the reason of it . . .

And the mob grew so great and so loud, I was frightened, and made my way back to the house to warn my son to make his escape, or hide himself for fear of the consequences.[13]

Irony then sees Sir Condy placate the mob with a few euphemisms about his retiring to the Lodge voluntarily, while the mob takes its last glass of whiskey at the Castle. The presence of a larger population is most powerfully felt in this scene, but it is not without influence elsewhere: Sir Patrick's body had been all but rescued from his debtors at his funeral by *the mob*, and that emotive eighteenth-century term appearing in the early pages of the novel warns us not to read *Castle Rackrent* as if its early episodes were prehistoric. Drink, gambling, and nuptial cruelty may constitute the surface of the lives of the three Rackrents of Part One, but Thady's narrative is fully alert to the history in which they are necessarily read. To speak as Thady does of Sir

[12] Maria Edgeworth *Tales and Novels* (London, 1832-3), vol. i, pp. 56-7.
[13] Ibid., pp. 74-5.

Patrick 'accommodating his friends and the public in general' is to acknowledge a social structure far from that feudal aristocracy retrospectively imposed by the Celtic Revival.[14] Politics is an interlude in the Rackrent saga, just as legislative independence was short-lived in Ireland. Far from drawing upon the facts and manner of the era before 1782, *Castle Rackrent* concentrates upon the illusions of that theatrical period.

More so than any other novel within the Anglo-Irish ambit *Castle Rackrent* has been turned to serve a Yeatsian purpose. Protestant Ascendancy had come to summarize a venerable and extended past with its heroes from Swift to Burke (or at least Grattan); the Sir Kits and the Sir Murtaghs and Sir Condys were the obverse of that long and distinguished pedigree, antithetical figures to the intellectual line of succession, essential embodiments of full-blooded life. Moreover, the sociology of Big House and Cabin found it easy to place the short-title version of Maria Edgeworth's novel into a convenient pigeon-hole. Finally, few noticed the pseudonymous status of the Rackrents, (*recte* O'Shaughlin), who inherit the estates on condition that they change their name. And the change of name is maybe the mute signal of a change of sectarian allegiance. Thus streamlined the novel had virtually become a unique sport, poised delicately on the date-line of the Act of Union, surveying a century and inaugurating a tradition. Instead of accepting as history the apparently extensive genealogy of the Rackrents, we discover in the genesis of the novel itself the intenser discontinuities and crises of an emergent literary form in an age of revolution.

2. A BURKEAN WORLD

An examination of *Wuthering Heights* has produced from that seemingly wild and woolly text a very strict line of transmission for the property involved, the laws of real estate and inheritance being strictly observed behind the strategies of a double narration. It is the work of a moment to apply

[14] Ibid., p. 4.

a similar technique to the story related by the devoted family retainer of the Rackrents. A cumbersome but revealing family 'tree' emerges:

Sir Tallyhoo Rackrent to his cousin Sir Patrick (O'Shaughlin)

                                               to his son

                                               Sir Murtagh to his brother Sir Kit

to a remote branch (Sir Condy) who sells to Jason Quirk, disputed by Isabella, widow

Thus, of the five proprietors bearing the name Rackrent only one inherits by primogeniture (Sir Patrick's son Murtagh). The frailty of the main line of Rackrents raises the possibility that only two generations at most separate Sir Tallyhoo Rackrent and the widow Rackrent (née Moneygawl). The estate changes hands five times, and though only the acquisition by Jason Quirk is effected basically by commercial means (buying up mortgages etc.) there is little prior experience in the family of direct inheritance by a son and heir. Moreover, it is not sufficiently noticed that Jason's title to the estate is not unchallenged, in that Thady tells us the widow Rackrent disputes his claim. Her own claim would appear on the surface to be virtually hopeless, but her making of it underlines the disputed nature of property transmission throughout the novel.

This concentration on the line of succession conventionally omits the women of the family. As to whether Sir Tallyhoo was married we know not; Sir Patrick had a legitimate son, but the mother is at no point mentioned; Sir Kit's wife was the 'Jewish', an outsider who, after her imprisonment in the Castle, outlived her husband and returned to England. With Sir Condy, we encounter a choice made between two possible wives — Judy M'Quirk 'who was daughter to a sister's son' of the narrator's, and Isabella Moneygawl whom by the toss of a coin he chose as wife.[15] Lady Rackrent is sent off to her relatives shortly before her husband's demise, and on her way

<hr/>

[15] Ibid., pp. 38, 40.

home suffers a near-fatal accident in the carriage. In short, the female line in *Castle Rackrent* endures a repression which is deliberate if arbitrary, and the combined effect of these dual *lacunae* in a pattern of human generation is to render the relation between property and human life peculiarly unstable. And in all this we must bear in mind the relentless pressure of Thady's distinctively human voice in the narrative, the deliberate mimicry in the written word of the narrator's accent. Humour and inhumanity jostle for supremacy, and the result might be aptly described as a dead heat. Yet there is one significant swerve which the narrative takes in its concluding pages. With the news of Lady Rackrent's death expected daily, the narrator has prompted his grand-niece to renew her closeness to Sir Condy; she instead indicates that the Castle will soon be another's and she will look in that direction. Jason, however, does not marry her, and by doing so avoids the faintest suspicion of Quirk family collusion. The new masters of the Castle, if new masters there are to be, will generate a different mode of property transmission. But the Rackrent genealogy will be transferred into the realm of literature where marital introversion and endangered succession will come to provide a potent theme in Anglo-Irish modernism.

The origins of that theme are not exclusively Irish, by any means; they may be traced in European romanticism, in Wordsworth, Goethe, Chateaubriand, Novalis, Burke. In the case of *Castle Rackrent* such exotic names are rarely cited, and yet there is a poignant moment where Thady's artless narrative brings his characters into contact with the heights of European literary fashion. Condy is shaving with an unpaid-for razor, when he asks his wife what she is reading: '"The Sorrows of Werter" replies my lady, as well as I could hear'.[16] The intense emotion of Goethe's romance contrasts starkly with the disappointed mercenary base of the Rackrents' marriage. The solitary literary allusion of Maria Edgeworth's novel should not be seen in isolation. The entire fabric of the novel derives from one dominant romantic metaphor, that of the house as temple of the human spirit.

[16]   Ibid., p. 61.

It is not exclusively a romantic image, for romanticism itself has its own lines of communication with the Renaissance and with neo-classicism. As Burke's *Reflections* amply shows, the image of the house, or the Great House, carries with it every possibility of irony. One consequence of the reduction of Maria Edgeworth's title to *Castle Rackrent* is to minimize the reader's alertness to the question of irony. Within the novel itself there is a body of evidence which casts shadows upon the short title; within the larger area of Irish culture one can find the material for an ironic interpretation even of the short title.

The Great Houses of Ireland are comparatively few in number. There is no equivalent of Castle Howard or Blenheim, and the larger Irish houses — Castletown and Carton west of Dublin, Russborough and Powerscourt in County Wicklow, Mount Stewart in County Down, Florence Court in Fermanagh, or Lissadell in Sligo — would appear well down the lists of houses graded by size in the British Isles. The reasons for the relatively small size of the Irish Great House are complex, but certainly include the prolonged absenteeism of the very great landowners in the eighteenth and nineteenth centuries. The result is that the Irish notion of the 'Big House' — a more familiar term in Ireland — is based on the houses of the county grandees rather than the aristocracy of a nation. Moreover, by reason of the great disturbances in Irish life throughout the sixteenth and seventeenth centuries there were few surviving old buildings of a purely domestic nature. With the greater stability and prosperity of the country from the mid-eighteenth century onwards, house building expanded and the image of Georgian Ireland generally accepted in the world is based on the architecture of the last half of the eighteenth century and of at least three decades of the nineteenth.

Maurice Craig has demonstrated with a mass of illustration the impact of medium-sized houses upon the Irish landscape in the years after 1750.[17] A large number of these were

---

[17] Maurice Craig, *Classic Irish Houses of the Middle Size* (London: Architectural Press, 1976).

glebe-houses built for the clergy of the Established Church, designed to accommodate a family and servants but not to adorn an extensive estate. In addition to the limited degree of standardization imposed by the Church's building programme, Irish house architecture was profoundly affected by the work of professional builders and designers. Two in particular deserve notice: Richard Morrison published his *Useful and Ornamental Designs in Architecture* in 1793 offering five types of houses and villas. The central design, for a 'Villa or Country House':

> was the plan that would have suited most small country gentlemen. Indeed, apart from the refinements of Morrison's facade it is the essential arrangement of the mass of box-like Georgian houses that dot the Irish countryside.[18]

The cost was between £1,000 and £1,100; there were seven bedrooms, four living rooms, an entrance hall, and servants' quarters. Much earlier The Reverend John Payne published *Twelve Designs for Country Houses* in 1757 where similar attention is paid to the needs of the middle class.[19]

All of this would appear irrelevant to castles, even fictional ones; but Craig's introductory remarks ought to be engraved on the desks of all inquirers into Irish literature:

> the 'big house' of Irish traditional ways is not always very large: the term denotes the fact that it was the house of a substantial, and usually resident, landowner, rather than its mere size. As well as these 'big houses' there were and are considerable numbers of houses, built by or lived in by minor gentry or prosperous farmers, or by manufacturers and traders, or occupied as dower-houses, agent's houses or as glebe-houses. The gulf between the 'big house' and the cottage has perhaps been over-emphasised by historians, and too much has been made of the absence of a middle class.[20]

In order to approach the aesthetics of the house in *Castle Rackrent* it is necessary to grasp the architectural context in which the language of 'Big Houses' and 'Castles' operates. If

---

[18] Brian de Breffny and Rosemary ffoliott, *The Houses of Ireland: Domestic Architecture from the Medieval Castle to the Edwardian Villa* (London: Thames and Hudson, 1975), p. 169.

[19] See Craig, op. cit., pp. 39–49.

[20] Ibid., p. 3.

the novel is steered towards its historical moment in the 1790s rather than its fictional setting in some unspecified past, then the proliferation of design-book houses in the late decades of the eighteenth century is at least relevant. Castles, perhaps, can plead exemption from these cheeky considerations. Or can they?

One feature of the cultural history of the eighteenth century which conditions this issue is the Gothic Revival, with its proliferation of mock-ecclesiastical and mock-military architecture. In addition to the larger achievements of the revival architects, the fashion for 'gothick' reached down to relatively modest householders, and gothicized cottages and villas became familiar across the landscape. Castle Ward, for example at Strangford in County Down has a Gothic Front and a Classical Front — it was built in 1760/73. Dunsany Castle in Meath is a medieval core, with gothic detail added in the eighteenth century. Lord Belvedere built the largest gothic folly in Ireland, the Jealous Wall, to blot out the sight of his brother's residence at Rochfort in Westmeath. All of these are substantial houses, 'big houses' even by Dr Craig's exacting standards.

One effect of the gothic movement, and of the antiquarian strand in eighteenth-century sensibility, was to encourage the application of antique terms to latter-day developments. Thus, in the index to Craig's *Classic Irish Houses of the Middle Size* we find fifteen houses listed with names of the 'Castle . . .' format: eleven of these were built in the eighteenth century, and one in the nineteenth; all, by definition, fall well below the stature of the Great House. 'Castle Rackrent' then resembles Castle Ffrench in County Galway (built 1779) as much as it resembles Castle Carbery which is a fortified Jacobean manor-house in Kildare. The inversion, by which 'Castle' precedes the family- or site-name, though it has genuine precedents among ancient buildings, is also typical of the affectations of antiquity practised by gothic revivalists. None of this exploration of Irish architecture in its surviving detail is intended to establish any neat revisionist view of the Rackrent seat as a *bijou* bungalow or gothic folly. It is however intended to indicate the ambiguity of Maria Edgeworth's title, the variety of social and cultural patterns suggested by the short title, and the particular implications of an architectural boom in the period of the novel's genesis. 'Castle Rackrent', therefore, does not automatically imply an age-old and rambling pile of essentially military character: it *may* also point to bourgeois expansion, and bourgeois colonization of the past as an ideological bulwark.

Only the recurrent image of the house in *Castle Rackrent* justifies this excursion into architectural history. The novel's portrayal of the house has not gained the attention it deserves, and a methodical tabulation of the evidence reveals greater variety and contradiction than is generally admitted. Our first encounter with the house occurs when Thady recounts the festivities which Sir Patrick (O'Shaughlin) Rackrent provided to mark his inheritance. Men of the first consequence, when there was no further room in the Castle 'made it their choice . . . to sleep in the chicken-house, which Sir Patrick had fitted up for the purpose of accommodating his friends . . .'.[21] This colourful detail derives from a period beyond Thady's own experience – he never knew Sir Patrick – and it is assimilable to the conventional notion of Irish hospitality and rackety ingenuity in overcoming problems. Yet the strategic effect of Thady's narration is to uncover the *real* function of the building commandeered for the guests. Being a chicken-house, it is further seen to be part of a complex of farm buildings (with residence) rather than the outer reaches of a mansion. This style of residence, with farm offices etc. tucked behind the house or behind the (largely decorative) wings, was common among houses of the middle size. Thady's deft exposure is modified by his immediate reference to a family portrait 'now opposite to me'; the portrait connotes a degree of self-esteem and social status which is itself questioned by Thady's easy access to the picture – where does it hang, *now?* With Sir Patrick's death and the arrival of the skinflint Murtagh, Thady laments the emptiness of the cellars, and so provides a further architectural detail of the house. With so many Irish houses of all sizes built upon a basement, to which light is admitted by an excavated *area*, the presence of cellars is unremarkable,

---

[21]   *Tales and Novels,* vol. i, p. 4.

certainly less than a guarantee of castle-like scale in Castle Rackrent.

Murtagh's successor, Sir Kit, arranges 'a great architect for the house, and an improver for the grounds' but then departs for Bath.[22] Before he returns with his Jewish wife, he instructs all concerned to have the house painted 'and the new building to go on as fast as possible'.[23] It is true that Thady tells us of the couple 'walking together arm in arm after breakfast, looking at the new building and the improvements', but the ensuing remarks divert our attention from what these innovations may have been.[24]

'Is the large room damp, Thady' said his honour. 'Oh, damp, your honour! how should it be but as dry as a bone', says I, 'after all the fires we have kept in it day and night? It's the barrack-room your honour's talking on.' 'And what is a barrack-room, pray, my dear?' were the first words I ever heard out of my lady's lips.[25]

The uncertainty as to the names of rooms underlines Thady's controlling role in the irony; through it we are given access to the turf stack and newly-planted trees or shrubs which constitute the view from Castle Rackrent. Lady Rackrent is locked in her bedroom for refusing to hand over her diamond cross — Jewish fidelity here ironically showing up Christian greed — and her husband is finally shot in a duel which results from a false rumour of the lady's death. Indeed, not only does the woman's perspective on the house tend to reduce its scale in the reader's eyes, but her falsely reported death — as in the case of her successor — prompts the real death of her husband. Illusion, once again, is a means towards clarification of vision.

Under the rule of Sir Conolly Rackrent all these images of the house are advanced once again, but now in an integrated shape rather than in the discontinuous sequence of allusions which characterized the first part of the history of the Rackrents. Condy had previously lived 'in a small but slated house, within view of the end of the avenue'. The passage continues directly:

[22] Ibid., p. 14.
[23] Ibid., p. 18.
[24] Ibid., p. 21.
[25] Idem.

I remember him, bare footed and headed, running through the street of O'Shaughlin's town, and playing at pitch and toss, ball, marbles, and what not, with the boys of the town, amongst whom my son Jason was a great favourite with him.[26]

The Castle now is seen to have an avenue, and simultaneously it is seen to be in close contact with other houses — albeit small but slated — and with the town which memorializes the family's abandoned name. The occasion of Lady Isabella's arrival provides a further conjuncture of disagreements as to the style of the house:

her feathers on the top of her hat were broke going in at the low back door, and she pulled out her little bottle out of her pocket to smell to when she found herself in the kitchen, and said, 'I shall faint with the heat of this odious, odious place.' 'My dear, it's only three steps across the kitchen, and there's a fine air if your veil was up', said Sir Condy . . .[27]

If Condy's 'three steps' is simply a coaxing reduction of the distance across the smelly kitchen, Thady still confirms that the back door of the house leads into the kitchen, and that the door is low. Lady Isabella's response to the house is to turn the barrack-room into a theatre, to acknowledge the role of pretence and role-playing in the life of Rackrent, as if in unconscious preparation for her husband's sham death. But if her ladyship 'had a fine taste for building, and furniture, and playhouses' and insisted on calling the long passage 'the gallery', Thady's narrative breaks through with references to 'the back stairs' and other details of the architecture as he sees and describes it.[28] The alert reader is obliged to compare these diverging sets of terms, to assess the extent to which each party presents the house within his or her own conventions. There is no objective view of the house, but the pervasive irony of *Castle Rackrent* lies in Thady's disinclination to accept the 'Big House' view: a servant, dependent on the

[26] Ibid., p. 33.
[27] Ibid., p. 42. This is preceded by Condy's offer to carry his bride from the back gate to the back door — as if the distance were a threshold? — 'for you see the back road is too narrow for a carriage, and the great piers have tumbled down across the ruins of the front approach, so there's no driving the right way by reason of the ruins.'
[28] Ibid., pp. 44, 61.

goodwill of the hereditary masters of Rackrent, he declines to advance a worm's eye perspective.

Just as the mob is shown to converge rapidly on Thady when Jason has finally taken over at the Castle, so the Castle is shown to be vulnerably close to the town. At the beginning of the second Part, Condy comes from a house within view of the avenue, he has played in the street: now that proximity threatens his successor. To be specific, Thady goes to 'the street door' of the Castle — without reference to the avenue — where 'the neighbour's childer' gather around him. This topographical exactitude should not tempt us into drawing maps of the battlefield, for the fiction carefully exploits its *written*, rather than a visual, character to create thematic foci: 'and when the report was made known, the people one and all gathered in great anger against my son Jason, and terror at the notion of his coming to be landlord over them . . . .'.[29] From this recognition of the insurgent Jason's formidable position as master, Thady has to make his way back to the house to warn his son; that is, distance is now exploited to suggest ironic reluctance or difficulty for Thady in his mission to save Jason from the mob. Throughout *Castle Rackrent* the size or crampedness, the isolation or integration, of the house is exploited for thematic purposes. The Castle shrinks to a low back door; the disguised villa echoes in the absence of its new elected master with vast loneliness; the view is alternately of desolate bogs and crowded streets; the Castle has neighbours and empty cellars. At a time when the 'Big House' as museum and tourist attraction all but monopolizes our view of the Irish past, or at least of Irish class imagery of the past, this elusive protean Georgian castle concentrates attention on the complexity of social and cultural dynamics in the age of the French revolution.

The prominence of a sectarian vocabulary in the reporting of violence in Ulster since 1969 has prompted some commentators to engage in wholesale revisionist interpretations of Irish culture, according to which issues previously related to

---

[29] Ibid., p. 75.

such chimeras as class, economics, and social reality may be rewritten to conform to the 'Two Nations' of immemorable glory. Maria Edgeworth has not been immune to such developments, and the context of her writing *Castle Rackrent* certainly requires some attention to the question of Catholic–Protestant antagonism. It is reported that, in 1976, the International Association for the Study of Anglo-Irish Literature was informed the Rackrents 'are, in fact, Catholics and that this involves Maria Edgeworth in a significant flight from the historical facts of her period'.[30] John Cronin's discussion of this theory is itself all rather hypothetical, and the subject is sufficiently important for aesthetic reasons to earn attention here. The heart of the argument is declared to be, in effect, two sentences from Thady's account of Sir Murtagh's career; these are:

She was a strict observer, for self and servants, of Lent, and all fast-days, but not holidays. One of the maids having fainted three times the last day of Lent, to keep soul and body together, we put a morsel of roast beef into her mouth, which came from Sir Murtagh's dinner, who never fasted, not he; but somehow or other it unfortunately reached my lady's ears, and the priest of the parish had a complaint made of it the next day, and the poor girl was forced, as soon as she could walk, to do penance for it, before she could get any peace or absolution, in the house or out of it.[31]

This is as close to the terminology of Protestant and Catholic as Maria Edgeworth reaches in the novel. Thomas Flanagan has suggested that Sir Patrick changed his creed with his name in inheriting from Sir Tallyhoo, an inference which is strengthened by the novel's reference to his doing so 'by Act of Parliament'.[32] The legitimization of a loss of identity, and the acquisition of the descriptive name Rackrent in place of the aboriginal O'Shaughlin, amounts to an imposing change: if it does signify apostasy it is vital to stress that Maria Edgeworth's method is suggestive allegory, at the most. Beyond this initial allusion to such a change, only the two sentences quoted above specify in words such as 'Lent' and

[30] John Cronin, op. cit., p. 32, reporting on and summarizing an unpublished paper by Maurice Colgan.
[31] *Tales and Novels,* vol. i, p. 7.
[32] See Flanagan, op. cit., p. 70.

'penance' religious practices associated with Catholicism rather than Protestantism. Anyone with the slightest knowledge of Irish history will not find the presence of Catholic servants in a Protestant house remarkable — so much for the maid. As to Lady Rackrent's fasting and her evident contact with the priest of the parish, it is worth noting that mixed marriages between Catholic and Protestant were not unknown, especially where the husband was a Protestant and so able to inherit and bequeath real estate. For what it is worth, then, Lady Rackrent may have been a Catholic, just as Lady Macbeth may have been the mother of dozens.

The point energetically missed by proponents of this argument relates to the novelistic character of the document they are analysing. To argue that, the Rackrents being Catholics, Maria Edgeworth is in 'significant flight from the historical facts of her period' is to mistake *Castle Rackrent* for a tract. First, one should note that the traces of a possible Catholicism in the Rackrent family occur very early in the novel, and that such traces are impossible in the era of Sir Condy Rackrent, MP. There is then a reading of *Castle Rackrent* according to which it contains the possible interpretation outlined above, in relation to a specific moment in the family chronicle and including intermarriage as well as apostasy. That the novel should, accordingly, be read as evolving towards a more polarized — and always unspecified — sectarian sociology is in keeping with the altering developments of the period of its genesis (the 1790s) and of late eighteenth- and nineteenth-century history broadly. Personally, Maria Edgeworth's attitudes towards religious belief were modified along rather similar lines — though at a slower pace: while her father was alive she appears to have shared his Enlightenment views, whereas the demands for Catholic Emancipation and O'Connellite agitation from 1820 onwards hardened her attitudes towards Catholics.[33] *Castle Rackrent* has nothing to say of Catholic Relief or Protestant Ascendancy, and it is certainly no simple reflection of the facts of its period. On the contrary, it enacts in its deployment of such

[33] For her social attitudes see Michael Hurst, *Maria Edgeworth and the Social Scene: Intellect, Fine Feeling and Landlordism in the Age of Reform* (London: Macmillan, 1969).

traces as we have analysed a resistance to the sectarian
sociology embryonic in the '90s. Just as the building at the
heart of the novel displays the flexible, anxious negotiations
between castle and gentleman's box, so the plot admits both
the tensions and bonds of Catholic/Protestant relations.

One of the renowned features of *Castle Rackrent* is its
account of money as the base of marriage. The eighteenth
century would hardly have found that unusual, and within
the novel it is the transition from property as the motive for
changes of identity and name (in marriage and otherwise) to
the operations of commercial and legal means to acquire
property which is significant. Jason is thus the insurgent
representative of a money-economy taking over from an
older culture in which property 'in great masses of accumulation' held a preserving inertia. In Greek mythology, of
course, Jason's uncle had usurped the throne of Iolcos, and
set the boy the impossible task of recovering the Golden
Fleece. If we are to see Jason Quirk's ousting of the Rackrents
as a modern retelling of the legend, then he starts with the
advantage of a professional education and access to the
cash through which he can fleece his fellow-lawyer Condy
Rackrent. Again, attempts have been made to argue that
Jason is an impossible character in the Ireland of pre-1782,
on the grounds that Catholics were not admitted to the legal
profession until 1793.[34] Here again, the real historical point
is missed: the novel demonstrates the different ways in which
membership of the legal profession operated in a society
undergoing quite rapid transition; in the case of Condy, being
'bred to the bar' was part of a landowner's education rather
than a professional training; in the case of Jason, the law is
an instrument fully understood as a means of effecting
change. The irony of Jason is that his father, the usurped
'king' of the legend, should benefit nothing from the changes
wrought by lawyer Quirk.

The world of *Castle Rackrent* is small but restless. Its dominant images alter in their import throughout the developing
narrative. The Great House is so far from being a Penshurst
that the only allusions to literary culture detectable in the

[34] See Cronin, op. cit., p. 33, who gives the date wrongly as 1782.

novel — Goethe's *Werter* and the fashion of amateur theatri-
cals — reflect on their own credibility.[35] As with Burke's employment of the House in the *Reflections on the Revolution
in France,* dilapidation rather than grandeur shines through
ironically. So too, money is seen to sustain a way of life
ostentatiously condemned but none the less acknowledged
by the narratives. The dejected state of *Castle Rackrent's*
narrator at the outset of the novel (dressed in a ragged
coat and annotations from Spenser) is one measure of the
extent to which social change involves the ironic victimiz-
ation of those whose sons succeed.[36] Borrowing words from
Burke again, and alert to the ironies of quoting Burke in the
context, we might see Thady 'cast forth, and exiled, from
this world of reason, and order, and peace, and virtue, and
fruitful penitence, into the antagonist world of madness,
discord, vice, confusion, and unavailing sorrow'.[37] The difference is of course that Maria Edgeworth's satire dispenses
with any idea of a norm, presents no image however dimmed
by time or distance of a world of reason, order, and peace.
Castle Rackrent investigates one Burkean world without
pretending that the other exists. Its parade of Anglo-Irish
follies and vices could be annotated from Burke's writings
on the effects of the Penal Laws as well as his scornful comments on the Jobb-ascendants. The *Reflections* utilizes
techniques which will subsequently be associated with the
historical novel, and *Castle Rackrent* purports to be a history
of the Rackrent family. Each work stands Janus-like at its
historical juncture: Burke is no more a thoroughgoing foe of
bourgeois revolution than Maria Edgeworth is a whole-
hearted supporter of Catholic Relief. The sensibility which
directs her activities as a novelist is not a constant position, a
fixed star, but a particular openness to the historical quality
of contemporary experience.

There is one pervasive metaphor for history which both

---

[35] A performance of *Romeo and Juliet* is evidently intended at Mount Juliet's
Town, with the future Lady Rackrent as Juliet, see *Tales and Novels*, vol. i, p. 38.
[36] Ibid., pp. 1-2; the notes draw on Edmund Spenser's *View of the State of
Ireland.*
[37] Edmund Burke, *Reflections on the Revolution in France* (Harmondsworth:
Penguin, 1968), p. 195.

Burke and Maria Edgeworth allude to, a metaphor which pervades *Castle Rackrent*. In the *Reflections* Burke declares that 'people will not look forward to posterity, who never look backward to their ancestors' and continues to categorize freedom (in the British sense) as a 'liberal descent . . . which prevents that upstart insolence . . . it has its gallery of portraits . . .'.[38] Posterity, ancestors, descent . . . such an invocation of ancient British liberties, gradually drawn into the image of a genealogy legitimizing the present, and illustrated in all its stages, is not unique to Burke: in *Castle Rackrent* it is sufficiently active to require a telling rebuke. Only by attending to the genesis of the fiction can we recover that critique of genealogy and pride in genealogy which characterizes the short-lived Rackrents. Yet if *Castle Rackrent* thus appears remarkably ironic in its treatment of genealogy then *The Absentee* (1812) is its counter-truth. *Castle Rackrent* manages for the most part to avoid the topic of human generation. In the first part, wives are effectively imported though never to breed: in the 'continuation' (a significantly awkward term) even more haphazard arrangements are recorded — Sir Condy (descendant of the O'Shaughlins who are presumed Catholic) decides by the toss of a coin against marrying Judy M'Quirk, his social inferior and a Catholic, only to be succeeded by her brother.

The plot of *The Absentee* is very different. The hero, Lord Colambre, will resist marriage to one who is tainted with social dependency and (it is hinted) a Catholic background. Yet in ultimately marrying her, he unites himself not only to his own estates but also to his aristocratic cousin; pedigree and property achieve a romantic union. That plot is unfamiliar to readers, and its unfamiliarity facilitates our concentration on the modes of writing — allegoric and schematic, rather than narrative and ironic — by which Maria Edgeworth seeks to establish the doubleness which lies at the heart of Anglo-Irish literature.

[38] Ibid., pp. 199, 121.

4. THE ABSENTEE

Time is no longer primarily a gulf to be
bridged, because it separates, but it is
actually the supportive ground of process in which the present is rooted.

(Hans-Georg Gadamer)[1]

The Act of Union, coinciding with the publication of *Castle
Rackrent*, lends an air of spurious neatness to Irish literary
history. As we have seen, the composition of the novel had
begun years before the Union became a lively issue and
before the Edgeworths were involved in the parliamentary
manœuvres which culminated in the Union. Nevertheless, the
attractiveness of round numbers and tidy coincidences has
directed inquiries away from the genesis of *Castle Rackrent*
into the context of its public appearance. This bias not only
ignores the origins of the novel but also seriously distorts
the relationship between text and context by emphasizing
a highly immediate notion of context. Both in chronological
and geographical terms the stress on immediacy can obscure
the wider context — of European as well as British experience, of the eighteenth century as well as the year 1800 — in
which Maria Edgeworth worked. At the heart of the matter
there is the problem (never easily resolved) as to when the
past ends and the present begins. The question is best tackled
by a challenge to the assumption that past and present are
categorically distinct, or that (like links in a chain) they are
comparable but separate in themselves. To take a more
dynamic range of terms, history is not confined to the past:
the historical perspective is a manner of interpretation which
may legitimately include contemporary experience. It is
therefore advisable to keep this flexible or expanding context
before us as we read Maria Edgeworth's fiction.

It would be relatively easy to outline an immediate context
for *The Absentee*, to sketch the relevant events of 1811-12,

---

[1] Hans-Georg Gadamer, *Truth and Method (Dichtung und Methode)*, trans.
Garret Barden and W. G. Doepel (London: Sheed and Ward, 1975), p. 264.

and of Maria Edgeworth's personal experience during this period. Indeed some such outline is unavoidable. But the over-all objective of the present chapter is to place the novel in its broader historical context and to illustrate that these extended boundaries permit us to see the fiction as an active agent in an imaginative debate of lasting significance. We may begin, however, with local matters.

The Act of Union had been passed amid promises of emancipation for Catholics; these promises were not kept. At first Catholic spokesmen were inclined towards a waiting game. The Prince Regent seemed friendly, and his accession could not be long delayed; the governments of Portland, Perceval, and Liverpool were so determinedly anti-emancipationist that petitions were better postponed for a happier day.[2] But as early as 1804 leading Irish Catholics had met to organize their efforts to secure release from the Penal code. The composition of this first lobby reveals a social division which was to have important repercussions both in politics and literature: on the one hand there were representatives of the surviving Catholic gentry and nobility (Lord Fingall, Sir Thomas French, and the wealthy landowner, Elias Corbally), and on the other hand merchants and professional men such as Denys Scully, James Ryan, and Randall McDonnell. (To the tuned ear Irish surnames ring with social and denominational overtones, a circumstance which Maria Edgeworth happily exploits.) Others who assisted in these councils were John Keogh (a veteran of the previous century) and Lords Kenmare and Trimleston. The prominence of the titled members, and the influence of the merchants, marked the poles of a transformation of the Catholic question from a matter of eighteenth-century petitioning to full-blooded machine politics: Daniel O'Connell was soon to throw his abilities behind the younger and more aggressive faction. It is, however, worth noting that the conflict between nobleman and merchant, between style and substance, is present in *The Absentee* in the figures of Count O'Halloran and Mrs Raffarty, figures whom we will find to be instinct with historical nuances.

[2] R. B. McDowell, *Public Opinion and Government Policy in Ireland 1801–1846* (London: Faber, 1952), pp. 83–108, esp. pp. 88–91.

By the second decade of the century, the Catholic question had attracted the attention of English liberals and radicals, including Shelley and Byron. By February 1812 O'Connell was virtually the leader of the movement for emancipation, and though Lord Trimleston and one or two others were yet to retain some prestige among the Catholics the struggle had decisively gone against the noble party. At a meeting in Dublin on 28 February, O'Connell was the principal speaker, but Shelley was one of the few non-Catholic participants. In the *Dublin Evening Post*'s account of his speech, there is an allusion which bears on an aspect of *The Absentee*'s symbolism; referring to the conversion of the old parliament house into a bank, he declared that 'he saw the *fane of liberty converted into a temple of Mammon. (Loud applause)'.*³ Shelley as a good (certainly an earnest) revolutionary saw Catholic emancipation only as a tactical necessity beyond which national freedom became a possibility: his tribute to the corrupt Irish parliament as a 'fane of liberty' must be taken as a gesture towards that sentimentalizing of the past which characterized Irish politics after 1800. Had Shelley lived to 1829 he would have been dismayed to note that O'Connell accepted emancipation on terms which placed the temple of Mammon before the rights of the cabin-dweller. His 1812 speech — together with the *Address to the Irish People* — economically makes one vital point, that the local and temporary cannot be absolutely distinguished from the wider context of British and European culture. More particularly, if the loud applause of Messrs Scully, Ryan, and McDonnell (or their equivalents) for Shelley's attack on Mammon indicates the unresolved state of Catholic opinion on the relationship between class and denomination — the Dublin banking fraternity was of course overwhelmingly Protestant — it also suggests that those with views diametrically opposed to Shelley's might also favour emancipation. It is in this light that we approach *The Absentee*'s discussion of the status of Catholics and the significance of the past, in the light of contemporary anti-revolutionary liberalism. The background to Shelley's presence in Dublin, as to Maria

³ Quoted in Kenneth Neill Cameron, *The Young Shelley: Genesis of a Radical* (New York: Macmillan, 1973), p. 146.

Edgeworth's novel, is of course the war against Napoleon, and the British government's need to placate Papist opinion at home in furtherance of the war effort.

A more detailed account of the events of 1812 is entirely feasible — the 'great series of county meetings'[4] in favour of unconditional emancipation in the summer months, which gave promise of the mass-politics of the 1820s. But fiction deals with the particular as a manifestation of the typical, and Maria Edgeworth's imagination was primarily historical. Of Shelley's existence in 1812 she was most likely happily ignorant. Nevertheless, as our account of *The Absentee* will concern itself with the precise historical associations of certain names and places (O'Halloran, Trimleston, Tusculum, O'Raffarty) there is something to be gained by looking briefly at some of Shelley's Irish contacts. John Philpot Curran he met, and William Hamilton Rowan he failed to meet: they had fallen away from their radicalism. Roger and Arthur O'Connor he approved of whole-heartedly, and with John Lawless (O'Connell's left-tenant) he planned to run a newspaper.[5] However, both Percy and Harriet Shelley were particularly impressed by a veteran of the 1798 rebellion, Catherine *Nugent*. Without suggesting the slightest debt on Maria Edgeworth's part to this energetic woman, we should remark a similarity between her and Grace *Nugent*, the heroine of *The Absentee* — both depended upon others for their subsistence despite an evident superiority of mind (and perhaps of breeding). Harriet Shelley wrote of the actual Catherine Nugent:

This excellent woman, with all her notions of Philanthropy and Justice, is obliged to work for her subsistence — to work in a shop which is a furrier's; there she is every day confined to her needle. Is it not a thousand pities that such a woman should be so dependent upon others?[6]

The point here is certainly not that Maria Edgeworth drew upon this friend of the 1798 prisoners, Shelley's political

---

    [4] McDowell, op. cit., p. 95.
    [5] Cameron, op. cit., pp. 142-4.
    [6] Harriet Shelley to Elizabeth Hitchener, 18/3/1812; quoted by Cameron, op. cit., p. 144.

associate in 1812. Instead we should note in Harriet's letter that tone of surprise at Miss Nugent's low estate; indeed it is the combination of inherited or innate dignity and circumstantial dependence which unites Catherine Nugent and 'Grace Nugent'. That the name Nugent carried very particular connotations is a proposition which awaits proof: that the collocation of Jacobin and Jacobite loyalties (i.e. contemporary and revolutionary with historical and reactionary) is possible in *The Absentee* is a further demonstration of the unsettled attitude to 'Mammon' evident in Shelley's reception by the Catholic delegates in February 1812. We approach *The Absentee* therefore informed of the restless and ambiguous state of opinion not only in Ireland but throughout Britain.

1. METHODS, NOT SOURCES

The Absentee is a tale of contemporary events. There are three moments in the fiction on which some light might be cast, three significant allusions which are in danger of neglect, being less than self-evident to the modern reader. This is not to supply sources which demonstrate how Maria Edgeworth wrote her tale, but rather to show how the public would have read it in 1812. She did not expect her readers to recognize originals for her details; instead her method facilitated general associations in the reader's mind. The first hidden moment illustrates the point quite economically.

A pamphlet, *An Intercepted Letter from China,* is recommended to Lord Colambre, the returning absentee, as a reliable account of social life in Dublin. This clearly is a late reference to the fashion of satire through pseudo-oriental travellers' reports, a fashion now recalled principally in the case of Goldsmith's *Citizen of the World* (1762). But in *The Absentee* the pamphlet's satirical nature is played down; it features as part of the evidence, which Sir James Brooke presents to Lord Colambre, of the amelioration of Dublin society since the immediate post-Union years. Though suspiciously little description of the city itself is provided, and its citizens make no direct intervention into the narrative, one might see this discrepancy between Brooke's avowed aims and the implications of the pamphlet's title as merely the result of Maria Edgeworth's ignorance of 'oriental' satire. But the Edgeworth style was vigorously rational, practical, and literate; footnotes abound in the fiction generally, and *Ennui* explicitly draws on a travel-book. In *The Absentee* every other item on Lord Colambre's reading list is authentic and exemplary — works by Edmund Spenser, Sir John Davies, Arthur Young, and D. A. Beaufort. In the circumstances, it would be obtuse to doubt the seriousness of Maria Edgeworth's citing the *Intercepted Letter*. Moreover, there is much evidence to identify the pamphlet with an actual satire, *An Intercepted Letter from J- T- Esq;, Writer at Canton, to his Friend in Dublin, Ireland,* published in Dublin in 1804, evidence in the form of shared social views, incidents, and analyses in the actual pamphlet and *The Absentee*.[7] The 1804 publication was anonymous, but it has been long attributed to John Wilson Croker. In *The Absentee* Sir James Brooke speaks of the pamphlet's 'slight, playful and ironical style', a description which does not accord with Croker's heavy-handed satire. In fact, the Irish capital as seen by readers of the tale more closely resembles Croker's satire than the effusive ambiguities with which the *characters* discuss *An Intercepted Letter* and its analysis. The tale provides in now submerged details such as an allusion to pseudo-oriental satire a more critical account of Dublin than that articulated by the characters.

Following the encounter with Sir James Brooke, Lord Colambre visits a villa called Tusculum near Bray, the property of Mrs Anastasia Raffarty. The hospitality he receives there constitutes the second impressive incident of his sojourn in Dublin and its environs. Mrs Raffarty, delighted to include a noble lord in her lunch party, puts on a show of parvenu vulgarity, a mercenary appreciation of art, a grotesque taste in landscaping, and a ridiculous pretension to relaxed opulence. *The Absentee* is here quite unambiguous:

The dinner had two great faults — profusion and pretension. There was, in fact, ten times more on the table than was necessary; and the

---

[7] See W. J. Mc Cormack, '*The Absentee* and Maria Edgeworth's Notion of Didactic Fiction', *Atlantis*, vol. 5 (1973), pp. 123-35. The author no longer accepts the final critical verdict on *The Absentee* expressed in this article.

entertainment was far above the circumstances of the person by whom it was given: for instance, the dish of fish at the head of the table had been brought across the island from Sligo, and had cost five guineas; as the lady of the house failed not to make known. But, after all, things were not of a piece; there was a disparity between the entertainment and the attendants; there was no proportion or fitness of things; a painful endeavour at what could not be attained, and a toiling in vain to conceal and repair deficiencies and blunders.[8]

The gardens are in keeping with the interior; they contain:

a little conservatory, and a little pinery, and a little grapery, and a little aviary, and a little pheasantry, and a little dairy for show, and a little cottage for ditto, with a grotto full of shells, and a little hermitage full of earwigs, and a little ruin full of looking-glass, 'to enlarge and multiply the effect of the Gothic'.[9]

This intrusiveness and inversion of nature is neatly dramatized when a stuffed ornamental fisherman on a Chinese bridge is pulled into the water by a living fish.

Unlike the encounter with Sir James Brooke, this scene can offer Lord Colambre no ambiguous reason for settling in his native land. The Raffartys, however, cannot have the effect of sending him hot-foot back to London, for they speak with a voice disturbingly similar to that of his parents, Lord and Lady Clonbrony. In narrative terms, the Tusculum scene brings the hero to a halt; it forces him to consider his surroundings and his domestic background, to *relate* Irish and English experience. But a continuity exists between this episode and earlier and later developments. Though he admitted that immediately after the Union vulgarity flourished in the wake of the annihilated parliament, Sir James had assured Lord Colambre that *now* in Dublin:

you find a society ... composed of a most agreeable and salutary mixture of birth and education, gentility and knowledge, manner and matter; and you see pervading the whole new life and energy, new talent, new ambition, a desire and a determination to improve and be improved ...[10]

---

[8] *Tales and Novels* (London, 1832-3), vol. ix, pp. 128-9. All quotations from Maria Edgeworth's work are taken from this 18-volume collected edition, henceforth cited as *Tales* with volume and page numbers.

[9] Ibid., vol. ix, p. 127.

[10] Ibid., vol. ix, p. 120.

The trouble is that the reader sees none of this benign synthesis of the faculties and the classes; he sees instead Mrs
Raffarty, a grocer's wife, living in a simulacrum of refined
ease.

Croker's pamphlet in 1804 had described just this swift
advance of the mercantile classes — it was a commonplace
criticism of post-Union Dublin — but also added as a climactic symbol an account of the despoilment of the parliament
house after the Union. (This is Shelley's fane of liberty *cum*
temple of Mammon.) The new owners of the building,
the Bank of Ireland company, pulled down a magnificent
colonnade, according to Croker who observed:

I thought at first that the money brokers expected the colonade to
refund in the pulling down, the prodigious sums which had been
expended in building, but I am informed that they have no such
mercenary motives, and that this lamentable destruction is a pure effect
of their *taste*.[11]

Croker is being satirical of course, but the historian W. E. H.
Lecky records details of the deliberate alteration of the old
parliament, the two objectives being to render it unfit for use
ever again as public debating chambers and to transform the
people's image of it by ornamentalizing the exterior.[12] The
satirist, for his own purpose, blames taste; the historian
reveals motivation. Between the two a contemporary commentator, John Carr, recorded his somewhat foolish opinion
of the architectural meddling, 'If at first that elegant screen
were improperly raised, the error of its situation has been increased, by the violation of its chaste and beautiful columns;
if it were judiciously erected, it is now spoiled.'[13] Now
Croker (whose satire is indirectly invoked elsewhere in *The
Absentee*) and Carr (whose Irish travels the Edgeworths,
father and daughter had hostilely reviewed) both fix on the
details of the columns or colonnade as an example of the

---

[11] [John Wilson Croker], *An Intercepted Letter from J—— T—— Esq., Writer
at Canton to his Friend in Dublin, Ireland* (Dublin, 1804), p. 5.
[12] W. E. H. Lecky, *A History of Ireland in the Eighteenth Century* (London,
1892), vol. v, p. 418 n.
[13] John Carr, *The Stranger in Ireland* (Shannon: Irish University Press, 1970),
p. 80 (photolithographic fascimile of the 1st ed.).

tasteless improvement or 'de-functionalizing' of the old parliament house. In *The Absentee*'s account of Mrs Raffarty's
villa we learn only one feature of its architecture:

> There had been a handsome portico in front of the house; but this
> interfering with the lady's desire to have a viranda, which she said could
> not be dispensed with, she had raised the whole portico to the second
> story, where it stood, or seemed to stand, upon a tarpaulin roof. But
> Mrs. Raffarty explained, that the pillars, though they looked so prop-
> erly substantial, were really hollow and as light as feathers, and were
> supported with cramps, without *disobliging* the front wall of the house
> at all to signify.[14]

Without thinking of the parliament as a source for Tusculum,
we may see that details from Croker's satire, though evidently neutralized in Sir James Brooke's summary, are
acknowledged and transformed in a later episode of *The
Absentee*. Nor does Maria Edgeworth allow the implication
to remain inert, for in a late reference to the Raffartys she
points out that the house passed to them 'that time the
parliament *flitted*'.[15]

The view that the despoilment of the old parliament house
is reflected in Mrs Raffarty's juggling with porticoes and
cramps is made more plausible if we consider the manifestations of taste available to Maria Edgeworth in creating
Tusculum. This is not to suggest an original for the ghastly
hostess — apart from Lady Clonbrony. The location of her
villa, however, is undoubtedly exact, and to contemporary
readers assuringly real. Tusculum is near the town of Bray,
and evidently on the Wicklow side of the town. At the
beginning of the nineteenth century, the principal villa in this
picturesque area was Bellevue, with a sizeable demesne
straddling the hill between the Glen of the Downs and
Delgany, the property of Mr and Mrs Peter La Touche. La
Touche was one of Dublin's leading bankers; that is to say,
of the profession who inherited and disfigured the old parliament house. Bellevue of course was not unique in the area,
but travellers made a point of including it on their itinerary.
Bellevue was special in several ways; it was open to the public

14   Tales, vol. ix, p. 126.
15   Ibid., vol. ix, p. 211.

at certain times of the year, as a model of its mistress's osten-
tation and public spirit, being thus already regarded as representative of a type. When John Ferrar published his
account of Dublin in 1796 he gave Bellevue prominence even
on the title-page. Some of his detail is suggestive to readers of
The Absentee — a conservatory 254 feet in length, a superb
orangery, a peach-house, and a pinery. 'The Gothic dining-
room — which is extremely curious and seems like a rock —
was added in the year 1788.'[16] Two years after this account
of Bellevue was published, insurrection broke out about
fifteen miles further south, and travel in Wicklow became
temporarily unfashionable.

In 1801 Robert Fraser published a *General View* of
Wicklow in which he devoted five pages to Mrs La Touche's
establishment, stressing that lady's munificence 'in this time
of uncommon scarcity', and seemingly anxious to rebut any
notion of Bellevue as pointless extravagance:

Here the barren mountain's side has been forced by its cultivation, to
afford subsistence and comfort to thousands, and to present an example to men of rank and fortune, which, if universally followed would
render Ireland the elysium of the world . . . The benevolent possessors
do not content their feelings with even amply rewarding the labour of
the peasants they employ. They attend even to the prevention of their
wants, and the increase of their comforts. Every article of subsistence
is procured for them . . .[17]

This tourist was in no danger of courting La Touche dis-
pleasure, though the attitude towards the peasantry (never an
Edgeworthian term) was one which the practical Edgeworths
could not have accepted. To Richard Lovell Edgeworth and

[16] John Ferrar, *A View of Ancient and Modern Dublin with its Improvements
to the Year 1796, to which is Added a Tour to Bellevue, in the County of
Wicklow, the Seat of Peter La Touche, Esq.* (Dublin, 1796), p. 111.

[17] Robert Fraser, *A General View of . . . County Wicklow* (Dublin, 1801),
pp. 63-4. For a modern account of the picturesque as manifested in County
Wicklow villas see Edward Malins and The Knight of Glin, *Lost Demesnes: Irish
Landscape Gardening, 1660-1845* (London, 1976), esp. pp. 168-78, 187-8.
Bellevue is discussed in some detail, and a watercolour drawing of one of the glass-
houses is reproduced. Malins and Fitzgerald also discuss the distribution of
cottages ornés ('more common in Ireland than in England') which are condemned
in *The Absentee*; in this connection they specify a cottage on the La Touche
estate at Marlay, County Dublin as representative (see pp. 119-20, and p. 123).

his daughter, the provision of prettified cottages and incongruous luxuries was likely only to confuse and distress the Irish tenant. They believed in inobtrusive adequacy, the reward of effort, but not the general improvement of conditions irrespective of individual deserts. In *The Absentee* this indiscriminate and sporadic passion for improvement is found at Kilpatrickstown:

Lord and Lady Kilpatrick, who had lived always for the fashionable world, had taken little pains to improve the condition of their tenants: the few attempts they had made were injudicious. They had built ornamented, picturesque cottages, within view of their park; and favourite followers of the family, people with half a century's habit of indolence and dirt, were *promoted* to these fine dwellings. The consequences were . . . everything let to go to ruin for the want of a moment's care, or pulled to pieces for the sake of the most surreptitious profit: the people most assisted always appearing proportionally wretched and discontented.[18]

But it was the egregious John Carr, in *The Stranger in Ireland*, whose account of Bellevue was in its enthusiasm for the useless and merely decorative most likely to infuriate the Edgeworths:

I believe in England and Ireland the green and hot-houses of Bellevue are unrivalled. This palace of glass, which looks as if it had been raised by Aladdin's lamp, is six hundred and fifty feet in length, and includes an orange, a peach, a cherry-house and a vinery, and is filled with the most precious and beautiful plants from the sultry regions of Asia, Africa and America, which, tastefully arranged and in the highest preservation, banquet the eye with their voluptuous perfume. As I was roving through the delicious spot, some steps led me into the chapel . . . festooned with Egyptian drapery . . . the seats are covered with scarlet cloth, the decorations are in the highest style of appropriate elegance, and the entrance opens into the conservatory.[19]

For prose like this Carr was ridiculed by the Edgeworths in the *Edinburgh Review*, but the impression persisted with Maria Edgeworth to contribute to her image of Mrs Raffarty's emporium. Ferrar, Fraser, and Carr were all writing prior to *The Absentee*, but the reputation of Bellevue lived on for

---

[18] *Tales*, vol. ix, pp. 155-6.
[19] Carr, op. cit., pp. 199-203.

many years. G. N. Wright, for example, describes the ornamental cottage at the northern extremity of the demesne as
containing 'a number of apartments; one on the ground floor
is appropriated to the purposes of a museum, and a second is
used for a banqueting room, where Mrs. La Touche sometimes entertains her friends at luncheon.' Close by, 'a few
cottagers reside, whose chief support is derived from supply-
ing parties from Dublin with accommodations, either in their
cottages or on the green turf before them, to enjoy their cold
collation.'[20] Wright's *Guide to County Wicklow* offers a
strangely muffled analysis of the local economy, for the area
is 'thickly inhabited by gentry'.[21] Brewer is more frank,
suggesting that the banqueting-house 'might, perhaps, have
been rendered more consonant to the unusual character of
the surrounding circumstances', and the modern plantations
'might possibly, have been withheld to advantage in some
places'.[22] If Brewer admits the excessive interference with
Nature over which Mrs La Touche presided, Wright records
details which are equally significant for us — a stuffed
panther, a collection of shells, a tottering wooden temple
presumably full of earwigs.[23] In *The Absentee* the excesses
of Tusculum remind Lord Colambre of his mother's debased
taste, her reception rooms in London being contrived to resemble a Turkish tent, a pagoda, and the Alhambra. According to Lewis's description of the actual estate at Bellevue, Mrs
La Touche's shrines included a solid Turkish tent and an
Octagon House.

Maria Edgeworth's method is not to copy Tusculum from
Bellevue, but rather to build on the assumption that her
readers will respond, not to a generalized idea of the fashionable villa, but rather to known and actual types. The general
idea of the villa, therefore, is engendered in the reader's mind
in the reading of *The Absentee*, and not in the tale itself.
Tusculum is not extensive like Bellevue; it is compact,
cramped (literally), and overcrowded; that is how Maria
Edgeworth conveys the shape of Mrs Raffarty's imagination.

[20]   G. N. Wright, *A Guide to the County of Wicklow*. (London, 1822), pp. 33–4.
[21]   Ibid., p. 35.
[22]   J. N. Brewer, *The Beauties of Ireland* (London, 1825), vol. i, pp. 294–5.
[23]   Wright, op. cit., p. 37.

Similarly, Carr's mixed metaphors and obsequious journalese
are not sources for *The Absentee*, at least not in any artistically important sense; the palace of glass raised by Aladdin's
lamp may become an appropriate image of Mrs Raffarty's
career, her imminent downfall, and her spurious eminence
in society. But in another sense Tusculum is pervasive, because through a recognition of its relationship with — say —
Bellevue, the reader of the fiction can see the Tusculum style
at work both in the Clonbrony's London home and in the
phoney Kilpatrick improvements. The Tusculum scene takes
up only part of one chapter in the tale, and its essence is
caught in the emblem-like stuffed fisherman dragged into the
living stream. That image is not simply the author's irony; it
prepares us for Mrs Raffarty's bankruptcy and the destruction of her brother, Nicholas Garraghty, whose regime as
land-agent at Clonbrony Castle is a perversion of a political
'norm'. The relationship between Tusculum and Bellevue is a
kind of dialectic — the precise location and concentrated
emblems of the fictional villa suggest to the reader districts
and villas he knows. Knowing more than the detail present at
Tusculum, he proceeds to recognize the same style elsewhere
in the tale, in London drawing rooms and deep rural cabins.
For it is not by studying Tusculum itself that we see its
relationship in *The Absentee* to London and Kilpatrickstown;
it is rather in the implied social context of such *typical*
effects. A distinction can be made between the reader of
1812 and the reader of today; the latter may come to regard
Bellevue as a source for *The Absentee*, but the contemporary
reader existed in a different consciousness. There is no
equivalence between Bellevue and Tusculum; instead, in *The
Absentee* a concrete typicality draws the reader's knowledge
into action. But the full implications of the contemporary
reader's view of Mrs Raffarty's villa can only be appreciated
within a comprehensive account of the fiction as a whole.
The relationship between Tusculum and Bellevue does not
just illustrate a method of composition; it exemplifies an
important theme in *The Absentee*, the transformation of
knowledge into action.

The third moment in the tale which may be drawn into its
proper focus has already been discussed in some detail by

Thomas Flanagan in *The Irish Novelists 1800-1850*, the
scene in which Lord Colambre visits the crumbling home of
Count O'Halloran. Though this theatrical depiction abounds
in what Flanagan calls allegorical meanings, the narrative does
not stand still. The Count is an antiquarian, and in his library
the returning absentee (as yet a mere sightseer) discovers
memorials of the ancient Nugent family. Remaining on the
narrative level, we can see that Colambre is drawn to these
memorials because his attractive and witty cousin, Grace, is
a Nugent. But his fellow visitors, English army officers for
the most part, seize on no such guiding star, and so are lost
amid the clutter of emblems which surround the Count — 'an
odd assembly: an eagle, a goat, an otter, several gold and
silver fish in a glass globe, and a white mouse in a cage'.[24]
These strange pets' behaviour is described in terms remi-
niscent of heraldry — 'the eagle, quick of eye but quiet of
demeanour, was perched upon his stand; the otter lay under
the table, perfectly harmless; the Angora goat . . . was walking
about the room . . .'.[25] The entrance of the strangers disturbs
this careful composition, but the subsequent arrival of the
Count sets all aright once more. When O'Halloran enters he
immediately refers to his menagerie in a phrase which Lord
Colambre courteously interrupts: ' "mouse, a bird, and a fish,
are, you know, tribute from earth, air, and water, to a
conqueror —" "But from no barbarous Scythian!" said Lord
Colambre, smiling'.[26] As the Count's allusion to Herodotus is
recognized and cancelled, Maria Edgeworth becomes more
explicit metaphorically in describing the reconciliation between pets and visitors:

The count looked at lord Colambre, as at a person worthy his attention;
but his first care was to keep the peace between his loving subjects and
his foreign visitors. It was difficult to dislodge the old settlers, to make
room for the new comers: but he adjusted these things with admirable

[24] *Tales*, vol. ix, p. 164.
[25] Ibid.
[26] Ibid., vol. ix, p. 166. The allusion is ultimately to Herodotus; see *The
Histories*, trans. A. de Selincourt (Harmondsworth: Penguin, 1972), rev. ed. by
A. R. Burn, pp. 313-14; the incident (in Bk. IV) relates to the ambiguous intention lying behind the Scythian gifts to the Persian invader, Darius.

facility; and, with a master's hand and master's eye, compelled each favourite to retreat into the back settlements.[27]

The terms of the metaphor are — each considered in isolation — innocuous; it is their accumulation which emphasizes a political context — 'to keep the peace' between 'loving subjects' or 'the old settlers' and 'foreign visitors', and to 'retreat into the back settlements', etc. As self-styled Scythian, Count O'Halloran had referred to the emblems of homage, casting himself as the conquered, and Lord Colambre (by implication) as the conqueror. The absentee's interruption, therefore, is much more than courteous; it indicates something of the terms on which he arrives back on his estates, and suggests that his contribution *alters* the historical role of the Count. Lest these implications be missed, there follows an incident in which the officers (or 'foreign visitors') before whom the master diplomat defers, mistakenly refer to him as *mister*. Given such emphatic signals, the reader cannot but reflect on O'Halloran's status and the proper mode of address he commands; he is a retired soldier, bearer of a continental title. In the argot of eighteenth-century Jacobitism, he is a Wild Goose, one of those high-born followers of King James who sought military service with the Catholic monarchs of Europe. Flanagan goes no further in analysing this strange scene than to stress O'Halloran's isolation in his homeland, his being the 'survivor of a long-dead Ireland'.[28]

Yet if the Count's title proclaims his loyalties, his surname is no less informative. Count O'Halloran is surrounded by genealogies, funeral urns and the skeletons of extinct animals; one of the outstanding antiquarians of Maria Edgeworth's age was Dr Sylvester O'Halloran. In *The Essay on Irish Bulls* (1802) Maria and her father had gently ridiculed the antiquarian movement, naming only O'Halloran as exemplar of the vocation. There are similarities, apart from the identical surname, to suggest that Dr O'Halloran contributed at least his name to the fictional Count O'Halloran — similarities of

---

[27] Ibid.
[28] Thomas Flanagan, *The Irish Novelists 1800–1850* (New York; London: Columbia University Press, 1959), p. 89.

continental association, even of dress.[29] But we have good
authority — Edgeworth family tradition, in fact — to believe
that another aspect of the Count was drawn from a different
quarter. Probably at the suggestion of her relative D. A.
Beaufort, whose *Memoir to a Map of Ireland* featured on Sir
James Brooke's reading list, Maria Edgeworth based the
Count's curious household of pets on that of the twelfth
Baron Trimleston, Robert Barnewall.[30] Trimleston had been
a Catholic, of Jacobite sympathies, who had spent years in
exile and had been coldly received on returning to Ireland.
In 1762 he had organized a petition to the Lord-Lieutenant
from notable Catholics, asking for a relaxation of the law
forbidding them to bear arms, and specifically requesting
permission to join the (Hanoverian) king's service.[31] At the
instigation of the exclusively Protestant Irish parliament,
this movement towards reconciliation was thwarted. However, Trimleston was long dead before Maria Edgeworth set
foot in Ireland, and his presence in the tale is of secondary
importance. Certain important associations and assumptions
went into the creation of the synthesis which is Count
O'Halloran. The exotic household is provided by family
stories of an eccentric neighbour, but the animals are so
disposed of in the prose as to become a heraldic tableau
vivant rather than a grotesque extension of a personality.
Baron Trimleston had practised medicine in France, and in
searching for a name for her character Maria Edgeworth reviews the names of those who share this characteristic. One
such is Sylvester O'Halloran, whom she has already mildly
satirized. Trimleston and Barnewall do not appear as names
in *The Absentee*, but that family had intermarried with
another important Irish sept, the Nugents, whose name is
borne by the heroine. It is not surprising therefore that Grace
Nugent's marriage to Lord Colambre is made possible by the
Count's intervention — antiquarianism brought up-to-date to

[29] See W. J. Mc Cormack, 'Sylvester O'Halloran and Maria Edgeworth's
Absentee', *Long Room* (No. 9, 1974), p. 41 for a contemporary description of
Sylvester O'Halloran's dress (cf. description of Count O'Halloran in *Tales*, vol. ix,
p. 162).
[30] Marilyn Butler, *Maria Edgeworth: A Literary Biography* (Oxford: Clarendon
Press, 1970), p. 378 n.
[31] Lecky, op. cit., vol. ii, p. 69.

serve the present. And in 1812 (when *The Absentee* was written) a renowned member of the Nugent family carried the title of Count of the Holy Roman Empire, thus completing the synthesis of the fictitious 'Count O'Halloran'. These associations — the Jacobite with the antiquarian with the latter-day continental soldier — become more potent in the light of Sylvester O'Halloran's attitude to the Act of Union. Maria Edgeworth's synthesis draws together Jacobite and anti-Union feeling, and launches a myth of incalculable potency in modern Irish literature and politics.

2. THE HEROINE

Inevitably an inquiry into these allusions must focus attention on Irish references, but before reaching any conclusion about them, we should consider a further context in which *The Absentee* should be read — that of Maria Edgeworth's fellow novelists in Britain. As we shall see, the tale pays impatient attention to landscape and 'improvement', while *Mansfield Park* (1814) used the ill effects of a master's absence from the Great House to describe a wider moral concern. In *The Heyday of Sir Walter Scott* Donald Davie compares Miss Edgeworth and Miss Austen, an exercise in which the Irishwoman is by no means disgraced. For him, the common factor is not the theme of absenteeism, but the heroine's dilemma:

Miss Edgeworth's Grace Nugent is, like Fanny Price in *Mansfield Park*, a ward and a dependent, but the Irish novelist doesn't penetrate this predicament as Miss Austen does, nor does she realise what a very advantageous station this was for the author, through her character, to inspect society from.[32]

---

[32] Donald Davie, *The Heyday of Sir Walter Scott* (London: Routledge, 1961), p. 72. In a more recent study of the novel in this period, *Jane Austen and the War of Ideas* (Oxford: Clarendon Press, 1975), Marilyn Butler devotes a lengthy chapter to Maria Edgeworth's fiction. Mrs Butler, however, is principally concerned with 'Maria Edgeworth's peculiarly sharp perception of the ethical content of feminine lives' (p. 132) and has little to say about *The Absentee*. In addition her use of the terms 'Jacobin' and 'anti-Jacobin' for warring parties in English literary life renders difficult any simple correlation of our findings. Readers especially interested in Miss Edgeworth's place in English literature cannot afford to ignore this absorbing study.

Characters and roles cannot be totally abstracted from a complex fictional world even for comparison with Fanny Price. Nevertheless, Davie's point is useful if it obliges us to show that Grace Nugent, within her own novel, is a fully integrated and articulate character. This has rarely been admitted by critics, and even Edgeworthians have expressed reservations about Grace's role. Marilyn Butler, in the definitive biography declares that:

> the concluding section of *The Absentee* is almost exclusively taken up with disentangling a sub-plot about the good name of the heroine's mother. It is not relevant to the theme of absenteeism, and indeed can scarcely be made intelligible without reference to *Patronage*. As a whole, therefore, *The Absentee* is very uneven, and in its treatment of Ireland is by far the least successful of Maria Edgeworth's four Irish tales.[33]

The role of the heroine is clearly central, not only to the task of illuminating the curious household of Count O'Halloran, but to the success of the tale as an artistic unity. Although Grace Nugent is absent from the page for much of the action, she is unquestionably as important to the theme of the tale as the hero himself. Given the apparent simplicity of the plot as customarily summarized, and the strictures of Donald Davie and Marilyn Butler on the heroine's role, it may be revealing to construct our account of *The Absentee* round her.

We first see Grace Nugent in the Clonbrony's London home, attractive but somewhat cool to her suitors. She has no parents, no fortune; her chief assets are an intelligent insight into her guardians' pretension and folly, and a loyal sense of embarrassment on their behalf. The first allusion to her name arises from Lady Clonbrony's admission that she had tried to persuade Grace to drop 'Nugent', to disguise the *Iricism*.[34] But Grace has evidently refused, perhaps because she has no other possession truly her own. A further consciousness of her name is amusingly conveyed when two guests at the Clonbrony gala attempt to discuss Grace's background without mentioning their victim:

[33] Marilyn Butler, *Maria Edgeworth*, p. 375.
[34] *Tales*, vol. ix, p. 22.

'Speak low, looking innocent all the while straight forward, or now and then up at the lamps — keep on in an even tone — use no names — and you may tell any thing.'

'Well, then, when Miss Nugent first came to London, Mrs. Dareville —'

'Two names already — did not I warn ye?'

'But how can I make myself intelligible?'

'Initials — can't you use — or genealogy?'[35]

The exchange stresses, by its fractured syntax, the impossibility of telling anything without resorting to names. Indirectly it informs us that names may tell a great deal about characters.

And the name 'Nugent' carried particular associations in Anglo-Irish circles at the beginning of the nineteenth century, had carried them for several previous centuries. The Nugents had been among the first Norman families to settle in Ireland after the twelfth-century invasion. Together with Plunketts, Dillons, and Barnewalls, they dominated Norman-Irish society in the northern midlands. At the Reformation these families remained Catholic, and continued to play a prominent part in Irish affairs, being known as the 'Old English' to distinguish them from later, Protestant planters. At the close of the seventeenth century, they adhered to the Jacobite cause, and lost lands, titles, limbs, and lives in the service of King James. The county of Westmeath, which borders on Longford, was the centre of Nugent influence, and the degree of their Jacobite commitment can be gauged from outlawry statistics; of those outlawed for high treason committed in Ireland against King William, two hundred and sixty-eight had homes in Westmeath, and of these forty-seven (or 17.5 per cent) were Nugents; of those outlawed for treason committed abroad, Westmeath accounted for ninety-two, fifteen of them Nugents.[36] As a result of these declarations many Irish Jacobites (and almost all of them Catholics) went into continental military service. At the battles of Ramillies, Oudenarde, and Malplaquet, a Christopher Nugent commanded a regiment which bore his name. He accompanied

---

[35] Ibid., vol. ix, p. 54.

[36] These calculations are based on a list of Irish Jacobites which is preserved in Trinity College Dublin, and published by J. G. Simms in *Analecta Hibernica*, vol. 22 (1960), pp. 11–230.

the self-styled James III to Scotland in 1715, a spontaneous act of Jacobite enthusiasm which led to disagreements with his French superiors. Nugent had married Bridget Barnewall, daughter of the ninth Baron Trimleston, another of whose daughters married another Irish Nugent.

Among a group for whom the possibilities of advancement were legally restricted, it is not surprising to find familiar patterns and habits emerging. A second Christopher Nugent (of the same Westmeath family) shared with the twelfth Baron Trimleston a French medical education, this later Nugent becoming in 1757 the father-in-law of Edmund Burke. Though he remained a strict and sociable Catholic, he was a member of Doctor Johnson's circle in London, and Johnson is said to have greeted news of Nugent's death with a sad apostrophe to their ritual Friday omelettes. By and large, the name Nugent implied an Irish, aristocratic, Jacobite background, though the defeat of King James had led to the demotion of the name in Irish society in the eighteenth century. All nineteen Nugents in the *Dictionary of National Biography* are connected with the Westmeath family, though not all were so pious or so loyal to tradition as Johnson's friend. For as the eighteenth century progressed, there were movements by both sides towards a reconciliation between some of the Jacobite exiles and the Hanoverian regime — which needed professional soldiers, and might stomach Popery in men of such reactionary political views. Trimleston's initiative of 1762 was of this kind. In a number of cases a *rapprochement* was achieved by an individual act of apostasy; Robert, the Earl Nugent (1702–88), was the family's most famous convert to the reformed religion and political success; his mother was Mary Barnewall. In the latter part of the eighteenth century, as the French Revolution overturned the alliances of a previous age, pressing reasons of state encouraged an understanding between the British government and the descendents of Jacobite traitors. In the Austrian service, Lavall, Count Nugent (1777–1862) combined a brilliant military campaign against Napoleon with diplomatic initiatives in London, initiatives which earned him the respect and confidence of Sir Arthur Wellesley, later Duke of Wellington, a fellow-Irishman with Westmeath/

Longford connections. Count Nugent was in London in 1811
and 1812, the months preceeding *The Absentee*'s publication, in quest of an agreement with the regime which had
banished his forefathers. Lady Wellesley being a friend of
Maria Edgeworth's and a native of Westmeath, it is not
unlikely that a report of the Count got through to Edgeworthstown. Even in Maria Edgeworth's childhood some
forty years earlier, the name Nugent conjured up particular
and embarrasing assumptions; an incident is recorded in a
later letter between members of the Edgeworth family:

> There was company one evening and tea and cakes of which Maria eat
> so much that being desired to buckle her shoe she could be no means
> stoop to reach her foot and looking for help she saw a Miss Nugent who
> having been playing on the fiddle her natural instinct taught her must
> be an underling — and called her to do it for her . . .[37]

A pointless reference, were it not for the fact that, in *The
Absentee* Grace Nugent is a dependent in the household, and
is finally accepted to the accompaniment of tune-players.
And even before 1812, Maria Edgeworth had drawn on the
status of the Nugent name to provide a typical incident in the
career of Sir Murtagh Rackrent, who had been very sanguine
about a lawsuit with the Nugents of Carrickashaughlin.
O'Shaughlin having been originally the Rackrent family
name, before Sir Patrick's apostasy, the lawsuit in *Castle
Rackrent* encapsulated an entire century of political conflict.
Names, as the nameless gossips of the London salons recognized, are everything in this fiction.

To the casual reader it is clear that Grace and her cousin
are destined for a happy marriage. Grace's reluctance is
generated by a distaste of placing herself in a position where
she might appear as a gold-digger. The dominant topic of the
opening chapters is advantageous marriage and the best
means to achieve it. A Mrs Broadhurst insists that the young
should be given opportunities to nurture affection on which
their parents have already agreed; she advises 'Propinquity! —
Propinquity! — as my father used to say — And he was married

---

[37] See M. Butler, *Maria Edgeworth*, p. 48, quoting a letter from Harriet Butler
to Michael Pakenham Edgeworth, 3 January 1838.

five times, and twice to heiresses.'[38] Grace's delicacy of
feeling on this point is implicated in her name; Goldsmith's
friend, the Earl Nugent to whom 'The Haunch of Venison'
was presented, had won fame and fortune by marrying a
succession of rich widows. Horace Walpole coined the verb
'to nugentise' to describe this mercantile attitude to marriage.[39] The opening chapters do not simply see the heroine
sitting aside from the fashionable and trivial — as Fanny
Price sits aside — but present Grace Nugent surrounded by a
society dedicated to enacting before her the idiomatic
meaning of her name. Her name is potentially a slight, on
grounds of politics and ethics; being poor she must avoid
the application of the name in the idiomatic sense. Consequently she must remain reserved towards her cousin, despite
her feeling for him.

But Colambre is even more stubbornly resistant to the
love-match. Through the scheming Lady Dashfort he learns
that Grace's mother had been a St Omar, a family of whom
none of the women was *sans reproche*.[40] Repeatedly he
muses on this disgrace, and repeatedly the name St Omar
figures as a short-hand for the offence. St Omer, of course,
was the French seminary at which a large proportion of
Catholic priests were educated in the eighteenth century,
when education was denied them at home. St Omar, in the
context of 1812, is as obvious a reference as would Harvard
be in a modern novel. Daniel O'Connell spent a brief period
in the St Omer seminary, and both Edmund Burke and Lord

---

[38]   *Tales*, vol. ix, p. 63.
[39]   Walpole to Horace Mann, 22 July 1744; see *Horace Walpole's Correspondence with Sir Horace Mann*, ed. W. S. Lewis *et al.* (London: Oxford University
Press, 1955), vol. ii, p. 481.
[40]   *Tales*, vol. ix, p. 157. For evidence that Maria Edgeworth was aware of the
sectarian associations of the name St Omer we have only to turn to the glossary
appended to *Castle Rackrent*. The narrator, Thady Quirk, has said of his son 'I
thought to make him a priest', and the 'editor' of Thady's memoranda comments:
'It was customary amongst those of Thady's rank in Ireland, whenever they could
get a little money, to send their sons abroad to St. Omer's, or to Spain, to be
educated as priests. Now they are educated at Maynooth ...' (*Tales*, vol. i, p.
109). That she should specify St Omer on this occasion when she sought to make
a purely technical point about the habits of Irish Catholics underlines the significance of the name in *The Absentee*; writing the glossary she saw St Omer as the
representative college of its kind, though in fact it was not an Irish but an English
(Jesuit) foundation dating from 1593.

Chancellor Fitzgibbon were maliciously accused of being alumni. To have a St Omar mother, therefore, was to be labelled with the badge of Catholic tenacity; Nugents might compromise or conform, but St Omars, having the fixity of place, could not change. To recognize the connotations of the name is to understand the real motives behind Colambre's hesitation in marrying Grace. The combination of Nugent and St Omar marks her as a symbol of Catholic resistance; he on the other hand bears a 'union title', a product of the corrupt and exclusively Protestant Irish parliament.[41]

It is worth pausing in this analysis of names to anticipate one or two details of a critical assessment of the evidence. Maria Edgeworth does not allow her concern with names to paralyse the narrative; the use of names is dramatic and occasional as well as emblematic and pervasive. Through Count O'Halloran's researches Grace's legitimacy is proved, her grandfather traced, and her wealth recovered. Her father, however, had been a soldier in Austria; that is, he too had been an exiled Jacobite. His name being Reynolds (and not Nugent) the nugentizing taint has been removed. These reassurances are adequate and the narrative moves on. The contemporary crisis of revolutionary and Bonapartist war makes Jacobitism politically acceptable, Count Nugent demonstrating the point in his reconciliation with Arthur Wellesley. In such circumstances the St Omar taint can be transformed into legitimacy, just as in 1795 the British government had sanctioned at Maynooth a college to rival the continental seminaries. At several levels, then, the theme of Maria Edgeworth's tale is the return of absentees, but not all were voluntary emigrants or careless landlords — some had been banished, some were disgraced.

Miss Nugent, however, is specifically *Grace* Nugent. When the entire family returns to Ireland we see little of the heroine; instead we overhear a harper playing a song called 'Gracey Nugent'. It is of course an actual tune, as

---

[41] Maria Edgeworth never specifically declares Clonbrony to be a 'union lord', but the discussion between the young ladies at the gala (*Tales*, vol. ix, pp. 45-6) implicitly condemns their host and hostess in terms of 'bought rank'. Colambre, being only 20 years old, cannot be personally accused though he bears a courtesy title as his father's heir.

recognizable to an Irish reader in 1812 as 'Green Sleeves' to the English, a tune composed by the greatest of Irish harpers, Torlough O'Carolan. It has been freely translated by Austin Clarke:

> And so I raise my glass, content
> To drink a health to Gracey Nugent,
> Her absence circles around the table.
> Empty the rummer while you are able,
> Two Sundays before Lent.[42]

The heroine is drawn into a folk tradition, an embodiment of excellence and dignity. According to Maria Edgeworth's design, she is present once again, a restored and restoring influence in the broad and inclusive network of social alliances in the tale.

Despite the historical and social substance of these discoveries, they have in fact been made primarily by an examination of the fiction itself. If it is objected that we have taken liberties with Miss St Omar by seeing her name as a place-name rather than a personal one, it is worth recalling how deliberately Maria Edgeworth named a series of minor figures who surround Grace Nugent — Mr St Albans, Mr Salisbury, Mr Martingale of Martingale, Mr Soho. The significance of the heroine's name is not that it is a 'real' one — all names in fiction must to some extent be so chosen — but that its connotations are directly pertinent to the theme of the tale. To read *The Absentee* as an autonomous document without relation to an external world is especially difficult, because it insists on the value of relation, exploration, and reconciliation. The problem of method may in fact be largely an illusion, the difficulty arising from the conscious effort which modern readers must make to recognize various references. What may appear as the application of external criteria (social relevance, topographical consistency) is really an examination of the fiction itself, of the hidden allusions within it, and the manner in which these are related one to another and to the tale as a whole. To scrutinize Miss Nugent for the implications of her name may prove very revealing,

---

[42] Austin Clarke, *Flight to Africa and Other Poems* (Dublin: Dolmen Press, 1963), p. 77.

and certainly offers a refreshing perspective on the hero; yet the words which constitute her presence in the fiction are part of a larger and wider pattern, a pattern which can be observed in various ways — in terms of symbol, reference or narration. A character cannot be isolated from a fictional context, because 'he' or 'she' is defined by and remains part of a continuous entity.

3. A CULTURAL CONTEXT

A literary work exists in a multiple context. Yeats's *Last Poems,* for example, may be regarded as part of a tradition including Thomas Davis, James Clarence Mangan, and Sir Samuel Ferguson, and as a successor to neo-Platonists such as Boehme, Swedenborg, and Blake. He is a contemporary both of Parnell and of Rilke. His measure may be taken from the fact that none of these irreconcilable figures is irrelevant to an understanding of Yeats: the great artist creates a new context for himself.

Here we shall confine ourselves within narrower limits. Techniques developed by exponents of comparative literature provide a means to relate Maria Edgeworth's work to European and British traditions, but for the most part the emphasis will remain Irish and historical. With *The Absentee* in mind, one might look for a chronology from the Norman invasion to the campaign of the Provisional IRA, from the arrival of the first Nugent in Ireland to the murderous results of the Provisionals' adherence to a neo-Jacobite contempt for the *reality* of existing institutions. While it is tempting to explore parallels between the eighteenth-century loyalty to a monarch over the waves (and a thoroughly reactionary monarch at that) and the loyalty of latter-day Provisionals to 'the first Dáil Éireann', such extensive contexts are rarely useful for they dilute, rather than concentrate, the bonds between the text under scrutiny and the world in which it lives and to which it gives meaning. But given the particular self-consciousness of Irish history, it is quite proper to relate *The Absentee* to the course of events in Ireland (and elsewhere) from 1688 onwards, from the Glorious Revolution which unseated King James. After a succession of military disasters at 'Derry, Aughrim, Enniskillen and the Boyne', the Irish Jacobites were forced to accept terms in the Treaty of Limerick (1691). Such guarantees of their rights as they received proved inadequate, and the Penal code of the next few decades progressively restricted Catholics in their administration of property and the practice of their religion, as well as in a host of minor but irritating aspects of social life. Legends of Jacobite suffering and endurance enlivened much Gaelic literature and music during the period. Thus, the harper's greeting of Grace Nugent is as important a recognition scene as that in which Mrs Raffarty proclaims Colambre's presence in the castle. Considered from the historical point of view, it reverberates with great intensity in that she is recognized by a communal anthem which speaks of a pattern reaching beyond any single individual. 'Gracey Nugent', of course, was available to Maria Edgeworth in several published sources — not to mention its currency in the Irish countryside.[43]

It would indeed be extraordinary if the tale did not reveal a familiarity with eighteenth-century tradition and nomenclature; the aspect of *The Absentee* which is artistically relevant here is its consistent relation of terms and names in such a way as to enrich the narrative stratum. The song's integrating function may be appreciated if we pay attention to Donal O'Sullivan's notes to his study of O'Carolan, especially where he quotes a letter of Charles O'Conor's, identifying the historical Grace Nugent as 'a worthy lady, the sister of the late worthy John Nugent of Castle Nugent, Culambre'.[44] Thus the union between the fictional characters — Nugent and Colambre — is implicit in the provenance of the song. Indeed, O'Carolan's compositions include many references to the Nugent family which are germane to an analysis of *The Absentee*; apart from 'Gracey Nugent' there are at least three

[43] See Donal O'Sullivan, *Carolan: The Life, Times and Music of an Irish Harper* (London: Routledge and Kegan Paul, 1958), vol. ii, pp. 3-4 for a list of sources including several printed prior to 1812.

[44] Charles O'Conor to Joseph Cooper Walker, 14 October 1785 — 'You enquire about Grace Nugent: a worthy lady, the sister of the late worthy John Nugent of Castle Nugent, Culambre. She lived in our own neighbourhood with her sister Mrs. Conmee when Carolan addressed her with the ode and piece of music . . .'. Quoted by O'Sullivan, op. cit., vol. ii, p. 69.

other pieces celebrating members of the family. In Lee's *Favourite Collection* (1780) we find 'John Nugent of Colamber' and 'Mrs. Nugent', the latter also appearing in Thompson's *Hibernian Muse* (*c*.1786). A third song, 'Elizabeth Nugent' is preserved in manuscript, and printed by O'Sullivan (1958). All four Nugents thus commemorated were members of the same branch of the family, the Nugents of Coolamber, County Longford. And the occasion of 'John Nugent' is identical with that in *The Absentee* when the harper greets Lord Colambre's bride, for it was written to 'Welcome to Ireland, and to Castle Nugent, a lady who has come over from France and who is apparently the bride-to-be . . .'.[45] In the fiction, Grace Nugent may be said to have 'come over' from French loyalties and principles in being cleared of the St Omar taint. 'Mrs. Nugent' includes the line:

's tú oidre an Chuil Omra, an bréagán san tseomra

which may be translated:

And you are heiress to Coolamber, the allurement in the room.[46]

Such details emphasize the close association, not only in family annals but also in the popular art of Jacobitism, of the names Nugent and Coolamber. Thus, the sub-plot of *The Absentee* which steers hero and heroine into marriage is far from aimless or irrelevant; it takes its direction immediately from history.

The Nugents were not the only family celebrated in song, nor were they without extensive connections by marriage in the north midlands. Grace Nugent, in *The Absentee*, is discovered to be really a Reynolds and, in Lord Colambre's words, 'there are so many Reynoldses.' Nugent and Reynolds, however, were conjoined in the names of two moderately well-known Irishmen of the period before the Union. The first, George Nugent Reynolds, was murdered in 1786 in a rigged duel.[47] The second, also George Nugent Reynolds, a

---

[45] O'Sullivan, op. cit., vol. ii, p. 66.

[46] Ibid., vol. ii, p. 67.

[47] See G. J. Browne, *A Report of the Whole of the Proceedings previous to, with a Note of the Evidence on, the Trial of Richard Keon, for the Murder of George Nugent Reynolds, and also of the Charges of the Judges thereon* (Dublin, 1788).

minor poet, died in 1802. Though the exact relationship
between them is difficult to establish, their ancestor was
George Reynolds of Letterfian, who had been O'Carolan's
first patron, about the year 1692. Reynolds therefore was
a name associated with both O'Carolan and Nugent; we
find among the composer's titles 'George Reynolds' (or
'Planxty Reynolds' as it is sometimes known) and 'Madame
Reynolds'.[48] James Hardiman went so far as to suggest in his
Irish Minstrelsy that 'Gracey Nugent' was a first cousin of
'George Reynolds'.[49]

These details are not irrelevant to Maria Edgeworth's
fiction, for they indicate that her choice of names conformed
to patterns well established in Irish society, particularly in
the region (Westmeath and Longford) from which she hailed.
Popular music, from as early as 1692, preserved the collocations of Nugent and Coolamber, Nugent and Reynolds; the
protracted conclusion of *The Absentee* enacts and extends
this eighteenth-century pattern in a new context defined by
the claims of landlordism and the military life — that is, residence or exile. The tale conforms to the historical pattern,
not only in its collocations of names, but also in relating
specific themes to the names. Seeing Grace Nugent as exemp-
lifying the dignity of the 'Wild Geese' we can look also to the
depiction of Count O'Halloran, to the contribution he makes
to the deciphering of Grace's past, to St Omar as the suspect
past and Reynolds as the rehabilitated past. Confirmation of
the St Omar symbolism and its idiomatic meaning in Irish life
may be conveniently found in a letter of George Nugent
Reynolds, the younger. The poet had been dismissed from
his magistracy by the Lord Chancellor, John Fitzgibbon.
Apostasy was prominent in Fitzgibbon's coat-of-arms, his
forebears being Catholics and his own dedication to Protestant supremacism near-fanatical. Fitzgibbon was much

---

[48] O'Sullivan, op. cit., vol. ii, p. 99.

[49] James Hardiman, *Irish Minstrelsy* (London, 1831), vol. i, p. xlviii. O'Sullivan
(vol. ii, p. 66) disputes this claim on the grounds that 'the Nugents of Carlanstown
were distinct from the Nugents of Castle Nugent.' Although the precise degree of
kinship may interest genealogists, the general association of the names Nugent
and Reynolds is authenticated in numerous instances. Several Nugents of earlier
generations composed Gaelic poetry — see Tomás Ua Bradaigh, 'Na Nuinnsionaigh
mór teaglach Gall-Ghaelach', *Ríocht na Midhe*, vol. 3, No. 3 (1965), pp. 211-21.

feared in Ireland, but Reynolds's response to dismissal was a flamboyantly frank letter in which he averred: 'Had your lordship, like your father been destined for the Popish priesthood, you would have had the benefit of a St. Omer's education, and, of consequence, known more decency and more good manners.'[50] It is important to note that this letter has no direct bearing on *The Absentee*, apart from illustrating the use of the seminary as a short-hand term for committed and principled Catholicism, for the tradition of foreign education which distinguished Jacobites and candidates for the priesthood. In the last quarter of the eighteenth century, the eclipse of Scottish Jacobitism and the improved condition of Ireland resulted in a reconsideration of the Catholic education issue: Edmund Burke was prominent among advocates of a more liberal policy, and he recommended a separate establishment in Ireland for the training of priests. Then, as the historian Lecky put it, 'the French Revolution and the war of 1793 forced the question into sudden ripeness by making the foreign education of ecclesiastical students impossible.'[51] This revolutionary alarm came much nearer home when rebellion broke out in Ulster and south Leinster, and French troops invaded Connaught. In 1798 the Edgeworths saw and heard within a mile or so of their home the terrible effects of those French principles which R. L. Edgeworth had been advocating as late as 1795. It was a decade in which a generation of liberals in Britain learned to swallow their enthusiasm for the Revolution, but nowhere was the process more distasteful and inevitable than in Ireland. George Nugent Reynolds, who had scolded a lord chancellor (albeit ironically) for lacking the St Omer virtues, reacted vehemently to the French invasion; his musical piece 'Bantry Bay' is written in loyally anti-Jacobin terms. Though he is merely a convenient external point of reference in discussing *The Absentee*, Reynolds in these few details embodies a combination of attitudes implicit in Maria Edgeworth's

---

[50] Quoted by J. R. O'Flanagan, *The Lives of the Lord Chancellors and Keepers of the Great Seal of Ireland* (London, 1870), vol. ii, p. 251. For a short account of Fitzgibbon, including a comment on his relations with Reynolds, see Terence de Vere White, *The Anglo-Irish* (London: Gollancz, 1972), pp. 94–110.

[51] Lecky, op. cit., vol. iii, p. 348.

plot — generosity to the Jacobite past, hostility to radical interference with existing class structures, and a concern for a broadly based reunification of the kingdom.

The revolutionary present informs *The Absentee* obliquely, in keeping with the diffused evidence of the past. The London of the Clonbronys' gala is swirling with the excitement and prosperity of a war boom, and though Napoleon Bonaparte is never mentioned, the revolutionary emperor's influence is felt by the guests in Grosvenor Square. When Colambre crosses to Dublin his first acquaintance is a professional soldier whose presence mutely points to the military crisis. Soldiers accompany Lady Dashfort on her tour, and doing so not only indicate her political loyalties but also exemplify the anxious co-operation of the newly united countries — Britain and Ireland — in the wake of rebellion. At Halloran Castle, the Count welcomes Captain Williamson, Major Benson, and Colonel Heathcock as potential allies:

turning to the officers, he said, he had just heard that several regiments of English militia had lately landed in Ireland; that one regiment was arrived at Killpatrick's town. He rejoiced in the advantages Ireland, and he hoped he might be permitted to add, England, would probably derive from the exchange of the militia of both countries: habits would be improved, ideas enlarged. The two countries have the same interest; and, from the inhabitants discovering more of each other's good qualities, and interchanging little good offices in common life, their esteem and affection for each other would increase, and rest upon the firm basis of mutual utility.[52]

In the light of these professions of common purpose, the soldiers' embarrassment in addressing O'Halloran (as *Mister* instead of *Count*) is seen to be more than ignorance or gaucherie; it is their blundering attempt to assimilate the Jacobite into their scheme of things. Insisting on her character's continental title, Maria Edgeworth indicates that the common interest of Ireland and England shall not be advanced by ignoring the past, but by positively acknowledging it: the Count comes to play a crucial part in tempering Colambre's later military ambitions. His welcome to the soldiers, however, is couched in the same indirect mode of

[52] *Tales*, vol. ix, p. 167.

expression which marked Sir James Brooke's discussion of Dublin society; at this stage of the tale it remains inert, merely intentional.

Like Brooke, O'Halloran introduces the returning absentee to a book which is more effective than the characters' indirect testimony:

> Lord Colambre, with the count's permission, took up a book in which the count's pencil lay, 'Pasley on the Military Policy of Great Britain;' it was marked with many notes of admiration, and with hands pointing to remarkable passages.
>
> 'That is a book that leaves a strong impression on the mind,' said the count.
>
> Lord Colambre read one of the marked passages, beginning with 'All that distinguishes a soldier in outward appearance from a citizen is so trifling —' but at his instant our hero's attention was distracted by seeing in a black-letter book this title of a chapter: 'Burial-place of the Nugents.'[53]

The alternatives of present and past are placed before Colambre in such elemental terms as these, and though he chooses to be distracted by history from policy, his motives are those of clearing up the obscurities of Grace Nugent's origins, of removing the obstacles to their union and the reconciliation of their loyalties. Charles William Pasley had published several editions of the first part of his *Essay on the Military Policy and Institutions of the British Empire* prior to 1812, and in the emergency of the war against Napoleon the essay was constantly revised and never completed. In 1812, the year of *The Absentee*, his practical contribution to the war effort was acknowledged by the establishment of a training school for non-commissioned engineers at Chatham.[54] Count O'Halloran is a scholar of the most modern and utilitarian tactics as well as of historical and antiquarian values.

If the reader expects these references to the current military crisis to disappear from view as the hero moves further into the countryside, then his expectations in this regard — as in so many others — are disappointed. Colambre's

---

[53] Ibid., vol. ix, pp. 168-9.
[54] For a brief account of Pasley see *The Dictionary of National Biography*.

journey, from the village which gave him his title towards his father's seat, sees the first appearance of Larry Brady, the postillion whose letter draws the tale to its curious conclusion. The evacuees whom Colambre and his driver meet on the road are on their way to England, forced to emigrate in involuntary imitation of the fashionable absentees. The fate which awaits Brian O'Neil and his beloved Grace, should they fail to meet the agents' demands, is a similar banishment to America. The good agent in Colambre village has already applied a global image to the absentee Lord Clonbrony:

he's a great proprietor, but knows nothing of his property, nor of us. Never set foot among us, to my knowledge, since I was as high as the table. He might as well be a West India planter, and we negroes, for any thing he knows to the contrary — has no more care, nor thought about us, than if he were in Jamaica, or the other world.[55]

This imagery lends an ironic substance to Larry's casual condemnation of the bad agent as a 'neger', a term which he uses as meaning in some way both 'negro' and 'niggard'.[56] Allusions to exploitation in the Caribbean and to enforced absenteeism among the lower classes have the effect of transforming the drab countryside between Colambre and Clonbrony Castle into a negatively universal site; there is much bustle and deception, confusion and accident which serves to bring out the consequences of a landowner's absenteeism, consequences which reach beyond Ireland, as Larry's brother in the London coachmaker's yard exemplifies. The Jamaican allusion also takes up the implications of O'Halloran's interest in Pasley's *Military Policy*, for the Caribbean was a theatre of war in which Britain opposed France. The Napoleonic campaigns have left their mark on the balladry of Ireland, especially in the form of exotic names and distant destinations, and the images employed by Mr Burke and Larry Brady are not in themselves implausible. But there is a further cogency to the Jamaican reference, in that George Nugent, who had commanded one of the northern regions during the Irish rebellion of 1798, had left

---

[55] *Tales*, vol. ix, p. 187.
[56] Ibid., vol. ix, p. 212. The footnote reads: '*Neger*, quasi negro; meo periculo, *niggard*'.

Ireland to become Lieutenant-Governor of Jamaica in 1801.
The point is not simply that the name Nugent once more
contributes some link between disparate elements in *The
Absentee*; both Ireland and Jamaica were important theatres
of conflict in which Britain faced revolutionary violence.[57]
These casual invocations of West Indian exploitation and
cursory allusions to a manual of military tactics cannot be
said to be integrated into the fiction, as a comparison with
Jane Austen's *Mansfield Park* must confirm. There, the
contemporary crisis is never so obviously invoked as to reveal
a copy of Pasley on Sir Thomas Bertram's table. Nevertheless,
Sir Thomas is temporarily cast as an absentee himself when
he is detained in Antigua, and Fanny's brother follows a
successful career in the Royal Navy; neither detail can be
fully appreciated without reference to the war at sea. Jane
Austen is content to leave these allusions on the periphery of
her fiction, and to concentrate on the moral consequences
of Sir Thomas's enforced absenteeism and on developing
Fanny's proper assumption of her importance at Mansfield.
Maria Edgeworth, on the other hand, displays a nervous
insistence in placing Pasley and Jamaica before the reader.
Even though we may feel that the atavism of the blind harper
is to some extent counterbalanced by this emphasis on the
urgency of a contemporary crisis, it cannot be denied that
the texture of *The Absentee* fails to absorb all of the author's
devices.

It is in fact only in the final chapters that she attempts to
reconcile the opposing values represented by the books on
Count O'Halloran's table, and once again these chapters
reveal their relevance to the theme of absenteeism. When
O'Halloran arrives in London, he explains his movements to
Lord Colambre:

[57] George Nugent's wife, Lady Maria Nugent, published a journal in which she
deplored the state of Ireland after 1798, and adopted an enlightened attitude to
the black population of the West Indies; see *Lady Nugent's Journal of her Residence in Jamaica from 1801 to 1805,* new ed. by Philip Wright (Kingston: Institute of Jamaica, 1966). Though the significance of the name Nugent cannot be
ignored, Lady Nugent's *Journal* cannot be regarded as a source for the tale, as it
was not published until after 1812; both writers moved in similar social circles
during their visits to London.

A relation of mine, who is one of our ministry, knew that I had some maps, and plans, and charts, which might be serviceable in an expedition they are planning. I might have entrusted my charts across the channel, without coming myself to convey them, you will say. But my relation fancied — young relations, you know, if they are good for any thing, are apt to overvalue the heads of old relations — fancied that mine was worth bringing all the way from Halloran Castle to London, to consult with *tête-à-tête*. So, you know, when this was signified to me by a letter from the secretary in office, *private, most confidential*, what could I do, but do myself the honour to obey?[58]

The Count is now at last receiving from the authorities the courteous address which Lady Dashfort and her soldier companions found so difficult to convey at Halloran Castle. He is not only an 'old head'; he is the head of an old order with whom the Government is now anxious to co-operate in 'an expedition'. In bringing his expertise and his charts to London, Count O'Halloran is fulfilling much the same role as the historical Count Nugent had done in the months preceding the publication of *The Absentee*. The tale, however, does not pursue the Count's mission on the level of verisimilitude; instead it begins to integrate the incident into a broader pattern that involves both Colambre and Grace Nugent. For we hear nothing further of O'Halloran's relatives in the Ministry; or rather, the purpose of his visit is assumed into the hero's dilemma concerning the St Omar taint, and the Count is next discovered advising Colambre on the merits and demerits of a military career. Why then does Colambre reject the military life? First of all, the discussion of an officer's existence is a part of the transformation of the Count's London mission into the reconciliation of Nugent and Colambre; it is part of a process by which verisimilitude becomes emblem, a process implicit in the music of Turlough O'Carolan. And secondly, the military life — as the Count knows only too well — is a life of exile, and it has occurred to Colambre primarily as an escape from his feelings for Grace, his cousin. The transformation of this dilemma can only be achieved by a renewed attention to the past rather than the military future. The harking (or harping) back evident in Larry Brady's account of the celebrations at Clonbrony Castle is not only counterbalanced by the imagery of contemporary crisis, but an attempt is made to relate past and present through the changing symbolism of the retired soldier's mission to London, a mission ostensibly concerned with maps and charts but ultimately fulfilled in the discovery of a marriage certificate.

That Maria Edgeworth in her fiction was concerned with contemporary revolutionary alarms cannot be doubted. In the first series of *Tales of Fashionable Life* (1809), 'Ennui' (which bears a close resemblance to *The Absentee* in that the hero leaves England for Ireland and discovers his real self) includes an Irish attempt at rebellion; 'Emilie de Coulanges' which appeared with *The Absentee* in the second series of the *Tales*, features refugees from revolutionary France. The Edgeworths had toured France during a lull in the hostilities with Britain, and Maria absorbed her experiences so deeply as to draw on them freshly when she wrote *Ormond* in 1817. Moreover, her brother had failed to leave France in time, and spent eleven years in prison; he was not released until 1814, and was therefore still in French hands when *The Absentee* was written. And if the tale of 1812 seems remote from specifically Irish disturbances — 1798 or 1803 — there is some evidence to suggest that it was either conceived at an earlier date or deliberately constructed with earlier material in mind. Croker's pamphlet of 1804, Hoare's travels of 1807, Carr's of the same year — all these are indirectly invoked in *The Absentee*. Mrs Butler, in the definitive biography, notes that 'Emilie de Coulanges' was devised as early as 1803.[59] Although Maria Edgeworth wrote virtually all her Irish fiction in great haste, its allusive density points to a proportionally long period of gestation.

The year 1798 differed from previous crises in many ways. Edgeworth interest in Longford was now the centre of the family, English holdings being regarded as peripheral. R. L. Edgeworth, as a Member of Parliament, occupied a more explicitly political position than many of his resident forebears. Previous military campaigns had been focused on

---

[59] Marilyn Butler, *Maria Edgeworth*, p. 322.

conflicts of a less clearly ideological kind: 1798, by reason of
its revolutionary context, demanded an intellectual as well as
a domestic response. Since the Jacobite wars of a century
earlier, no such crisis had arisen in Ireland. A French army
was marching through the midlands, supported spasmodically
by bands of rebels whose inspiration was more often local
vengeance than abstract ideological zeal. The rebellion had
indeed broken out elsewhere on the island, but the French
presence was limited to the west and the north midlands.
Thus, where the Edgeworths were uniquely isolated, the
French troops stimulated in their enemies a unique response
of slaughter, cruelty, rumour-mongering, and treachery.
R. L. Edgeworth's political isolation was near-complete; by
reputation an eccentric if not a radical (and certainly no
friend of the new Orange element in the county), he was
suspect in the eyes of the local gentry and their armed
militia; by breeding and by his social role cut off from the
tenantry, he became overnight transformed from radical
anchorite to fool-in-the-middle. The war against Irish rebels
was conducted with the utmost barbarity: about two hundred ill-equipped wretches were butchered in the demesne at
Wilson's Hospital, though the invading French army remained
intact. Its destination was Dublin, and its course lay just
north of Granard. A government force under Lord Cornwallis
camped in the parish of Clonbroney early in September, and
met Humbert's troops at Ballinamuck on 8 September. Out-
numbered by about five to one, the invading revolutionaries
were finally defeated. The alarm in Longford/Westmeath had
lasted a little over a fortnight, but the advance of professional
French soldiers, in league with a desperate western tenantry,
had brought the Edgeworths closer to extinction than they
had been for over one hundred years. The boundary of their
survival was the short distance between Edgeworthstown
and Ballinamuck; from it father and daughter had fled to the
town of Longford for safety. There, with the camp-fires of
the French visible from the walls, the citizens tried to lynch
R. L. Edgeworth as a spy. The grounds — as Edmund Burke
might put it — of their survival must be studied carefully,
for the map of this patch of land bears a number of names
immediately relevant to *The Absentee* — the townlands of

Coolamber and Coolamber Manor, the townland and parish of Clonbroney (the latter including Firmont), the townland of Castlenugent. Clonbroney includes both Ballinamuck (where the French were finally halted) and St Johnstown (the borough which R. L. Edgeworth represented in the Irish House of Commons.)[60] In creating the character of Clonbrony Maria Edgeworth dramatized the history of her own landed interest in Ireland, emphasizing the conflicting loyalties which had gone into the making of her heritage. The Williamite element is perhaps taken for granted, though its sectarian excess is deplored or depreciated. But the Jacobite and French connection was even more dramatic; Louis XVI's confessor had been the Abbé Henry Essex Edgeworth, who took his title 'de Firmont' from his birthplace in the same district. That a novel of reconciliation should take up these names, and use them to analyse the effects of absenteeism in moral rather than political terms, indicates the confident strength which Maria Edgeworth brought from her experience of the moral tale to the writing of fiction. *The Absentee* makes no explicit reference to the violence of 1798; the task of literature was not simply to reflect the past, but to generate the transformations which it required. *The Absentee* is not didactic in its argument, but in its symbolic demonstrations.

The heroine's function as emblem of a renovated past, the inner coherence of the characters' names taken as a group, the contemporary relevance of the reconciliation theme to the author's experience (both immediate and familial), these elements possess a multiple dependence on each other which contributes to an over-all artistic integrity. Setting, character, metaphor are not separable items in a physical reaction which

---

[60] According to Lewis's *Topographical Dictionary*, Clonbroney possessed excellent resources of limestone, and in *The Absentee*, the disguised Colambre poses as a researcher in quarries. Lewis records, under Kilpatrick (cf. the tale's Kilpatrickstown) that this Westmeath parish includes 'the ruins of an old church, with the vestiges of a fortified building nearly adjacent; and part of another fort is on the lands of Tuitestown' (vol. ii, p. 161); Maria Edgeworth's Catholic ancestor was Jane Tuite. Topographical information embodied in this note is based on Ordnance Survey maps, and was tabulated for me by the staff of Longford–Westmeath County Library, to whom grateful acknowledgement is duly made. Estate papers relating to Edgeworth family possessions in the area are preserved in the Public Record Office Dublin.

may be reversed and cancelled; on the contrary they unite in a chemistry which is active and persistent. Nevertheless, the plot of *The Absentee* remains to be assessed; and here, we must take care not to accept plot as effectively the *summum* of the tale, but rather insist that plot — like character or setting — is part (but only part) of a larger artistic unity. Walter Allen has spoken of its ostensible relevance:

in *The Absentee* Maria Edgeworth had seized upon the essential situation of her country at the time of writing: the absence of its land-owners in England and the stranglehold their agents had on a helpless peasantry. And when we visit Ireland in the company of Lord Colambre, the Clonbronys' son, whose aim it is to induce his parents to return to their native land and take up their proper duties there, we might be in nineteenth-century Russia, in that world of sequestered petty land-owners, culturally almost indistinguishable from their peasants, among whom every kind of eccentricity flourished . . . *The Absentee*, then, has a theme that was of the highest importance in its day.[61]

There are good reasons, however, for seeing absenteeism not so much as the theme as the outward plot of the tale; and this is just as well, for contemporary relevance alone cannot raise itself into art.

Two kinds of ignorance are combated in the course of the narrative, two kinds of darkness dispelled. On the geographical plane, the worlds of London and the Irish midlands are brought into a tense relation through the conduct of the Clonbrony family, whose surnames and even Christian names are withheld from us lest the importance of place-names be ignored. The absentees learn to recognize Ireland as their home, not in any spiritual or romantically nationalist sense, but, as it were, logically: the anomaly of Colambre in London is rejected. This level of narrative has of course its contemporary aptness; the Dublin banker William Digges La Touche, at a meeting in 1798, laid much of the blame for the Insurrection on the absentees, declaring that

if these men had resided in their own country among their tenantry, it is more than probable that we would never have been afflicted by that rebellion by which we have been reduced to that state of

[61] Walter Allen, *The English Novel: A Short Critical History*. (Harmondsworth: Penguin, 1958), p. 105.

humiliation and weakness, which has subjected our liberties, our manners, and our name to insult and threatened attack.[62]

The threat was of Union with Britain. R. L. Edgeworth had
shared La Touche's contempt for the absentees, but after his
experiences in the Insurrection, he had supported Union on
principle (though he came to vote against it in practice!) La
Touche was quite frank in admitting his motives as an anti-
Unionist, and his ironical-rhetorical thinking sheds light on
Maria Edgeworth's depiction of Dublin's middle class. How,
demands the banker, would Union help us?

Is it to be an increase of our absentees and a decrease of our population? Is it by these our commerce is to be improved? ... I divest
myself of every feeling but those immediately connected with the
mercantile character ... I do say that in a Legislative Union with Great
Britain, we are certain of nothing but loss ...[63]

Neither Edgeworth nor La Touche had a monopoly of
wisdom or even consistency, for Edgeworth finally voted
against the Union in protest at the corrupt methods of the
authorities, and La Touche's bank survived the Union by
many prosperous years.

Only propaganda is plain and simple: the nexus involving
absenteeism, rebellion, and Union was infinitely more complex and unclear. *The Absentee* reflects this complexity in
placing before Colambre's eyes, on his arrival in Dublin,
evidence which cannot be read simply and plainly. The
contradictions which face him are of course selected, and
relate specifically to other areas of the tale, yet in this artistic
complexity there is an acknowledgement of the unsettled
debate in society. Far from being didactic in directing the
absentees homewards, Maria Edgeworth confronts them with
scenes which, through their moral condition, are transformed
into a fiction of reconciliation. Dublin society and rural
conditions — the ragged beggars, rootless soldiers, dreadful
parvenus, and slovenly landlords — are not simply a tableau
vivant existing independently of the principal characters. It is

[62] *Proceedings at a Meeting of the Bankers and Merchants of Dublin.* Dublin,
1798, p. 7. (The pamphlet is cited by R. B. Mc Dowell, op. cit., p. 252, as illustrating how highly the anti-unionists valued the gentry as a bond in society.)
[63] *Proceedings* etc., p. 6.

only when this society is perceived by Colambre, and incorporated into his experience, that it takes on artistic meaning. Indeed, the beggars, soldiers, parvenus, and landlords may be seen as potential extensions of Colambre's consciousness, roles which are so to speak open to him. It is precisely because of this conflicting evidence confronting Colambre that a second plane of reconciliation has to be considered, involving not a topographical or spatial dimension, but a historical one. Grace Nugent functions as the epitome of the Jacobite past on the eve of rehabilitation, O'Halloran as the necessary but outmoded *accoucheur* of this process. Reconciliation presupposes reassessment, and there is abundant evidence of a renewed interest in the past, a sensitivity to titles, a veneration of urns and genealogies, an eagerness to explore. Absenteeism, as the tale's plot, does not simply monopolize thematic concerns; the plot operates as emblem also, for the essence of the absentee's dilemma is that he denies connection, connection between place and person, community and individual, present and past. That the evidence inducing Colambre to abandon absenteeism is contradictory takes on a special significance when read as symbolic of a broader theme of reconciliation. For while much is learned of the Jacobite past, nothing is revealed of the Williamite inheritance. Perhaps this is a necessary limitation of Maria Edgeworth's method, a consequence of her choice of a hero without epic qualities. Yet these consequences cannot be ignored, and they include the very imperfect self-discovery of the absentees and their purely ceremonial integration into the rural community.

Having seen something of the historical context in which *The Absentee* was written, we can return to the final chapter to scrutinize the manner in which Maria Edgeworth describes the scene at Clonbrony Castle. If the tale were to reach its climax in the blind harper's playing of 'Gracey Nugent' without some counterbalancing imagery, the result would be to draw *The Absentee* away from its concern with contemporary society. For Grace Nugent functions in the last movement of the fiction (Larry Brady's letter) almost exclusively as historical emblem, the rapid development of her consciousness as character being apparently forgotten; her

spontaneous speech and expanding interior reflections do
not impinge in a single instance on Larry's letter. If the
O'Carolan tune were the sole unifying image of reconciliation, then the result very likely would be a sentimental
return to a past already declining in relevance. Though the
recognition of a revolutionary alarm behind O'Halloran's
mission to London counterbalances O'Carolan — just as
Pasley's policy and Nugent history divide his table between
them — the final movement lacks poise and conviction, its
uncertainties half-concealed behind Larry's racy dialect.
When style relaxes sufficiently to allow renewed contact with
a narrative line, we find that Lord Clonbrony and Colambre
can offer only fair play to their tenants — an arrangement
previously evident under the regime of the good agent, Mr
Burke, while their lordships were absentees. There is no
indication as to how Colambre and his wife will manage the
estate, no attention to the agricultural economy over which
they will preside. Detail of the kind which invigorated *Castle
Rackrent* cannot be provided; stylistically, this disability
stems from the disappearance of social satire from these
final pages — satire flourishing on vivid detail. In terms of
social analysis, the new situation of the landlords as resident
does not inaugurate any new relationship between tenant and
master. Ultimately *The Absentee* reduces social reality to
personal moral rectitude; a striking reversal has taken place in
the course of the tale for, commencing with an acknowledgement that morality is social, it finally suggests the very different proposition that moral intention can support a social
function. It is in fact Larry, the solitary spokesman of the
tenants, who points out the diminished role of the landlord
on the estate; directed by Colambre to bring his aged father
forward, Larry appreciates a passing whimsical reference:

he knows the *natur* of us, Paddy, and how we love a joke in our hearts,
as well as if he had lived all his life in Ireland; and by the same token
will, for that *rason*, do what he pleases with us, and more may be than
a man twice as good, that never would smile on us.[64]

Technically, this is a superbly controlled evasion, moving

[64]   *Tales*, vol. x, p. 52.

from the pleasantry of Colambre's joke to a very different implication that he will do 'what he pleases'. It is not merely the joke which was awkward, nor the admission that a jovial landlord may behave however he likes, may do more than a man *twice as good*. Colambre, in this final movement utilizes the last of the political metaphors already observed in O'Halloran's study and the Clonbrony office. On these occasions, Colambre resisted identification as invader or conqueror amid the emblems of O'Halloran's castle, and asserted control in ousting Nicholas Garraghty when the agent was presented as viceroy in the presence-chamber. Here, Colambre neither resists or asserts; he presides. And the political metaphor adopted is that of the chief-justice; initially Colambre jokingly says that he has a 'warrant' for Larry's father, and once again it is Larry who perceives the depth of the imagery:

'I've a warrant for you, father,' says I; 'and must have you bodily before the justice, and my lord chief justice.' So he changed colour a bit at first; but he saw me smile. 'And I've done no sin,' said he; 'and, Larry, you may lead me now, as you led me all my life.'[65]

With the blameless and infirm elder Brady led before him, Colambre's role as chief justice is seen as entirely vacant and nugatory, an image in keeping with other aspects of Larry's letter, the relegation of Grace Nugent, the indirect presentation of the other principals, and the special dispensation for jovial residential landlords.

Of course it is possible to see this as merely the slackening of pace necessary for a smooth conclusion to the tale, a *jeu d'esprit* immune to finicking analysis. Alternatively, it might be regarded as a further acknowledgement of the unfinished state of eighteenth-century hostilities. And like *Castle Rackrent*, *The Absentee* concludes by placing two representatives of the tenantry before the reader. But whereas Thady Quirk has given the lie on the Rackrents, and they in turn are about to be succeeded by Jason Quirk, in *The Absentee* it would appear that the initiative remains firmly with the Clonbronys and their heirs. This renewed confidence in the landlords,

---

[65] Ibid., vol. x, p. 53.

coupled with the curious morality of bringing blameless and hitherto neglected characters before a tribunal including the Clonbronys, surely marks a dramatic change in Maria Edgeworth's thought. The means which she recommends may be ostensibly progressive, but the motivation has become conservative. Thomas Flanagan has spoken in general terms of a dilemma of the Edgeworths and their fellow Anglo-Irish liberals, 'As a group they were to fail wretchedly, even on their own estates, for the Irish land problem was hopeless of solution at the level of private action, however self-sacrificing. On the level of national politics they were to be caught between their own class, callous and grasping, and a peasantry which had chosen its own leaders.'[66] The critic writes with the legitimate benefit of hindsight; the novelist creates with the flawed yet synthesizing gift of perception. *The Absentee* acknowledges the uncertainty of its context by withholding an ultimately conclusive reconciliation. In keeping with her family's secular outlook Maria Edgeworth rarely mentions the conflicting denominations of the Irish countryside, but rather concentrates on political implications. If Grace Nugent and Colambre stand in some way for these then *The Absentee* suggests, but does not impose, reconciliation through the symbol of marriage: their wedding is heralded but held back from the reader. Once again symbolic narrative and verisimilitude harmonize; the refusal to conclude with wedding bells avoids easy sentiment and acknowledges the persisting difficulties in bringing Catholic and Protestant, Jacobite and Williamite, together. Reservations dominate the final pages despite and through the dialect humour of Larry Brady. In dialectical terms, *The Absentee* advances antithesis rather than thesis.

It could not be said, then, that it presents a Burkean world in the manner of *Castle Rackrent*. There are however implicit Burkean longings — the rectification of past offence, the combination of rival goods to oppose drastic change, the identity of place and personality. It is surely no accident that the true agent of Lord Clonbrony's interests is named Mr Burke. In more profound ways also *The Absentee* looks back

---

[66] Thomas Flanagan, op. cit., p. 84.

to the author of the *Reflections.* Throughout his polemic
against the revolution in France, Burke used (as we have
seen) the image of the Great House, the estate, and the
garden as symbolic of a proper order and continuity in the
State. Such a continuity speaks of stability rather than
change, or when it requires change it insists on organic
growth and not artificial contrivance and re-forming. But, as
events in France had only too clearly shown, this model of
permanence was vulnerable to drastic change: nature in its
order had not excluded the possibility of disorder. Burke's
lamentations over the fall of France could be read as late
exercises in the style of the mutability ode — with this
proviso that the agent or vehicle of violent change (when it
is not 'your literary men, and your politicians') is money,
commerce, trade. These values must not be confused with
wealth or property which has a redeeming inertia and a
tendency towards unequal accumulations. Society is a
contract, Burke allows, but not a contract in mere goods and
chattels. The vocabulary of wealth inheritance and due legal
process is used to illustrate the impropriety of change:

One of the first and most leading principles on which the commonwealth and the laws are consecrated, is lest the temporary possessors
and life-renters in it, unmindful of what they have received from their
ancestors, or of what is due to their prosperity, should act as if they
were the entire masters; that they should not think it amongst their
rights to cut off the entail, or commit waste on the inheritance, by
destroying at their pleasure the whole fabric of their society; hazarding
to leave to those who come after them, a ruin instead of a habitation.[67]

Such language finds its supreme literary reflection in *Mansfield
Park* but it is clearly at one with Maria Edgeworth's intentions
also. A little further on in his *Reflections,* Burke concentrates
this imagery with much savagery on the responsibilities of the
limited individual in the Burkean world — 'No man can mortgage his injustice as a pawn for his fidelity.' This is not the
place to discuss the metaphoric use of commerce either in
Burke or in literature generally, nor to open up the possibility that such imagery reveals Burke's understanding (albeit

---

[67] Edmund Burke, *Reflections on the Revolution in France,* ed. Conor Cruise
O'Brien (Harmondsworth: Penguin, 1968), p. 192.

implicit) of the economic objectives of the revolution. Instead we should recognize that the symbolism of *The Absentee* mediates between the debate of noble and merchant in the Catholic cabals of 1812 and the world-view of *Reflections on the Revolution in France*. The juxtaposition of Mrs Raffarty and Count O'Halloran (the latter with his *ancien régime* manners) is more than local colour or contemporary verisimilitude. And is it not characteristic of much Anglo-Irish literature that it stands, or is given its precarious footing, between political action and political thought?

A second area in which Burke affects *The Absentee* may at first glance seem trivial. In the fragmentary 'Notes on the Genius & Style of Burke' Maria Edgeworth deals almost exclusively with literary technique rather than ideas, a significant response from a novelist whose work-sheets are for the most part factual and intellectual. She concludes that 'allusions in general [are] preferable to similies' and she particularly notes 'allusions by a single word'.[68] There is no form of allusion less comparable to simile that the proper names of *The Absentee*: the nominalist approach exploits the single word to the highest degree. But on the same page of jottings, she acknowledges that a 'popular writer must be regulated in choice of allusions by the actual state of knowledge in his country'.[69] Quite clearly, the majority of readers of *Tales of Fashionable Life* had never heard of such landmarks as Coolamber or Clonbrony, even if they recognized an allusive quality in St Omar. Has Maria Edgeworth interwoven a private meaning into her published fiction; do the allusive place-names suggest a *roman à clef*? The answer may be found either by returning to our opening remarks on the manner in which sources, in literature, are transformed into method, or by looking at the psychology of creativity in the particular case of Maria Edgeworth. Her training as a writer of moral tales encouraged a *positively* superficial approach to literature: the young (for whom she originally wrote) required an evident and discernible meaning rather than a

---

[68] The MS in the possession of Mrs Christina Colvin, of Oxford; I am grateful to her and to Mrs Marilyn Butler for a copy of the relevant pages which they supplied to me.

[69] Idem.

profound obscurity; characters bear transparent names like Frank or Lucy. As we have seen, *The Absentee* resembles this school of writing in some ways, but its explicit theme (the desirability and possibility of successful resident landlordism) is undermined by contradictions, evasions, and reservations — Sir James Brooke's ambiguous pamphlet, Larry Brady's concluding letter, etc. The pressure of these conflicts, and maybe a subconscious recognition of their intractability in the circumstances of the time, brought Maria Edgeworth in contact with (literally) the grounds of her experience. These allusions do not add any literary meaning to *The Absentee* which is not already discernible through an analysis of the plot, but they do authenticate that analysis by making specific a trauma which the fiction strives to transform. If there is any truth in Conor Cruise O'Brien's argument that the energy of the *Reflections* derives ultimately from Burke's Irish experience of the violence (and, in a sense, the necessity) of revolution, there yet remains the infinitely larger context of Europe in 1790 to which he explicitly addresses himself. So too with Maria Edgeworth we study the sources of her art in order to attend fully to the art itself.

5. MID-CENTURY PERSPECTIVES

1. FROM EMANCIPATION TO REBELLION

> Gabriel pointed to the statue, on which
> lay patches of snow. Then he nodded
> familiarly to it and waved his hand. —
> Good-night, Dan, he said gaily.
>
> (James Joyce)[1]

The Act of Union achieved two principal and perhaps contradictory ends — it removed Irish parliamentary representation
from a separate institution in Dublin to Westminster where
all Members of Parliament for the British Isles were now
united together; it placed the discussion of distinctively Irish
issues in the context of an assembly where Irish representatives were necessarily a permanent minority. The first consequence is usually commemorated with some comment on the
disappearance of resident dignitaries from Dublin which
declined to the status of a provincial town. It is important to
qualify this implied condemnation of the Irish MPs' remoteness from their constituents by emphasizing that, on the
crucial issue of Catholic Emancipation, a majority of the Irish
members had been in favour of relief long before Westminster
conceded the issue in 1829. Majorities at Westminster had
priorities other than Irish ones, and British governments had
to consult the complex politics of an industrialized nation before adjusting some anomaly in Irish local affairs. Behind the
intricacies of party politics, and the deeply reactionary mood
inherited from the Napoleonic period, the question of Catholic Emancipation challenged a newly aggressive evangelical
element in British Protestantism.

Apart from Emancipation, the history of Ireland in the
1820s and after has been primarily written with specific
reference to land occupation and agrarian problems, with the

---

[1] James Joyce, *Dubliners*, corrected text ed. Robert Scholes (London: Cape,
1967), p. 245.

tithes a largely Catholic tenantry paid to Protestant rectors forming a contentious link between the two agitations. The literature of the period is best remembered in the fiction of the brothers John and Michael Banim and of Gerald Griffin. Their cautious attention to the values of a depressed Catholic middle class is characteristic of one skein in the pattern of Daniel O'Connell's long campaign for emancipation. A need to trim the material so as to soothe the excited temper of the times is often visible in their work. The result is often at once tendentious and evasive; one has little sense of a distinctive and coherent *literature* in the 1820s, merely a dossier of workmanlike illustrations. This is not to say that the disturbed decade leading up to emancipation was without influence. Indeed the immediate cause and seat of the agitation associated with 'Captain Rock' — gross mismanagement and violence on the Courtenay estate in County Limerick — will reappear in a subversive and vestigial form in Sheridan Le Fanu's 1864 novel, *Uncle Silas*. A comparison of John Banim and Le Fanu might suggest that the historical influence is most creatively absorbed when it is tensely drawn across a long span of years and when it links conditions which are acknowledged as altering. Immediacy, a consciousness of living in important times, can produce a literature which is totally non-reflexive.

Though the reforms of the 1790s had given Catholics the right to vote, and the 1829 Act gave them the right to sit in parliament, local government remained essentially closed. A conservative historian has described the hundred-odd Irish municipal corporations as 'exclusively and arrogantly protestant ... with petty peculation and jobbery, bigotry and incompetence as their outstanding characteristics'.[2] It was of course the Corporation of Dublin who had given the lead in 1792 with its resolutions on the theme of Protestant Ascendancy. The larger context of the post-assembly debates in William Street was European revolution, and at the beginning of the revolutionary 1840s the Corporation of Dublin was once again the focus for a discussion of Protestant Ascendancy. History occurs twice, we are told, first as tragedy and

---

[2] R. B. Mc Dowell, *Public Opinion and Government Policy in Ireland 1801–1846* (London: Faber, 1952), pp. 180–1.

then as farce: in 1840 our witness to the Ascendancy debates
is not Edmund Burke with his scrupulously ironic analysis of
language, but The Reverend Tresham Dames Gregg.[3]

Prior to the Irish Municipal Act of 1840, the peculiar
character of the corporations created a distinctive area in
Irish society where Catholics experienced the weight of the
old mastership. Responding to the 'Captain Rock' agitations
in the early 1820s, Thomas Moore distinguished carefully
between the anxieties of Catholics living in the Ulster
countryside 'surrounded by armed Orangemen' and the
anxieties of 'the Catholic inhabitants of towns and cities,
whom the spirit of Corporation Ascendancy haunts through
all the details of life'.[4] Back in the 1790s Moore had been
within an inch of involvement in radical, even revolutionary,
politics, and he remained no friend of the Irish Establishment. His student days were 'the glorious days of Protestant
jobbing . . . the Golden Age of the Ascendancy when jobs
and abuses flourished in unchecked luxuriance'.[5] Moore
effectively retains a perspective on Protestant Ascendancy
which acknowledges its recent, urban, and bourgeois origins.
In contrast, we may look at *The Rockite*, an evangelical and
fictionalized tract by Charlotte Elizabeth: here the object of
Catholicism is defined:

To overthrow the abhorred ascendancy of Protestantism, and once
more to reign unrivalled and unchecked, became the sole object of that
aspiring apostasy, which would, as God, ever sit in the temple of God,
shewing itself to be a god.[6]

What is evidenced here is not so much the valorization of the
phrase, Protestant Ascendancy, as the logic by which Henry
Grattan's assumption of possible universal salvation for
Catholics and Protestants alike is reduced to an exclusivist

[3] Karl Marx, 'The Eighteenth Brumaire of Louis Bonaparte', *Surveys from
Exile; Political Writings*, vol. ii ed. and introd. David Fernbach (London: Allen
Lane and New Left Review, 1973), p. 146.

[4] [Thomas Moore], *Memoirs of Captain Rock . . . Written by Himself*
(London: Longman, 1824), 5th ed., pp. 348-9.

[5] Ibid., p. 290.

[6] Charlotte Elizabeth, *The Rockite: An Irish Story* (London: Nisbet, 1829),
p. 254. An Englishwoman by birth, she married as her second husband Lewis
H. Tonna: she lived for many years in County Kilkenny, and wrote voluminously
for the evangelical movement.

evangelicalism. The comparison between Moore and Charlotte Elizabeth is revealing, not of some innate sectarian distinction, but of Moore's resistance to Protestant Ascendancy as ideology and the novelist's indulgence of it.

The Famine of 1845–7, and the rebellion of 1848, are the dominant events of the decade in Irish history. Yet both can only be understood in the context of political assumptions which permitted them: Whig *laissez-faire* economics contributed as much (or rather, as little) to the fate of the Irish population as the potato blight, and revulsion against Daniel O'Connell's collaboration with English Whiggery played its part in creating the Young Ireland group and William Smith O'Brien's rebellion. Naturally, the political context cannot be appreciated solely in Irish terms: the 1840s are also the decade of Chartism in Britain and revolution in Europe. The restlessness of working people in England and France was not without parallel in Ireland, and though there was little prospect of a coherent working-class movement emerging in Dublin or Belfast, other political elements were keen to bind the working population to them. Industry in Dublin had suffered a decline, and the Reform Act of 1832 (while it fell far short of universal franchise) had the effect of bringing parliamentary electioneering within the experience of a substantial proportion of the citizenry. O'Connell's movement to repeal the Act of Union, launched in July 1840, provided a grand cause requiring a heightened rhetoric of all the protagonists.

Jacqueline Hill has written of the manner in which Protestants among the working class declined to accept the Repealers' arguments that the Union had caused the city's reduced prosperity.[7] Though conservative newspapers were primarily directed towards a middle-class readership, *The*

---

[7] Jacqueline Hill, 'The Protestant Response to Repeal: the Case of the Dublin Working Class', in F. S. L. Lyons and R. A. J. Hawkins, eds. *Ireland Under the Union: Varieties of Tension. Essays in Honour of T. W. Moody* (Oxford: Clarendon Press, 1980), pp. 35–68; in addition to Dr Hill's discussion of The Revd Tresham Dames Gregg's influence on the Dublin Protestant working class, an ecclesiastical and theological perspective may be obtained from Desmond Bowen's *The Protestant Crusade in Ireland 1800–1870* (Dublin: Gill and Macmillan, 1978), esp. pp. 108–13.

Warder took pains to report the activities of Protestant working-class groups. Of these the most important was the Dublin Protestant Operatives Association, founded by Tresham Dames Gregg. Since September 1840, Sheridan Le Fanu had had a share in the direction both of *The Warder* and of *The Statesman*. *The Warder* was a solid, respectable weekly paper in which Le Fanu retained an interest until 1870, whereas *The Statesman* — in part owned by T. D. Gregg — was flamboyant and aggressive. It ceased publication in 1846, though Le Fanu had not written for it in its last twelve months.[8]

As the creation of Gregg, *The Statesman* became the principal voice of the Dublin Protestant Operatives Association. In 1840, Gregg proudly reported the differences between his paper and the conservative press generally:

When *The Statesman* commenced its career, it avowed Protestant Ascendancy as its guiding principle. Some of the *soi disant* Protestant newspapers laughed us to scorn — told us that we were behind the spirit of the age. We should be glad to see which of them would venture to murmur against us now — which of them would presume to say that we are unreasonable in looking for all that is demanded by high principle. The question has, in truth, made way. If a proof of this be required, we need only refer to the complaint of Mr. O'Connell — no inferior testimony on such a subject — that gentleman alleges as the most effectual barrier to his anti-union projects, the existence of a strong 'Protestant Ascendancy' party. He is right.[9]

The strong Protestant Ascendancy party was not, of course, orthodox Toryism but the network of fringe groups which had sprung up in the 1830s. The causes of this recrudescence of Protestant Ascendancy as a crusading political force are many — Catholic Emancipation, Tithe War, the suppression of the Orange Order, Melbourne's reforming government, and Thomas Drummond's scrupulous regime as Under-Secretary (1835–40). O'Connell's success in bargaining within the conventions of the united parliament added to the Irish Tories'

---

[8] W. J. Mc Cormack, *Sheridan Le Fanu and Victorian Ireland* (Oxford: Clarendon Press, 1980), p. 87.
[9] T. D. Gregg, *Protestant Ascendancy Vindicated and National Regeneration Through the Instrumentality of National Religion Urged in a Series of Letters to the Corporation of Dublin* (Dublin: Bleakley, 1840), p. 86.

sense of remoteness from Westminster. For the middle class, the Dublin Metropolitan Conservative Association provided one outlet for their disillusion and ardour, with Gregg's Dublin Protestant Operatives Association directing itself to the lower classes. Tension between these bodies was noted by others, apart from Gregg. The difference was one of manners as much as theory: Le Fanu writing home to his father complained of the embarrassment he felt in being involved with Gregg's paper:

My vote is overruled by the other two [proprietors] ... *I* proposed converting the paper into a merely political one, but was overruled. *I* proposed changing it into a staunch Church paper but was *overruled.* I have no power over the Statesman and wash my hands of all responsibility for its tone in point of style & of feeling.[10]

Manners and theory are not absolutely distinct of course. Gregg's harangues to the faithful masses may have offended the son of the Dean of Emly, but the real grounds of their dispute *were* political. Le Fanu believed that a paper should either devote itself to politics or to Church affairs: the combination necessarily veered towards the vulgarly enthusiastic — as with Gregg's accusations of fornication brought against a Catholic priest and his attempt to 'rescue' a convert-novice from a convent.[11] This is not to suggest that Le Fanu accepted any separation of Church and State, far from it: but he expected a certain decorum of public discussion.

Gregg's notion of Protestant Ascendancy, if it offended Le Fanu, would have mortified Edmund Burke. Burke's opponents in the Corporation of Dublin openly acknowledged the conjunction of 'the security of property in this kingdom' and 'the Protestant ascendancy in our happy constitution'.[12] The Ascendancy was defined by reference to specific political and administrative priorities and privileges. Gregg's definitions, however, accentuated the Protestantism

[10] Sheridan Le Fanu to T. P. Le Fanu, undated; quoted in *Sheridan Le Fanu and Victorian Ireland*, p. 87.
[11] See Bowen, op. cit., pp. 108–9.
[12] 'Address of the Corporation of Dublin to Lord Henry Fitzgerald and Henry Grattan', *Calendar of Ancient Records of Dublin*, ed. Lady Gilbert (Dublin: Dollard, 1909), vol. xiv, p. 243. See pp. 00–00, above.

of Protestant Ascendancy in a series of published letters addressed to the Corporation of his day:

My Lord Mayor and Brethren — 'PROTESTANT ASCENDANCY!' — A sore point this with the popular Conservative politicians of the day; they don't know what to make of it. The age is so imbued with mock philosophy — this has become so much the standard that regulates every thing, and the thought of God and of religion is so much driven from us, that the man who confesses himself an advocate for Protestant Ascendancy is looked upon as infatuate, and laughed at as behind the intelligence of the times.

Still the principle of Protestant Ascendancy is a sound principle which must and will be acted on. How? — it is impossible! 'All things are possible to them that believe' — 'By the help of my God I will leap over the wall.' Why, what can poor abandoned Protestants do? Revolutionise the age — make the current of popular opinion run in the right channel, and pour out large blessings on the world, 'not by might nor by power, but by my Spirit, saith the Lord.'

It is absolutely essential that there should be sound views on this subject. So long as the nonsense which exists on it at present has place, so long as we find Protestants meally-mouthed about it, so long as we find such worthies as Sir George Murray and Alderman Warren, in the plentitude of their good nature coming forward, and saying, 'we don't require any ascendancy over others' — so long nothing good will be effected. No! no! Let these excellent personages be well assured that the old Protestants who made ascendancy their rallying cry in the time of William the Third, were neither fools nor blind — that we may suspect our philosophy when it compels us to the adoption of a language so very different from theirs.

I can, however, justify these gentlemen. I know that in *their own* sense of the words they mean a right thing. What *they* mean to express is this, 'we seek not to act the part of tyrants; we renounce the idea of any unreasonable domination over our Roman Catholic countrymen.' They conceive that such is meant by 'Protestant Ascendancy.' Such an ascendancy they abjure, and so do I, and so does every Christian Protestant. The most strenuous advocates of the principle would abhor such an application of it. No; *this* were its abuse. In the renunciation of this, we agree with the worthy Alderman and the gallant General, and we only find fault with their language because it is capable of being mistaken.

Still our cry is *'Protestant Ascendancy!'*[13]

[13] Gregg, op. cit., pp. 62-3.

Thus on the eve of their eclipse, the city fathers are exhorted to hold tenaciously to ascendancy, in the name of a Williamite rallying cry. 'Unreasonable domination' is abjured but the military triumph of Protestantism is strategically recalled. Gregg opposes any democratic reform of the Corporation, and offers instead an amalgam of evangelical fervour and pseudo-historical allusion. The 'Golden Age' to which Moore mockingly alluded as the period of Protestant jobbing is pressed back in time: on this occasion not only to include the eighteenth century *in toto* but also to associate itself with the origins of the Whig Revolution. Hand-in-hand with this sweeping historical revision, Gregg presents his own definition of a contemporary Protestant Ascendancy, by which he means 'the making of the Word of God, as it ought to be, supreme in the councils of the state', with the effect of overturning O'Connell's 'Apostate Church'.[14] It is hardly necessary to add that the Corporation was reformed, and indeed O'Connell became the first Catholic lord mayor of the city since 1688.

In terms of party politics Gregg's influence may have been negligible, but his significance cannot be measured solely in terms of immediate impact. The messianism so often attributed to Catholic nationalism in later years is latent in his Protestant war-cry. Basically, it utilizes that rare sense of nationalism, meaning the doctrine 'that certain nations (as contrasted with individuals) are the object of divine election'.[15] If a charge of this kind may be levelled at Patrick Pearse with his ideas of blood sacrifice, and at some latter-day saints, it is entirely explicit in Gregg's *Protestant Ascendancy Vindicated and National Regeneration Through the Instrumentation of National Religion Urged* ... For a nineteenth-century Irish Protestant Unionist to invoke *national* regeneration he had need of a considerably long perspective on history. The 'Protestant Nation' of Grattan's phrase had surrendered its identity in 1800, and increasingly the pace of Irish politics had been determined by Catholic

---

[14] Ibid., p. 87.
[15] See the *Oxford English Dictionary*, which cites as its example of the sense G. S. Faber on the primitive doctrine of election published in 1842, two years after Gregg's pamphlet.

problems if not always Catholic energies. By referring to the Catholic Church as apostate, Charlotte Elizabeth and The Reverend Mr Gregg sought to emphasize that the original church of Saint Patrick could be identified theologically with the Established Church of Ireland. In this sense the Church of Ireland was, so to speak, aboriginal and national, and Catholicism a series of aberrations provoking the sixteenth-century Reformation. In the context of the 1840s, the essence of the argument was its anti-democratic assumptions, hence Gregg's assiduous attention to the emotions of Protestant operatives. Indeed, Gregg was not so much anti-democratic as anti-political: the ideology he proffered repeatedly substitutes Biblical quotation for social analysis or documentation. In *Protestant Ascendancy*, for example, having defined that term as the word of God supreme in the councils of the state, he proceeds:

I call the attention, especially, of the humbler classes to the promises made by God himself to the nation which thus exalts and honours his Word. 'It shall come to pass if thou shalt (i.e. as a nation) hearken diligently unto the voice of the Lord thy God . . .'.[16]

The quotation is taken from Deuteronomy 28: 1, and Gregg proceeds to quote *in extenso* all of God's promises to Israel of material prosperity:

Blessed shalt thou be in the city, and blessed shalt thou be in the field. Blessed shall be the fruit of thy body, and the fruit of thy ground, and the fruit of thy cattle . . .[17]

Irish Protestants, then, are identified with the children of Israel: the Williamite settlement is their promised land, 'and he shall bless thee in the land which the Lord thy God giveth thee. The Lord shall establish thee an holy people unto himself . . .'.[18] Apocalyptic language of this kind has many precedents. The distinctive feature of Gregg's rhetoric is his presentation of social reward in return for an abjuration of social action. And the underlying strategy is to promulgate a false consciousness of history in which Saint Patrick, the

[16] Gregg, op. cit., p. 87. Original parenthesis.
[17] Idem.
[18] Idem.

Old Testament prophets, William of Orange, and Gregg himself (speaking God's lines) are conjoined. To this alliance, other Protestants rather than other operatives were cordially invited.

Gregg's exhortation to the doomed exclusivist Corporation may be unmemorable in the university seminar, though it will sound familiar enough to many in Ulster gospel-halls. Sociologists and partisans have striven to describe the emergence of a reactionary Protestant working class, and the task is best left to them.[19] But the process of assimilating the Whig Revolution to the rhetoric of nineteenth-century Protestant Ascendancy has specifically literary consequences. Writing in 1934, W. B. Yeats spoke of four bells, 'four deep tragic notes, equally divided in time, so symbolising the war that ended in the Flight of the Earls; the Battle of the Boyne; the coming of French influence among our peasants; the beginning of our own age . . .'[20] William's victory at the Boyne led to 'the establishment of a Protestant Ascendency which was to impose upon Catholic Ireland, an oppression copied in all details from that imposed upon the French Protestants'.[21] In the following paragraph Yeats utters his more familiar tribute to 'the Protestant Ascendancy with its sense of responsibility', and the shift in tone is implicitly a shift in historical focus: oppression is acknowledged in the early eighteenth century, responsibility is posited for the late. Here, Yeats may have taken his cue direct from Grattan himself: addressing the Irish parliament in February 1793, he noted three policies towards Catholics — 'the first was that of Cromwell — extermination by operation of the sword; the second was that of Ann — extermination by operation of the laws; and the third was your's — which allowed them a qualified existence!'[22] The process by which Protestant Ascendancy is extended backwards from 1792 to embrace the age

---

[19]   The bibliography of the Irish question, or the Ulster question, is vast and still growing. Liam de Paor's *Divided Ulster* (Penguin Special, 1970) is perhaps the best introduction to a contentious subject.

[20]   Peter Allt and Russell K. Alspach, eds. *The Variorum Edition of the Poems of W. B. Yeats* (New York: Macmillan, 1977), 7th printing, p. 832.

[21]   Ibid., p. 833.

[22]   Daniel Owen Madden, ed., *The Speeches of the Right Hon. Henry Grattan* (Dublin: Duffy, 1865), 2nd ed., p. 203.

of Swift is particularly ironic if we take Swift's excoriating dictum on Queen Anne's Irish viceroy as evidence, 'He is a Presbyterian in politics, and an atheist in religion, but he chuses at present to whore with a Papist.'[23] The multiple innuendo, a mixture one might say of Augustan paradox and hydrochlorate, reaches its most extended form in Swift when he characterizes the Duke of Marlborough, hero supreme of triumphant Whiggery, in his *History of the Four Last Years of the Queen.*

When Tresham Gregg eulogizes the victor of Blenheim he runs the risk of a thunderbolt from Swift's ghost in Saint Patrick's Cathedral. When he associates Protestant Ascendancy indiscriminately with King William, the Corporation, the eighteenth century, he creates a shapeless synthesis in which other imaginations may yet discern irony and order. Gregg's uneasy partner on *The Statesman*, Sheridan Le Fanu, was already composing his early stories and novels at the time of the Irish Municipal Act: indeed, as a member of the Irish Metropolitan Conservative Association he was doubly active as radical conservative and as secret novelist. His first novel, *The Cock and Anchor* (1845), is set in Dublin in the last year of Thomas Wharton's viceroyalty: Swift and Joseph Addison make brief appearances as foils to the genial, venial Wharton. If this is not Swift's first appearance as fictional character, it is certainly an important early contribution to the mythic figure of Yeats's pantheon. But, perhaps the most striking aspect of Le Fanu's treatment of the early eighteenth century is his deployment of 'ascendancy' for a complex and ironic effect: conspiring Catholic Jacobites declare that

over-ridden, and despised, and scattered as we are, mercenaries and beggars abroad, and landless at home – still something whispers in my ear that there will come at last a retribution, and such a one as will make this perjured, corrupt, and robbing ascendancy a warning and a wonder to all after times.[24]

---

[23] Jonathan Swift, 'Short Character of His Ex— T— E— of W—', *The Examiner and Other Pieces 1710-11* (Oxford: Blackwell, 1940), p. 179.

[24] [Sheridan Le Fanu], *The Cock and Anchor* (Dublin: Curry, 1845), vol. i, p. 20. For a discussion of this novel, and its relation to the author's politics, see Mc Cormack, *Sheridan Le Fanu and Victorian Ireland,* pp. 97-100.

Le Fanu has chosen to exploit the anachronism of ascendancy meaning, in 1710, the governing élite in Ireland, and the motivation may well be connected with his recognition that in 1845 his own class was on the point of eclipse. For one of the symbolic implications of accepting ascendancy to do the work of aristocracy (albeit on behalf of a disguised bourgeoisie) is the attendant notion of a rising and falling pattern: the star which in the ascendant must fade or fall, the Protestant Ascendancy must be succeeded by some other social order. By Yeats's day, the usage of ascendancy as élite was well established, but it is characteristic of his sensitivity to the inner dynamics of a word that he should ally his pride in ascendancy to a cyclical notion of history in which one order is succeeded by another in a perpetual pattern of rising and falling civilizations. Etymologically, as J. M. Synge noted in his reading of Trench's *On the Study of Words*, ascendancy is derived from the language of astrology, and sardonically he summarized the discovery by noting that ascendancy involved a *belief* in astrology. Yeats, less satirical in his attitude to his ancestry, composed his own astrology in *A Vision*. That arcane philosophy speaks principally of world history, of the renaissance, and the loss of 'unity of being'. Yet to a considerable extent it is facilitated by Yeats's experience of the Anglo-Irish Protestant Ascendancy in the nineteenth century, the social experience of that élite, and the evolution of that linguistic term.

The Cock and Anchor is best approached as a late Irish contribution to the historical novel as founded and developed by Sir Walter Scott. The two-team structure of Jacobites and Williamites, with a hero and heroine drawn from opposing sides, the blending of violent incident and romance, preserve the outward appearance of the Scottish novel. But Le Fanu's first exercise in fiction has also to be read in relation to his politics: accordingly, we find a species of ventriloquism in which the privations of eighteenth-century Catholics may be decoded as symbolizing the indignation of nineteenth-century middle-class Protestants. And this in keeping with the altered association of words, as between 1688 and 1840: Whiggery for the generation of Le Fanu's fictional heroes was the Protestant Succession, the Penal Laws, Ascendancy:

Whiggery for Le Fanu's political associates was now closely allied with Catholicism, with the *hoi polloi* and detestable Dan O'Connell at their head. *The Cock and Anchor*, with its neglect of that supernaturalism which had characterized Le Fanu's earlier short stories, with its posited union of Protestant and Catholic, accorded well with the attitudes of Young Ireland. Indeed Le Fanu's second novel, *Torlogh O'Brien*, concludes with two interdenominational weddings, while simultaneously the author was carried over into some collaboration with Young Irelanders such as Charles Gavan Duffy, Thomas Francis Meagher, and John Mitchel.[25] The motion towards Young Ireland and nationalism was prompted by dread of further reform imposed by an English government, combined with outrage at British reactions to the Irish Famine. But there were necessarily reservations, and when Meagher and Mitchel, with William Smith O'Brien, became implicated in conspiracy, treason, and rebellion in 1848, Le Fanu's sense of self-betrayal was overwhelming. Instead of the harmonies and reconciliations of *The Cock and Anchor*, Le Fanu's fiction of 1848, the long three-part tale 'Richard Marston', is riddled with solitude and division.[26] With this, we note also the re-emergence of the nervous supernaturalism which Le Fanu had purged from his first two novels. In Ireland 1848 brought to an end the minor renaissance of literature associated with Thomas Davis, James Clarence Mangan, and *The Nation*, a company with whom Yeats claimed a touching affinity. More significant, ultimately, however, was the foundation of the Encumbered Estates Court to begin the dismemberment of a landed estate system fatally shaken by the Famine and its consequences. The development of the Ascendancy as a cultural entity is closely related to the decline of landed estate.

---

[25] Details of this episode are provided in *Sheridan Le Fanu and Victorian Ireland*, pp. 100–6.

[26] 'Richard Marston' is extensively analysed in W. J. Mc Cormack, 'J. Sheridan Le Fanu's Richard Marston (1848): the History of an Anglo-Irish Text', in *1848: The Sociology of Literature*, ed. Francis Barker and Others ([Colchester]: University of Essex, 1978), pp. 107–25; see also *Sheridan Le Fanu and Victorian Ireland*, pp. 106–10.

2.   UBI LAPSUS? QUID FECI? SHERIDAN LE FANU AS SUBVERSIVE

> the house, in its silence, seems to be
> contemplating the swell or fall of its
> own lawns.
>
> (Elizabeth Bowen)[27]

Between *Castle Rackrent* and *Ulysses* only one Irish novel approximates to a total apprehension of social reality, and given that its setting is Derbyshire its totality is necessarily problematic. *Uncle Silas* is in many ways flawed, but it nevertheless represents a bold inquiry into the nature of literary form and its bearing upon reality. Regarded as delinquent in the lists of respectable novels about castles and cabins set in a cloth of green, and consequently accommodated among the sensationalist productions of Wilkie Collins, Charles Reade, and Le Fanu himself at his more common second-best, *Uncle Silas* calls for analysis in less easily predictable terms. Its thorough-going symmetry, and hermetic completeness, has been established primarily by means of detailing Le Fanu's structural use of Swedenborgian doctrine.[28] Swedenborgianism, with its elaborate system of correspondences, aligns itself with allegory, and the present inquiry will concentrate on an account of how and why Le Fanu should choose to write in the allegorical mode in his finest fiction. However, allegory is itself in need of some restitution and a preliminary digression is in order.

In his magisterial study of German baroque tragedy, Walter Benjamin initiated a reassessment of the aesthetic status of allegory, which has not been sufficiently assimilated to other areas of European literature. Allegory had been relegated to the level of mere ciphering and deciphering by the romantic insistence on transcendence in the symbol: 'even great artists and exceptional theoreticians, such as Yeats, still assume that allegory is a conventional relationship between an illustrative image and its abstract meaning.'[29] The priority, for Benjamin,

---

[27] Elizabeth Bowen, 'The Big House', *Collected Impressions* (London: Longmans, 1950), p. 196.
[28] See ch. 5 of *Sheridan Le Fanu and Victorian Ireland*.
[29] Walter Benjamin, *The Origins of German Tragic Drama*, trans. John Osborne (London: New Left Books, 1977), p. 162.

was not simply the restoration of allegory to respectability as a technique, rather it was the elaboration of a comprehensive typology in which tragedy is distinguished from *trauerspiel*, myth from history, transcendence from immanence. Insisting on the dialectical nature of allegory in this typology, he speaks of its 'worldly, historical breadth':

Whereas in the symbol destruction is idealised and the transfigured face of nature is fleetingly revealed in the light of redemption, in allegory the observer is confronted with the *facies hippocratica* of history as a petrified, primordial landscape.[30]

Such speculations may appear to be remote from the birth pangs of Anglo-Irish literature. Yet, if we look forward to Yeats's 'Purgatory' or 'The Words Upon the Window-Pane', we will find the distinction between tragedy and *trauerspiel* may help to relate those plays to earlier Yeatsian drama. Furthermore, Patrick Diskin has pointed out resemblances between J. C. Mangan's translation of Zacharias Werner's 'Der Vierundzwansigste Februar' in *The Dublin University Magazine* and Yeats's 'Purgatory' — Werner's play is part of Benjamin's argument.[31] The culmination of this present inquiry will be an examination of the way in which 'Purgatory' succeeds in revealing the inauthenticity of the history its characters proclaim. One Irish antecedent to 'Purgatory', in its association of the Big House and Swedenborgian patterns, is *Uncle Silas*. And if we look back over the earlier history of Anglo-Irish literature, *The Absentee* stands out as an example of allegory rendered too palpable by the historical failure of the programme to which it referred. (One might offer the embarrassing comparison of Spenser's *Faery Queen* in which the allegory of Elizabethan *realpolitik* is transformed by the success of that *realpolitik*.)

Our principal focus on Le Fanu's allegory will be to examine the manner in which it assimilates and transforms the materials of history, and relates that history to other forms of order. It is significant that the sources are exceedingly diverse — Chateaubriand and 'Captain Rock' — for there is

---

[30] Ibid., p. 166.
[31] Patrick Diskin, 'Yeats's "Purgatory" and Werner's "Der Vierundzwanzigste Februar", *Notes and Queries* (August 1979), pp. 340-2. See below, pp. 369-70.

a formal logic to the manner in which allegory deliberately seeks to incorporate such disparate elements. Benjamin speaks of 'the violence of the dialectical movement'[32] in allegory; and, though he has in mind the plots of his baroque *Trauerspiel*, it is proper to consider this violence as a structural principle in allegorical forms. Dickens's novels, violent enough in their details, met much opposition from a neoclassicism which arrogates to itself an exclusive access to the Sublime. In being fully accepted as consummate art, they revealed a central and controlling dualism. It is often argued that the causes of Dickensian dualism were biographical, but the Anglo-Irish instance may be explored in less subjective terms. Client cultures tend to employ imitative forms, and do so for two reasons. First, by modelling their art upon that of the dominant 'mother' culture, they acknowledge the source of their identity and definition. In the heightened consciousness of a colonial society imitation tends to veer at times towards pastiche or even parody: thus, the second motive for the imitative nature of colonial literature is a need or ability to resist the imposition of identity. Irony binds the positive and negative elements of this stance: irony distinguishes the work of Swift, Sheridan, and Burke in the eighteenth century. In moving from *Castle Rackrent* to *The Absentee* we note the displacement of irony by a different mode of dual focus, which closely resembles allegory. And the impetus behind this altered literary practice of Maria Edgeworth's is her realization that Union had *not* achieved its object of dissolving Irish identity: that double-edged identity survived in ever more complex and overt forms of social practice. Closing the gap between Colambre and Nugent is not simply a matter of healing sectarian divisions: it is a longing to unite past and present, to transcend the conditions of social existence. In this problematic manner, the uneasy alliance of allegory and didactic is revealed. If *Uncle Silas* is unique among Irish novels appearing between *Castle Rackrent* and *Ulysses* in approaching what Georg Lukács would term totality, it is because in Le Fanu's novel allegory flourishes untrammelled by fond didactic

[32] Benjamin, op. cit., p. 166.

ambitions. Instead of such harmony in unity we have violent dialectic.

To test these speculations, let us begin with a single passage from *Uncle Silas* in which the narrator Maud is speaking of her father, Austin Ruthyn:

It was his wont to walk up and down thus, without speaking — an exercise which used to remind me of Chateaubriand's father in the great chamber of the Château de Combourg. At the far end he nearly disappeared in the gloom, and then returning emerged for a few minutes, like a portrait with a background of shadow, and then again in silence faded nearly out of view.[33]

What Maud has been reminded of is the following passage (translated) from Chateaubriand's *Mémoires d'outre tombe:*

My father would then set off on his walk, which would end only when it was time to go to bed. He was dressed in a white Petersham gown, or rather a sort of coat that I have seen only him wearing. His half-bald head was covered with a large white cap, held straight in position. As he walked about he would take himself away from the hearth, the vast room being so dimly lit by a single candle that he could no longer be seen: he was only heard still walking about in the shadows: then he would come back slowly towards the light, emerging little by little from the darkness like a ghost, with his white gown, his white cap, and his long pallid face.[34]

Here too the narrator's father walks in a room so as to appear and disappear from and into the darkness. There is, however, a prominent element in Chateaubriand's account which is absent from Maud Ruthyn's. Indeed it is a integral part of the picturesque effect of the *Mémoires* — the reiterated whiteness of the father's appearance. Readers of *Uncle Silas* will know that this element, though absent from the account of Austin Ruthyn, is insinuated repeatedly elsewhere in the novel — not in the description of the narrator's father but in that of her uncle. When she gives us her first impression of Silas, he is an 'apparition, drawn as it seemed in black and white'. Trying to sleep in Bartram-Haugh on that first night under her uncle's roof, she visualizes his face as 'ashy with a

---

[33] J. S. Le Fanu, *Uncle Silas* (Oxford: World's Classics, 1981), p. 2.

[34] Trans. Julia Marshall; for the original see René Chateaubriand, *Mémoires d'Outre-tombe* (Paris: Flammarion, 1948), vol. i, p. 110.

pallor on which I looked with fear and pain'. In a crucial scene he is 'dressed in a long white morning gown ... with the white bandage pinned across his forehead ...'.[35] Such cameos of Silas's whiteness and paleness could be multiplied by other citations. What is already evident is that Chateaubriand's pallid and perambulating father is reflected in *two* characters in *Uncle Silas*, Austin Ruthyn complying with the manner of walking in and out of the narrator's vision, his brother Silas carrying very many images of bloodless, pallid, white, and ghostly appearance.

We may conclude, therefore, that Le Fanu's allusion to *Mémoires d'outre tombe* is not just simply the kind of casual name-dropping which flatters the reader's vanity. It is, however, less clear-cut than the acknowledgement of a debt or a source. The curious, vestigial presence of this borrowed image has its relevance for Chateaubriand also, for there were really two personalities in the author of the *Mémoires*: on the one hand the astute politician who reverted to Christianity just at the right moment, and on the other, the poet and libertine.[36] These polarities are reflected in the pious austerity of Austin Ruthyn, and the suspected criminality and licence of Silas. The structure of the novel as a whole is a vast series of symmetrical details, often dislocated from their immediate context but corresponding with details secreted elsewhere in the text. It is a two-part symmetry with Austin at Knowl 'corresponding' with Silas at Bartram-Haugh, with life continuing in death, rectitude revealed as guilt, truth replaced by conspiracy. Benjamin has summarized the conventional notion of allegory as a relation between an illustrative image (in the work of art) and its abstract meaning (lying outside the work of art). In *Uncle Silas*, this pattern is raised to the second power, so to speak, in that a Swedenborgian reading establishes the novel as a self-referring allegory: assumptions of virtue *are* vices, the soul's experience in death is indistinguishable from the events of life. Thus, one part of *Uncle Silas* provides an allegorical reading of the other, ensuring that an extended allegorical reading —

[35] *Uncle Silas*, pp. 190, 194, 279.
[36] Michel Butor, *Inventory* (London: Cape, 1970), p. 59.

by which the novel as a whole is allegorically related to 'external' reality — is reflexive. By an internal analysis of character disposition, we may say that Silas is the post-humous revelation of the real guilt which lies behind Austin's pious rectitude: if we are to read Austin as allegoric of the Big House philosophy, then that philosophy is also reflected in Silas's homicide, fraud, corruption, and suicide. This identity of opposites in the fiction is ultimately deducible from an analysis of the novel as a whole, but it is offered in the first chapter in that cryptic allusion to Chateaubriand's father both ghostly and pedestrian.

One allusion does not make a novel. For most readers Maud Ruthyn's comparison of her father to Chateaubriand's father remains a decoration sustaining their confidence in the narrative as articulate and well-informed. It is crucial to Le Fanu's curious achievement in *Uncle Silas* that further investigation should undermine this confidence, should reveal a bifurcated response to the source of the allusion which threatens the separate identities of separately named charac-ters. If this were the only instance of its kind in the novel, we might conclude that Le Fanu intended it perhaps as a sardonic joke, perhaps did not intend it at all. Other literary allusions — to Swift's Struldbruggs in *Gulliver's Travels* and to the wizard Michael Scott in Walter Scott's 'Lay of the Last Minstrel', for example — do suggest a consistency of intention: these references to figures who 'survive' death so as to teach a lesson to the living contribute metaphorically to the sense of Silas as a revelation of Austin's real moral condition. Often such references are integrated smoothly to a character's particular circumstances — Silas, for example, reels off verses from French poets with a fluency which we are meant to see as beguiling. Austin, on the other hand, is highly economical in his recourse to such devices, and this is in keeping with his withdrawn personality. In the important scene where he confides in his daughter on the matter of Silas's bad reputation, he allows himself a few Latin tags. Having won her agreement that she should assist in some future recovery of the family's honour — sullied by Silas's suspected crimes — he moves from an unyielding painterly pose into veritable eloquence:

He turned on me [i.e. Maud] such an approving smile as you might fancy lighting up the rugged features of a pale old Rembrandt.

'I can tell you, Maud; if my life could have done it, it should not have been undone — *ubi lapsus, quid feci*. But I had almost made up my mind to change my plan, and leave all to time — *edax rerum* — to illuminate or to *consume*.'[37]

Austin's notion of doing nothing, of leaving all to Time, calls forth a Latin tag of no great obscurity: 'Tempus edax rerum' (Time, the destroyer of all things) comes from Ovid's *Metamorphoses*.[38] But 'ubi lapsus, quid feci' seems, at first glance, inscrutable.

Burke's *Peerage* and similar works of reference tell us that the motto of the Courtenays of Powderham is 'Ubi lapsus? Quid feci?' translatable as 'Where is my fault? What have I done?' These words which express astonishment at a sudden and undeserved fall are said to have been adopted by the family when they lost the earldom of Devon.[39] More immediately relevant to our problem is an additional note in Burke's to the effect that, in 1585, Sir William Courtenay (thirteenth *de jure* Earl of Devon) 'was one of the undertakers to send over settlers for the better planting of Ireland, and thus laid the foundation of the prodigious estates in that kingdom enjoyed by his posterity'.[40] We have then some thematic relevance in Austin Ruthyn's citing the Courtenay motto: the actual Courtenays and the fictional Ruthyns have suffered a reversal of fortune through no fault — they feel — of their own. And we have a rudimentary link between the Courtenays as Irish planter landlords and Le Fanu as an Irish novelist. The latter link can be immediately confirmed in that the principal Courtenay seat in Ireland was The Castle, Newcastle, Limerick, while Le Fanu was raised at Abington Glebe in the same county.

In critical terms we have reached a stage similar to that when the passage from *Mémoires d'outre tombe* was seen to

---

[37] *Uncle Silas*, p. 102.

[38] Ovid *Metamorphoses*, xv. 234; see notes to the World's Classics edition for the range of allusion drawn upon by the author.

[39] *Handbook of Mottoes*, ed. C. N. Elvin (London: Heraldry Today, 1963), p. 205.

[40] *Burke's Peerage* (London, 1959), 102nd ed., p. 670.

resemble Maud's account of her father, and *before* its resemblance to her account of Silas was noticed. In other words, the Courtenay motto has a sort of broad relevance to the context in which it appears — like the Courtenays, Austin wonders where he has made his mistake that he should feel his family's honour tarnished. Its critical contribution to a more diffused and subversive reading of the novel has yet to emerge. If 1585 seems remote from 1864 (when *Uncle Silas* appeared) we should recall that the novel evolved from a short story written in 1838 while Le Fanu was still living in County Limerick. Furthermore in 1838 the Courtenays were variously in the news, and their motto had an ironic propriety.

Le Fanu's father had been appointed to the parish of Abington in 1823, but he postponed his removal thence for some years due to the disturbed state of the county. These disturbances were soon widespread in Munster, and formed part of the background to the Catholic Emancipation crisis. Their origins in Limerick were quite specific and notorious. In late 1821 the county was 'in a very desperate state', according to Matthew Barrington, the Crown Solicitor for Munster.[41] In evidence to a House of Commons committee he said that 'murder, burnings, breaking houses, outrages of every description were committed there'.[42] Asked whether the disturbances had originated on the estate of any particular proprietor, he answered 'It was on the Courtenay estate, and in that neighbourhood.'[43] Numerous other witnesses confirmed this identification of the Courtenays' estate at Newcastle as the starting-point of the widespread violence of 1821-3. The central outrage had been the murder of Thomas Hoskins, son of Alexander Hoskins, the agent on the Courtenay property. This agent, a new appointment and an Englishman unfamiliar with Irish conditions and Irish customs, had established a rigorous and (for him) profitable regime on the estate, and his determination to profiteer through his office was affirmed by witnesses ranging from the

[41] House of Commons, '4th Report on the State of Ireland' (1825), p. 121.
[42] Ibid.
[43] Ibid.

parish priest of Michelstown to the Earl of Kingston.[44] In
the expanding wave of violence which followed the murder
of Thomas Hoskins, 'Captain Rock' emerged as the epony-
mous leader of the agitation and the conspiracy — the
'system' as it was called. Thomas Moore's *Memoirs of Captain
Rock*, Mortimer O'Sullivan's *Captain Rock Detected*, and
Charlotte Elizabeth's *Rockite* are only three ephemeral
monuments to the nation-wide consequences of the Courtenay
estate disturbances. Blue Books from 1824 to 1832 repeat,
with much affecting detail, the role of Hoskins in stimulating
the violence.

If we look at the vestigial reference in *Uncle Silas* to this
episode in Irish history, we may feel that it is curiously exact
and remote; it has about it an abstract air which is potentially
hostile to fiction. At the theoretical level one might counter
by arguing that allegory is concerned to relate precisely such
intractable evidences of abstract consciousness, and that this
kind of consciousness is typical of colonial cultures. Yet the
remoteness we speak of in *Uncle Silas* is not simply formal, it
is thematically central to the depiction of the Ruthyn
brothers who are cut off from county politics, Church affairs,
even neighbourhood activities. This is voluntary in the case
of Austin, and the result of ostracism in the case of Silas —
here again are those binary oppositions which so intimately
connect the brothers while seeming to distinguish between
them. In terms of society as depicted in the novel, we see a
landowning class at once wealthy and endangered, remote
from other strata of the community. There are servants of
course in the Big Houses, but these are either stage-hands
as far as the action is concerned or they are extensions of the
conspiring, endangered aspect of the master. Tenants on the
estate do ultimately play a part in the heroine's escape but
their contribution is entirely mechanical and unrelated to any
depiction of their lives and values. In other words, *Uncle Silas*
could be interpreted as presenting an intensified version of
the isolated Anglo-Irish ascendancy for whom local affairs
and the religious life of the community were closed. And

---

[44] House of Lords, 'State of Ireland' (1825), pp. 513 and 696. See also
Appendix D.

looking back to the origins of *Ubi lapsus?* in the murder of
young Hoskins there would seem to be confirmation of this
sense of a conflict of extremes, resulting in Le Fanu's novel
in a depiction of one of those extremes — the ascendancy —
against a darkened and empty background. To interpret this
incident as a fatal conflict between castle and cabin, landlord
and peasant would be to accept uncritically the blurred
sociology implicit in such terms as 'ascendancy'. That
Hoskins Senior was agent for an absentee landlord — William
Courtenay being obliged to live abroad at the time — contributes a further element to a stereotyped response. The facts
are more various in their implications. After the Napoleonic
War, agriculture was greatly depressed; provincial banking
collapsed, and the economy entered a deep recession.[45] The
Reverend John Kiely, parish priest of Mitchelstown, County
Cork, described to the Commons committee the social effects
in Munster of the post-war depression:

The times were very bad for the farmers, and there was a peculiar kind
of gentry, a kind of middle order between the rich gentry of the
country and the peasantry; persons who were generated by the
excessive rise of the agricultural produce during the war, and got the
education of persons above their rank; by the fall of the times these
were reduced to their original level. Without the habit of labour, they
associated with the lowest description, and in order to keep themselves
in the possession of their lands, and so forth, they deferred to the
system [i.e. of agrarian conspiracy], and, hence, I believe arose the
organisation in the system itself, that could not have been devised by
the lowest order of the peasantry.[46]

It is worth confirming this diagnosis by reference to an article
appearing in the *Quarterly Journal of Agriculture* in which
the earlier notoriety and present quiet prosperity of the
Courtenay estates in Ireland are noted.

The discontents were fomented by persons of a much higher class [than
the actual assailants], who, being themselves in arrear, perhaps from
bad management and extravagant housekeeping, were apprehensive of
being called on peremptorily to discharge them.[47]

    [45] See ch. 5 of L. M. Cullen, *An Economic History of Ireland since 1660*
(London: Batsford, 1972).
    [46] House of Commons, loc. cit.
    [47] *Quarterly Journal of Agriculture* 1838, p. 394.

'Captain Rock', therefore, may be characterized as a middling farmer, short of money and in danger of losing his leases, at the head of a peasant band. Questioned on the murder of young Hoskins, Matthew Barrington told the committee that 'some of the under-tenants on the Courtenay estate did encourage the lower orders' and hired an assassin to kill the agent's son.[48] These middle-men, far from being the simian figures later invented by *Punch*, may also be found in the novels and tales of Gerald Griffin. No feudal lord nor noble savage is at the heart of the Hoskins affair: it would be more accurately seen as an incident in the annals of an insecure middle class.

Ubi lapsus? Quid feci? The insensitive management of Viscount Courtenay's estate in Limerick in the 1820s can hardly in itself explain the motto in *Uncle Silas*. The short story version of the novel, 'Passage in the Secret History of an Irish Countess' had appeared in 1838, and Courtenay had died just three years earlier. William Courtenay, the third viscount, was the only son of William Courtenay and Frances Clack, a Wallingford tavern-owner's daughter. Young Courtenay had been seduced and corrupted by William Beckford of Fonthill: later in life the third Viscount was obliged to reside outside England to avoid prosecution. Despite this, in 1831 at the prompting of his third cousin (regrettably another William Courtenay) Beckford's 'Kitty' was declared to be the twenty-ninth *de jure* Earl of Devon by a questionable decision of the House of Lords.[49] Thus, the exiled 'Kitty' Courtenay succeeded in reversing the loss of honour which had led his ancestors to adopt their distinctive motto. The irony of this was not lost on contemporaries: Lord Chancellor Brougham was advised that Courtenay was one 'who ought to think himself happy that his titles and estates have not been forfeited or himself paid the debt to the law like the Lord Hungerford of Heytesbury' [beheaded in 1540].[50] When a bill was found against him, he remained abroad, afraid to take his seat in Parliament, his motto raising

[48] House of Commons '4th Report on the State of Ireland', p. 121.
[49] See *The Complete Peerage*, ed. George Edward Cokayne; rev. Vicary Gibbs (London: St Catherine's Press, 1916), vol. iv, p. 336.
[50] Ibid.

'a question which its owner avoids to leave to a tribunal of his country to answer'.[51]

Austin's complacent ejaculation, *Ubi lapsus? Quid feci?*, thus contributes to the structural identification of pious Austin and depraved Silas, for the motto is borrowed from one who was least fitted to bear it. 'Kitty' Courtenay, the twenty-ninth Earl of Devon died in the Place Vendôme, Paris, in May 1835, and was succeeded by his namesake and third cousin. In the history of this remarkable family — three ancestors had been attainted by the sixteenth century — reversal's reversed at a stroke, and the thirtieth Earl proved to be a model landlord. Indeed between 1843 and 1845 he was chairman of a government commission investigating land tenure in Ireland, its evidence the most revealing indictment of landlordism in the nineteenth century. Naturally, despite the improvements at Newcastle, Sheridan Le Fanu and the Irish Metropolitan Conservative Association deplored the Devon Commission's findings. Like Smith O'Brien's rebellion of three years later, it could be drastically interpreted as treachery, a blow struck from within at the 'security of property in this kingdom' and 'the Protestant ascendancy in our happy constitution'.[52]

But how can we relate the irony of *Ubi lapsus?*, now decoded, to the opacity of 'Chateaubriand's father in the great chamber of the Chateau de Combourg'? If Le Fanu's allegory is to be anything more than occasional external parallels lodged in the density of inner symmetries, some dynamic organization of the allusions is required to integrate the plot and texture of the fiction as a whole. Of the plot Elizabeth Bowen has observed that it is really a fairy-tale — the Endangered Heiress, the Wicked Uncle, and so forth.[53] But if it is fairy-tale, it is fairy-tale wrought in Victorian embroidery, at once garish and restrained. Miss Bowen has also remarked the sexlessness of the heroine, indeed 'no force from any

[51]   Ibid.
[52]   See pp. 72 ff. above for the Corporation of Dublin's use of the catchphrase in 1792.
[53]   Elizabeth Bowen, 'Introduction' to Sheridan Le Fanu, *Uncle Silas* (London: Cresset Press, 1947), p. 7 *et passim*.

one of the main characters runs into the channel of sexual feeling.'[54] This is true, provided that we allow its opposite also to be true — that the novel is deeply concerned with the force of sexual feeling, and employs much of its energies ensuring that evidence of this concern is deeply buried in its structure. For these forces are disguised or inhibited on the surface of the action: when Maud's loutish cousin Dudley makes a pass at her, his technique is a rugby-player's and not a roué's. Miss Bowen's contemporary among Anglo-Irish novelists, Francis Stuart, remarked in conversation that, if *Uncle Silas* were written *now*, Silas and his niece would be locked in sexual *mésalliance*, incestuous intrigue.

Certainly, on the level of sexual implication the novel produces remarkably ingenious responses in readers: the Knight of Glin has recently suggested that the story of the brothers Ruthyn is based on that of the Rochfort family in Westmeath. Robert Rochfort, Lord Bellfield, married for love as his second wife Mary, the daughter of Richard, Viscount Molesworth. They had four children, the last a boy born in 1743. Shortly after this date, his lordship was

privately informed that she co-habited unlawfully with his younger brother. Upon which he put the question to her, and she with consummate impudence owned the fact, adding that her last child was by him, and that she had no pleasure with any man like that she had with him.[55]

---

[54] Ibid., p. 9.

[55] Letter of Lord Egmont, 2 May 1743; quoted by the Knight of Glin in 'Foreword' to a sale catalogue published by Messrs Christie's on the occasion of the sale of Belvedere, County Westmeath on 9 July 1980 (p. 1). I am grateful to William O'Sullivan, sometime Keeper of the Manuscripts, Trinity College, Dublin, for drawing my attention to this source. In addition to the general resemblance between the houses and brothers of the Rochfort saga and those of Le Fanu's Ruthyn family in *Uncle Silas*, there is a further area in which the possibility of Le Fanu's debt to the saga is enhanced. Jonathan Swift was a frequent visitor at Gaulstown, the premier Rochfort house, and composed several poems describing the household. Le Fanu, by way of his Sheridan family connections, had inherited some of Swift's papers, wrote about Swift, and generally regarded himself as an indirect literary descendant of the Dean's. Moreover, the title of his first 1860s' novel, *The House by the Church-yard*, echoes in its title a poem by Swift 'On the Little House by the Churchyard of Castlenock' — Castleknock, being on the northern side of the Phoenix Park in Dublin, and the setting of the novel (Chapelizod) being on the south-west. For the Swift poems see *The Poetical Works* (London, 1866, in 3 vols.), vol. iii, pp. 96–8, 167–72. The Castleknock poem is discussed by John P. Harrington in 'Swift Through Le Fanu and Joyce', in *The Irish Tradition in Literature*, ed. Daniel S. Lenoski (Winnipeg: University of Manitoba Press, 1979), pp. 49–58.

Arthur Rochfort fled to England, but eventually languished in a debtors' prison until death separated him from his brother. The incestuous wife was locked up in Gaulstown, a house just six miles from her husband's seat at Belvedere. Another brother, George, lived in another neighbouring house, and when Lord Bellfield quarrelled with him, he built the largest Gothic sham ruin in Ireland — the 'Jealous Wall' — to blot out the view of the offending brother's residence.

The Knight of Glin admits that the similarity is not very great, and that Le Fanu's novel is 'roughly based' on the Rochfort saga. In seeing a resemblance, he implicitly makes certain assumptions. First, two houses in the neighbourhood of Belvedere, that which imprisons the woman and that which is the offending brother's home, are conflated in order that they resemble Bartram-Haugh, Silas's home and Maud's prison. Second, the relationship between Arthur Rochfort and his sister-in-law is comparable to that between Silas Ruthyn and his niece: both are of course forms of incest — if one admits that sexual bond which Francis Stuart prescribed and which Elizabeth Bowen denied. The violation of sexual taboo had a place in the Courtenay saga also, and even Chateaubriand contributes to the undercurrent of sexual offence in that, at the time his father perambulated in the shadows, the future author of the *Mémoires* was passionately in love with his sister. (Michel Butor traces this passion in the incestuous patterns of Chateaubriand's fiction.[56]) These offences against custom and the law may be said to have one common factor, they were *overvaluations* of blood-relationship (brother/sister) or sexual similarity (male/male).

In *Uncle Silas* nothing so explicitly sexual is admitted. Nevertheless, Silas does attempt to marry off Maud to his own son, her first cousin. While such marriages were not within the tables of forbidden affinity, they were generally disapproved of as genetically short-sighted. The motive behind Silas's scheme is as economically self-centred as it is maritally introverted — the preservation, to his own heir, of Maud's wealth. Moreover, the patterns of overvaluation of blood etc. are counterbalanced by other patterns of

[56] See Michel Butor, *Inventory, passim.*

undervaluation. Silas's dead wife had been the daughter of a Denbigh innkeeper, and the proposed marriage between Maud and his son Dudley is frustrated by the discovery that Dudley is secretly married to Sarah Mangles of Wigan.[57] 'Kitty' Courtenay's mother had been the daughter of a Wallingford innkeeper, while the unfortunate Lady Bellfield, on appeal to her father was ignored 'because she was only his bastard by his wife before he married her'.[58] Of course these are more offences against class and custom than against taboo or even law: yet they illustrate an urge to sexual alliance *outside* certain prescribed limits, thus they undervalue these limits. Overvaluation in sexual introversion, undervaluation in social *mésalliance* — *Uncle Silas's* sources reveal a complex network of sexual forces unconfessed upon the surface of the novel.

All of this is entirely in keeping with our findings in other areas. A literary allusion attaching to Austin describes Silas also. A claim of innocent bemusement, an invitation of public scrutiny, is itself revealed to be an accusation. The dual level at which these allusions to Chateaubriand and Courtenay operate parallels the nineteenth-century Anglo-Irish myth of an Augustan Golden Age. *Uncle Silas*, we should remember, grew from 'Passage in the Secret History of an Irish Countess', a story solidly lodged in the Irish eighteenth century. Le Fanu's method is to contribute to this myth by means of expansive evocations of neo-classical architecture which, in the latter half of the novel, is revealed to be echoing, decayed, ruinous. The contribution to myth is simultaneously a subversive critique of assumed rectitude and validity. The suggestion that the story of Knowl and Bartram-Haugh is based on the Rochfort family houses is substantiated further if one notes the exemplary extinction of their honours and titles with the Act of Union. Lord Bellfield having been created Earl of Belvedere, he died in 1774 and was succeeded by his son George. The second Earl was said in 1775 to have been 'left very embarrass'd in his Circumstances, & from his Distress must consequently be dependent

---

[57] *Uncle Silas*, p. 328.
[58] Letter of Lord Egmont, quoted by the Knight of Glin (p. 1).

on the Crown, likely to quarrel with his Brother Robert, a respectable amiable man.'[59] Here we have two elements familiar from *Uncle Silas* — security and property is succeeded by dependence and discord, and (for the second time in two generations) brother quarrels with brother. The second Earl died in 1814 and, by the terms of the Act of Union, all his titles became extinct.[60] The history of the earldom of Belvedere is exemplary in that it is explicitly terminated by the last decision of the Anglo-Irish Protestant parliament: more specifically, it is characterized by the over-valuation of blood in incestuous adultery, and by the under-valuation of blood in the repeated conflict of brothers.

Le Fanu's fiction shows the present as a repetition or indeed a higher confirmation of the past: the past, by producing the degenerate and self-extinguishing present, is condemned as the fount of corruption. In terms of character and action, suicide is the dominant pattern — self-regarding and violent, character destroys itself. Ostensibly, the fault (*lapsus*) lies in a noble propensity to mate with innkeepers' daughters, and this should be read not so much as an echo of eighteenth-century habits but as a nineteenth-century sensitivity among the Anglo-Irish ascendancy on the topic of disagreeable exogamy. Behind this lies a largely unacknowledged code of inbreeding, intensified in the various forms of sexual introversion discernible in the material we have considered. It is the function of Le Fanu's remarkable use of allegory that the decoration of French literary reference and secreted evidences of Irish local and family history may be integrated to the over-all contours of the novel. There is much in *Uncle Silas* to distress the fastidious reader, yet the novel preserves a negative totality in its reflection of social reality. The absence of any middling order of characters, the apparent monopoly of master and servant, is not only a reflection of

---

[59] *The Irish Parliament 1775 from an Official and Contemporary Manuscript*, ed. William Hunt (London: Longmans; Dublin: Hodges Figgis, 1907), p. 66.

[60] For the text of the Act of Union see Edmund Curtis and R. B. McDowell, edd., *Irish Historical Documents 1172–1922* (London: Methuen, 1977), 2nd ed., pp. 208–13. Between 1761 and 1800 a member of the Rochfort family had represented Westmeath continuously in the Irish House of Commons; thus, the Union and the death of Lord Belvedere combined to extinguish the family's political role.

the false sociology which went into the making of 'ascendancy', it is also a critique in lurid terms of that opting for
ideology over an imaginative rationality.

3. CHARLES LEVER: FROM *HARRY LORREQUER* (1939) TO *LUTTRELL OF ARRAN* (1865)

I stood in Luttrell's Glen. Ash saplings tossed
And Zephyr sullenly came, churning the dust.
A path let in, out of the clash of the light,
Ferns shivering towards a stream. Broken, as slight
As flesh, weak with leaves,
Stone arches bedded in the slope; disused
Forges withered, half in sight,
Their cold lids clumsily slammed; moss on smashed eaves.

(Thomas Kinsella)[61]

Le Fanu's trilogy of the 1860s is the most concentrated
Victorian examination of the eighteenth century, the Irish
eighteenth century as distinct from the Augustan compromise of Pope, Fielding, and Johnson. Yet the morbid
psychology of his fiction has attracted less attention than the
comic extravagances of his friend, Charles Lever. Yeats
acknowledged that Lever has 'historical significance' because
he so vividly 'expressed a social phase' of 'frieze-coated
humanists, dare-devils upon horseback'.[62] The extent to
which the eighteenth century has been interpreted all but
exclusively in terms of Jonah Barrington's *Recollections* and
Buck Whaley's *Memoirs* would serve as a reliable measure of
our need for a genuine literary history and *Kulturgeschichte*.
Le Fanu's sensationalist plots and Lever's picaresque comedies

[61] Thomas Kinsella, 'Lead', *Another September* (Dublin: Dolmen Press,
1962), p. 44. The poem is one of several — 'Phoenix Park', 'Nightwalker', and the
several poems of *Notes from the Land of the Dead* among them — in which
Kinsella utilizes the historical landscape of the area lying between the western
purlieus of Dublin city and the Phoenix Park. Luttrellstown, once the seat of
Colonel Simon Luttrell and acquired by his apostate brother under the penal
laws, is an estate near Lucan in County Dublin. As I write, it is aptly the centre of
controversy with regard to corruption in the planning of land for housing development.
[62] W. B. Yeats, 'A Parnellite at Parnell's Funeral', printed with notes to the
Variorum Edition of the Poems (New York: Macmillan, 1977), p. 834.

are merely the twin strategies of evasion and confession which characterize the Victorian attitude to the Irish past. This is not to say that Lever's comedy constitutes evasion and Le Fanu's sensation enacts confession: each novelist combines in different proportions both attitudes. If Le Fanu has been hitherto neglected because his dominant tone has been interpreted as pathological, Lever may have been the victim of a grosser misinterpretation in being presented as a thoughtless jester. It is true that recent commentators have pointed to a deepening of Lever's involvement with his material in the later novels: what requires emphasis is that both the picaro-heroics of *Harry Lorrequer* (1839) and the sombre depiction of society in *Lord Kilgobbin* (1872) proceed from Lever's response to altering conventional views of the eighteenth century.[63]

The plot of his early novels revolves round the adventures of a young soldier whose relationship to the society he encounters is both privileged and ignorant. Any possibility of a more intense involvement in social reality, of the kind posited for Colambre in *The Absentee*, is turned aside by excursions to the Peninsular War, to Brussels or the German spas. Half a dozen of Lever's novels of the 1830s and 1840s fit this description, with only the minimum adjustments required to differentiate one novel from another. The base of these novels is Victorian picaresque — an apparently shapeless quest by the hero through unfamiliar and yet entertaining landscapes and through incidents which never threaten real violence or any real offence to moral decorum. Irish readers, influenced by Daniel Corkery, have taken offence at the English hero whose ignorance of Irish ways they deem to be a mark of patronizing *ascendancy* attitudes in the author. This is mistaken, for the comic irony of Lever's early novels is that the hero is officially travelling *at home* within the United Kingdom and his bewilderment is an index of the

---

[63] See A. N. Jeffares, *Anglo-Irish Literature* (London: Macmillan; Dublin: Gill and Macmillan, 1982), pp. 121-5. Though it only deals with a few novels, the best recent treatment of Lever is to be found in George O'Brien's doctoral thesis, 'Life on the Land: The Interrelationship between Identity and Community in the Irish Fiction of Maria Edgeworth, William Carleton, and Charles Lever' (unpub. Ph.D. thesis, University of Warwick, 1979).

Union's failure. Moreover, the Victorian picaresque hero's ultimate destiny — success in the world apart — is honourable marriage, and Lever's choice of brides for his heroes has a symptomatic interest. In *Harry Lorrequer* (1839), the young English officer ends up married to Lady Jane Callonby just as her father is appointed Viceroy of Ireland. *Jack Hinton* (1843), Lever's third novel, follows the formula closely though it has the added attraction of including Mrs Paul Rooney, the author's version of Maria Edgeworth's Mrs Anastasia Rafferty — indeed one illuminating way to read Lever's picaresque is to interpret it as *The Absentee* drained of social function as to plot, with military pranks provided as a substitute. Jack Hinton, however, finally marries Louisa Bellew whose name encapsulates more than a hint of Catholic nobility.[64]

By the time we reach *Luttrell of Arran* (1865) this pattern has for us a further dimension to its meaning. For Lever's early fiction offers a clear-cut demonstration of the difference — crucial to the practice of literary history — between past significance and present meaning. To say that the comic irony of *Harry Lorrequer* or *Jack Hinton* lies in its *exposé* of the Union is to emphasize the present meaning of the novel read within our latter-day literary history; to speak of the conclusive marriages is to emphasize the significance of the fiction in its day as part of the ideological reinforcement of Union. But, as we have seen already in the case of Lever, these functions of the work — significance and meaning — necessarily interact through the contradictions inherent in each. In the case of both Le Fanu and Lever these contradictions are manifested in formal terms. *Harry Lorrequer* was intended by its author as a series of monthly sketches, but the pressures of serialization in the conservative *Dublin University Magazine* combining with the renewed vitality of the novel-form in the London markets drew the material

---

[64] Several members of the Bellew family were active in movements for Catholic relief between 1790 and 1820. During the period of the novel's setting, Sir Edward Bellew represented a moderate wing of the movement: see R. B. McDowell, *Public Opinion and Government Policy in Ireland 1800–1846* (London: Faber, 1952), pp. 90, 95, 100, 105; also McDowell, *Ireland in the Age of Imperialism and Revolution 1760–1801* (Oxford: Clarendon Press, 1979), pp. 410, 412, 559.

into the shape of moralized picaresque. In both Le Fanu's and Lever's novels, there is a generic pressure within the fiction towards an acknowledgement of a shorter, interpolated fiction, a tale within a tale. And here again, *Harry Lorrequer* provides a typical example.

In the thirty-ninth chapter the irrepressible O'Leary tells the story of 'the Knight of Kerry and Billy M'Cabe'. A synopsis can be reconstructed from O'Leary's words:

Well, it seems that one day the Knight of Kerry was walking along the Strand in London, killing an hour's time till the House was done prayers . . . his eye was caught by an enormous picture displayed upon the wall of a house, representing a human figure covered with long dark hair, with huge nails upon his hands, and a most dreadful expression of face . . . he heard a man . . . call out 'Walk in, ladies and gentlemen. The most vonderful curiosity ever exhibited — only one shilling — the vild man from Chippoowango, in Africay — eats raw wittles without being cooked, and many other pleasing performances.' The knight paid his money, and was admitted . . . to his very great horror, he beheld . . . a man nearly naked, covered with long, shaggy hair, that grew even over his nose and cheekbones. He sprang about, sometimes on his feet, sometimes all fours, but always uttering the most fearful yells, and glaring upon the crowd in a manner that was really dangerous. The knight did not feel exactly happy . . . and began to wish himself back in the House, even upon a Committee of Privileges, when suddenly the savage gave a more frantic scream than before, and seized upon a morsel of raw beef which a keeper extended to him upon a long fork like a tandem whip . . . Just at this instant some sounds struck upon his ear that surprised him not a little . . . conceive, if you can, his amazement to find that, amid his most fearful cries and wild yells, the savage was talking Irish . . . There he was, jumping four feet high in the air, eating his raw meat, pulling out his hair by handfuls; and amid all this, cursing the whole company to his heart's content, in as good Irish as ever was heard in Tralee. . . . At length something he heard left no further doubt upon his mind, and turning to the savage, he addressed him in Irish, at the same time fixing a look of most scrutinizing import upon him.

'Who are you, you scoundrel?' said the knight.

'Bill M'Cabe, your honour.'

'And what do you mean by playing off these tricks here, instead of earning your bread like an honest man?'

'Whisht,' said Billy, 'and keep the secret. I'm earning the rent for your honour. One must do many a queer thing that pays two pound ten an acre for bad land.'

This was enough: the knight wished Billy every success, and left him . . . This adventure, it seems, had made the worthy knight a great friend to the introduction of poor-laws; for, he remarks very truly, 'more of Billy's countrymen might take a fancy to the savage life, if the secret was found out.'[65]

No doubt there are echoes of Don Quixote in this tale of 'the worthy knight' of Kerry; but Billy M'Cabe's pretence, the fiction of an African within the fiction O'Leary relates to Lorrequer in Lever's novel links literary convention to economic *exposé*. Most of the elements are immediately evident — the rent, the malingering knight ticking-off his hard-working tenant, the Irish speaker as savage on the Strand. The interpolated tale whimsically displays an image of social relations which the enfolding tale generically rejects. And yet, if O'Leary's story reveals an aspect of truth, the invitation is there for the reader to see some further measure of truth in Lorrequer's conquest of the future Viceroy's daughter. To read *Harry Lorrequer* requires decisions by the reader as to proportions of revelation and concealment enacted in the fictions of the novel.[66]

But every novel is composed from the language which remains outside that novel, and the tale-within-the-tale is often structurally a return to that larger social dimension by means of an appearance of microcosm. Certainly in 1839 there was a Knight of Kerry alive and well; what is more, he had been a Member of Parliament for over thirty years, though he was finally unseated in the aftermath of the 1832 Reform Act. Maurice Fitzgerald (1774–1849, eighteenth Knight of Kerry) had represented Kerry in the Irish and later the Westminster parliament, and had held various government offices in Tory governments. Though he had ceased to be an MP by 1838, the Knight of Kerry was a vigorous opponent of the government's attempt to extend the Poor Law system to Ireland, holding (as an Irish landlord) that the estates could not afford the charge on the rates. Thus, when Lever was writing his chapter in August 1839, his comments on the

    [65] [Charles Lever], *Harry Lorrequer* (Dublin, 1839).
    [66] In *Our Mess*, vol. i, *Jack Hinton the Guardsman* (Dublin, 1843), the 6th chapter, 'The Sham Battle' (pp. 37–47), provides another illustration of pretence within the fiction veering towards symbolic reportage.

salutary effect of the Billy M'Cabe encounter upon the
Knight's friendship towards the introduction of the Poor
Laws are ironical. Moreover, Lever's official setting of the
novel in the second decade of the century is simultaneously
undermined, and the contemporary function of historical
fiction laid bare.[67]
The example of the Knight of Kerry's indirect appearance
in *Harry Lorrequer* encourages a similar approach to *Luttrell
of Arran*, where historical allusion is even more devious.
Before passing to the later novel, one further aspect of the
thirty-ninth chapter is unavoidable. The Knight and his
tenant are able to converse confidentially, as it were, in the
middle of London by virtue of their sharing the Irish language. Triumphantly, the wretched M'Cabe can silence his
landlord while simultaneously cursing the ignorant audience
whom he entertains. Yet the Irish language cannot be
admitted into the discourse of Lever's fiction; it stands
beyond the bar of tolerance for such a novel, just as if it
were a wild man from Chippoowango. The exchange — here,
not an entirely Yeatsian one — between beggar and nobleman
successfully leaps over any intervening social element by
a combination of shared intimacy (language) and shared
displacement (the Strand). When we return to the larger
fiction of Harry and Lady Jane etc., the action moves
through France, Canada, Strassburg, and eventually Munich
where Lorrequer is married to the new Viceroy's daughter.
The unreality of such a consummate Union is not mute.
Whether through residual Irish, or the exotica of a German
mis en scène, such intimacies of beggar and nobleman, picaro
and Viceroy, require specific ideological mediations.
By the end of the 1840s, Lever's fiction had grown more
sombre in tone, partly as a result of criticism directed at
the capers of Harry and Jack, and partly as a consequence
of the sociological/political disaster of the Famine. The
contrast therefore between *Harry Lorrequer* and so late a
novel as *Luttrell of Arran* is only startling if one passes over

[67] For Maurice Fitzgerald see *DNB* and John S. Crone, *A Concise Dictionary
of Irish Biography* (London: Longmans, 1928). His attitude to the question of a
poor law for Ireland is discussed in Angus Macintyre, *The Liberator: Daniel
O'Connell and the Irish Party 1830–1847* (London: Hamish Hamilton, 1965).

the intervening development. Nevertheless, the novel of 1865 does possess characteristics which demand our attention by way of a comparison with *Lorrequer*. Lever's dedication-page in *Luttrell of Arran* provides a neat initial point of reference through which we can begin a broader analysis.

The novel is dedicated 'To Joseph Sheridan Le Fanu Esq., — He who can write such stories as "Wylder's Hand" or "Uncle Silas" . . .'. It is true that the two men had been friendly in the 1840s, and that in 1863 Le Fanu had resumed novel-writing after a sixteen-year-interval — here are grounds for a dedication, surely. Yet in 1865 the two had drifted apart, the one to Italy, the other to a reclusive life in Dublin. What prompts the examination of this gesture towards Le Fanu is Lever's choice of name for one group of characters, the Courtenay sisters, Laura and Georgina. To find, in a novel dedicated explicitly to the author of *Uncle Silas* — which had appeared the year before — characters called Courtenay goes some way towards confirming the analysis of 'Ubi lapsus? Quid Feci?' which assimilated it to Le Fanu's complex allusive system. Yet the Courtenays play a relatively minor part in *Luttrell of Arran*, and that unconnected with the aspects of Courtenay family history drawn upon by Le Fanu.

Though very specific details of the novel detonate its meaning, a summary by synopsis and quotation is unavoidable. John Hamilton Luttrell was engaged to marry Georgina Courtenay, having initially fallen for her sister Laura. Prompted to inquire about his rapid exit from 'the Irish university' Georgina discovered that he has been a United Irishman. Pressing him for details to reassure her family she learned from him that many eminent men in public life had been Luttrell's fellow revolutionaries. Mr Courtenay, a friend of Castlereagh in his time, went to the Government: there were investigations, resignations and, in Ireland, demands for the traitor's name:

'Why not Luttrell?' said one writer in a famous print. 'His father betrayed us before.' This was an allusion to his having voted for the Union. 'Why not Luttrell?' They entered thereupon into some curious family details, to show how these Luttrells had never been 'true blue' to any cause.[68]

[68] Charles Lever, *Luttrell of Arran* (London, 1865), p. 20.

The wedding was cancelled, Luttrell wounded in a duel:

> He would seem to have mixed himself up with the lowest political party
> in Ireland — men who represent, in a certain shape, the revolutionary
> section in France — and though the very haughtiest aristocrat I think I
> ever knew, and at one time the most fastidious 'fine gentleman', there
> were stories of his having uttered the most violent denunciations of
> rank, and inveighed in all the set terms of the old French Convention
> against the distinctions of class. Last of all, I heard that he had married
> a peasant girl, the daughter of one of his cottier tenants . . .[69]

Mrs Luttrell was never publicly acknowledged as his wife by
Luttrell; her family had its own long record of subversion,
albeit of a more agrarian than aristocratic kind. Her sister's
daughter, Kate, is taken up by Laura Courtenay's husband
who educates her alongside his own daughter, Ada. The
'romantic' element in the novel concerns Kate's social
advancement, her seduction by Adolphus Ladarelle, and her
ultimate marriage to Harry Luttrell, her aunt's son, by now
an honest sailor. Kate has been adopted by old John Luttrell
as his daughter and his heir, in the belief that his son is dead,
and Ladarelle's object in the fraudulent marriage is her
inherited estate. The final marriage, however, brings together
the son and the adopted daughter of the ostracized aristocrat-
rebel.

Summarized thus, the novel does not amount to much.
Yet there are intriguing patterns even in the summary. The
husband of the woman Luttrell originally loved 'adopts'
Kate, who is subsequently adopted by Luttrell himself — she
has thus been the surrogate child of the original couple. Kate
is falsely married to Ladarelle — an inadequate bonding —
and will be truly married to her cousin/'brother' — a double
bonding. Ladarelle has virtually appeared from nowhere,
conveniently during Harry's absence (presumed death) at sea.
As the similarity of the names suggests 'Ladarelle' is a false
Luttrell, attracting into his function that hereditary falseness
to all causes which the name symbolized to John Luttrell's
comrades. From the drastic social *mésalliance* of the fine
gentleman John Hamilton Luttrell and Sally O'Hara of Arran,
the novel moves to the introverted marriage of Kate Luttrell

---

[69] Ibid., p. 22.

and Harry Luttrell: '"The Luttrell spirit is low enough, I take it, now," said she, blushing.' 'If their pride can survive this, no peasant blood can be their remedy."'[70] In contrast to the central hero's marriage to Lady Jane or Lady Louisa, his marriage into Viceregal or quasi-recusant circles, the absent hero of *Luttrell of Arran* marries into the peasantry, albeit a peasantry represented by a society-trained heroine. And whereas the picaresque novels had flitted through Paris in 1814 and Bavaria in no time at all, *Luttrell of Arran* finally focuses on an *ur*-Gaelic Ireland, a western isle located rather uncertainly somewhere near the coasts of Galway, Mayo, and/or Donegal. We thus have several kinds of inward motion in a plot which decisively commences with the eclipse of the hero in suddenly exposed (and yet hereditary) guilt. As in *Uncle Silas* this guilt is associated with exclusion from politics; and whereas Le Fanu presents the marriage of first cousins as one threat which hangs over his heroine, Lever employs an intensified form of this inward movement within a family as the climax to his plot. Luttrell, like Silas Ruthyn, has married 'beneath' him; whereas this *dis*graced Le Fanu's hero/villain, Luttrell's marriage into the O'Hara family is doubly the means of grace — at least as far as the narrative endorses the conclusive marriage of Kate and Harry.

Narrative form, or forms, constitutes an important aspect of these mid-century novels. Le Fanu's sustained use of a female narrator in *Uncle Silas* in part reflects the eclipse of traditionally male heroics in its Anglo-Irish provenance, and in part also contributes actively to that eclipse. In Lever's novel of the following year, the anecdotal method of *Harry Lorrequer* is replaced by a more comprehensive multi-vocal narrative. Lever liked writing dialogue, and though *Luttrell* is officially an impersonal narrative a great deal of it indeed reaches the reader through the words of specific characters. The retrospective account of Luttrell's exposure of his political activities and the results of that exposure appears at times to have the tone of impersonal narrative, but the first-person pronoun strategically bursts this appearance towards the end — 'the very haughtiest aristocrat I think I ever

<hr />

[70] Ibid., p. 503.

knew ...'. The reader commences to read aware of the particular speaker, is then drawn towards an interpretation of what he reads as narrative rather than speech, and is again redirected towards the speaker's perspective. The technique is far from original in Lever — consider the drastic application of such a working on and against the reader in *Wuthering Heights* — but it derives its significance by its bearing upon the altering views of history advanced in the altering narrative.

Arran is not precisely located for the reader where a map-reader would expect it. It is unlikely that many readers will have paused to worry over such imprecision, finding the reflection of ecclesiastical ruins, the Irish language, and occasional references to County Galway an adequate guarantee that they do not err drastically if they call Inis Mór to mind. Yet such excursions to the topographical world vitiate the strategies of fiction and its reading. Less easily accommodated to this kind of reading are references to the site of Luttrell's alleged treason as 'the Irish university'. True, such locutions may represent a speaker's unfamiliarity with Ireland and its institutions — thus he avoids the idiomatic 'Trinity College' or 'Dublin University' because he is unaware that there is only one university in Ireland at the time of the alleged events. Yet this explanation only shifts the significance of the phrase from the author to the character or narrator. Furthermore, there was a notorious inquiry into subversion in Trinity College, conducted by Fitzgibbon and Dr Patrick Duigenan on the eve of the United Irishmen's rebellion.[71] Among those examined by the inquisitors were Thomas Moore, the future melodist, and an obscure friend called Dacre Hamilton.[72] No Luttrell can be found implicated in these proceedings, while in the novel the imposition of an oath on the young John Luttrell evidently was attempted after the rebellion. The fictional hero is subsequently denounced as an informer on his former comrades, and there had indeed been many informers placed

[71] For an account of this episode see J. W. Stubbs, *The History of the University of Dublin* (Dublin, 1889), pp. 297-301.

[72] See L. A. G. Strong, *The Minstrel Boy: A Portrait of Tom Moore* (London: Hodder and Stoughton, 1937), p. 52. Dacre Hamilton was among the 19 students expelled as a consequence of the inquisition.

in the ranks of the United Irishmen — the most famous being
Francis Higgins ('the Sham Squire') and Leonard MacNally.
As for the associations of the name Luttrell in 1798, one
figure of note bearing that name was Lord Carhampton
(Henry Lawes Luttrell, 1743-1821), Commander-in-Chief of
the forces in Ireland from 1796. (His illegitimate son sat in
the Irish parliament from 1798 to 1800, and subsequently
became a wit and man of fashion in London.)

Neither of these Luttrells of the period invoked at the
opening of Lever's novel seems a likely candidate for the
reclusive, embittered aristocrat-rebel. Cautiously, one might
notice that there is a blurred resemblance in the circumstances
of the novel to some discrete aspects of the Rebellion — the
presence of informers, the presence of Luttrells, the inquisition at Trinity — but circumstances and aspects fail to line
up in any neat pattern. Pressing such searches for pattern,
one might desperately seize on Lord Carhampton's seduction
of a gardener's daughter near Woodstock, Oxfordshire, as
an original to the *mésalliance* (in Society's terms) with a
Catholic peasant girl from Arran. It is true that Carhampton
at first vehemently opposed Union, and then supported it,
but such a change of heart is not unique or even remarkable
in one of his military background.[73]

Two developments are in progress in this 'blurring'. The
first is simply a new adjustment between folklore and
history, the second a rewriting of the United Irishmen's
rebellion in the decade of Fenian rebellion. For the Luttrell
family had a larger and more defined place in the folklore of
the eighteenth century than in the history of 1798. Two
brothers Luttrell were prominent in the ranks of King
James's forces prior to the Battle of Aughrim. Simon Luttrell
(d. 1698) sat in the Jacobite parliament of 1689 representing
the county of Dublin together with Patrick Sarsfield, James's
premier Irish general. After the Jacobite defeat, he was
attainted for treason and died in exile — his treason was

---

[73] Jonathan Swift wrote to Charles Ford on 2 February 1718-19: 'We have
found out the Fellow that killed Harry Lutterel, but cannot hang him. No doubt
you know the Story, but it is very odd that he who hired the murderer should
confess in hope of the Reward . . .'. *Correspondence*, ed. Harold Williams (Oxford:
Clarendon Press, 1963), vol. ii, p. 313.

therefore the result of a change of regime and not a change
of loyalty. His brother, Henry (1655?–1717), however,
defected to the Williamites immediately prior to the Battle of
Aughrim, and took advantage of the terms of the Treaty to
secure his position with the new regime. He was shot dead in
his sedan-chair on 3 November 1717 in Stafford Street,
Dublin; and his grave was violated some eighty years later
during the period of the United Irishmen rebellion when his
grandson's high-handed methods in putting down discontent
had excited popular feeling. According to Macaulay (no
friend of Jacobitism), the perpetrators were 'descendents of
those whom he had betrayed'.[74] Of the grandson, the Lord-
Lieutenant, Camden, wrote that he 'did not confine himself
to the strict rules of law'. From a position of unimpeachable,
twentieth-century impartiality, *The Complete Peerage* comments of the Luttrells 'they seem to have been an unlovely
race.'[75]

Popular opinion of the eighteenth century, therefore, is
radically modified and yet exploited in the pre-history of
Luttrell of Arran, Luttrell treachery as Jacobites or to
Jacobitism being subliminally drawn upon to justify the
third-hand observation that the family had never been true
blue to any cause, the cause on this occasion being *Jacobin*
rather than *Jacobite* in its leanings. The third Earl of
Carhampton (John Luttrell-Olmius, died 1829, aged about
84) was the last of his line, with whom all his titles became
extinct. Like the shadow of the Rochfort family which may
shine behind the dark patterns of *Uncle Silas*, we encounter
here a noble ancestry now extinct. Like the fictional Ruthyns
and the historical Rochforts, Luttrell notoriety involves
sibling conflict, the self-division of a family to whom pride
and depravity jointly adhere. It may seem that Lever's novel
misses this sibling rivalry, for we hear nothing of disputatious
brothers as such; instead, however, there is the otherwise
inexplicable villain Ladarelle who substitutes for honest

---

[74] Thomas Babington Macaulay, *The History of England*, ed. C. H. Firth
(London: Macmillan, 1914), vol. iv, p. 2073.

[75] For Camden's letter see W. E. H. Lecky, *A History of Ireland in the
Eighteenth Century* (London, 1898), vol. iii, p. 419; see also *The Complete
Peerage*, ed. George Edward Cokayne; Rev. Vicary Gibbs (London: St Catherine's
Press, 1913), vol. iii, p. 24.

Harry during the latter's presumed death. The *Doppelganger* of Ladarelle/Luttrell resembles the Ruthyn brothers' relationship in that villainy and virtue are never presented at once, though their presence (separately) in the novel requires a patterned symmetry to be at all explicable. But the significance of Lever's treatment of Luttrell notoriety is its contribution to the notion of identity consolidated in hereditary guilt. Whereas, the discrete material lying behind Le Fanu's allegory points to guilt in the binary offence of overvaluation and undervaluation of sexual and blood bonds, Lever's historical traces serve to point to the coexistence of antagonist political loyalties — Jacobite and Williamite, originally.

That synthesis had been anticipated in Irish historical fiction through the influence of Walter Scott upon — amongst others — John Banim and Sheridan Le Fanu. The ventriloquism of Le Fanu's *Cock and Anchor* (1845) had presented the anxieties of the author's Protestant Ascendancy caste through the humiliation and suffering of Jacobite heroes of a bygone age. Lever's implied synthesis of the Jacobite and Williamite past is merely a further stage upon the same progression. That progression is, of course, the alignment of history in resistance to the threats of a reformist government in Britain (for Le Fanu in the 1830s and 1840s) or to the threat of Fenian and Mazzinian outrage in the 1860s. The renowned shift in Lever's sympathies (from a mockery of the native Irish in early novels to a near-nationalist position in *Lord Kilgobbin* etc.) is simply another statement of that rewriting of history; rebellions of the past may be rehabilitated, indeed 'romanticized', so as to be a bulwark against contemporary unrest; the phenomenon is familiar even today in circles to whom the Provisional IRA are an embarrassment. The United Irishmen are presented at the opening of *Luttrell of Arran* as an honourable conspiracy, or at least which it would be dishonourable for a gentleman to betray. The novel's narrative holds at a distance the confirmation of Luttrell's membership, and also fails quite to confirm that he betrayed anyone. Lever was living in Florence at the time of writing, and he conceded a curious unease about the novel:

I do not believe 'Luttrell' will do, and my conviction is that the despair

that attaches to Ireland, from Parliament down to 'Punch', acts injuri-
ously on all who would try to invest her scenes with interest or endow
her people with other qualities than are mentioned in police courts.[76]

The police court exactly identifies the change between the
context of pre- and post-Famine. The administration of order
had by the 1860s reached a point of public organization in
which the pervasive informer system of the 1790s was less
effective. In *Luttrell of Arran* the change is acknowledged
in the contrasting styles of subversion associated with John
Luttrell and his adopted daughter's grandfather, Peter
Malone. Luttrell is to be seen, it is hoped, as an aristocratic
United Irishman, a testy Philippe Egalité: Malone and his
associates are presented as vindicative or misled malefactors,
in a mode ostensibly of the eighteenth-century Whiteboys
but more recognizably a product of contemporary fears of
Fenian secrecy. The police court is the administrative counter
to a political conspiracy which cannot be penetrated by
noble democrats or sensitively ambiguous informers. In the
face of a new republican conspiracy, now *petit bourgeois* and
predominantly Catholic in composition, *Luttrell of Arran*
offers an image of the United Irishman in aristocratic embrace
of a refined peasantry. The Celtic Revival will press home this
holy alliance of guilt-ridden Ascendancy and marginalized
Gaelic peasantry as a bulwark against the politics of class and
the sociology of an industrialized metropolitan colony. Its
subscribers shall include some unlikely partners.

4. W. E. GLADSTONE

How little reaped where they had sown —
The generous Ascendancy.

(Leslie Daiken)[77]

The significant element, culturally speaking, in the fiction

[76] Lever to Dr Burbidge, 26 December 1863, from Cara Capponi Florence;
Edmund Downey, ed., *Charles Lever: His Life in his Letters* (Edinburgh:
Blackwood, 1906), vol. i, p. 393.
[77] Leslie Daiken 'Lines Written in a Country Parson's Orchard'; see Kathleen
Hoagland, *1000 Years of Irish Poetry* (New York: Grosset and Dunlap, 1962),
pp. 759-60.

of Sheridan Le Fanu and Charles Lever which we have
examined is the technique of subterfuge. Feelings of personal
guilt or compromise do not satisfactorily account for the
means by which allegories of ascendancy culpability are
unveiled and veiled again. If guilt is repeatedly a hallmark of
ascendancy there is nevertheless some uncertainty as to the
precise location of this identifying guarantee. A guilty past
satisfies on two levels — it establishes the reality of one's
identity and at the same time sanctions a latter-day derelic-
tion. To the old-style nationalist, convinced of the moral
depravity of 'the Anglo-Irish Protestant Ascendancy', we
must break the unwelcome news that the Ascendancy to a
large degree invented its depravity as a small price to be paid
for its continued viability as a social entity.

The abashed nationalist has powerful allies, however, and
they emerge precisely in the wake of that fiction we have
been examining. The 1860s were years of Fenian anxiety,
and traditionally the conversion of William Ewart Gladstone
to the reformist solution of the Irish question is attributed
(grudgingly) to the impact of Fenianism and attendant
discontents. The long-awaited extinction of Palmerstonian
Whiggery finally came in the election of 1868, and within a
few years the Irish established Church and the Irish landlord
system were in the crucible, and Home Rule poised on the
rim. The October 1868 election campaign saw Gladstone
touring in Lancashire, delivering a series of immensely long
speeches on the priorities of new-style liberalism. The resulting
collection of election addresses is impressive not so much for
its material — which is naturally somewhat repetitive — as for
the ultimate identification of a symbolic focus for a new Irish
policy. On 23 October, Gladstone spoke at Hengler's Circus,
Wigan; his main themes were already familiar but the climactic paragraph of this final Lancashire rally broke new ground:

It is clear the Church of Ireland offers to us indeed a great question, but
even that question is but one of a group of questions. There is the
Church of Ireland, there is the land of Ireland, there is the education of
Ireland: there are many subjects, all of which depend upon one greater
than them all; they are all so many branches from one trunk, and
that trunk is the tree of what is called Protestant ascendancy. Gentlemen, I look, for one, to this Protestant people to put down Protestant

ascendency which pretends to seek its objects by doing homage to religious truth, and instead of consecrating politics desecrates religion . . .
We therefore aim at the destruction of that system of ascendency
which, though it has been crippled and curtailed by former measures,
yet still must be allowed by all to exist. It is still there, like a tall tree of
noxious growth, lifting its head to heaven and darkening and poisoning
the land as far as its shadow can extend; it is still there, gentlemen, and
now at length the day has come when, as we hope, the axe has been laid
to the root of that tree, and it nods and quivers from its top to its base.
It wants, gentlemen, one stroke more — the stroke of these elections.[78]

This is Gladstone's most trenchant attack upon the causes,
as he sees them, of the Irish Question. In earlier speeches of
the campaign he has condemned the trailing of political
insignia in Protestant churches and ceremonies, but at Wigan
Orange practices are virtually conflated with the dignities of
Protestant Ascendancy. Though the future prime minister is
unlikely to have had The Reverend T. D. Gregg in mind as he
spoke, he too assumes ascendancy to have an ancient pedigree, an outmoded history. Gladstone's central image of
course is the tall tree of noxious growth which, though he
does not specify it, is the Javanese upas. The implications of
this metaphor were not lost on commentators: Lord Edmond
Fitzmaurice, speaking on an Irish education bill in 1873,
declared that:

It was perfectly certain that a man who possessed a great deal of imagination might, if he stayed out sufficiently long at night, staring at a small
star, persuade himself next morning that he had seen a great comet; and
it was equally certain that such a man, if he stared long enough at a bush,
might persuade himself that he had seen a branch of the upas tree.[79]

[78] 'Speech Delivered in Hengler's Circus, Wigan October 23rd. 1868', *Speeches
of the Right Hon. W. E. Gladstone Delivered at Warrington, Ormskirk, Liverpool,
Southport, Newtown, Leigh, and Wigan in October 1868* (London, [c.1868]),
pp. 97-8.
[79] Quoted in Henry Yule and A. C. Burnell, *Hobson-Jobson: A Glossary of
Colloquial Anglo-Indian Words and Phrases, and of Kindred Terms, Etymological,
Historical, Geographical and Discursive* (London: Routledge and Kegan Paul,
1968), new ed., rev. W. Crooke, p. 959. Cf. Sir William Gregory in 1869: 'Mr.
Gladstone lost no time when Parliament met in cutting down the branches, as he
termed them, of the upas tree; and immediately brought in a bill for the suppression of the Irish State Church.' *Sir William Gregory, K.C.M.G., Formerly
Member of Parliament and Sometime Governor of Ceylon: An Autobiography
edited by Lady Gregory* (London, 1894), 2nd. ed., p. 255.

There is great aptness in Gladstone's image, for the upas is both a tree which exudes a poisonous juice (*Antiaris toxicaria*) and a legendary or fabulous tree which is so poisonous as to destroy all life around it for many miles. Like the vampire (bat), it connotes a real and specific thing, and a fantasy of the human mind woven from that thing. There is no doubt that upas trees were saved from the axeman on the strength of their legendary powers, and the Protestant Ascendancy is likewise girded round with magical protection. And yet the tree-image has other kinds of ambiguity attaching to it also; just as Burke's notion of the State as an organism indivisible as a tree coexists with the fashion of planting liberty trees symbolic of man's freedom to initiate as well as to perpetuate, so Gladstone's upas comes to mimic Burke's great-rooted blossomer. The assault upon Protestant Ascendancy at Wigan in 1868 absolved Lever from the need subliminally to insinuate a guilty past into his fiction — Lever's late novels are far more explicit in their condemnation of the past than *Luttrell of Arran* — and it lent the dignity of a prime minister's outrage to what had been previously nervous and ill-defined. It is fair to say that, without the consensus encapsulated in Gladstone's denunciation, the process by which Yeats takes Protestant Ascendancy and renders it as cultural tradition would not have been possible. Gladstonian reform of the Irish Church and the system of land tenure provided the evidence of political renunciation and denial by the Protestant Ascendancy, upon which cultural compensation by way of tradition would eventually build.

The image of Protestant Ascendancy reflected in the Wigan speech had reached the status of public opinion, with all the elusive ramifications this involved. Gladstone's ability to enunciate a statement of Protestant Ascendancy lay largely in his unfamiliarity with the society in which this transformed ideology operated. In Ireland, testimony of a similar scale and intensity is less available. To the Protestant Ascendancy, Protestant Ascendancy required no elaboration or definition; while to the Catholic population — whom Burke had warned so many years earlier — the currency of the *acceptance* of this distinctive sociology was its own validity. Nevertheless, there were of course denunciations of the monopoly Protestants enjoyed in public offices and the professions, and complaints as to the limited extent of Catholic emancipation in a society where an élite regulated the distribution of reward within its own ranks. By 1868, such complaints, allied to a recognition of the Church Establishment and (more remotely) land tenure as political issues embittering the Union, were common enough. What makes *Protestant Ascendency in Ireland: Its Cause and Cure* worthy of attention is the manner in which ascendancy is related to the development of a sectarian sociology.

Its author, Mulhallen Marum, was a Queen's County justice of the peace, a barrister by profession. His recurring concern in the pamphlet was to recommend the concept of *copyhold* as a reform of Irish land tenure, and the commentary on Protestant Ascendancy is partly incidental to that concern. The history of Ireland's woes is extended back to the Reformation and before, with Protestant Ascendancy granted at least a Cromwellian provenance.[80] The resolutions of the Corporation of Dublin in 1792 are quoted *in extenso*, but they are accepted simply as a confirmation of an acknowledged and venerable concept. Marum's notion of Protestant Ascendancy in 1868, then, was simply the dominance of wealth, office, and dignities by Protestants, a state of affairs requiring no differentiation by historical period as to degree, intensity or any other factor. While his title speaks of causes, these are so remote in history as to be virtually a *primum mobile*; as for cures these degenerate into atomized proposals, the product of a campaigner's enthusiasm, mere schemes. Thus, Protestant Ascendancy came to symbolize not simply the permanence of a state of affairs (say, like the monarchy), but its apparent *necessity* whether enjoyed or resented. Burke's metaphor had been 'abracadabra', and indeed the mid-nineteenth-century invocations of Protestant Ascendancy had the tone of magical spells. The crucial stage leading to this experience of Protestant Ascendancy as some inevitable dimension of existence in Ireland was the loss of its history, the process of back-dating the phrase to

[80] E. Mulhallen Marum, *Protestant Ascendency in Ireland: Its Cause and Cure, and the Right of Irish Tenants, under the British Constitution, to Fixity of Tenure, Vindicated* (Dublin, 1868), p. 12.

encompass first of all the eighteenth century generally, then the Williamite wars and the Settlement, and ultimately Cromwell and post-Reformation society *in toto*. That latter position may never have been held or expressed by serious historians — history can be falsified but it cannot actually be annulled — but the tactics were sufficiently widespread to produce what amounted to an eternal image, an iconic representation of history.

Marum's pamphlet links this significantly with the antagonism not only of creeds but of races also. Like the *Dublin University Magazine* of 1837, he compared the interaction of peoples and cultures in England and Ireland, but came to different conclusions. Catholicism, he insisted, was the element in pre-Reformation England which facilitated the amalgamation of Saxon and Norman etc; Protestant Ascendancy in post-Reformation Ireland effected a racial schism: 'The fell spirit of Ascendency stalked through the land, establishing religion as the criterion of race, and smiting the Roman Catholic as of inferior caste — even as the black man on the new continent.'[81] This rather ambiguous period piece of prejudice is a timely reminder that the corollory of Protestant Ascendancy became in due course the revival of Celticism as an exclusive, identifying theory by which the repression of class enacted in Protestant Ascendancy was unwittingly complied with. Marum can refer in passing to 'the Celtic race and creed', unconcerned by the *linguistic* area of reference involved in 'Celtic'.[82] The sociology of Ireland was to be propagated thereafter in a binary scheme which implied both mutual exclusion among a categorized population and a de-historicized model of dominance/ subservience. The ruins of Le Fanu's and Lever's fiction are not simply remnants of Englih romanticism preserved in a provincial literature too undeveloped to throw off such anachronisms: they are the static and shattered, the exclusive and radically divided image of colonial Ireland.

Facies hippocratica is no longer remote from the petrified, primordial landscape encountered in the ruined houses of Le

----

[81]   Ibid., p. 42.
[82]   Ibid., p. 33.

Fanu or the shanty-abbeys of Lever. In a culture which fossilizes history as unchanging condition, historical allegory becomes a means of subversion by which anachronism and dislocated identity draw attention to the reader's task of reading relations between various levels of allusion. Chateaubriand *and* Courtenay, Luttrell as United Irishman — these are not to be taken as fictional exotica uncertainly controlled by a wayward writer. In the business of reading, within a coherent literary history, *Uncle Silas* and *Luttrell* present a challenge not categorically different from *Finnegans Wake* or *Ulysses* where multiple allusion and so-called 'misinformation' also proliferate. The mid-nineteenth century is not a degeneration of romanticism so much as it is the early manifestation of modernist anxieties. And Ireland is less a backward and marginal culture than it is a central if repressed area of British modernism. An area of *British* modernism by virtue of its place in the British colonial system, of British *modernism* by virtue of its intimate place in the United Kingdom, the flagship of high capitalism in the nineteenth century.

Yeats's view of the Irish nineteenth century was otherwise. It is well known, and in due course will be subject to scrutiny. In declaring the century void he demonstrates the romantic priorities of symbolic unity, of which cultural nationalism was but one expression. No equally extensive Joycean diagnosis is available though arguably 'The Dead' is an anatomy of Victorian Ireland in which the (im)balance of the sects is more accurately adjudged than in complaints such as Mulhallen Marum's. By the time Joyce wrote *Dubliners*, of course, many of the issues raised by Marum had been resolved. Thomas Kinsella's summary of an alternative to the Yeatsian view inevitably employs Joyce:

Joyce, with a greatness like Yeats's, was able to reject (that is, accept) the whole tradition as he found it — as it lay in stunned silence, still recovering from the death of its old language. Joyce's isolation is a mask. His relationship with the modern world is direct and intimate. He knows the filthy modern tide, and he immerses himself in it to do his work. His relationship with Ireland is also direct and intimate. In rejecting Ireland he does so on its own terms . . . He is the first major Irish voice to speak for Irish reality since the death of the Irish language . . .

The filthy modern tide does not only run in Ireland, of course, and
Joyce's act of continuity is done with a difference: he simultaneously
revives the Irish tradition and admits the modern world . . . So, the Irish
writer, if he cares who he is and where he comes from, finds that Joyce
and Yeats are the two main objects in view; and I think he finds that
Joyce is the true father. I will risk putting it diagrammatically, and say
that Yeats stands for the Irish tradition as broken; Joyce stands for it as
continuous, or healed — or healing — from its mutilation.[83]

Even in a diagnosis which so signally declines to prescribe
Yeats the tendency to write criticism and literary history as
a paraphrase of Yeatsian history is not absent.

[83] Thomas Kinsella, 'The Irish Writer', *Davis, Mangan, Ferguson? Tradition
and the Irish Writer. Writings by W. B. Yeats and by Thomas Kinsella* (Dublin:
Dolmen Press, 1970), pp. 64–5.

6. THE QUESTION OF CELTICISM

Standish O'Grady supporting himself between the tables
Speaking to a drunken audience high nonsensical words;

(W. B. Yeats)[1]

No account of Anglo-Irish literature can be complete without some attention to the question of its relation to Gaelic culture, the nineteenth-century decline of Gaelic as a vernacular, and the movement to revive it. An inspection of most books in the field will readily establish that such an attention is rarely granted. In so far as Anglo-Irish studies have been dominated by American and British critics, or by specialists whose academic training has steered them away from the necessary competence in the Gaelic language, this state of affairs can only be noted in silence. There is in addition, however, a symptomatic value in the studious neglect of Gaelic: it mutely signals the extent to which Anglo-Irish literature required the eclipse of Gaelic culture, and signals also the conflicting assumption of self-sufficiency on the part of the Gaelic Revival movement.

The movement associated with the foundation of the Gaelic League in 1893 should be seen in a European perspective of at least a century in duration. The underlying assumptions of the Gaelic Revival, in relation to nationality, culture, and language, form a distinctive part of the legacy of German romanticism. Doubtless there are unique and local factors at work in the Irish experience, just as the romantic origins of its philosophical formulation are not exclusively German. Nevertheless, the name of Johann Gottfried von Herder economically focuses the drastically new view of language initiated by his publication in 1772 of *On the Origins of Speech*. The comparative study of philology, which developed from Herder's work, in turn gave rise to the indefatigable industry of Celtic philologists (many of them German).

---

[1] W. B. Yeats, 'Beautiful Lofty Things', *Collected Poems* (London: Macmillan, 1963), p. 348.

There is no doubt that scholarship in the area of Celticism constitutes perhaps the most refined and intellectually demanding exercise of the academic mind, but this should not blind us to the specific ideological and historic origins and affiliations of the discipline. No more than Practical Criticism, or sociology, can Celticism boast of an immaculate conception.

Professor Edward Said has written a provocative and persuasive analysis of the ideological investment of European colonial and imperial ambitions in the academic study of *Orientalism*.[2] No comparable account of Celticism exists, nor indeed is there even any extensive history of the study of the Celtic languages written from within the assumptions of the discipline. There are certainly overlapping areas of impact — the poets who wove the Oriental theme into their work included (with Byron, de Nerval, etc.) Thomas Moore whose *Lalla Rookh* was published in 1817. More substantially, Yeats's early use of Indian imagery does have a specific (if concealed) line of communication with the British interest in the Indian Empire. These will seem isolated examples and unconvincing as such, for our criticism has inculcated in us a respect for the luminous integrity of texts, which are merely sullied by attempts to string up lines of communication with the equally atomized world of events. The totality lying behind the romantics' exploitation of the East, or the modernist commitment to the primitive, can only be recovered by the incorporation of every aspect of human production, behaviour, and speculation into a comprehensive history. Such an endeavour is repeatedly jeopardized by the discovery of potent, guilty, silences — questions which cannot be asked, let alone answered. Said enumerates a series of these in relation to 'western' attitudes to Arab culture, and a similar project is long overdue in the area of Celticism and the Gaelic revival which is its populist equivalent.

One Oriental theme which has a long and orthodox history in Europe, a history transformed and rendered problematic in the nineteenth century is, quite simply, Christianity. Three particular aspects of the notorious Victorian crisis of belief

---

[2]   Edward W. Said, *Orientalism* (London: Routledge and Kegan Paul, 1978).

deserve attention here, though their provenance lies well beyond that normally implied by the term 'Victorian'. With the undermining of religious faith as a philosophical position, the sense of comprehensibility which religion had provided was in part replaced by an increased valorization of *race* as the living guarantee of the reality of the past and the cohesion of a secular society. The erudition of Ernest Renan and the violent irrationality of Julius Langbehn were alike assimilable to the nineteenth-century preoccupation with race, and Renan is particularly relevant in that his scholarly interests included Celtic literature.[3] A further area of comparison between France and Ireland might be identified in the doctrines of political messianism optimistically enounced by Edgar Quinet in 1848 and the pervasive symbolism of messianic sacrifice and redemption found in Patrick Pearse's life and works.[4] Finally, and more familiarly, in Matthew Arnold (and others) there is the investment in literature and in culture generally of the sublime Hope which religious belief had previously entertained. All three of these aspects of Christian decline have a bearing on the emergence of Anglo-Irish literature and its relations with Celticism.

1. ERNEST RENAN AND MATTHEW ARNOLD

Ernest Renan (1823-92) is best known in the English speaking world as the author of the *Vie de Jésus* (1863), a humanist biographico-romance which led one inspired reader to deplore the absence of a climactic marriage at the end of the story. Renan had studied for the priesthood, and his abandonment of the Church resulted from doubts raised by his philological study of the scriptures. Essentially a humanist who perceived definite laws of progress in Nature and Man, he embarked on a vast examination of the evolution of languages, cultures, and religions as manifestations of the

[3] For Langbehn and the German strand of racist thought see George L. Mosse, *The Crisis of German Ideology: Intellectual Origins of the Third Reich* (London: Weidenfeld and Nicolson, 1970). Said deals quite extensively with Renan's orientalist preoccupations.

[4] See in this connection Ceri Crossley, 'Edgar Quinet and Messianic Nationalism in the Years preceding 1848', in Francis Barker *et al.*, edd., *1848: The Sociology of Literature* (Chelmsford: University of Essex, 1978), pp. 265-76.

development of the human mind. Philosophically he owed much to Hegel, and while he spoke respectfully of science he was no positivist of the Comtean kind. In turning to examine the remains of Celtic civilization within France, he had available to him conventions as to the desolate beauty of Brittany but his treatment of them is distinctive:

> Every one who travels through the Armorican peninsula experiences a change of the most abrupt description ... A cold wind arises full of a vague sadness, and carries the soul to other thoughts; the tree tops are bare and twisted ... a sea that is almost always sombre girdles the horizon with eternal moaning. The same contrast is manifest in the people: to Norman vulgarity, to a plump and prosperous population ... succeeds a timid and reserved race living altogether within itself, heavy in appearance but capable of profound feeling, and of an adorable delicacy in its religious instincts. A like change is apparent, I am told ... when one buries oneself in the districts of Ireland where the race has remained pure from all admixture of alien blood. It seems like entering on the subterranean strata of another world, and one experiences in some measure the impression given us by Dante, when he leads us from one circle of his Inferno to another.[5]

The essentially linguistic term Celtic is here seen almost fully clothed in its new usage — the Celts are a race, living virtually outside history, materially disadvantaged but, wonderfully spiritual and poetical. Although 'reserved' and 'living altogether within itself', this race is in practice established by a process of comparison — the Celt is different from the Norman or the Briton, he lacks certain attributes of these more mundanely successful races and possesses other characteristics in greater proportion or in an intenser form, *by comparison.* The Celt vicariously maintains a piety and nobility now rendered impossible for Norman and Briton obliged to live in the world of time, happiness, plenty, and vulgarity. He is a godsend.

Renan's evocation of the Celtic other-world is punctuated with comments which acknowledge to some degree the strategies at work. Its religious genius is noteworthy because 'nowhere has the eternal *illusion* clad itself in more seductive

---

[5] Ernest Renan, *Poetry of the Celtic Races and Other Essays,* trans. W. G. Hutchinson (London, [1896]), pp. 1-2.

hues' [my emphasis]; and, for all its eternality, 'alas! it too is doomed to disappear, this emerald set in the Western seas.'[6] Seductive appearance, spirituality, impermanence — it is not surprising to find that the Celt has a distinctive place in the sexuality of politics:

> If it be permitted us to assign sex to nations as to individuals, we should have to say without hesitance that the Celtic race . . . is an essentially feminine race. No other has conceived with more delicacy the ideal of woman, or been more fully dominated by it. It is a sort of intoxication, a madness, a vertigo.[7]

Sex, nationhood, and race blur in this passage in a manner which is not characteristic of Renan, but still characteristic of the intellectual movement of which he was usually a more cautious proponent. It is at first reassuring to read that race, though 'of capital importance to the student who occupies himself with the history of mankind . . . has no application in politics'.[8] Renan's concern with race, then, is to be seen as part of a historical enterprise without any practical application in contemporary affairs: it is a category of research and not an objective. Yet the difference between this academicism and the followers of Langbehn is less great than first appears: the practical racists simply deny that there is a politics other than that of race, and Renan's research ultimately is no counter to the philosophical application of Zyklon.

Poetry of the Celtic Races indicates one strand of European thought in mid-century already evident in rough narrative form in Lever's *Luttrell of Arran*. Districts of Ireland where the race has remained pure from all admixture of alien blood provide the guilty, harassed gentleman of the world with a bride, and will provide his son with another: the virtue of Arran, sullied by John Luttrell's intervention, will be restored by his son's marriage to his cousin/sister. Through the lectures of Henri d'Arbois de Jubainville which J. M. Synge attended at the Collège de France in 1898, Renan and Lever are held in continuity with the more renowned Aran of the

---

[6] Ibid., p. 2.
[7] Ibid., p. 8.
[8] Ibid., p. 74; this quotation comes from the essay 'What is a Nation?'

Celtic Revival. More than any figure of his generation Synge was aware of the bearing, not to say overbearing, of Herder, Renan, the *Revue celtique*, and *Zeitschrift fur Celtische Philologie* on the local endeavours of Douglas Hyde, Tomás O Criomhthain, and others.[9]

Renan's essays then form a meeting point between the high sophistication of comparative philology as developed in Germany, France, and Britain from the initiative of Herder, and the popular perception of a Celtic fringe as an aesthetic survival in the industrial age. German scholarship has its part in that transition, but is less immediately documentable in its ideological negotiations. In Britain, where philology was dominated by Max Müller and the controversies he excited, Celticism became not so much an academic discipline — though there are important Welsh, Manx, and Scots Gaelic areas of inquiry — as it became the idiom of a new exchange between the elements of the United Kingdom, notably in the great election of 1868.

Matthew Arnold's Oxford lectures *On the Study of Celtic Literature* (published 1867) stand at a junction between the German philology of Zeuss and Meyer and the 'Celtic Twilight' of Yeats. Though Arnold begins with memories of a holiday in Llandudno, and alludes to conditions in Ireland, the real source of his inspiration is Renan's essay on Celtic poetry, at that time as yet untranslated into English.[10] These lectures, together with the later *Irish Essays* (1882) present a fascinating insight into changing British attitudes towards Ireland. Notoriously, Arnold speaks of the Celt 'always ready to react against the despotism of fact' but, as he acknowledges, the phrase properly belongs to Henri Martin.[11] The Gallic debt should not persuade us that Arnold is here indulging yet another of his preferences for continental authority so as to show up the paucity of local examples: Arnold's Celticism is British through and through in its priorities and in its objective function, but his allusion to

[9] See Declan Kiberd, *Synge and the Irish Language* (London: Macmillan, 1979).

[10] Matthew Arnold, *Lectures and Essays in Criticism*, ed. R. H. Super (Ann Arbor: University of Michigan, 1962).

[11] Ibid., p. 344 n.

Henri Martin neatly indicates that Celticism is a strategy not exclusively British.

Seamus Deane has remarked the *racial* connotations of Arnold's vocabulary, and this is only to be expected given its sources and antecedents. It is however an oversimplification to suggest that 'Celtic Ireland did not in fact die with Lady Morgan or with Thomas Moore. It simply removed itself to England, encased in Burke's capacious reputation, then blossomed there again in Arnold's essays.'[12] The opening of *On the Study of Celtic Literature* dramatizes the diverse elements in Arnold's strategy: echoes of Renan and Burke are simultaneously adjusted so as to produce a new synthetic and British Celticism:

> The summer before last I spent some weeks at Llandudno, on the Welsh coast. The best lodging-houses at Llandudno look eastward, towards Liverpool . . . At last one turns round and looks westward. Everything is changed. Over the mouth of the Conway and its sands is the eternal softness and mild light of the west; the low line of the mystic Anglesey, and the precipitous Penmaenmawr, and the great group of Carnedd Llewelyn and Carnedd David and their brethren fading away, hill behind hill, in an aerial haze, make the horizon; between the foot of Penmaenmawr and the bending coast of Anglesey, the sea, a silver stream, disappears one knows not whither. On this side Wales, — Wales, where the past still lives, where every place has its tradition, every name its poetry, and where the people, the genuine people, still knows this past, this tradition, this poetry, and lives with it, and clings to it; while, alas, the prosperous Saxon on the other side, the invader from Liverpool and Birkenhead, has long ago forgotten his. And the promontory where Llandudno stands is the very centre of this tradition; it is Creuddyn, *the bloody city*, where every stone has its story . . .[13]

The rhetorical exploitation of a topographical stage has rarely been so strenuously attempted. As in Renan's opening paragraph, the scene is divided between a prosperous horizon represented by lodging-houses (temporary dwellings) and an eternal horizon represented by the philology of stones, places, names. Arnold's second paragraph is just as deft in its manœuvres:

---

[12] Seamus Deane, 'An Example of Tradition', *Crane Bag*, vol. 3, No. 1 (1979), p. 46.

[13] Matthew Arnold, op. cit., p. 291.

As I walked up and down, last August year, looking at the waves as
they washed this Sigeian land which has never had its Homer ...
suddenly I heard, through the stream of unknown Welsh, words, not
English, indeed, but still familiar. They came from a French nursery-
maid with some children. Profoundly ignorant of her relationship,
this Gaulish Celt moved among her British cousins, speaking her polite
neo-Latin tongue, and full of compassionate contempt, probably, for
the Welsh barbarians and their jargon. What a revolution was here![14]

It is not excessive to see the maid as Arnold's reworking of
Burke's Marie Antoinette, and indeed what a revolution there
is in such a transformation. The maid is royal Celt compared
with her hosts, the incomprehensible Welsh: for Arnold, she
speaks a language which can be variously related to that
which he speaks and that which he hears around him at the
Llandudno eisteddfod. In the strict sense, then, he is not
racialist in his thinking in that he stresses the fusion of
peoples and the reduction of linguistic frontiers:

The fusion of all the inhabitants of these islands into one homogeneous,
English-speaking whole, the breaking down of barriers between us, the
swallowing up of separate provincial nationalities, is a consummation to
which the natural course of things irresistibly tends; it is a necessity of
what is called modern civilisation, and modern civilisation is a real,
legitimate force ...[15]

The function of the Celtic element in this homogeneous
United Kingdom is clear — as with Renan, Arnold sees the
Celt as poetically unsuccessful, spiritually intense but dis-
organized, an embellishment without which 'the Philistinism
of our Saxon nature' would be intolerable.[16] Celticism is,
therefore, part and parcel of the larger campaign mounted in
Culture and Anarchy, a campaign directed against middle-
class Philistines in high places. In 1865 when Arnold delivered the lectures — and even more so in 1867 when they
were published — the Celtic lands of Wales and Ireland
distinguished themselves drastically. Wales, as the holiday
interlude demonstrates, is happily non-political: all that can
be safely said of contemporary Ireland is hedged in regret:

[14] Ibid., p. 292.
[15] Ibid., pp. 296–7.
[16] Ibid., p. 295.

I know my brother Saxons, I know their strength, and I know that the Celtic genius will make nothing of trying to set up barriers against them in the world of fact and brute force, of trying to hold its own against them as a political and social counter-power, as the soul of a hostile nationality. To me there is something mournful (and at this moment, when one sees what is going on in Ireland, how well may one say so!) in hearing a Welshman or an Irishman make pretensions, — natural pretensions, I admit, but how hopelessly vain! — to such a rival self-establishment . . .[17]

It is striking how little of contemporary Ireland Arnold allows his readers to see, allows himself in contrast to the panorama of Llandudno. Though he had been private secretary to the Marquis of Lansdowne when that great Irish land-owner was Lord President of the Council in Lord Russell's government (1846-52), Arnold knew nothing of Ireland at first hand. The despotism of fact was unlikely to influence his view of the Irish Celts whom he increasingly identified with Irish Catholics. Indeed, the central strategy of Arnold's Celticism is not racial in any sense that Langbehn would have accepted, but a modernized synthesis of imperialist and sectarian tactics. A most revealing passage in *On the Study of Celtic Literature* demonstrates the way in which comparative philology could be turned to such purposes, and in the course of it we see how unconsciously Arnold accepts the government of India as a Saxon responsibility, a matter of 'brute fact':

when Mr. Whitley Stokes, one of the very ablest scholars formed in Zeuss's school, a born philologist, — he now occupies, alas! a post under the Government of India, instead of a chair of philology at home, and makes one think mournfully of Montesquieu's saying, that had he been an Englishman he should never have produced his great work, but have caught the contagion of practical life, and devoted himself to what is called 'rising in the world', — when Mr. Whitley Stokes, in his edition of *Cormac's Glossary*, holds up the Irish word *triath*, the sea, and makes us remark that, though the names *Triton, Amphitrite,* and those of corresponding Indian and Zend divinities, point to the meaning *sea*, yet it is only Irish which actually supplies the vocable, how delightfully that brings Ireland into the Indo-European concert![18]

[17] Ibid., p. 298.
[18] Ibid., p. 334.

It is a pity that the proponents of Practical Criticism shunned the examination of such prose passages as this, for the very shape of the sentences is instinct with subliminal meanings — consider how the regret at Stokes's purely useful exile in India, followed by the allusion to French authority, postpones and then sanctions the bringing of Ireland into the concert; and consider how gracefully 'concert' serves to indicate and conceal what modes of incorporation are ultimately invoked.

Though Arnold emphasizes what he regards as the Celtic element in English literature, and reveres the sanctity and poetry of the Celtic genius, it goes without saying that his assumed norm is industrial, nineteenth-century England. This may seem paradoxical in the author of *Culture and Anarchy,* the apostle of European culture to a philistine people, but the comparative study of Celt and Saxon obliges him to take up a distinct position. The 'steady-going habit' of the Saxon leads up at last 'to the comprehension and interpretation of the world', a world fortunately supplied with 'doors that open, windows that shut, locks that turn, razors that shave, coats that wear, watches that go, and a thousand more such good things . . . the invention of the Philistines'.[19] Flippancy cannot be dismissed as irrelevance, and the drift of Arnold's totting-up of the comprehended world is that it is the world of commodities, all that the Celt has been blessedly unable to master. Thus Celticism serves not only to impose a certain identity on the Irish who are seen entirely outside history and outside any rudimentary sociology, it also serves to legitimize the activities of British industrial capitalism in the world. Far from being the soul of national resistance Celticism, as Arnold presents it, is a consolation, anodyne, or opium.

2.   STANDISH O'GRADY

One of the irritating and yet instructive features of Irish cultural life in the nineteenth century is the proliferation of similar or identical names among different individuals.

[19]   Ibid., p. 348.

Savants are irritated by the outsider's confusion of George Thomas Stokes (author of *Ireland and the Celtic Church*) and Whitley Stokes (co-editor of *Thesaurus Paleohibernicus*), or the fusion of Standish Hayes O'Grady (1832–1915) and Standish James O'Grady (1846–1928). Outsiders, on the other hand, are more likely to inquire as to the significance of this repetitious pattern. More closely defined, the area involved was the Protestant gentry and professional middle-class, a small and energetic aspect of Irish society. It is easy to accept the elevated and self-referring memoirs of members of this élite at face value, but Victorian Ireland was in practice a more various and complex society than is often admitted. Reiterated names indicated a desire to confirm identity and demonstrate continuity, just as the acquisition of property and a country 'place' enacted the need for secur-ity. In the aftermath of the Famine, and the Encumbered Estates Court sales of property, William Wilde built a villa on the shores of Lough Corrib, and named it Moytura after the legendary battle of the gods and aboriginal Irish. He and his wife christened their famous son, Oscar Fingall O'Flahertie Wills Wilde.

When Lord Chacellor Fitzgibbon and Dr Patrick Duigenan conducted their visitation in Trinity College early in 1798, the central figure in their investigation was Whitley Stokes (1763–1845), then a fellow of the college attached to the medical school. Stokes had been friendly with members of the United Irishmen, including Wolfe Tone, and was sus-pended from his fellowship for two years. Whether or not Lever had Stokes in mind as he wrote in *Luttrell of Arran* of subversion and discrimination in 'the Irish university' is an unanswerable question, but by the time the novel was published the Stokes family — like the fictional Luttrells — were looking towards the west of Ireland for mental susten-ance. William Wilde led a party from the British Association to the Aran Islands in 1857 which included Samuel Ferguson, George Petrie, and William Stokes, son of the suspect United Irishman. While Lever's novel contributes to one transform-ation of the United Irishmen in the Victorian imagination by inserting an aristocratic participation in his fictionalizing of the movement, the descendants of those essentially middle-class radicals were channelling their disaffection with the Union into antiquarianism. William Stokes of 1857 was by profession a medical man and his antiquarian interests were those of a gifted amateur; his son, Whitley Stokes (1830–1909), completed the transformation in classic style by combining a career in the Indian civil service with a brilliant scholarly achievement as Celticist. Practical orientalism and philological rigour come together in a paradigm of 'patriotism without nationalism'.

It would be wrong to dismiss such patterns as simply the haphazard product of a small community. They are neither accidental at the social level nor deliberate at the biographical level. Instead they should be seen as visible features of a largely concealed totality in which the broader activities of the United Kingdom of Great Britain and Ireland take place. One insistent advocate of this latter point of view was Standish James O'Grady who — it must be conceded — was as much victim as author of the politics he espoused. Here again, the duplicity of names is symptomatic — while Standish O'Grady (as I shall call *him* exclusively) was a historical explorer, novelist, and political propagandist, his cousin Standish Hayes O'Grady was a meticulous Celticist, editor of *Silva Gadelica* (2 vols., 1892). In the O'Gradys the immaculate non-politics of Celticism sets off its opposite like the distant explosion caused by a serene grenadier.

Standish O'Grady (1846–1928) was born in County Cork, at Castletown Berehaven. His father, Viscount Guillamore, was rector there, but the boy's education at the local school and Tipperary Grammar School, followed by Trinity College Dublin and the Irish bar, was not the usual course for one of his class. In 1899 he recorded a more pertinent educational experience:

I think I was in my 24th year when something happened which has since then governed the general trend of my life, and through me that of others. In a country house in the west of Ireland, near the sea, I had to stay indoors one rainy day, and though my appetite for literature was slender enough then, in default of other amusements I spent the time in looking over the books in the library. So I chanced upon O'Halloran's History of Ireland, in three volumes — the first History of Ireland into which I had ever looked. He wrote, I think, in the second decade of this century and before the rise of the Vallency School.[20]

Although the material is obscure to most readers, here is a dramatic conflict between the significance of form and that of content. Psychologically, the passage conforms to many of the conventions of the evangelical testimony — the inauspicious occasion, previous ignorance, the chanced-upon all-changing text. Such considerations might prompt the inquiry as to why the Anglo-Irish Revivial was called a 'revival' — is it not in several of its personalities (Yeats, Synge, and O'Grady himself, and in a varied form, Lady Gregory) the achievement of displaced Irish evangelicals? Certainly, on the basis of the passage quoted, O'Grady is likely to fare better in a discussion of formal rhetoric than of intellectual content, for his remarks on Sylvester O'Halloran and Charles Vallancy are a tissue of impossible dates.[21]

Fired by his reading of O'Halloran, and later of Eugene O'Curry, O'Grady became a Victorian Sage. Carlyle and Marx featured in his reading as diversely as polemic, fiction, history, and journalism featured in his writing. It is easier to classify his work without regard to genre, and then subsequently to consider his drastic demolition of generic distinctions in the light of his outlook. First, O'Grady became preoccupied with early Irish history and epical material: in this area he wrote what purported to be histories as well as ostensibly fictional material set in this historical setting. Second — and this is not a chronological list of O'Grady's works — there are his various writings on Elizabethan Ireland, including his edition of *Pacata Hibernica*, a contemporary account of the war in Munster. Finally, there are his polemical works commencing with *The Crisis in Ireland* (1882)

---

[20] Standish O'Grady, *Selected Essays and Passages*, ed. Ernest A. Boyd (Dublin: Talbot Press [n.d.]), p. 3. The quotation comes from a fragmentary autobiography, 'A Wet Day', first published in *The Irish Homestead* in 1899.

[21] For O'Grady's carelessness and unreliability as a scholar see V. H. S. Mercier, 'Don Quixote as Scholar: The Sources of Standish James O'Grady's *History of Ireland*', *Long Room*, vols. 22/23 (Spring/Autumn 1981), pp. 19-24. In this particular connection, note that Sylvester O'Halloran's *General History of Ireland* was published in 1774, and Charles Vallancey published what the *DNB* rightly calls 'worthless tracts on Irish philology and history, 1772-1802'.

and including the editing of *The Kilkenny Moderator* and the
All Ireland Review.

O'Grady has been called the father of the Anglo-Irish
revival, and in this regard his versions of the Cuchulain
epic have a historical importance in their influence upon
Lady Gregory and hence on W. B. Yeats.[22] His writings on
Elizabethan Ireland are extensively cast in stories and novels
of an adventurous kind, principally intended for a juvenile
readership. But the distinctions between history and fiction
are jeopardized in the telling inscriptions O'Grady regularly
added to presentation copies of his books. *Red Hugh's
Captivity* (1889) is described in its subtitle as 'A Picture of
Ireland, Social and Political in the Reign of Queen Elizabeth',
but an inscription added by O'Grady on the copy he presented
to John Quinn reads 'This book is history very slightly
dramatized and historical fiction', a remark which can hardly
have guided the recipient excessively. On the other hand, *The
Bog of Stars* (1893) is annotated by the author 'All the
tales . . . may be read as History except the first . . .'. Or
again, *The Story of Ireland*:

I wrote this outline of Irish history rapidly in less than a month;
looking up no authority during its composition except for the Battle
of the Boyne. I wrote it thinking that the things I remembered because
I felt an interest in them, might be interesting to the reader.[23]

This is hardly encouraging to those who are in search of a
literary history in which some kind of methodological
procedure will be maintained. And yet O'Grady, for all his
slipshod enthusiasm and missionary heat, is a useful indicator
of the interactions of Ascendancy and Celticism in the last
quarter of the nineteenth century.

'The things I remembered because I felt an interest in
them, might be interesting to the reader . . .'. True it is
merely an annotation hastily scribbled perhaps as he posted

---

[22] See Ernest A. Boyd's *Ireland's Literary Renaissance* (New York: John
Lane, 1916), pp. 26-54; V. H. S. Mercier points to O'Grady's acknowledgement
of a debt to Whitley Stokes's edition and translation of one Cuchulain source in
the *Revue celtique*; see Mercier, loc. cit., p. 21.

[23] These transcripts of O'Grady's annotations are printed in John R.
McKenna, 'The Standish O'Grady Collection at Colby College: a Checklist',
Colby Library Quarterly, series 4, vol. 16 (November 1958), pp. 291-303.

the book to John Quinn in America. Nevertheless, it implies
a greater importance lying in the subjective consideration of
material than in the material *per se*: clearly O'Grady as
historian has no truck with the von Ranke school of documented fact. In a further annotation on a copy of *In the
Gates of the North* (1901), O'Grady comments: 'As to
the manner of composition — I read all the old stories of
Cuculain that I could find and the tale found here just
emerged out of the consequent memories and meditations'.[24]
(Original emphasis). No historical writing of any worth descends direct from the facts in a simple and wholly straight-
forward manner — so much may be agreed. But O'Grady's
recurrent emphasis on the emergence of his writing 'out of
the consequent memories and meditations' which follow his
encounter with the latter-day evidences of history should be
distinguished from any dialectical notion of history as
mediation. As the passage recording his first discovery of
Irish history (or was it literature? He is unsure) O'Grady's
forte is a kind of style. He admires the heroic gesture of
Cuchulain, and is uninterested in the distinction between
myth and chronicle. The validity of words is established by
the memories they evoke; time is essentially conceived as the
barrier between inner and outer worlds rather than the index
of change and process in an objective social existence.

   A predictable assessment of Standish O'Grady is that,
in attempting many things, he failed in all. As a scholar he
is frankly incompetent; as a novelist, he is concerned only
with rudimentary aspects of the form; as a political writer, he
is intermittently loud and silent. A more telling analysis
might suggest that O'Grady symbolized in an uncanny way
an incompleteness of social character which is highly relevant
to the consequences of the ideology of Protestant Ascendancy. The O'Gradys of Limerick (where the family originated) were emerging in the years from 1820 onwards as a
politically powerful and active family.[25] His father having
taken holy orders, Standish O'Grady grew up in Castletown
Berehaven rectory at a time when the Church, as a profession

[24] Ibid., p. 295.
[25] See R. B. McDowell, *Public Opinion and Government Policy in Ireland,
1801–1846* (London: Faber, 1952), pp. 43–44.

and a source of income, was staggering out of the disaster of the Tithe War and staggering towards Disestablishment. The family's legal background in the late eighteenth century placed them above the level of corporation politics where Protestant Ascendancy first took root, but landlordism on a small scale combined with dependence on a clerical income in the nineteenth steered the O'Gradys (or at least this branch of them) precisely towards those areas of Irish society in which the metamorphoses of Protestant Ascendancy were to take place. With an irony I fear unconscious, O'Grady's political writings expose the pretensions of Protestant Ascendancy in late Victorian days while his researches into the past demonstrate the allurement of Celticism at its least rigorous. These alternating commitments in his work are as it were the rival identities between which he never ultimately chose, not out of weakness but out of an apprehension of their partial unreality. The Standish O'Grady we meet in Yeats's writings is largely a creation of the poet's, the poet having experienced a similar self-division but having also pressed it to the point of dramatic confrontation.

Absurdity is all too easy to find in O'Grady. Take the episode of his editing *The Kilkenny Moderator*: in 1898, O'Grady took control of this thoroughly obscure and undistinguishedly loyal newpaper at the behest of a local magnate, Otway Cuffe, heir to the earldom of Desart, and within months he had involved his patron and his paper in a tea-cup scandal touching upon two continents. At the height of the Boer War, O'Grady decided to recruit an embryonic army through whom Irish consciousness might assert itself: with the militia training to fight for the British in the Transvaal and an 'Irish Brigade' recruiting support for the Boers, O'Grady was obliged to look elsewhere for his recruits and lighted upon the Church Lads Brigade, the Boys' Brigade, and the local Foxhounds. So far, the business was merely pathetic, but when the Colonel of the Kilkenny Militia was discovered to have appropriated £6,000 from the Desart estate (of which he had been agent) local passions were raised. The Bishop of Ossory then invited the Colonel (in his official capacity) to address a review of the Church Lads Brigade, and O'Grady's newspaper intervened wrathfully:

We are not at war with the Bishop but with the great and dominant social power in our midst, reaching up to the Throne and down to the smallest Kilkenny huxter, a power which has almost obliterated a sense of honour and public morality in the minds of a few and dulled and paralysed the conscience of the community . . .[26]

The great power was the Marquis of Ormonde who had indeed been recently visited by the future George V and his wife and was shortly to receive Edward VII and his queen. Not surprisingly libel writs were thick in the air. O'Grady had earlier accused the Marquis of neglecting important political interests, and the Church Lads Brigade provided a convenient but ludicrous focus for the quarrel. More coldly considered, however, the episode exposed the largely decorative nature of Irish class terminology and the futility of cultural enterprise within the preserves of what was assumed to be the Protestant Ascendancy. It was O'Grady, however, rather than the Marquis who represented the Ascendancy, and his class rather than any residual aristocracy which led the movement known as the Celtic Revival.

O'Grady's political writings *per se* commenced with *The Crisis in Ireland* (1882) in which he exhorted the landowners — or ex-landowners as they were soon to be — to take real heed of the existence and reality of the Land League and the epochal changes implied for Irish society. This was followed by *Toryism and the Tory Democracy* (1886) in which he took his lead from Randolph Churchill's perception of the conservatives' need to protect landlordism from a combination of capital and labour: this extended pamphlet is classically evangelical in its approach, addressing Irish landlords first as a group and then singling out one nameless representative who is earnestly exhorted to take up his cross. The third political booklet, *All Ireland* (1898), deals with the revelations of the Childers Commission, a governmental body whose report proved the over-taxing of Ireland under the Union by a gross amount. All three works, in common with the novels and the 'histories' are obsessed with the notion of leadership, a quality singularly absent in the Ireland O'Grady

---

[26] My source for this incident, and quotations from the *Kilkenny Moderator*, is Hubert Butler, 'Anglo-Irish Twilight: the Last Ormonde War', *Journal of the Butler Society*, vol. 1, No. 8 (1978/9), pp. 631–41.

sees around him, where no one is willing to forgo simple
pleasures in order to assume the role of national saviour. Two
subsidiary elements, however, are in truth of great significance — the first is O'Grady's recurrent attention to the
condition of Irish aristocracy, and the second is his recurring
metaphor of illusion.

In his introduction to *Pacata Hibernica* (1896) he condemned as doubly false 'Mr Froude's picture of the upright,
God-fearing, and civilized Englishman contending against a
flood of Celtic barbarism' in the Tudor period.[27] The Celtic
element, identified here with the Irish population as a whole,
is seen as elevated, civilized, and yet demotic. And when
he is seeking to explain the condition of Ireland under the
Union, he alludes to 'The Stupefaction of the Ultonians',
one of his favourite episodes from primitive literature in
which a great enchantment is at work:

> The political understanding of Ireland to-day is under a spell and its
> will paralysed. If proof be demanded for this startling assertion, how
> can proof to any good result be supplied? It is the same spellbound
> understanding which will consider the proof.[28]

The imagery of spells, enchantments, and phantoms pervades
the entire work, and the operations of ideology are well
described in such terms:

> We worship phantoms, and phantoms powerless *per se* once worshipped
> — so they tell me — become endowed with a terrible and malignant
> vitality and activity ... Heavy as lead, cold as death, the Great En-
> chantment obsesses the soul of the land, and not one but all classes lie
> supine under its sway — supine under the fanning of gigantic wings.
>
> It covers the whole land, every class and order of men in this Island
> are held inescapably in the grip of that dead hand. With such a docu-
> ment in our possession as the Report of the Childers Commission, with
> such a preponderating political power as ours, and with such hosts of
> good British friends, why can we do nothing? — strengthless, purpose-
> less and resourceless, as were the Ultonians sunk under the curse of the
> great mother and queen whom they had outraged, drowned in the
> avenging tides of that fountain of their life which they had polluted.[29]

---

[27] Standish O'Grady, *Selected Essays and Passages*, p. 163.

[28] Ibid., p. 174.

[29] Ibid., pp. 178-9.

Paralysis and pollution are metaphors which will reappear in more familiar contexts in Joyce's *Dubliners* and Yeats's 'Purgatory' — here at least their political sense is inescapable. Politics, in such a condition as he sees Ireland, is described by O'Grady in two further metaphors emphasizing the unreal or partly apprehended nature of reality — Ireland is confronted by 'the Veiled Player', or her cards are in the hands of 'the Unknown Dealer'. The implication O'Grady obsessively strives to convey is the hidden or but partly known nature of that which confronts him. The spells and enchantments which have woven this condition are located, he claims, in the imperial parliament, 'that seemingly august yet really absurd assembly'. Parliament is the forum of class conflict, says O'Grady, and class conflict detracts from the national unity which is required in the crisis. Yet, this contempt for class politics is followed immediately by the most passionate outburst of the essay in which a specific class is denounced at length:

> Aristocracies come and go like the waves of the sea; and some fall nobly and others ignobly. As I write, this Protestant Anglo-Irish aristocracy which, once owned all Ireland from the centre to the sea, is rotting from the land in the most dismal farce-tragedy of all time, without one brave deed, one brave word. Our last Irish aristocracy was Catholic, intensely and fanatically Royalist and Cavalier, and compounded of elements which were Norman-Irish and Milesian–Irish . . . Who laments the destruction of our present Anglo-Irish aristocracy? Perhaps in Ireland not one. They fall from the land while innumerable eyes are dry, and their fall will not be bewailed in one piteous dirge or one mournful melody.[30]

The meaning of ascendancy implies the inevitability of a fall, just as it had arisen like a star in the astrological charts. O'Grady's bitter condemnation of the Protestant Anglo-Irish aristocracy is remarkable in its total avoidance of the term Protestant Ascendancy, and its sarcastic insistence on the *aristocratic* status of the useless class under pressure. It remained to Yeats in particular to provide a suitable dirge and melody for the fall of the Protestant Ascendancy.

Ernest Boyd characterized O'Grady's politics as a 'detes-

[30] Ibid., pp. 180–1.

tation of triumphant commercialism'.[31] His separatism is
based on a rejection of middle-class hegemony in the Union,
and that founded on the notion that no such hegemony
operated in Irish society. Given the evidence of the rich shop-
keeper sailing at Kingstown while his son hunts with a
fashionable pack, 'the brewer and distiller, the successful
manufacturer and contractor, the stock-broker', such a
notion is at least unstable.[32] And at this point, the operations
of Celticism once again become evident, not as the regalia of
anti-imperialism but as the eternal source of an unassailable
aristocracy, unassailable because enchantingly unreal. In
George Bernard Shaw's *Man and Superman* (1903) Don Juan
observes that 'nothing is real here. That is the horror of dam-
nation.'[33] It would be rash to interpret Shaw as intending an
exposé of colonialism with its elaborate simulacrum of a
metropolitan society, its theatrical representations – in
Arnold's term – its concert. It would be rash so to interpret
Shaw, and yet he allows us to recall that curiously unnecess-
ary image in Renan's essay on Celtic poetry in which he
compares entrance into Brittany or Ireland to 'the impression
given us by Dante, when he leads us from one circle of his
Inferno to another'.[34] Truly it is Yeats's 'Purgatory' which
alone can rid us of such hellish notions.

[31] Ibid., 'Introduction', p. 16.
[32] Ibid., p. 203.
[33] Bernard Shaw, *Collected Plays with Their Prefaces*, vol. ii (London: Max
Reinhardt, the Bodley Head, 1971), p. 637.
[34] Ernest Renan, op. cit., p. 2.

ENTR'ACTE: MODERNISM, HISTORY, AND IRELAND

> It is a cramped little state with no foreign policy,
> Save to be thought inoffensive. The grammar of the language
> Has never been fathomed . . .
>
> (Richard Wilbur)[1]

The history of Marxist approaches to culture in recent years has seen a marked reluctance to endorse any single or universal theoretical perspective on the relation between literature and society, and this is indeed but a specific example of the re-examination of the much-abused model of base/superstructure which had dominated official pronouncements in this area.[2] The new interest in the work of the Frankfurt school, and that of Walter Benjamin, has provided a more penetrating and sophisticated account of the problem of historical necessity, and of the relationship of continuity to radical change.[3] Benjamin, in particular, stresses in 'Theses on the Philosophy of History' that 'thinking involves not only the flow of thoughts, but their arrest as well.'[4] For a

---

[1] Richard Wilbur, 'Shame', *Advice to a Prophet* (London: Faber, 1962), p. 33.

[2] The British discussion of the base/superstructure metaphor, while it has been invigorated recently by the work of Raymond Williams, was effectively initiated by E. P. Thompson in 'Socialist Humanism', *New Reasoner* (1957), vol. 1.

[3] The Frankfurt School is known in the English-speaking world principally through the work of Theodor Adorno, Max Horkheimer, Jurgen Habermas, Herbert Marcuse, and (more marginally) Walter Benjamin. Two anthologies are available — *The Essential Frankfurt School Reader*, edd. Andrew Arato and Eike Gebhardt (Oxford: Blackwell, 1978); *Critical Sociology*, ed. Paul Connerton (Harmondsworth: Penguin, 1976). The best critical account of the movement is Martin Jay, *The Dialectical Imagination: A History of the Frankfurt School and the Institute of Social Research 1923–50* (London: Heinemann, 1973). In addition to the various books by Adorno, Benjamin, and Habermas quoted elsewhere in this study, Adorno's essay on Arnold Schoenberg in *Philosophy of Modern Music*, trans. Anne G. Mitchell and Wesley V. Blomster (New York: Seabury Press, 1973), is most useful. The impact of Frankfurt on intellectual discussion in Ireland has been slight, though some traces of recent interest may be found in the various numbers of the Dublin-based journal *Crane Bag*.

[4] Walter Benjamin, 'Theses on the Philosophy of History', *Illuminations*, ed. and intro. Hannah Arendt, trans. Harry Zohn [n.p.]: Fontana/Collins, 1973), p. 264.

historical materialist such as Benjamin it follows that the same is true of history itself. Far from constituting an un-interrupted flow of events, history for him is conceptualized as specific and concrete movements, and discontinuities between these provide the opportunities for revolutionary intervention. The classic instance of such an opportunity is the year 1848.

Nineteenth-century Irish history — within the context of the United Kingdom — appears to break neatly into two such movements, with the Famine of the 1840s and its attendant political aspects acting as a demarcation line between the old and the new. Language change, emigration, and so forth are indicators of the contrast. Yet the younger Irish historians today are busy arguing for a recognition of the *moderniz-ation* of Irish society even before the Famine.[5] While this argument is ostensibly directed against an older, nationalist view that nothing flourished under the foreign yoke, it should be noted that the new historiography also serves to conceal the 'arrest' of history which Benjamin for one would require. Literary modernism, which follows so promptly in Ireland upon the heels of those modernizing developments documented by the historians, acts with a similar masking effect upon our engagement with the past. Yet it is character-istic of literature (and other forms of cultural production also) that, when subjected to a thorough critique, it yields up both its own strategies and the past it seeks to represent. In Ireland, where literature is pre-eminent among forms of cultural production and where literature has been long attuned to a so-called national psyche, the demarcation lines and discontinuities can be conveniently traced in psycho-logical terms.

One of the central experiences of Anglo-Irish literature is embarrassment. In narrative terms this may be traced in fictions of shame such as *Castle Rackrent, Uncle Silas* or, later, Somerville and Ross's *Big House of Inver*. As one advances through the nineteenth century and into the

---

[5] A useful introduction to this area is Joseph Lee, *The Modernisation of Irish Society 1848–1918* (Dublin: Gill and Macmillan, 1973). But compare the concept of modernization employed in Marshall Berman, *All that is Solid Melts into Air: The Experience of Modernity* (London: Verso, 1982).

twentieth, sectarianism translated into quasi-racial terms, provides a vocabulary for this theme. But, in a more basic sense, embarrassment characterizes that advance itself — embarrassment at the nearness of Yeats to Aubrey de Vere or William Larminie. So great a poet, so merely competent his precursors. Whether one focuses on Yeats or Joyce, poetry or prose or drama, the sequential history of Anglo-Irish literature reproduces these embarrassing antecedents. George Moore, in whom competence and greatness compete for attention, made such *frissons* the material of *Hail and Farewell* — 'dear Edward' Martyn, with his sublime folly, is truly a central idol in the Anglo-Irish pantheon. But for Yeats and Joyce a history of embarrassment became a matter of artistic pride, the pride of heroic overcoming in Yeats, of devious transfiguration in Joyce. This is not to deny the persistence of a problematic history in the work of both authors, but rather to emphasize the manner in which the two, considered as a binary and mutually dependent cultural production, confront the totality of history.

Taking up, say, McHugh and Harmon's *Short History of Anglo-Irish Literature from its Origins to the Present Day,* one encounters a sequence of discontinuities — the 'older civilization and its literature' (in Gaelic) . . . 'the Irish Literary Revival' (in English) . . . 'Contemporary Writing' (in English) . . .[6] When literary history accepts chronology as its model, unspoken and unanswered questions necessarily proliferate. Eighteenth-century antiquarianism, vigorously employed to bridge some of these discontinuities — is it not as much a German or British phenomenon as a 'Celtic' one? And beyond this particular issue, perhaps the most accessible general assumption is the unchallenged nationalism of such chronologies. Yet in noting the dislocation of Yeats and Joyce from Irish chronology we are really acknowledging their place in European modernism. To move from a discussion of Charles Lever to the work of Joyce, or from a discussion of early Irish lyrics to the poetry of Yeats, is to cross seismic lines of demarcation.

---

[6] Roger McHugh and Maurice Harmon, *Short History of Anglo-Irish Literature from its Origins to the Present Day* (Dublin: Wolfhound Press, 1982).

Modernism – the term is misleadingly unified. While it has its eighteenth-century usage, 'modernism' is decisively altered by the controversy within Catholicism which led in 1907 to *Pascendi gregis*, Pope Pius X's encyclical 'de modernistarum doctrinis'. Modernism, here, is a mode of theological inquiry according to which the Bible and the doctrines of the Church are examined in the light of modern thought. Far from being a unified philosophy or even a single attitude, modernism challenged such unities in a spirit of inquiry and disclosure. Marx, Nietzsche, and Freud were not so much advocates of modernist approaches as they were channels through which the historical moment of modernism was variously defined. The eclipse of the human individual as conscious and self-regulating shaper of his existence was a common element among these contending reinterpretations of human society. Literary modernism, it need hardly be remarked, manifested itself in different ways in Germany, Austro-Hungary, Italy, Britain, and America, and this largely in relation to the differing forms of individual consciousness in these societies.

Yeats and Joyce are exemplary in this multifarious context in that each denies his inherited orthodoxy and strives to re-create a specifically literary heterodoxy. But the orthodoxy they had lost was itself radically fractured, and fractured in a manner increasingly articulated as a sectarian sociology. A disproportionately large Irish contribution to English-language modernism is central to the elaboration in the nineteenth century of Protestant Ascendancy as ideology. In addition to the imperfect schism achieved by Yeats and Joyce in their rejection of (an already shattered) orthodoxy, it is worth noting that both were sons of men who had in their generation distanced themselves from the conventions and loyalties of their churches. Yeats and Joyce are not primary rebels in any simplistic Oedipal pattern, and when we come to study the father/son bond in Yeats's drama this factor should be recollected.

To return to broader matters, the comparison with English modernism is illuminating. Recognizing that Henry James, T. S. Eliot, and Ezra Pound remain essentially American figures (at least up to the moment of Christian conversion in

Eliot's case), and recognizing that Conrad cannot be domesti-
cated without great difficulty, and that E. M. Forster and
Ford Madox Ford were never really modernist in their practice (whatever their sensibility) — recognizing all that, we
are left with D. H. Lawrence and Virginia Woolf as English
modernists. Now, the important point relates not to their
marginal or exposed position within the dominant British
system (Lawrence as border-line lower middle-class, Woolf
as woman) but rather to the contrasting literary histories
into which English and Irish modernists might be placed.
Lawrence had Hardy and Dickens to look back to; and beyond that, Blake and even Milton provided lines of legitimate
descent. Virginia Woolf could cite Jane Austen, in addition
to her own family network. They had, in other words,
various means of disguising their exposed position even if
these did not soothe the wounds inflicted upon them by the
bourgeois suburbia of Edwardian Britain. In contrast, Yeats
and Joyce found the drafting of a literary pedigree highly
taxing. Joyce, in his early days, acknowledged debts to Defoe
and Blake, but his place in English literature can scarcely be
defined in terms of lineage.[7] Yeats, it is true, came to a
striking statement of the complexities of 'lineage' seen as
the symbol of literary tradition:

The 'Irishry' have preserved their ancient 'deposit' through wars which,
during the sixteenth and seventeenth centuries, became wars of extermination. No people, Lecky said at the opening of his *Ireland in
the Eighteenth Century*, have undergone greater persecution. Nor did
that persecution altogether cease up to our own day. No people hate as
we do in whom that past is always alive. There are moments when
hatred poisons my life and I accuse myself of effeminacy because I
have not given it adequate expression. It is not enough to have put it
into the mouth of a rambling peasant poet:

> You ask what I have found and far and wide I go,
> Nothing but Cromwell's house and Cromwell's murderous crew,
> The lovers and the dancers are beaten into the clay,

---

[7] For treatment of this question of Joyce's place in English literature see the
contributions of Philip Brockbank (pp. 166-84) and Timothy Webb (pp. 30-55),
in W. J. Mc Cormack and Alistair Stead, edd. *James Joyce and Modern Literature*
(London: Routledge and Kegan Paul, 1982).

And the tall men and the swordsmen and the horsemen
> where are they?
And there is an old beggar wandering in his pride
His fathers served their fathers before Christ was crucified.
> *O what of that, O what of that*
> *What is there left to say?*

Then I remind myself that though mine is the first English marriage I know of in the direct line, all my family names are English, and that I owe my soul to Shakespeare, to Spenser and to Blake, perhaps to William Morris, and to the English language in which I think, speak, and write, that everything I love has come to me through English; my hatred tortures me with love, my love with hate.[8]

The manner in which Yeats advances from the notion of a historical memory to details of his own family tree, and from that to a literary tradition incorporating Shakespeare and Blake is a graph of specific conceptual shifts in the background to Anglo-Irish literature and its emergent definition. The romantic organicism of the first stage (history to pedigree) is followed by the elaboration of a sequential literary chronology of the classic nineteenth-century kind, and this finally elevated in the passionate, Yeatsian antinomy of love and hate. The interpolated verse from 'The Curse of Cromwell' contributes far more than a mere illustration of hatred, or reason for hatred: being a imaginary translation from Gaelic it reflects with venom upon its own linguistic status as English. Moreover, the title of the poem also enacts a drastic transference — the dramatic speech which follows is *not* the curse but the words of one who is victim of Cromwell's curse. In all this we see the degree to which Yeats's employment of his own verse adds complexity to what is on the surface a casual commentary on the relation between art and history. The pseudo-translation, which is victim to its own title, encapsulates Yeats's own entanglement in the history he aspires to summarize.

---

[8] W. B. Yeats, 'A General Introduction for my Work', in Edward Callan, *Yeats on Yeats: The last Introductions and the 'Dublin' Edition* (Mountrath: Dolmen Press, 1981), New Yeats Papers, XX, p. 59–63. Callan's editing of the General Introduction is important in that he demonstrates Yeats's intention to include the lines from 'The Curse of Cromwell' (omitted in the standard text): see above, 'A Note on Sources and References'.

While Yeats became increasingly articulate on the topic of his own relation to Ireland as he advanced in years, Joyce's comments on such matters nearly all date from his apprenticeship as an author. Yet even a passage from 'Ireland, Island of Saints and Sages' (1907) can establish Joyce's antithetical relation to Yeats:

> to exclude from the present nation all who are descended from foreign families would be impossible, and to deny the name of patriot to all those who are not of Irish stock would be to deny it to almost all the heroes of the modern movement — Lord Edward Fitzgerald, Robert Emmet, Theobald Wolfe Tone and Napper Tandy, leaders of the uprising of 1798, Thomas Davis and John Mitchel, leaders of the Young Ireland movement, Isaac Butt, Joseph Biggar, the inventor of parliamentary obstructionism, many of the anticlerical Fenians, and finally, Charles Stewart Parnell.[9]

In due course these names will undergo different metamorphoses in Yeats's poetry (e.g. 'September 1913') and in *Finnegans Wake*. But whereas Yeats's citations are predominantly liturgical in form or intention, Joyce's historical allusions from 'Ivy Day in the Committee Room', the 'Cyclops' episode of *Ulysses*, to the *Wake* itself deliberately act upon the reader to demand of him that he relate once again the elements of his knowledge. This courteous insistence on the reader's active participation in the *work* of art generates a serene absence of kinetic anxiety in the prose — nothing is at risk in Joyce's prose. In *A Portrait of the Artist as a Young Man* the famous disquisition on 'funnel' and 'tun-dish' shows Joyce's fictional representative calmly acknowledging — in English — that the language belonged to the English Dean of Studies *before* it belonged to the Irish undergraduate. If this repeats the Yeatsian concern with the chronology of Irish history and the place of language

---

[9] James Joyce, 'Ireland, Island of Saints and Sages', in *Critical Writings*, edd. Ellsworth Mason and Richard Ellmann (New York: Viking Press, 1959), pp. 161-2. Dominic Manganiello, *Joyce's Politics* (London: Routledge and Kegan Paul, 1980), and Colin MacCabe, *James Joyce and the Revolution of the Word* (London: Macmillan, 1978), are the two most influential treatments of this topic: Manganiello concentrates on political attitude as announced by Joyce and his characters, while MacCabe is concerned with a post-modernist politics of writing. Neither pays much attention to the question of history.

displacement in that chronology, Joyce's fiction takes us further in highlighting some of the crucial strategies of Anglo-Irish modernism — its recourse to a 'primitive past' and a primitive hinterland, its invention of/dependence on a vestigial, other culture in the west. In this, as in many other respects, Joyce appears as a critical modernist, embodying in his own work a critique of the larger movement within which that work takes on its local significance.

This sense of modern embarrassment in the face of a nobler past is closely linked to Ireland's closely administered ability to give evidence of a primitive *ur*-culture within the United Kingdom. The Scottish clearances had too thoroughly affected the Gaels of North Briton, while the perseverance of the Welsh language was linked to 'progressive' features such as mining and Methodism. Only in Ireland did the demographic and economic developments of the nineteenth century permit the recognition of an endangered (and hence valorized) older culture open to aesthetic rather than industrial investment and exploitation. The Famine, far from paralleling the clearances, had the effect of rendering Irish linguistic change traumatic, and that will be shown to have immense repercussions within Joyce's prose. ('Uneven development' provides a classic Marxist account of the Irish question, and much could be said along these lines in relation to the economics of the United Kingdom: the transference of this dynamic into the cultural arena has been neglected however.) In relation to development and retardation, Ireland exemplified at many levels the identity of opposites, the paradox of the 'disunited kingdom', the sociology of Protestant Ascendancy. Pursuing an exhaustive account of the political unconscious in Conrad and others, Fredric Jameson has pointed to an uneven development, a non-synchronous overlap in Conrad's own values and experience (feudal Poland, capitalist England); and a reading of *Lord Jim, Heart of Darkness,* and *Nostromo* (fictions of colonial and imperial activity *par excellence*) would acknowledge that overlap.[10] Where Conrad is a special case, a unique biographical dossier,

---

[10] Fredric Jameson, *The Political Unconscious: Narrative as a Socially Symbolic Act* (London: Methuen, 1981), esp. pp. 206–80.

the Anglo-Irish modernists constitute a socially extensive and interrelated structure of cultural productions emanating from a far more central and crucial overlap within the terms of the most advanced capitalist and imperialist economy on the globe. In its very incompleteness, its inability to clothe the fissures in its ideological claims, Protestant Ascendancy is both the political and the unconscious element in this uneven development within the United Kingdom in the period leading up to High Capitalism's crisis in 1914–18, the period of modernist efflorescence.

From these preliminary remarks about the two great Anglo-Irish modernists upon which this inquiry soon will concentrate, it is possible to proceed to consider the altering shapes of historical experience involved in the shift from the generation of Maria Edgeworth to that of Joyce. A brief, comprehensive account of the shift could be summarized in tracing the changes in British capitalism from the era of the Napoleonic wars to that of J. M. Keynes, Earl Haig, Lenin, and Hitler. More locally, it seems of course that we are in touch with a concrete social reality when we watch John Giffard and his associates coin 'Protestant Ascendancy', or when we note Maria Edgeworth's use of her family history in the details of *Castle Rackrent* and *The Absentee*. There is a loss of this accessibility as the nineteenth century advances, and this despite the well-known attention of Yeats to the doings of his contemporaries, the well-known attention of Joyce to the minutiae of his native environment. What has really altered of course, in this question of accessibility, is the relation between the individual participant in the historical process and the possibility of articulating an account of this participation. The framework of the Protestant Ascendancy debates — whether in the Irish parliament or the Common Council of Dublin Corporation — is the third-person report, the seemingly olympian record of utterances and observations categorically distinct from those who utter and from those who hear and read. That epistemology is central to Maria Edgeworth's lifelong notion of fiction and fictional narrative — with the crucial exceptions of the narrator in *Castle Rackrent* and the final chapter of *The Absentee*. It is central but threatened, and the recourse to nomenclature in

the latter novel is a recognition of the complex interactions
between different levels of narration — contemporary or
historical, ethical or analytical — and between different areas
of reception, British, Irish, enlightened rationality, romantic
mythologizing, etc. In mid-century, the work of literature
which succeeds in establishing a critical dialectic of art and
reality does so by means of a highly organized reflexivity
(*Uncle Silas*) in which seemingly casual allusion (Chateaubriand, Courtenay, etc.) colludes with absent characterization. The striking instances of a 'concrete social reality' in
Le Fanu's fiction are precisely those details which do not
appear, those references which either float like unanchored
ectoplasm away from their contexts or which are suppressed
and denied. Those who cleave to the theory that history tells
us what actually happened are hampered by such theory
when the crucial questions revolve round the issue of what
palpably does not happen. And, as will become clear shortly,
the first emergence of a coherent Anglo-Irish literature comes
with the binary opposition of Yeats/Joyce in which the one
body of work opposes or qualifies the other. Protestant/
Catholic, therefore, is not simply a question of what happened in history, it is an aspect of generic form, of the
deployment of novel and lyric to the distinctive poles of a
sociology in which religious sect rather than class is increasingly invoked.

It is possible now to explain certain omissions from
Ascendancy and Tradition. First, we are not dealing with
'Joyce's attitude to history', which was, as it happens, fairly
conventional. We are instead concerned to distinguish between the rival forms of history encountered by, and in,
Yeats and Joyce. (Given this preference, there's an inevitable
avoidance of sequence in the modernist chapters — in no
important sense does Joyce come *after* Yeats.) Certainly,
Wilde and Synge offer an opportunity to relate comedy and
tragedy to specific political perspectives: certainly Moore
and Shaw provide similar opportunities to extend the discussion. The omission of these figures, however, does not
alter the discussion: instead it concentrates it upon central
issues — literary history, the Irish contribution to modernism,
the relation between the Emerald Isle and the Continent of

Europe. On the question of omissions, of course, the possibilities are limitless. Memoirs of the Protestant Ascendancy,
from Wynne's *An Irishman and his Family* (1937) to T. R.
Henn's *Five Arches: A Sketch for an Autobiography* (1980)
offer abundant evidence of the conceptual merger (conspiracy?) between a late nineteenth-century rural bourgeoisie
and its hypothetical eighteenth-century forebears to produce
another endangered aristocracy awaiting its laureate. Together with Shaw's sporadic autobiographical writings and
Elizabeth Bowen's gravely impressive *Bowenscourt*, these
might provide a further argument concerning the moments
of transition from encumbered estate to flourishing tradition.
Here, we shall concentrate on the concept of tradition itself,
its ambiguous place in modernist apologetics, and the construction of Yeats's particular tradition of Irish Augustanism.

  If the perception of history changes between 1800 and
1900, and with it the possibility of literary history, so Ireland
alters in a variety of complex ways. Too much has been made
of its 'generally remarked upon lack of a capitalist bourgeoisie'. The growth of industry in Belfast and the Lagan
valley is only one aspect of a neglected development in
nineteenth-century Ireland. The musician Robert Stewart, in
bringing concert music from Dublin to 'Flaxopolis', underlined in his memoirs the practice of distinguishing between
industrial and (agri)cultural Ireland. According to this neg-
lectful but widespread view, the agricultural and the cultural
are virtually synonymous — industry being relegated to the
subconscious zone generally reserved for the poor and
uncivilized. This disdain of industry, however, is but a further
identifying feature of an essentially bourgeois society in
which profit and residence are separated in the growth of
suburbia, and production and the superstructures of society
are held apart. The significant characteristic of Irish industri-
alism is not its alleged non-existence, or its limited scale, but
its essentially nineteenth-century structures. Unlike British
industry, Irish industry is primarily post-Union in its origins
and organization. In Joyce's fiction, the particular concentration of the Dublin employers in the areas of mass consumption and communications is shown to striking effect.[11]

[11] See below, pp. 288-9.

The over-simplified identification of industry with capitalist advance and of agriculture with an underdeveloped
economy dogs Marxist commentary on Ireland as surely as
the nineteenth-century denial of industrial activity itself.
Birmingham and Ballyporeen existed together within the
economy of the United Kingdom: and if Birmingham displayed industrial advance, Ballyporeen saw alterations in
landownership which were deliberately limited to the smaller
island. From the 1850s onwards, the reform of the Irish
landlord system posed a threat to landed estate which British
spokesmen for property in great masses of accumulation were
not slow to resist.[12] And in the west of Ireland, the establishment of the Congested Districts Board introduced a degree of
state participation in the local economy without parallel
elsewhere in the Kingdom. Synge's Aran Islands, for example,
had a fishing industry using large trawlers from the east coast
and linked directly to the London markets. As in Conrad's
non-metropolitan world, it is the transitional status of 'the
west of Ireland', the tangible insecurity of its vestigial pre-
capitalist social relations, already shot through with practices
deriving from the metropolis and the developed world, which
is significant. One might say that for the full operation of
industrial capitalism in the United Kingdom, it was necessary
for one sector of its society to be non-industrialized, and
only subliminally capitalized. It was Ireland's historic destiny
to fulfil this aesthetic function.

The Ireland of C. S. Parnell and Michael Davitt, of the
Land War and the Home Rule campaign, was not the abject
primitive outback occasionally advanced for propagandist
purposes. It had a sizeable industrial sector, and an extensive
middle class — though both were hidden in part by the heavy
tapestry of Protestant Ascendancy ideologies. The social
composition of the Land League was *petit-bourgeois* rather
than peasant-based, and the very terminology of *Home*
Rule loudly proclaimed a domestic metaphor in keeping with
bourgeois attitudes. Moreover, the labour movement had
active links with Scotland, with the English ports and great

[12] See John W. Mason, 'The Duke of Argyll and the Land Question in Late
Nineteenth-century Britain', *Victorian Studies*, vol. 21, No. 2 (Winter 1978),
pp. 149–70.

cities. In America, the experience of Fenian exiles and other emigrants was — unlike the Germans of the mid-west for example — primarily urban and industrial. Ireland indeed had its place in the industrialized world, but it was a place conditioned in the consciousness of native and outsider alike by the contradictions of its role as a metropolitan colony.

Spectral facticity and abstract consciousness, these are one set of poles between which these contradictions may be detected in the cultural sphere. Such terms are unfamiliar, but the social realities which lie behind them have been with us for over a century. The nineteenth-century preoccupation with fact — cf. Mr Gradgrind, Burke's *Peerage*, positivism — had its obverse, phantom side in corporal punishment, the silver-spoon novel, theosophy: in this it displays its pervasive and systematic operations in the factory system and in philosophy. The experience of facticity with spectral intensity, and the increased abstraction of the individual consciousness, are both functions of reification, the process whereby relations between people take on the character of a 'thing'.[13] Whether one looks to Marx's analysis in *Das Kapital* or to the style of Dickens or Tennyson, the revelation of 'thingy-ness' in human relations is a familiar Victorian theme. While positivism held sway in crucial areas of intellectual debate — history, theory of knowledge etc. — in much of the developed world, and with it its valorization of 'fact'; abstract consciousness had its concentrations in certain metropolitan colonies where the double-vision of a society which is at once other-than and identical-with its mother

---

[13] Georg Lukács, *History and Class Consciousness: Studies in Marxist Dialectics*, trans. Rodney Livingstone (London: Merlin Press, 1971), pp. 83–222. The notion of 'spectral reality' arises from Lukács's discussion of E. T. A. Hoffmann (which in turn draws on Marx) in 'Fortschritt und Reaktion in der deutschen Literatur' (*Internationale Literatur*, 1945). If Hoffmann seems remote from Anglo-Irish literature, one should recall translations of his stories, and of other works of German romanticism, in the *Dublin University Magazine* in the 1830s and 1840s, when Sheridan Le Fanu and James Clarence Mangan were prominent contributors also. As for the particular problems arising out of Ireland's colonial status, these urgently require attention from literary historians. For Lukács etc. see his *Kurze Skizze einer Geschichte der neueren deutschen Literatur* (Darmstadt and Neuwied: Lachterland Verlag, 1975), esp. pp. 86-7. I am grateful once again to Dennis Tate for discussing with me aspects of Lukács's literary criticism and its bearing on Irish literary history.

culture requires a phantom objectivity so seemingly all-
embracing and absolute as to exclude evidence of its duality.
Ireland, Algeria, Hungary at different historical moments and
in differing political circumstances exemplify this cultural
condition.

The entire conjunction of High Capitalism in its imperial
phase, Ireland in its complex social development within the
leading capitalist economy, literature in Ireland shifting
qualitatively from the provincial margins to the centre of
Anglophone culture, the entire conjunction gives rise to
concepts and questions rarely aired in literary criticism of
the Revival. After so many pages hunting historical allusion
amid the tasteless productions of minor authors, or exploring
dark metaphors in obscure political pronouncements, may
we not now relax into the familiar attitudes of Practical
Criticism applied to familiar texts by undisputed genius?
Having sketched the background can we not now sit upon
the verandah of our culture and contemplate equally dislocated, autonomous poems and stories? Much could be
written on the violence implicit in such contemplation, its
violation of relation and reflection, its self-mutilating projec-
tions. And the truth is that Practical Criticism — as distinct
from close reading within a larger interpretive strategy — is
the logical extension of that epistemology by which text
is taken as an unchanging object of contemplation. If Leavis
is introduced to counter the sterility of Practical Criticism
in its post-war seminar, we should recall Leavis's own historically significant impatience with Joyce and the striking
inability of Leavisite critics to come to terms with the
Irish modernists. It is too late to re-integrate Yeats and Joyce
to the curriculum of English letters, except in the most
obscurantist denial of the European context in which the
academic discipline itself might be ultimately judged. It is
with Joyce that we can look for the first comprehensive
attempt to 'write through' the historical experience of
modernism, with a critical dimension which will subsequently
inform our several approaches to the poetry and drama of
Yeats.

7. JAMES JOYCE: BÁS NÓ BEATHA

The Irish language, Mahaffy said
Is a couple of books written clerkly,
A dirty word in a song or two —
'Matter a damn' says Berkeley.[1]

1. 'EVELINE'

In 1898, writing in the magazine *Outlook*, Joseph Conrad
observed drily: 'Life is life, and art is art — and truth is hard
to find in either'.[2] His official topic was the sea-fiction of
Captain Marryat and Fenimore Cooper, but the real object of
this thought was Kipling's notorious line:

> Oh, East is East, and West is West, and never the twain
> shall meet . . .[3]

Reading Conrad nowadays we find it easy to assimilate his
treatment of imperial expansion and exploitation to a comprehensive criticism of his fiction. *Heart of Darkness* is a set
text in schools and (as Lionel Trilling remarked of *Ulysses*)
it has lost its power to disturb. Comparing Conrad and Joyce,
we would want — initially at least — to locate their powers of
disturbance in different areas — Conrad's in his moral irony,
Joyce's in his stylistic disorientation. Here we should stress
the continuity which leads from the novels of Henry James,
Joseph Conrad, and Ford Madox Ford to the more distinctly experimental canon of modernist fiction.

In considering the Irish contribution to modernist literature in English, we have available an all-too-prominent
political timetable in the events which led from the demand
for Irish home rule within the United Kingdom to the establishment of the Irish Free State. The recent renaissance of

[1] Anonymous ballad quoted in Ruth Dudley Edwards, *Patrick Pearse: The Triumph of Failure* (London: Gollancz, 1977), p. 38. Its date is c.1899.

[2] Joseph Conrad, 'Tales of the Sea', *Notes on Life and Letters* (London: Grant, 1925), p. 57.

[3] Rudyard Kipling, 'The Ballad of East and West', *A Choice of Kipling's Verse*, ed. T. S. Eliot (London: Faber, 1967), p. 111.

interest in Joyce's politics has not, however, been characterized by any inquiry into the dominant political, social, and
economic relationships in which and of which he wrote.
Among these the role of language as at once the mirror and
lamp of social reality is crucial. In this regard we should stress
the essential unity — that is, historical continuity — of all
Joyce's fiction from *Dubliners* to *Finnegans Wake*. A casual
glance at pages from each of these books will apparently
jeopardize this claim, but only apparently so — continuity in
a period of revolutionary change and frustration may not be
confused with constancy. From 'Ivy Day in the Committee
Room' to the dream of Earwicker, Joyce strove to find forms
in which history and technique become a single *problem*. No
doubt a definition of modernism centred on technique could
be conveniently introduced here, but definitions in their
exhaustive length have the effect of excluding as often as
they include. Rather than deal in identifying characteristics, I
would approach the process of definition with the problematic relationship between text and world, a feature which is
found in diachronic form in the attenuated relation of past
and present manifest in various mechanical concepts of
history. Hugh Kenner, writing specifically about *Ulysses,*
alludes to 'the enchained determinisms in which Western high
thought was immobilizing itself at the century's turn', but
insists on restricting his insight to space and physics.[4]
Textual hermeticism and historical discontinuity — these are
not so much principles of modernism as they are underlying
anxieties.

In the preface to *The Political Unconscious*, Fredric
Jameson emphasizes the virtually trans-historical imperative
of dialectical thought, 'Always historicize!'[5] It is not enough
merely to place the object in its historical context: the
reader, the subject (so to speak) of criticism is also historically placed. The interaction of these historicized objects and
subjects is the proper concern of criticism. Conrad and
Kipling serve to remind us of the larger perspective in which
modernist literature in English has its genesis, crisis in the

---

[4]   Hugh Kenner, *Ulysses* (London: Allen and Unwin, 1980), p. 149.
[5]   Fredric Jameson, *The Political Unconscious: Narrative as a Socially Symbolic Act* (London: Methuen; Ithaca: Cornell University Press, 1981), p. 9.

Empire, commercial exploitation of Africa and Asia, the arms race in Europe. Joyce's early reading of socialist thinkers should not be seen solely as a personal trait, a sensitive rebel's response to the inadequacies of Irish nationalism. It is intimately part of the emergence of the nexus of political and aesthetic concerns which distinguish the Irish contribution to English modernism. As a metropolitan colony within the United Kingdom, Irish society was especially susceptible to the contradictory movements of British domestic and global policy.

Joyce's own account of the society in which he wrote is well known. Of *Dubliners* he said: 'My intention was to write a chapter of the moral history of my country and I chose Dublin for the scene because that city seemed to me the centre of paralysis.'[6] Conventionally, this analysis is taken as being somehow literally true; Dublin in 1904 was static, immobile, devoid of the ability to translate intention into action, that is, *paralysed*. The image was certainly one that appealed to Joyce, for on 7 January 1904 he had concluded the semi-fictional essay 'A Portrait of the Artist' with the declaration:

To these multitudes, not as yet in the wombs of humanity but surely engenderable there, he would give the word. Man and woman, out of you comes the nation that is to come, the lightning of your masses in travail; the competitive order is employed against itself, the aristocracies [*sic*] are supplanted; and amid the general paralysis of an insane society, the confederate will issues in action.[7]

What emerges from this curious manifesto is not so much an impressive politics — far from it — but our renewed apprehension of the metaphorical basis of Joyce's idea of society as paralysed. His devotion to Flaubert and the art of nineteenth-century France is more than a search for *le mot juste*, but implicates that French preoccupation with disease, especially socially reprobated disease, as a total metaphor for social

[6] Joyce to Grant Richards, 5 May 1906, *Letters of James Joyce*, vol. ii, ed. Richard Ellmann (London: Faber, 1966), p. 134.
[7] *The James Joyce Archive*, 'A Portrait of the Artist as a Young Man', *A Facsimile of Epiphanies, Notes, Manuscripts, & Typescripts*, ed. Hans Walter Gabler (New York, London: Garland, 1978), pp. 84-5.

reality.[8] The organicist metaphors which constitute Joyce's political longing culminate in 'the general paralysis of an insane society', which resounds with the medical shorthand for the terminal stage of severe syphilitic infection — general paralysis of the insane, GPI.[9] The artist portrayed in the essay, however, will give the word by which sexual generation and the birth of a sane society will issue. If the aetiology of this paralysis be considered, we discover that Joyce's theme is sexual excess as much as it is sexual decay and impotence, that behind the absence of motion implicit in paralysis there lies a history of uncontrolled — because unformulated — motion.

The interaction of sexuality and language in Joyce's fiction is immediately accessible in 'Eveline' which has a good claim to be representative of his short stories. The story is deliberately divided by a single asterisk into two parts. The first is based on a mental present within which Eveline is indirectly reported to meditate on past events in her life:

Even now, though she was over nineteen, she sometimes felt herself in danger of her father's violence. She knew it was that that had given her the palpitations. When they were growing up he had never gone for her, like he used to go for Harry and Ernest, because she was a girl; but latterly he had begun to threaten her and say what he would do to her only for her dead mother's sake.[10]

The indirect reporting of Eveline's recollection of her father's

---

[8] For an account of this dimension to 19th century French culture see Roger L. Williams, *The Horror of Life* (London: Weidenfeld and Nicolson, 1980).

[9] In *James Joyce: A Student's Guide* (London: Routledge and Kegan Paul, 1978), Matthew Hodgart cites (p. 45) an article by Burton A. Waisbren and Florence L. Walzl, 'Paresis and the Priest: James Joyce's Symbolic Use of Syphilis in "The Sisters",' *Annals of Internal Medicine*, vol. 80 (1974), pp. 758–62, in which symptoms are discussed and a diagnosis of tertiary syphilis advanced for Father Flynn. Hodgart makes the casual and yet positive remark that paralysis is a condition 'in which the majority of the human race has always found itself' (p. 46), which, if it is too easily universalist, nevertheless acknowledges the *symbolic* nature of Joyce's fiction. J. B. Lyons in 'Animadversions on Paralysis as a Symbol in "The Sisters"', *James Joyce Quarterly*, vol. 11, No. 3 (1974), pp. 257–65, engages in much special pleading on the question of priestly purity, and ignores the question of symbolism. John Garvin, in *James Joyce's Disunited Kingdom and the Irish Dimension* (Dublin: Gill and Macmillan, 1976), has far more sensible things to say on the topic (pp. 37–42).

[10] *Dubliners*, corrected text ed. Robert Scholes (London: Cape, 1967), pp. 38–9.

threat creates a stylistic feature of great opacity. One might have expected him to threaten in terms of what he would *not* do but for her mother's sake.[11] The particular form which Joyce has chosen both emotively intensifies the threat and formally suppresses it, and this is in keeping with Eveline's ultimate inability actively to quit this life with her father. Technically, the crucial feature here is the implication for Joyce's narrative of the different conventions governing spoken language and written language. If we say that, with Joyce, technique has thematic ambitions this is not to suggest some internalizing 'fiction-about-fiction' quality; on the contrary, this feature is one by which he draws the reader's attention to the possibilities of revitalized intercourse between language and social reality.

One reason for taking 'Eveline' as typical of *Dubliners* is precisely this feature. From 'The Sisters' to 'The Dead' the characters frequently become engaged in a false consciousness of some crucial moment in their past or conjure deliberately some anticipated moment in the future. Aware of the frailty of their mental present which, paradoxically, binds them with an iron control, they seek to establish their first-person-singular existences more objectively, even if that additional security should take the form of anguish or guilt or pain. In 'Eveline' this development is discernible on two levels: psychologically, the girl hears now in the mental present sounds which remind her of her mother's last night. Stylistically, the reader encounters 'the odour of dusty cretonne', a phrase with which the story has opened. Both levels initiate at this point a process of *recursus*:

As she mused the pitiful vision of her mother's life laid its spell on the very quick of her being — that life of commonplace sacrifices closing in final craziness. She trembled as she heard again her mother's voice saying constantly with foolish insistence:
— Derevaun Seraun! Derevaun Seraun!

[11] I have in mind the idiomatic 'What I wouldn't do but . . .!', where 'but' serves as a pseudo-negative negating 'not'. The point is discussed further in my paper, 'James Joyce's "Eveline" and a Problem of Modernism', in *Irland: Gesellschaft und Kultur* vol iii, ed. Dorothea Siegmund-Schultze (Halle: Martin-Luther Universität, 1982), pp. 252-64.

She stood up in a sudden impulse of terror. Escape! She must escape . . .[12]

Her ultimate topographical immobility — her inability to join Frank on the boat — is counterbalanced by this fluidity of movement on the temporal plane, 'she heard again her mother's voice.' Paralysis at the barrier is the counterpart of an excess of movement between past and present. And within the story this binary opposition is expressed at a further linguistic level, for Eveline who hears words when they are not spoken never speaks.

Eveline cannot be said to act: instead she *opts*. Her opting for the internally known and structured world of her father's house is consistent with the non-emergence of her ego (grammatically her 'I') in the narrative. At a further level it is consistent with the strategy adopted by Mr Duffy in that most chilling of the *Dubliners* stories, 'A Painful Case':

He had an odd autobiographical habit which led him to compose in his mind from time to time a short sentence about himself containing a subject in the third person and a predicate in the past tense.[13]

It would be quite feasible at this point to adopt Freud's distinction between the manifest and latent content of dreams as a means of analysing the critical and therapeutic function of Joyce's narratives. For, just as Freud takes over the model of a philological hermeneutic in developing the techniques of psychoanalysis — and this at the moment when philology was engaged in its own realignment with 'Celticism' — so Joyce creates within his characterization dreams of the past ('nightmares of history') of which only the manifest content is immediately intelligible to the characters. The reader's function of course involves the elucidation of a latent meaning according to which the narrative is transformed. By means of a technique introduced by Joyce at a late stage into 'Aeolus', a newspaper caption provides the title for the story involving Mr Duffy: 'A Painful Case' is the subtitle of a newspaper article fulsomely cited in the narrative. The phrase is of course a journalistic euphemism

---

[12] *Dubliners*, p. 41.
[13] Ibid., p. 120.

for suicide, and Duffy's conscious efforts are directed towards consolidating the euphemistic view, towards repressing the latent accusation of his own moral responsibility. In 'Eveline', the recollection of the heroine's mother's dying words results in their apparent meaninglessness, again involving the repression of a latent meaning.

The site of Eveline's traumatic and contradictory opting for escape is the inscrutable recollected phrase, 'Derevaun Seraun'. Brendan O Hehir has written that the words are 'probably gibberish but phonetically like Irish', and proceeds to offer possible original Irish Gaelic words of which these are corruptions.[14] The range of possibilities becomes teasingly wide, but one particular combination would reconstruct the dying mother's words as (with English translations):

dearbhán   seireán
(small) genuine thing, little sea-anemone

Here perhaps is a thematically relevant allusion to a creature who, like Eveline, clings to the rocks and will not breast the waves. The distortion of this ur-message might be located at either of two levels, on that of the old woman's deathbed confusion, or on that of Eveline's recollection. As with 'he had begun to . . . say what he would do to her' the reader has no access to the formal alternative of further information from the past. The narrative method of the stories mimics the dreamer's censorship of his or her dream, but in doing so by means of meaningless words draws attention to the act of censorship. The words, as Eveline recollects them, both stimulate and frustrate her wish to escape.

'Meaningless' is a relative term, and the corruption is more specific than a mere phonological inexactitude. Words of one language are recalled within another, a problem which diachronically involves the largest perspective of nineteenth-century Irish history, the displacement of Gaelic by English as the vernacular language. Nor can the insistent New Critic

[14] Brendan O Hehir, *A Gaelic Lexicon of* Finnegans Wake (Berkeley, Los Angeles: University of California Press, 1967), pp. 333-4. See also Johannes Hedberg, 'Derevaun Seraun – A Joycean Puzzle' *Moderna Sprach*, vol. 60 (1966), pp. 109-10; also, James MacKillop, 'Beurla on It; Yeats, Joyce, and the Irish Language', *Eire/Ireland*, vol. 15, No. 1 (1980), pp. 138-48, esp. p. 139.

protect 'Derevaun Seraun' from a dialectical relation to history: he can neither integrate the words to a formal analysis nor can he (with any confidence) declare them absolutely meaningless. Officially committed to denying the significance of linguistic change, he is confronted by an enactment of linguistic change at two levels — that of the displacement of one language by another within the story so as briefly to reverse the historical displacement, and that of the corruption of certain words into other words as to require the elicitation of some latent meaning.

The broader historical area in which this feature of Joyce's work should be read may be illuminated by reference to a hitherto unnoticed metaphor in the story. The first paragraph of 'Eveline' reads in its entirety:

> She sat at the window watching the evening invade the avenue. Her head was leaned against the window curtains, and in her nostrils was the odour of dusty cretonne. She was tired.[15]

The significant, neglected word is of course 'invade'; the rest of the paragraph can be seen as muted anticipations of the story's end. The active form of the first verb ('She sat . . .') alters after 'invade' to a series of passive and decreasingly concrete forms ('Her head was leaned . . .'). The military metaphor operates within the paragraph to initiate stages of Eveline's opting for inaction. Within the story as a whole it is taken up only once, in the second part, when the crowd on the quays is particularized as 'soldiers with brown baggages'.[16] Rather than conclude that the metaphor has simply been exploited in narrative terms, we should note the dialectical operation of technique and theme in Joyce's fiction, by which means we note also Joyce to be a *critical* modernist. For the last end of Eveline is a silence which transcends narrative method:

> He was shouted at to go on but he still called to her. She set her white face to him, passive, like a helpless animal. Her eyes gave him no sign of love or farewell or recognition.[17]

15 *Dubliners*, p. 37.
16 Ibid., p. 42.
17 Ibid., p. 43.

The invasion of the first paragraph marks the commencement of the English language's advance within the narrative of Eveline's reverie, which in turn centres upon a disruption of that advance. Richard Ellmann comments that Joyce's 'Eveline' is a counterpart to 'The Countess Cathleen': accordingly Yeats's play 'had extolled the virtue of self-sacrifice' and Joyce's story 'evokes the counter virtue of self-realization'.[18] Though this seems simultaneously to go too far in interpretation and not far enough, we can agree that behind both nominal heroines lies the personification of Ireland as Patient Woman, *an tsean bhean bhocht.* Yet Eveline's refusal to travel can only be ambiguously related to the troops with brown baggages, for the events of the narrative cannot be elevated to the level of theme if by such a reading we exclude once again the critical function of the therapeutic fiction. If they are departing invaders does Eveline opt for some domestic form of home rule in North Richmond Street; alternatively does she refuse to travel with them and by so refusing acknowledge their continuing power over her — is she an abstentionist?

While resisting such simplified allegories, we still may remind ourselves that in analysing the imagery of Joyce's fiction we attend positively to the concrete social realities both of the text's historical context and of our own historical condition as readers. Joyce was closer than Yeats or Synge to the social realities which made Ireland potentially revolutionary in this period of European crisis. One consequence of this intimacy might be described as Joyce's lack of illusion as to the odds-against chances of revolution in Ireland. A comparison with Yeats in terms of their attitudes to Hitler would be banal; a more profound comparison might focus on

---

[18] Richard Ellmann, *James Joyce* (New York: Oxford University Press, 1959), p. 170. I refer above to critical silence on the metaphoric 'invade' of 'Eveline's' opening paragraph: it may be useful to note one critic who has ventured an opinion on its tone. Warren Beek, in *Joyce's Dubliners: Substance, Vision and Art* (Durham, NC: Duke University Press, 1969), suggests that 'The word 'invade', especially connoting the dusk, suggests a suspended mood without stressing it' (pp. 112-13). Given the American presence in Vietnam at the time Beek was writing, it is only fair to point out that since those days academic criticism has provided a less myopic perspective on modernist fiction and global politics — cf. Conrad's Kurtz in full US army regalia in *Apocalypse Now*.

the manner in which each responded to the late nineteenth-
century legacy of imperialist formalism conveniently represented here by Kipling. 'The Ballad of East and West', with
its initial autonomous self-defining easts and wests, rapidly
moves to a fourth line assimilable to Yeats's Blue Shirt
melodies:

> But there is neither East nor West, Border, nor Breed,
> nor Birth,
> When two strong men stand face to face, though they
> come from the ends of the earth![19]

Deplorable sentiment apart, one notes conflict and cancellation as resulting from the unmediated valorization of east
and west. 'Eveline' poses equally unmediated and mutually
excluding alternatives: instead of conflict and cancellation,
we find paralysis.

2.   THE DEATH OF THE LANGUAGE

The short stories of *Dubliners* take their place in a field
already defined by Flaubert and Maupassant in France, and
concurrently by Chekhov in Russia. Such a generic context,
however, fails to place their author in a cultural context or,
rather, the irony of the fiction succeeds in undermining the
reader's faith in that possibility. The problem with Joyce,
therefore, was his apparent disjunction from any tradition
which touched upon his material. Certainly he could be
accounted for in terms of *genre* − but 'The Dead' brought
Dubliners to a climax in which genre was no longer an
adequate explanation. It was Joyce's tangential relation to
any Irish tradition which gave his early fiction its shock
effect for local readers. Nothing was self-evident, nothing
was concealed.

Traditionally, this state of affairs is translated into the
proposition that Joyce was a Catholic, and that Catholics
had little or no place in the Anglo-Irish Renaissance. But
Catholicism in Ireland was not (and to a degree, is not) a

---

[19]   Kipling, loc. cit.

matter of theology but of the relation between money and culture. In the literary critic's sense Edward Martyn was not a Catholic, despite his piety and his Palestrina choir. What distinguishes the Protestant from the Catholic in cultural terms is his relation with the past, his *possession* of a history. Protestant Ascendancy provided the late Victorian Irish middle class with an eighteenth-century pedigree in which material and cultural prosperity were rationally linked. It was left to Yeats to transpose this sociological phenomenon into a literary tradition. To the late Victorian Irish Catholic, the eighteenth century meant little apart from echoes of deprivation — the Nugents and the Barnewalls were lost to sight. Intervening between those costume figures and the generation of John Joyce, the nineteenth century dominated the scene. Instead of the ratifying sequence which Protestant Ascendancy supplied to the Protestant bourgeoisie as a possession, history possessed the Catholic imagination in a frenzy of simultaneity. Here, money — cash rather than capital in most cases — was a relatively new element connected to the collapse of a pre-Famine economy in which subsistence outweighed trade for the bulk of the populace. Here, culture found some degree of continuity through the Church and its offices, for the linguistic transformation of the nineteenth century inhibited sequential memory. (Joyce's notions of Irish history, at least prior to the artificially engendered inquiries which were involved in composing *Finnegans Wake*, were little more than commonplace.)

One recent commentator on this 'death of the Irish language' has tried to explain it as 'a millenial or utopian movement' characterized by 'panic, hysteria, or utopianism, or by any mixture of these emotions'.[20] High fertility, combined with dependence on an unreliable diet (based on the potato), produced not only famine but the recurring fear of recurring famine. According to the utopian explanation, the Irish rural population abandoned the Irish language because it stigmatized them as potential victims, and because the English language was the key to migration, employment, and

[20] Seán de Fréine, 'The Dominance of the English Language in the Nineteenth Century', in Diarmaid Ó Muirithe, ed., *The English Language in Ireland* (Dublin, Cork: Mercier Press/Radio Telefis Éireann, 1977), pp. 82-3.

security. The argument has many faults if it is taken as a causal explanation of socio-economic events, but it is entirely at one with the view that the nineteenth century provided for the Irish Catholic an experience of history as trauma. And by trauma we mean not simply shock but precisely that form of dream-work which evidently contradicts the wish-fulfilling function of dreams.

One problem of comparative analysis arises here. We want to bring together Joyce and some earlier cultural production in which the post-famine trauma is absent. But mid-eighteenth-century Irish-speaking Ireland had not possessed the social or technical opportunities to create a literature. It is true that the poetry of Aodhaghán Ó Rathaille (1670–1726) makes it clear that in Augustan Ireland the aristocrats remained *parvenus*, but Ó Rathaille's poetic conventions are far removed from the theme involved here. Brian Merriman's *Cuirt an Mhéan Oiche* (*c*.1780), with its employment of liberating dream as a means of permitting sexual frankness, suggests a possible comparison with the 'Circe' of *Ulysses*. Closer to Joyce, however, is the following passage from an autobiographical work in Irish which, for the sake of dramatic effect, I quote initially in the original:

Is cuimhin liom mé a bheith ar bhrollach mo mháthar. Ceithre bliana a bhíos sular baineadh de dhiúl mé. Is mé dríodar an chrúiscin, deireadh an áil. Sin é an réasún ar fágadh chomh fada ar na ciócha mé.

Bhíos i mo pheata ina theannta sin. Ceathrar deirféar agam agus gach duine acu ag cur a ghoblaigh féin in mo bhéal. Bhíos mar a bheadh gearrcach éin acu: Máire Dhónaill, Cait Dhónaill, Eibhlin Dhónaill agus Nora Dhónaill, Padraig Dhónaill agus Tomás Dhónaill.

I was born on St Thomas's day in the year 1856. I can recall being at my mother's breast, for I was four years old before I was weaned. I am 'the scrapings of the pot', the last of the litter. That's why I was left so long at the breasts. I was a spoilt child, too.

Four sisters I had, and every one of them putting her own titbit into my mouth. They treated me like a young bird in the nest. Maura Donel, Kate Donel, Eileen Donel, and Nora Donel — those were their names. My brother was Pats Donel, and I am Tomas Donel.[21]

[21] Tomás Ó Criomhain, *An t-Oileánach* (Baile Atha Cliath: Cló Talbot, 1973), p. 13: *The Islandman*, trans. Robin Flower (Oxford: Oxford University Press, 1978), 3rd ed., p. 1.

I intend no disrespect to the translator if I point to certain discrepancies between the original and the English version — there is no fixed rate of exchange between languages. But the most monoglot reader can see that the first sentence of the translation has no equivalent whatever in the original. It may be that Robin Flower was discretely providing his English reader with a necessary historical pointer in providing a date; alternatively, he is shaping the passage by implying a connection between the writer's birth-day and his name. What he has modified, however, is the simplicity with which suckling at the breast is established as primary memory, as memory which depends on no '*can* recall': 'I remember being on the breast of my mother. Four years I was before I was taken from suckling'.[22] Moreover, the list of siblings is by Flower modulated stylistically so as to break it down, reduce it. These are probably inevitable consequences of translation but they underline the immense psychic difficulty of rendering in English the potency of Ó Criomhthain's words. No English-language memoir of this kind was possible within Joyce's lifetime, and yet *An tOiléanach* was published in 1929.

The atmosphere in which Ó Criomhthain's book was received was conditioned by two powerful and contradictory motifs. One was the familiar (perhaps, tactically exaggerated) puritanism of semi-independent Catholic Ireland, in which official censorship was hyper-active. The other was the establishment of the Irish language as the inert *primum mobile* of the new state. But the embarrassment which this conflict of values generated from time to time had a larger and older source upon which to draw. That earlier reservoir was the propagation in the nineteenth century of a sectarian schematization of the emotions which reinforced the sense of history as trauma:

All Protestants are not virtuous, nor are Protestant peoples without their share of irregular sexual intercourse, self-stupifaction by alcohol, and so forth; but, bad as their backsliding may be, it is not as character-killing as the sensuality engendered by the Roman system; and whenever Protestantism is in the ascendant [*sic*], there also health, energy,

---

[22] Translated by the present writer.

integrity, and industry will be found in the ascendant. This is stated as
a fact, and not for the purpose of insulting the Catholics. Nothing could
be further from the thoughts of one, like myself, whose kith and kin
are all Catholics. Roman sensuality debases the mind, because it is more
in thought than in action . . .[23]

Thus, although Ó Criomthain was a native of the most
westerly islands and so might be dismissed as culturally
marginal or residual, the aftermath of linguistic trauma was
turned to provide the complementary ideology to Protestant
Ascendancy. If this sounds tiresomely like local broadcasting
from darkest Ulster, it is worth noting that, in the year of
Joyce's *hegira* (1904), Max Weber commenced publication
of *The Protestant Ethic and the Spirit of Capitalism.* Joyce's
greatest fiction, *Ulysses*, demonstrates how symbolically
effective marginal Dublin might be in the unmasking of
western capitalism.

In 1904 'the death of the Irish language' was already a
cliché, and attempts to revive Gaelic were already under way.
As a student at the Royal University, Joyce remained un-
impressed by the arguments of the Gaelic League though he
briefly attended League meetings. Pressure from this quarter
is not prominent among the difficulties young Stephen
Dedalus encountered. Though Stephen's diary records that
he fears the old man with red-rimmed horny eyes who had
spoken Gaelic to John Francis Mulrennan, the entry significantly ends, 'no. I mean him no harm.'[24] The controversies
aroused by the Gaelic League's revivalism produced significantly paradoxical reactions. Thus, two professors in Trinity
College sought to show that Gaelic was purely a scholarly
concern, involving venerable texts rather than contemporary
speakers.[25] The Gaelic League and associated revivalist language movement are significant not solely for some mystical
'*volk*-ish' quality inherent in the residual vernacular, but as
the corollary to the emasculation of English as spoken and
written in the metropolitan colony. Of course, related

---

[23] Michael J. F. McCarthy, *Irish Land and Irish Liberty: A Study of the New
Lords of the Soil* (London: Robert Scott, 1911), p. 196.
[24] *A Portrait of the Artist as a Young Man* (London: Cape, 1968), corrected
ed., p. 256.
[25] Ruth Dudley Edwards, op. cit., pp. 38–41.

developments affected Victorian England, where genteel
speech among the middle classes came increasingly to resemble the conventions of written language. But in Ireland
language change took place against the background of that
larger transformation — the displacement of Gaelic by
English. The historical causes of that larger phenomenon are
complex — the penetration of rural Ireland by commerce, the
demographic upheaval of the Famine, populist politics, and
journalism might be relevantly cited. However, if we look for
more than a descriptive analysis we should consider if the
underlying characteristic of the Gaelic language central to
its eclipse is not sexual. High fertility, illegitimacy, early
marriages, and large families were associated with those
southern and western areas in which the 1840s Famine had
been most devastating. For the most part, these were also
Gaelic-speaking areas. To speak Gaelic was to identify oneself
with the stricken, dangerously fecund community, to distance oneself from charity and relief. Moreover, the Gaelic
language did not distinguish — and English increasingly did —
between polite and coarse registers in describing bodily functions, in swearing, and so forth. (To speak Gaelic was to
make explicit aspects of human biology which English was
tending to disguise.) Within the United Kingdom, where its
political role was anomalous and its economy divergent,
Ireland experienced an intense cultural trauma through the
medium of linguistic change. Other areas of Britain underwent similar if less intense alterations of convention —
Thomas Hardy's fiction provides eloquent evidence on this
point — but the close bond between moral, economic, and
linguistic change is distinctively Irish. Nevertheless, this
pattern is not uniquely Irish nor is it the result simply of
famine: increased fertility in the nineteenth century was
common in Europe, and the abandonment of Gaelic necessi-
tated by migration had already commenced prior to 1845.
The Famine, however, provided a *traumatic* account of social
and economic change and rendered it capable of interpretation as cultural change.[26] In turn, the cultural significance

[26] The principal works on the famine are R. D. Edwards and T. D. Williams,
edd., *The Great Famine* (Dublin: Brown and Nolan, 1956), and Cecil Woodham-
Smith, *The Great Hunger* (London: Hamish Hamilton, 1962). Two important

of the Irish experience is not its uniqueness but precisely the manner in which it impinges upon the development of British society, both domestic and imperial, at the turn of the century.

The mobility engendered by mid-century famine and its consequences contributed signally to the perception of a Catholic middle class in Ireland as a category rather than as a formation. For the most part such 'perceivers' were of course members of a bourgeoisie which had since 1792 sailed under the colours of a Protestant ascendancy.[27] Yeats's Celtic Twilight sought a 'dream of the noble and the beggarman', and thus sought both to acknowledge the immiseration of the nineteenth century and to leap-frog back across the Famine to an era of Whiggish hegemony.[28] In more specifically linguistic terms, he sought a cultural synthesis under the guise of 'a written speech'.[29] This synthesis longed to exclude the middle classes and urban life, the material which Joyce chose for all his fiction. In *A Portrait of the Artist as a Young Man,* he integrates one potent image of rural life by way of Davin's account to Stephen of his encounter with the young woman in the Ballyhoura mountains. The fertility and guilelessness

books by Louis Cullen provide valuably broader contexts for the crisis — *An Economic History of Ireland Since 1660* (London: Batsford, 1972), and *The Emergence of Modern Ireland 1600–1900* (London: Batsford, 1981), the latter providing far more commentary and analysis on cultural matters than its title might initially suggest. In relation to the interaction of language and sexuality, such commentaries as McCarthy's are highly revealing. In Irish, Peadar Ó Laoghaire's *Mo Sgéal Féin* (1915) and the diary of Amhlaigh Ó Suilleabháin provide excellent primary material.

[27] The preface to E. P. Thompson's *The Making of the English Working Class* (Harmondsworth: Penguin, 1968) is a brief, and suitably challenging, introduction to the theory of class in which the notion that groups of people *as* groups constitute classes is countered by the Marxist view of class as based on relations. Below the argument about literature which is the present book's principal concern, there is a further argument according to which Protestant Ascendancy enters crucially into Irish class conflict, apparently to differentiate between unique Irish conditions and the norms of 19th-century social experience elsewhere. In this way, sectarianism provided a means of enforcing, or attempting to enforce, rigid categorization of classes on social process. There is nothing very new in this, but the discussion of literature and history may serve to show how central was the role of culture in this enforcement and in resistance to it.

[28] W. B. Yeats, 'The Municipal Gallery Revisited', *Collected Poems* (London: Macmillan, 1963), p. 369.

[29] W. B. Yeats, 'Upon a House Shaken by the Land Agitation', *Collected Poems*, p. 107.

of the woman, as described to him by Davin, prompts
Stephen to see her 'as a type of her race and of his own, a
batlike soul waking to the consciousness of itself in darkness
and secrecy and loneliness . . . .'.[30] The immediately succeeding pages chart important stages of Stephen's development —
his response to the slogan *Vive l'Irlande*, his acknowledgement that 'the Ireland of Tone and of Parnell seemed to have
receded in space', his discussion with the English dean of
studies first of Thomistic aesthetics and then of the notorious
discriminations on the English language itself, as spoken in
England and Drumcondra.[31]

In the days immediately prior to his 'flight' Stephen
returns in his diary to an image of residual Gaelic Ireland, this
time in the form of John Francis Mulrennan's interlocutor
rather than the bare-breasted revenant of Davin's recollection. By this point Stephen has achieved some solider hold
upon the ordinary world, and with it a more relaxed attitude
to the rural, recently-Gaelic world reported upon by
Mulrennan/Synge. Nevertheless, the aesthete has not been
dissolved, though his aestheticism is directed against a
specific target, the early poetry of W. B. Yeats:

April 6, later. Michael Robartes remembers forgotten beauty and, when
his arms wrap her round, he presses in his arms the loveliness which
has long faded from the world. Not this. Not at all. I desire to press in
my arms the loveliness which has not yet come into the world.[32]

Together with the parody of Synge and the paraphrasing of
Yeats, the recurrent tabulation of dates serves to draw attention to the historical moment of the novel's climax. Furthermore, Joyce's aesthetic (as distinct from Stephen's superficial
aestheticism) indicates that the meaning of the work of art
lies not only in its historical genesis but also in its future
reception.

3. NIGHTMARES OF HISTORY

Joyce's letters often give the impression of being written by
Gerty MacDowell; they hang their little displays of fabric and

---

[30] *A Portrait of the Artist*, pp. 186-7.
[31] Ibid., pp. 187-94.
[32] Ibid., p. 255.

fabrication on the most tenuous associative line. In this they also reveal their genuine profundity. Writing to his brother Stanislaus in January 1907, he recorded his reaction to Kipling's *Plain Tales from the Hills:*

If I knew Ireland as well as R. K. seems to know India I fancy I could write something good. But it is becoming a mist in my brain rapidly. I have the idea of three or four little immortal stories in my head but I am *too cold* to write them. Besides, where's the good. Ibsen, of course, may have liked that kind of sport [i.e. total absorption in his work regardless of his environment] . But then he never broke with his set. I mean, imagine Roberts or Fay, with an allowance from the Irish Republic moving round Europe with correspondence tied at his heels like a goat's tether and you have H[enrik] I[bsen] .[33]

Joyce did not live to see an Irish Republic established. The letter to Stanislaus, however, indicates that as early as 1907 he envisaged no very positive relationship between the artist as an old man and any newborn state. In 1922, after the publication of *Ulysses*, he was indeed approached by Desmond Fitzgerald (an Irish Free State minister) who proposed advancing Joyce's name to the Nobel Committee. Of this scheme he was highly sceptical, and in the event Yeats got the government nomination and the prize, Joyce being the first to send a telegram of congratulation.[34] The historical 'gap' between the setting of *Ulysses* (1904) and its eventual publication (1922) is crossed by the electrical charge of these altered relations between Joyce and his native land. The stories of *Dubliners*, like *A Portrait of the Artist as a Young Man,* posit a future by means of the placing of the reader in relation to the therapeutic narrative, a future which is in the simplest sense real. *Ulysses*, on the other hand, looks forward to the present. And (one is tempted to add) *Finnegans Wake* looks forward to what's past, or passing, or to come.

Joyce's fiction after *A Portrait of the Artist as a Young Man* consists of two historical novels. The point, a crude but necessary one, is clarified if juxtaposed with T. S. Eliot's familiar description of the Homeric parallel as a way of ordering 'the immense panorama of futility and anarchy

---

[33] James Joyce, *Letters,* vol. ii, p. 205.
[34] Ellmann, op. cit., p. 546.

which is contemporary history'.[35] Theodor Adorno's response to Georg Lukács's dismissal of Joyce as a decadent is worth recalling in the context of a discussion of the historical character of his fiction:

Even in Joyce's case we do not find the timeless image of man which Lukács would like to foist on him, but man as the product of history. For all his Irish folklore, Joyce does not invoke a mythology beyond the world he depicts, but instead strives to mythologize it, i.e. to create its essence, whether benign or maleficent, by applying the technique of stylization so despised by the Lukács of today. One is almost tempted to measure the achievements of modernist writing by inquiring whether historical moments are given substance as such within their works, or whether they are diluted into some sort of timelessness.[36]

Generally speaking, one welcomes this kind of discrimination, especially Adorno's insistence that 'art exists in the real world and has a function in it, and the two are connected by a large number of mediating links. Nevertheless, as art it remains the antithesis of that which is the case.'[37] However, 'man as the product of history' is one version of the overwhelming question that Stephen Dedalus asks himself on his visit to Dublin from Paris.

In 1908, during his pre-Marxist phase, Lukács defined a condition of emergent modernism which in his subsequent work he strove to dissolve sometimes with subtlety, sometimes with other means. 'Every written work', he observed, 'even if it is no more than a consonance of beautiful words, leads us to a great door — through which there is no passage.'[38] As a general principle this urgently needs to be historicized and particularized, first by emphasizing its reference to emergent modernism rather than 'every written work', and secondly by pointing to its status as a description of a condition implicit in the modernist aesthetic — as Lukács sees it — rather than as an objective account of modernist

[35] T. S. Eliot, 'Ulysses, Order, and Myth', Selected Prose, ed. Frank Kermode (London: Faber, 1975), p. 177.
[36] Aesthetics and Politics: Ernst Bloch, Georg Lukács, Bertolt Brecht, Walter Benjamin, Theodor Adorno (London: New Left Books, 1977), pp. 158-9.
[37] Ibid., p. 159.
[38] Georg Lukács, Soul and Form, trans. Anna Bostock (London: Merlin Press, 1974), p. 113.

texts. It is of course cognate with Conrad's dictum on the elusiveness of truth in either 'Life' or 'Art' when these are hermetically isolated and hypostasized. The essential quality which is jeopardized is that mediated access to history which Joyce's critical method in *Dubliners* had sought to re-establish. In seeking to historicize Joyce's contribution to European modernism we cannot afford to neglect the colonial condition of the society upon which he chose to concentrate, and its *potential* transformation in the years between 1882 and 1922. In the case of *Dubliners* and *A Portrait* the temporal discrepancy between historical setting and composition is minimal, though in the later of these it is perceptibly widening through the agency of the biographical narrative. With *Ulysses* the discrepancy achieved structural proportions — '16 June 1904' in *Ulysses* embodies a function far more significant than 'April 6, later' in *A Portrait*. In political terms, the transition encompasses the emergence of the Free State and the modification of Ireland's colonial relationship to Britain.

Hugh Kenner has likened one interpretation of *Ulysses* to Laplace's cosmos — 'all chains of action and reaction are folded in, coupled end to end, determined.' Such a cosmos, he adds in a telling metaphor, 'perpetually trembles in its sleep while undergoing no real events'.[39] When we meet Stephen in the opening episode of *Ulysses* he is 'displeased and sleepy'.[40] His night's rest has been disturbed by moans emitted by the dreaming Haines who shortly summarizes Anglo-Irish relations in the phrase 'It seems history is to blame.'[41] Haines is a Laplacian. Stephen, on the other hand, has a different account to offer though it is mediated only to the reader by means of the famous *monologue intérieure*:

In a dream, silently, she had come to him, her wasted body within its loose graveclothes giving off an odour of wax and rosewood, her breath, bent over him with mute secret words, a faint odour of wetted ashes.

Her glazing eyes, staring out of death, to shake and bend my soul. On me alone. The ghostcandle to light her agony. Ghostly light on the tortured face. Her hoarse loud breath rattling in horror, while all prayed

[39] Kenner, op. cit., pp. 149–50.
[40] *Ulysses* (Harmondsworth: Penguin, 1969), p. 9.
[41] Ibid., p. 27.

on their knees. Her eyes on me to strike me down. *Liliata rutilantium te confessorum turma circumdet: iubilantium te virginum chorus excipiat.*
    Ghoul! Chewer of corpses!
    No, mother! Let me be and let me live.[42]

The substance of this passage has reached us just five pages earlier:

Silently, in a dream she had come to him after her death, her wasted body within its loose brown graveclothes giving off an odour of wax and rosewood, her breath, that had bent upon him, mute, reproachful, a faint odour of wetted ashes.[43]

The repetition certainly constitutes one element of Stephen's developing rhythm in the prose, the curve of his emotion. But rhythm here is not simply a matter of musical approximation in verbal form; it has specific conceptual effects also. In addition to the newly introduced liturgical quotation, we are now given an intensified evocation of the ghostly figure, in phrases devoid of finite verbs and hence seeking temporarily to abolish time. When, in 'Circe', we encounter by way of phantasmagoric stage-direction another variation upon this passage, it is to inaugurate Stephen's apocalyptic reconciliation of Time and Space, the rigid polarities of both his aesthetics and his anxious metaphysics:

(*Stephen's mother, emaciated, rises stark through the floor, in leper grey with a wreath of faded orangeblossoms and a torn bridal veil, her face worn and noseless, green with gravemould. Her hair is scant and lank. She fixes her bluecircled hollow eyesockets on Stephen and opens her toothless mouth uttering a silent word. A choir of virgins and confessors sing voicelessly.*)
    THE CHOIR

Liliata rutilantium te confessorum ....
Iubilantium te virginum .....

[...]
    THE MOTHER (*with smouldering eyes*) Repent! O, the fire of hell!
    STEPHEN (*panting*) His noncorrosive sublimate! The corpsechewer! Raw head and bloody bones.
    [...]

    [42] Ibid., p. 16.
    [43] Ibid., p. 11.

THE MOTHER (*in the agony of her deathrattle*) Have mercy on
Stephen, Lord, for my sake! Inexpressible was my anguish when ex-
piring with love, grief and agony on Mount Calvary.
    STEPHEN *Nothung!*
(*He lifts his ashplant high with both hands and smashes the chandelier.
Time's livid final flame leaps and, in the following darkness, ruin of all
space, shattered glass and toppling masonry.*)[44]

Just as the grammatical immediacy of 'Her eyes on me to
strike me down' does not mimic a scene in the novel, so the
conclusive imagery of 'Circe' records no resolution of
Stephen's psychological difficulties — *Ulysses* is no pseudo-
biographical study in realism. These variations on the rhythm
of Stephen's nightmare serve, however, to relate other themes
in the fiction, and indeed the focus here is central to Joyce's
work as a whole: just as 'Let me be and let me live' recalls
Stephen's ultimate ability to face the horny-eyed Old Man of
the *Portrait* diary, so the deathbed recalls Eveline's mother
and her 'secret words'. Joyce had begun to orchestrate a
sentence on the theme of the revenant mother as early as
1904; its passage to 1922 is also its passage through the styles
of *Ulysses*.[45]
    These themes are in essence history and aesthetics which,
at the outset, are for Stephen the imposed starting-point and
longed-for destination of his search for authenticity. But,
as problematic hero, Stephen's most potent characteristic is
his recognition of the polar interaction of these values in his
particular situation. Dream, the involuntary experience in a
subjective present of events which ostensibly occurred in the
past, is the dominant metaphor employed in *Ulysses* to
represent this crucial condition. The novel opens with a dis-
agreement between the wakened dreamers, reaches its climax
in a stylistic transformation of matter into manner, quantity
into quality when the 'Circe' episode adopts the literary
equivalent of dream *and its analysis*.[46] Finally, Molly's

[44] Ibid., pp. 515–17. Bracketed ellipses mark omissions; the others are Joyce's.
    [45] For the 1904 origins see *The James Joyce Archive*: 'A Portrait . . .', etc.,
pp. 33, 47, 49, 53, 141.
    [46] Colin MacCabe, *James Joyce and the Revolution of the Word* (London:
Macmillan, 1978), p. 128; see also Hugh Kenner, 'Circe', in *James Joyce's* Ulysses:
Critical Essays, edd. Clive Hart and David Hayman (Berkeley: University of
California Press, 1974), p. 360.

soliloquy transforms the *monologue intérieure* (which has earlier detained Stephen within his search) into a renewed balance of past and present and future. Yet it is as early as 'Nestor' that Stephen makes explicit, with a grammatical precision we neglect at our peril, the importance of this pervasive metaphor:

— History, Stephen said, is a nightmare from which I am trying to awake.[47]

Commentators have been casual in referring to Joyce and 'the nightmare of history'. That misquoted phrase contains an ambiguity Stephen is anxious to avoid, though he explores its grammatical base in another context. Meditating on the words *amor matris* he notes and implies the coexistence of a subjective genitive (the love of a mother for X) and an objective genitive (the love of X for a mother) in the Latin construction. 'The nightmare of history' offers a parallel at least within the different conventions of another language: it may point to a nightmare which history endures (say, the Reign of Terror, Senator McCarthy's ascendancy, or the plagues of Egypt, according to your taste); or it may point to the enduring of history by X in the manner of a nightmare. The distinction is less than absolute, just as history and the life of an individual may not be absolutely distinguished — and here the parallel between Latin and English genitives reveals its limitations. But the form of words which Joyce has Stephen adopt, together with Joyce's obsessional elimination of perverted commas, makes it clear that Stephen refers to the second category. If we recall Stephen's recollected dream, we know that the revenant mother is his dominant image of history, and thus in speaking to Mr Deasy he identifies himself with a particular reading of Irish culture.

It is no accident that the Latin phrase on which Stephen effects his distinction of objective and subjective genitives invokes the maternal relationship, and the correlation greatly advances our attempts to historicize Joyce's fiction. Stephen's dream-revenant is implicitly cannibalistic, the vengeance wrought on the author of that aphorism which defined

[47] *Ulysses*, p. 40.

Ireland as 'an old sow that eats her farrow'.[48] Immediately
before the recollection of his dying mother's secret words,
Stephen recalls playing the piano for her: the song he has
played is Joyce's setting of a poem by Yeats:

> A cloud began to cover the sun slowly, wholly, shadowing the bay in
> deeper green. It lay behind him, a bowl of bitter waters. Fergus' song: I
> sang it alone in the house, holding down the long dark chords. Her door
> was open: she wanted to hear my music.[49]

The relationship between the poem in 'The Countess
Cathleen' and the decisive action of the titular heroine is
contrapuntal: Fergus has been king of Ireland but chose the
vocation of poet so as to find peace in the woods; the
countess sacrifices her serenity and risks her soul in order to
save a starving and plundered tenantry – she acts symbolically as mother to her people. Throughout *Ulysses* Stephen
is preoccupied with the larger implications of his mother's
death, for his 'nightmare' is located at the scene of her death
and his (non-)involvement in it. Stephen, to be sure, is faced
with less drastic alternatives than those personified in Yeats's
play by Cathleen and Fergus; but, just as he all but concluded
his diary in *A Portrait of the Artist as a Young Man* with an
allusion to Yeatsian nostalgia, so here at the beginning of
Ulysses we find his dilemma dramatized by reference to a
Yeatsian brooding on 'love's bitter mystery'. At the end of
the fourth chapter of *A Portrait* Stephen had resolved that
the artist's mission was 'to recreate life out of life'.[50] At
the beginning of the first chapter of *Ulysses* he is tempted
to the re-creation of second-hand art out of art.

Fergus's song is significant for Stephen because it may
be a point of departure from the world of history, process,
and consumption. Yet what it offers is not so much a retreat
from life as a conveniently arty terminology for nature – 'the
deep wood's *woven* shade'. Yeats's poem exemplifies in a
thoroughly unconscious way Lukács's diagnosis of art as a
great door through which there is no passage. Stephen's
introspection, intensified as the revision of the early episode

---

[48] *Portrait*, p. 208.
[49] *Ulysses*, pp. 15-16.
[50] *Portrait*, p. 176.

was effected, is a structurally introspective representative of the novel's latent hermetic closure. Traditional accounts of *Ulysses* have interpreted Stephen's meeting with Bloom as providing, for both men, a renewed access to reality and release from their interior preoccupations. But as Stephen has painstakingly revealed to Deasy, the material of his introspection is history itself: his experience within the novel will involve a comprehensive adjustment of relation both to text and world. These preoccupations are given their head in the third episode when Stephen walks on Sandymount Strand. Characteristically, his meditations on his family, his trip to Paris, his fellow lodgers in the tower, are introduced by a meditation on the nature of art:

Stephen closed his eyes to hear his boots crush crackling wrack and shells. You are walking through it howsomever. I am, a stride at a time. A very short space of time through very short times of space. Five, six: the *Nacheinander*. Exactly: and that is the ineluctable modality of the audible. Open your eyes. No. Jesus! If I fell over a cliff that beetles o'er his base, fell through the *Nebeneinander* ineluctably! I am getting on nicely in the dark. My ash sword hangs at my side. Tap with it: they do. My two feet in his boots are at the end of his legs, *nebeneinander*.[51]

The art of this episode, according to Stuart Gilbert's schema, is philology, and the second sentence is 'Signatures of all things I am here to read ...'.[52] The allusion to Jacob Boehme offers a possibility of dynamically rendering nature intelligible to a degree only approximated and mocked by nineteenth-century philology. Stephen in *A Portrait* had listened silently to Donovan's glib citation of Lessing's aesthetics: now he is led to recall his differentiation of the verbal arts which deal with objects one after another ('nacheinander') in time, and the visual arts deal with objects next to one another ('nebeneinander') in space.[53] By alluding to Hamlet, Stephen translates this distinction into an analogy of movement on two axes — if you walk over a cliff you cease to move on the horizontal axis though you move

[51] *Ulysses*, pp. 42-3.
[52] Ibid., p. 42.
[53] See Fritz Senn, 'Esthetic Theories', *James Joyce Quarterly*, vol. 2, No. 2 (1965), pp. 134-6.

with increasing rapidity through it, on the vertical axis. *Nacheinander*, we might say, characterizes that mechanical order which Kenner calls Laplace's cosmos; *nebeneinander* the simultaneity of all events in the 'nightmare of history'. In colonial Ireland sequence and simultaneity are rival experiences of history.

Stephen's aesthetic meditation has its complement in Bloom's recurring puzzlement by the phenomenon of parallax, by reference to which we explain the apparent displacement or difference in the apparent position of an object caused by an actual change or difference of the position of the observer.[54] In a sense, what Time is to Stephen, Space is to Bloom. One is tempted to see the novel as requiring a resolution based on a time/space concept similar to that proposed initially by Einstein in 1905, were it not for the fact that 'resolution' is precisely what such a continuum jeopardizes. As a consequence, many approaches to *Ulysses* are actually directed at a non-existent, or recently extinct, target. The reconciliation of father and son, which critics of the archetype-and-myth school fondly celebrate, is more properly considered as the effort of Joyce's critical modernism to overcome the urge towards autonomy that characterizes so many modernist texts. Strictly speaking, Stephen without Bloom is unthinkable, Bloom without Stephen unthinking; thus the structuralist may read *Ulysses* as Joyce's effort to bring together the problematic author (Stephen) and the problematic reader (Bloom). But in what sense is such fiction historical? None that Walter Scott would immediately recognize. If the composition of *Finnegans Wake* outlasts Scott's entire career as prolific novelist, that of *Ulysses* more clearly reveals the historical nature of the fiction. To Carlo Linati in September 1920 Joyce declared his attitude to the Greek myth in terms which make the point effectively, 'My intention is to transpose the myth *sub specie temporis nostri*.'[55] The contrast here is not between then and now but between Eternity and time, between the

---

[54] *Oxford English Dictionary*; Kenner in *Ulysses* traces the parallax allusions, p. 5 n. 11 etc.

[55] *Letters of James Joyce*, ed. Stuart Gilbert (London: Faber, 1957), pp. 146–7 (cited hereafter as *Letters I*).

metaphysical beyond into which Stephen fears he may walk
on Sandymount Strand and the world of historical time to
which the movement of the novel restores him. Fifteen years
earlier Joyce had conceived his Odyssey as a short story for
Dubliners, and its evolution as a long novel had necessarily
brought alterations of conception and execution. Kenner has
written of the ironic mood which the novel would have had
if it had ended with 'The Wandering Rocks', and written also
of the increasing uncertainty and unreliability of the nar-
rators' methods, as 'The Sirens', 'Cyclops', 'Nausicaa', 'The
Oxen of the Sun', and 'Circe' progressively illustrate.[56] To
demonstrate his point Kenner cites the cheating reference to
'Mr Bloom's dental windows'[57] which is only cleared up
eighty-five pages later with a denial that Leopold is any
relative whatever of Bloom the dentist. Such red herrings
certainly multiply – how can C. B. O'C. F. T. Farrell frown
at the Metropolitan Hall when he halts at Wilde's corner, for
the Hall is three-quarters of a mile away on the other side of
the river?[58] What has happened is not just that Joyce is
extending a naturalist novel (episodes 1–10) in a different
mode; the novel comes to acknowledge the historical nature
of its attention to 16 June 1904. With reference to Bloom
the dentist Kenner observes:

True, we can imagine a reader from whom 'Mr Bloom's dental windows'
would have instantly invoked the actual Marcus Bloom, dentist, who
practised in 1904 at 2 Clare Street: a reader who would have known that
vanished, pre-rebellion Dublin as intimately as do Joyce's Dubliners.
But not even in 1922 can there have been many left alive who both
commanded such lore and were capable of reading 250 pages into the
difficult *Ulysses*.[59]

Professor Kenner's fundamental anti-historicism here takes
the form of historical exaggeration: after all, the six years
between the Easter Rebellion and the publication of *Ulysses*
had not seen the death of so many Dubliners and potential
readers, nor had the Rebellion and its suppression caused the

[56] Kenner, *Ulysses*, p. 151.
[57] *Ulysses*, p. 249.
[58] See Appendix E.
[59] Kenner, *Ulysses*, p. 65.

city to 'vanish'. Such sentiment distracts us from a more
thoughtful consideration of events occurring between the
conception and publication of the novel — among them,
massive labour unrest in Dublin, the Rebellion, the murder
of Joyce's friend Sheehy-Skeffington, the Great War, the
internment of Stanislaus Joyce in Austria, Revolution in
Russia and Germany. Across Europe and within Ireland,
historical change had rendered 16 June 1904 no longer
contemporary. Seen in this light the changing styles of
Ulysses do not so much chronicle the events of one specific
day as they seek to come to terms with the changing perspectives upon a 'fixed' day which a revolutionary period
generated. *Ulysses* is thus historical in two senses, first in
that it takes as its setting a date which is progressively seen
as historical; and second, as a stylistic consequence, the
process of composition itself is historicized.

Both *Dubliners* and *A Portrait* posited a future reader
whom the texts awaited: Joycean irony and the conventions
of *Bildungsroman* contributed to that perspective. *Ulysses*,
on the other hand, is in danger of containing its author and
reader. Or to put it in different terms, *Ulysses* appears all
but 'posthumously': in 1922 old Troy of the D.M.P. is
virtually an anachronism and the Citizen is on the point of
assuming his functions. Joyce's youthful notions (of 7
January 1904) concerning the masses in travail and the end
of a competitive social order find no fulfilment in the Irish
Free State. This local timetable has its European tabulation
also in the irresolution of 1918 and the failure of revolution
in Germany and the West. To relate modernist literature to
the crisis of western society is hardly original: nevertheless
we await some dialectically satisfactory account of the
disproportionate Irish contribution. Yeats's Anglo-Irish
tradition is a classic instance of wisdom after the event, and
the Parnellite trauma the symbol (manifest content) rather
than the source of cultural energy. A dialectically thorough
analysis of the Anglo-Irish Renaissance would take into
account the contradictions implicit in the incorporation of
a colonial and metropolitan system within the *United* Kingdom, and relate this feature to the function of sectarian
ideologies in Ireland. The Great Famine, with the broader

socio-economic pattern of which it is part, assisted in translating these contradictions into cultural terms, indeed gave occasion to that linguistic disjunction we have noted in homeopathic form in 'Eveline'. At the aesthetic level such an account of the Anglo-Irish phenomenon would have many tasks, but in the present context we may specify one element. Yeatsian and Joycean paradigms are conveniently summarized in two slogans — the Celtic Twilight, the nightmare of history. These are of course problems to Yeats and Joyce as much as they are programmes, but they illustrate the centrality of the sectarian conflict to the elaboration of Anglo-Irish literature. For Yeats, typical of that self-conceived and self-deceived bourgeoise element known as the Protestant Ascendancy, history passively awaited formulation, invention, faith. For Joyce, urban inheritor of an abandoned language, history excelled itself, being prolific, obsessive, intolerable. To see these rival experiences of history in terms of *colon* and *colonisé* is tempting but grossly so; a more profoundly historical inquiry will reveal their mutual interaction within a larger political strategy.

Hence the significance of academic criticism's reluctance to consider Joyce and Yeats together in a fully comparative analysis. The uncritical acceptance of Yeats's rewriting of literary history, like the refusal to acknowledge the metaphorical nature of Joycean 'paralysis', perpetuates convenient myths. The role imposed on Joyce at least as far as his reception is concerned resembles that of the academic portrayal of Gaelic revivalism — he is at once pedant and pornographer, who gave us 'a couple of books written clerkly' and restored a dirty word or two. Similarly, we should note that *Ulysses*'s renowned openness to life is not without its problematic aspect, its contextual limitations, though here too we may take the opportunity to establish a Yeatsian comparison. It is specifically in 'Hades' that Bloom provides us with thoughts that at once qualify any naïve acceptance of the novel as celebration and reveal a positive disposition in any comparison with Yeats:

Plenty to see and hear and feel yet. Feel live warm beings near you. Let them sleep in their maggoty beds. They are not going to get me this innings. Warm beds: warm fullblooded life.[60]

        [60] *Ulysses*, pp. 116-17.

The parallel is obvious, the Old Man in 'Purgatory':

> I saw it fifty years ago
> Before the thunderbolt had riven it,
> Green leaves, ripe leaves, leaves thick as butter,
> Fat greasy life.[61]

The enclosure dreaded and desired by modernist literature is perhaps never so fully and awe-fully enacted as in Yeats's play where the speakers know not their own death. 'Purgatory' as a meditation on Irish history, the Big House, and sectarian *mésalliance* subversively and persuasively reveals the manner in which those who formulate their history and consciously invest their faith in it are ultimately enclosed in all that they unconsciously exclude and repress. Yeats's 'Purgatory' is Hell, and by a pleasing corollary Joyce's 'Hades' is processive, purgatorial. Bloom, by winding the adage 'The Irishman's house is his coffin' out of his funereal mood, puts both Englishmen and castles in their place; furthermore we note that Bloom returns to his house and to his warm bed. Yet the distinguishing, Joycean *mot juste* is Bloom's 'yet', a possible continuity of that critical modernism which history called forth and frustrated between 1904 and 1922.

4. *FINNEGANS WAKE* 13.04-13.19

Where is this continuity to be traced — in latter-day Irish literature written in English or Gaelic, in the *nouveau roman* of Robbe-Grillet and Beckett, in Joyce's own *Finnegans Wake*? Beyond these literary texts there lies a vast tract of critical discourse whose existence is scarcely conceivable without the *Wake* and the earlier Joycean preludes to the *Wake*. No adequate treatment of even one of these Joycean legacies can be attempted here: instead we may be content with emphasizing the continuity which links *Finnegans Wake* to the earlier work in which Joyce's critical modernism

[61] W. B. Yeats, 'Purgatory', *Collected Plays* (London: Macmillan, 1963), pp. 681-2.

first bravely manifested itself. In discussing the *Wake* one necessarily discusses its critics for Joyce's compositional method guarantees that every reading of his novel is a critical response and not a passive acceptance. Of course some commentators have striven to reduce their response to the level of a naturalist appreciation: J. B. Lyons, for example, labours sedulously to prove that Irish priests were immune to venereal disease and crowns his argument by citing as evidence of Joyce's modified and softened attitudes to his early environment the following passage from *Finnegans Wake*:

> Since the bouts of Hebear and Hairyman the cornflowers have been staying at Ballymun, the duskrose has choosed out Goatstown's hedges, twolips have pressed togatherthem by sweet Rush, townland of twinedlights, the whitethorn and the redthorn have fairygeyed the mayvalleys of Knockmaroon . . .[62]

To fear and yet practise a literal reading of 'The Sisters' leads Lyons to see this passage as 'vivid with life', a rebuke to those who cling to the stultifying idea of paralysis, and not to see that his example is Joyce's parody of Edgar Quinet's rhapsody on botanical survival and human mortality.[63]

Generally speaking, we may regard literalism as the least bothersome of the approaches adopted towards *Finnegans Wake*. The static application of the very philology Joyce strove to defeat is more characteristic. Adeline Glasheen, in the preface to *A Census of Finnegans Wake*, insists that 'Joyce did not forsake received religion in order to enslave himself, as most rationalists have done, to received history.'[64] Hence, in her interpretation of *Finnegans Wake* 'Waterloo and the Resurrection are events of the same order.'[65] From this dubious if seemingly harmless observation Miss Glasheen

---

[62] *Finnegans Wake* (London: Faber, 1964), pp. 14–15. This view of the passage as parody is reinforced if we note a similarity to the moment in *Ulysses* (p. 79) reporting Bloom's murmured version of Martha Clifford's love-letter, 'Angry tulips with you darling manflower punish your cactus if you don't please poor forgetmenot . . .', etc.

[63] J. B. Lyons, 'Animadversions on Paralysis as a Symbol in "The Sisters"', *James Joyce Quarterly*, vol. 11, No. 3 (1974), p. 265.

[64] Adeline Glasheen, *A Census of Finnegans Wake* (Evanston: Northwestern University Press, 1956), p. vii.

[65] Idem.

advances towards the dehistoricizing of all Joyce's work.
Let us take a sample passage:

So This Is Dyoublong?
Hush! Caution! Echoland!
How charmingly exquisite! It reminds you of the outwashed engravure
that we used to be blurring on the blotchwall of his innkempt house.
Used they? (I am sure that tiring chabelshoveller with the mujikal
chocolate box, Miry Mitchel, is listening) I say, the remains of the
outworn gravemure where used to be blurried the Ptollmens of the
Incabus. Used we? (He is only pretendant to be stugging at the juba-
lee harp from a second existed lishener, Fiery Farrelly.) It is well
known.[66]

In fairness, it should be noted that Miss Glasheen's annotation relies on information from another source, Mrs
Christiani's *Scandinavian Elements of 'Finnegans Wake'*.
Nevertheless, as the form in which the *Census* presents its
case is itself significant I quote Miss Glasheen verbatim:

FARRELLY, Fiery, and Miry Mitchel — Mrs Christiani says: 'Fiery' =
French *fier*, 'proud'; 'Farrelly' = Danish *farlig*, 'dangerous'; she, therefore, identifies FF with Nicholas Proud (q.v.), and Miry (Russian *mir*
= 'peace') Mitchel (q.v.) with St Michael (q.v.). I am sure there is a lot
of truth in this explanation.[67]

As Nicholas Proud is identified with the Devil (Nicholas =
Old Nick = Lucifer = Pride), this reveals Fiery Farrelly and
Miry Mitchel to be an eternal opposition of Devil and
Archangel, as in Milton (q.v.). Not only does the lexico-
graphical arrangement of information mimic the metaphysical interpretation it implies, it also suppresses the
indicative shapes and tones of Joyce's prose. Rhyme (cf.
'miry') tells us to pronounce 'Fiery' as adjectival of English
'fire', and Fiery Farrelly thus begins to sound and look like
a plausible Irish name. In the *Annotations*, Roland McHugh
glosses it as 'Feardorcha O'Farrelly (fl. 1736), Ir. poet' and

    [66] *Finnegans Wake*, p. 13.
    [67] Adeline Glasheen, *Third Census of Finnegans Wake* (Berkeley, Los Angeles,
London: University of California Press, 1977), p. 90; see also Dounia Bunis
Christiani, *Scandinavian Elements of Finnegans Wake* (Evanston: Northwestern
University Press, 1965), p. 92. (Miss Christiani is a mite more tentative in her
interpretation than Miss Glasheen acknowledges.)

offers no suggestion for Miry Mitchel.[68] He does however
interpret 'So This is Dyoublong?' as an allusion to M. J.
MacManus's *So This is Dublin* (1927) which derides Joyce.
However, 'Hush! Caution! Echoland!' echoes a passage in
George Moore's *A Drama in Muslin* (1886) which, significantly, is set in Dublin in the year of Joyce's birth, 1882; the
paragraph parodies characteristic stylistic flourishes of
Moore's.[69] If this echo is recognized, it becomes feasible to
see in Miry Mitchel a reflection of Susan Langstaff Mitchell
(1866–1926) who satirized Moore in verse and who wrote
a mock biography of him.[70] As rhyme links Miry and Fiery,
Fiery Farrelly might then be treated as an allusion to Agnes
O'Farrelly, a Gaelic League enthusiast and sometime professor at University College, Dublin. Both women are gently
mocked in Moore's *Hail and Farewell*, thus forming a perfect
circle of literary allusion.[71]

The result of this exegesis is not some claim that *Finnegans
Wake* is about Irish literary skirmishes rather than the war in
Heaven. It is however salutary if we recognize that the crucial
element in reading *Finnegans Wake* is not the identification
of referents but the elucidation and advancement of relationship between various levels of allusion. That Joyce should
refer to a novel dealing with 'the moral idea of Dublin in
1882' indicates the degree to which his last great novel
conforms to the programme announced to Grant Richards
in 1906 — 'to write a chapter of the moral history of my
country'. Superficially, the *Wake* looks unlike *Dubliners*,
and yet the technique of forcing the reader to change roles
(and become momentarily, a speaker) so as to perceive the
relationship between Fiery Farrelly and Miry Mitchel was
employed by Joyce as early as 1904 in writing 'Eveline'.

[68] Roland McHugh, *Annotations to Finnegans Wake* (London: Routledge and
Kegan Paul, 1980), p. 13.
[69] See Appendix F for 'the moral idea of Dublin' etc.
[70] See S. L. Mitchell, *Aids to the Immortality of Certain Persons in Ireland*
(Dublin; London: Maunsell, 1913), and *George Moore* (Dublin;London: Maunsell,
1916; also reissued by Talbot Press, 1929). If purists argue that *Finnegans Wake*
refers to Miry Mitchel (not Mitchell), it might be pointed out that Miss Mitchell
misspells John Mitchel as Mitchell, thus endorsing Joycean error — see Mitchell's
George Moore, p. 60.
[71] George Moore, *Hail and Farewell: Ave, Salve, Vale*, ed. Richard Cave
(Gerrards Cross: Smythe, 1976), pp. 587, 644, 748, 751.

Moreover, between 1904 and 1939, Joyce's country had undergone drastic historical adjustments. It had, to be sure, failed to realize the liberation of the 'masses in travail' and it still laboured within the competitive order of western capitalism: nevertheless it had formally inaugurated the revolt against the imperial and colonial system of the great powers — Joyce's interest in African colonialism is manifest in *Finnegans Wake*, and rubs shoulders with deft allusions to the fratricidal violence of post-1921 Ireland.[72] *Finnegans Wake* is necessarily cryptic, obscure, and baffling, because its underlying concern is subversive and its tactics those of retrenchment and renewed silence, exile and cunning. *Finnegans Wake* extends Joyce's critical modernism not in its alleged 'experimentalism' but in its self-conscious examination of the processes of history and language, history in language. Once again one might emphasize that Joyce's method may employ the rituals of philology but his ends are far removed from such scholasticism; so too his theme in *Finnegans Wake* is guilt and failure for the very reason that such a rendering articulate is a stage within the process of liberation. The naïve programme of release from 'the general paralysis of an insane society' announced in 1904 is itself subjected to a scrutiny of its sexuality in the festive comedy to which *Finnegans Wake* looks forward.

Speaking at the third Conference on Irish Politics and Culture at the University of Halle-Wittenberg, Professor Joachim Krehayn charted the turning tide of Marxist attitudes towards Joyce. He had been unfairly neglected in the past, and now editions of his works were in progress: Joyce had been reconsidered, and reissued, but in the long run he remained distinctively an Irish author whose relevance in the German Democratic Republic must be limited. As editor

---

[72] I am grateful to Dr Pieter Bekker for his comments in conversation on African elements in *Finnegans Wake* and on Joyce's interest in the history of colonialism. Some time around 1909–10 Joyce ironically noted in an address-book:

England
She is successful with savages, her mind being akin to theirs (*James Joyce Archive* 'A Portrait . . .', etc., p. 123).

As in so many other areas, Joyce's relation with the primitivist side of modernism is deeply critical.

of the new edition of *Dubliners*, Krehayn was clearly not
speaking from a position of hostility or reluctant approval.[73]
His relegation of Joyce as distinctively an Irish writer has a
symptomatic value which extends far beyond the frontiers
of Germany. And this must stimulate a confession of deep
unease on the part of the present writer. For, if Joyce is
rescued from the New Critics, the mythologists, and the
philologists, and is instead regarded as an exemplary subject
of literary history, should not one concede the *marginality* of
the history which he in turn works upon? Certainly, English
critics have been notoriously reluctant to commit themselves
at length, as if their commentary might constitute some form
of trespass in the affairs of a friendly and neighbouring state.
Dr Leavis on Joyce scarcely amounts to a slim pamphlet, and
much of it repetitious as if the bother of considering a
second example were excessive.[74] The same might be said
of Raymond Williams, who transfers the *aperçus* of *The
English Novel* (1970) to *The Country and the City* (1973)
almost verbatim.[75] Such embarrassment in confronting Joyce
might in itself form the material for an analysis of cultural
relations between Britain and Ireland, but for the moment
we should concentrate on the immediate issue of Joyce's
obsessive exploitation of the minutiae of Irish topography,
the arcana of local affairs in Dublin, the sounds and smells of
Chapelizod, all that an outsider might justifiably complain
he cannot master.

In what sense — or, perhaps one should say, to what
ends — can Susan L. Mitchell, the Metropolitan Hall, and
'Derevaun Seraun' concern the contemporary reader and
writer? An answer could be provided at length, in which the

[73] Joachim Krehayn, 'James Joyce, Nationalautor und Weltliteratur', *Irland:
Gesellschaft und Kultur*, vol. iii, pp. 265-71. See also Wolfgang Wicht's provoking
and impressive paper, 'Yeats and Joyce: Some General Remarks' (pp. 204-12 in
the same collection) which relates Joyce to the international nature of the transition to monopoly capitalism rather than to the cosmopolitan decadence of
modernism as denounced by Lukács.
[74] See, e.g., *The Great Tradition* (1948) (London: Chatto, 1973), pp. 25-6,
and *The Common Pursuit* (1952) (London: Chatto, 1965), p. 284. Leavis's most
extensive commentary on the topic was 'James Joyce and the Revolution of the
Word', *Scrutiny*, vol. ii, No. 2 (1933), pp. 193-201.
[75] *The English Novel from Dickens to Lawrence* (London: Chatto, 1970),
pp. 164-8; and *The Country and the City* (Frogmore: Paladin, n.d.), pp. 291-5.

culture of 'secondary' nations is shown to have been crucial
in shaping twentieth-century cosmopolitan art — Strindberg's
Sweden, Sibelius's Finland, and Picasso's Spain are not the
'great powers' of August 1914. But this indiscriminate listing
of small nations and irredentist provinces is really little
more than sentimentality. More precisely, one should point
to Ireland's early experience of independence and neo-
colonialism and the prior history of that status, and to
Ireland's *late* experience of linguistic trauma in the colonial
period. This, together with the contradictions of the disunited kingdom,[76] provides the crude framework for an
analysis in terms of Althusserian 'overdetermination'. Of
course, all this is true of Yeats as well as Joyce; as we have
seen, the two Irish authors adopted drastically different
attitudes towards history, genre, and language. Approaching
Joyce's texts more closely, one might specify a particular
feature of Irish colonial experience which is taken up in
Ulysses and which is given structural status there. In the
prolonged and bitter 'lock-out' of 1913, the leader of the
Employers' Federation was William Martin Murphy, a newspaper magnate: in 1916, the same Murphy used his press to
insist upon the execution of the socialist James Connolly
who was consequently shot in his wheel-chair. Ireland's
under-developed industrial sector was well known, and the
absence of genuine workers in *Ulysses* cause for complaint by
primitive Marxists. But the centrality of the press in the
organization of Irish capitalism in the revolutionary period is
at once a sign of industry's undeveloped state and its
advanced consciousness, for control of communications takes
the place of the steel-mills or the manufactories. Joyce's
Citizen knows Murphy as 'the Bantry jobber', and Murphy's
hostility to Parnell is the cause of his animus. The 'Aeolus'
episode, however, transcends the simple attention to the
press as topic, and its language achieves the 'ruination of
the referential powers of language'.[77] Moreover, 'Aeolus'

[76] *Finnegans Wake,* p. 188. For a stimulating essay on some aspects of the
colonial/national timetable see L. M. Cullen, 'The Cultural Basis of Modern Irish
Nationalism', in Rosalind Mitcheson, ed., *The Roots of Nationalism: Studies in
Northern Europe* (Edinburgh: Donald, 1980), pp. 91-106.
[77] Colin MacCabe, op. cit., p. 115.

perfectly demonstrates the historical quality of Joyce's composition for, having published the episode in *The Little Review* in October 1918, Joyce further expanded it and its catalogue of rhetorical devices and broke it up with sixty-three journalistic captions or headlines. 'Aeolus' opens with tram-men's cries, Guinness barrels, and advertisements: communications and consumerism dominate with all their unreal promises of fulfilment. Far from missing the essential features of industrial society, *Ulysses* concentrates upon the most potent features of life in such a society.

The development of language implicit in Joyce's radical revision of 'Aeolus' totally undermines the classic notion of the work of art as an end in itself, the sort of creation the Stephen of *A Portrait* aspires to. In terms of character, we have seen that the Stephen of *Ulysses* does not simply achieve a renewed access to reality via Bloom's kitchen. But Joyce's revolutionary practice here distinguishes him drastically from Yeats, and the distinction embraces concepts of history as well as art. In Yeats one finds repeatedly that, within a poem or play, a figure is presented as achieving form by assimilation to some further level of art; thus, in 'Easter 1916', the concluding lines of the poem ritualize names which, by being written out in verse, are changed utterly.[78] This metaformalism does indeed undergo a sea-change in the later work (where its effects are more ironic), but in 'Cathleen ni Houlihan' its compensatory function is clear. The Old Woman, having prophesied that 'many that are red-cheeked now will be pale-cheeked', proceeds to move from prose to verse and with this shift to offer an aesthetic immortality in legend for those who support her cause:

> They shall be remembered for ever,
> They shall be alive for ever,
> They shall be speaking for ever,
> The people shall hear them for ever.[79]

Considered in terms of plot, this curtain line of the disguised Countess anticipates the imminent defeat of the rebels — the setting is Killala, 1798. If Yeats's late plays reveal the manner

---

[78] W. B. Yeats, 'Easter 1916', *Collected Poems*, p. 203.
[79] W. B. Yeats, 'Cathleen ni Houlihan', *Collected Plays*, p. 86.

in which those who formulate their history and consciously
invest their faith in it are ultimately enclosed in all that
they unconsciously exclude and repress, then 'Cathleen ni
Houlihan' (written on the eve of Yeats's explicit adoption of
the *Ascendancy* view of Irish history) lays the ground for this
ultimate irony. The play attempts to advance two unrelated
and unrelatable perspectives upon history; for the family in
the cottage there is all the freedom and unpredictability of
the future, the sense of potential and participation; for the
lyrical Countess, there is the metadramatic knowledge of
history and its closures, the certainty, indeed predetermi-
nation of an illusory future. And here we find in Yeats the
counter-truth to Stephen's experience of history; for, having
observed that *colon* and *colonisé* are too exclusivist in their
implications to describe the formulator and the recipient of
history respectively — and Stephen is recipient by virtue of
his nightmares — we find in Yeats an antithetical statement
of the polarity. The Old Woman's song is a significant point
of reference and comparison because it too lies behind the
passage from *Finnegans Wake* we have taken as our focus;
the paragraph continues:

Lokk for himself and see the old butte new. Dbln. W.K.O.O. Hear?
By the mausolime wall. Fimfim fimfim. With a grand funferall. Fumfum fumfum. 'Tis optophone which ontophanes. List! Wheatstone's
magic lyer. *They will be tuggling foriver. They will be lichening for
allof. They will be pretumbling forover. The harpsdischord shall be
theirs for ollaves.*[80]

McHugh's *Annotations* offer real aid here, for he tells us that
Wheatstone invented a box 'shaped like a lyre, into which
piano's vibrations passed, & which then appeared to play
itself'.[81] In other words, the Aeolian Harp in mass-produc-
tion. The art of Moore and the early Yeats offers illusory
compensations for the disappointments which its history
imposes. Joyce's critical modernism fully acknowledges the
defeat of his idealistic 1904 programme of culture liberation,
yet it proceeds through *Ulysses* and *Finnegans Wake* to

---

[80] *Finnegans Wake*, p. 13; emphasis added to parallel the four lines of Yeats's
play.
[81] Roland McHugh, op. cit., p. 13.

interrogate the terms of that defeat and to assume (and so render possible) a future readership.

I have spoken of Joyce as offering a possible continuity of that critical modernism which was called forth and frustrated in the years between 1904 and 1922. Continuity, of course, is not simply a matter of futurist extension, and it may be equally valid to look to an earlier moment of literary history for an effective placing of Joyce's achievement. 'Wise passiveness in time' is in part a definition of Wordsworth's Christian stoicism, but it also catches the frustrations of a young man whose faith in revolution was (in his view) betrayed. That the great revolution of Joyce's time was Bolshevik rather than bourgeois must be noted, together with the confusedly bourgeois-and-more promptings of the Irish rebellion. Yet while it was never Bolshevik, Joyce's attitude to revolution, as to history, was not permitted to be one of privileged faith. The dialectical transformation of quantity into quality, function into symbol, is seen in essentially romantic terms in lines from 'Michael' which may none the less be quoted in this Joycean context:

> The length of full seven years from time to time
> He at the building of this Sheep-fold wrought,
> And left the work unfinished when he died.[82]

In the more exposed position of Irish modernist in the age of Russian revolution, Joyce's image of literary conscience, literary conservation cannot be the sheep-fold. In *Ulysses* we have seen that even in Hell, Bloom can assert the dignity of the common man, though in a style which we should progressively read for its limitations. Wordsworthian pastoral, which might be called the formalism of Nature, similarly claims to be the language of men speaking to men. At the conclusion of the second chapter of Book III in *Finnegans Wake*, the narrator provides a superficially similar and attractive vision of natural rhythms re-emerging:

Brave footsore Haun! Work your progress! Hold to! Now! Win out, ye divil ye! The silent cock shall crow at last. The west shall shake the

---

[82] William Wordsworth, 'Michael, a Pastoral Poem', *Poetry and Prose*, ed. W. M. Merchant (London: Rupert Hart-Davis, 1969), p. 205.

east awake. Walk while ye have the night for morn, lightbreakfast-
bringer, morroweth whereon every past shall full fost sleep. Amain.[83]

It is true that west and east are here restored to some mutually defining rhythm, and true too that the 'lightbreakfast-
bringer' lightly knocks on the head that domesticating myth
of *Ulysses* interpretation whereby Leopold's patriarchal
stature is restored in his ordering of breakfast from Molly.
But Book III is described by Campbell and Morton as 'the
book of the *desired* future; not the future *really* germinating
in the nursery upstairs . . . but the mirage-future of the
idealizing daydreams of the half-broken father'.[84] Once
again, Joyce obliges the reader of *Finnegans Wake* to change
roles, this time in order to recognize the specific *speaker* of
the words on the page. It is true that the passage is comic,
but with this higher recognition its comedy approaches that
critical revelation of a festive conclusion which is the end of
history. In the first version of the passage Shaun is hailed
'heart & soul you are of Shamrogueshire'[85] and the entire
rhetoric here is a parody of *biedermeier* Free State self-
sufficiency, a hermetic and deluded protectionism. Joyce's
mimicry, in *Dubliners* as much as in *Finnegans Wake*, mocks
a mockery. Thus it draws the reader towards his creation of
an order which is not competitive and in which life and art
positively define each other.

[83] *Finnegans Wake*, p. 473.
[84] Joseph Campbell and Henry Morton Robinson, *A Skeleton Key to
Finnegans Wake* (London: Faber, 1947), pp. 211–2.
[85] David Hayman, ed., *A First Draft Version of Finnegans Wake* (London:
Faber, 1963), p. 227.

8. W. B. YEATS: TWO APPROACHES

Dead on the sand dead Arabs and dead Jews.
Dead in the mud all kinds of Vietnamese.
After commercials and comedians
The Irish kill each other on the news.

Matthew Mead[1]

The impact of T. S. Eliot's famous endorsement of the
English metaphysical poets as exemplary for the contemporary writer has been sufficiently great to mask the tensions
within that historical strategy. Modernism, so deeply associated with Eliot's achievement in English poetry, and
Tradition, so effectively nourished by Eliot's and Grierson's
presentation of John Donne, are antagonistic terms — or so it
would seem. A concern with the modernity of their generation's experience does not immediately sanction that
attention to the value of a past literature which Tradition
tabulates. And yet, it is undoubtedly true that Yeats, Eliot,
and Pound acknowledged the crisis of their time by a particular emphasis on the culture of the seventeenth century
(in England), the eighteenth century (in Ireland) or the
medieval period generally.

Modernism — a catch title if ever there was one — is not to
be identified with any easy acceptance of the contemporary
experience. Its accepted dates — say 1880 to 1930 — mark a
period of transition, of change, and revolution. And Tradition may yet be shown to be less than frank and respectful
in its attitude to the past. One crucial area in which these
tensions were manifest was *the primitive*, that paradoxical
discovery of high European civilization in its violent imposition upon the globe. The confident belief in European
superiority was never shared by a Cézanne or a Conrad;
nevertheless, the artistic obsession with primitive cultures
remained ambiguously related to the gunboats and syphilis

---

[1] Matthew Mead, 'And Later this Evening', *The Midday Muse* (London:
Anvil Press, 1979), p. 19.

of official negotiations. That ambiguity, in turn, contributes to the truly central place of Yeats in Anglophone Modernism, for Yeats's Ireland provided access to an allegedly primitive society which was still European. The unique political and economic structure of the United Kingdom of Great Britain and Ireland left Birmingham and Ballina open to each other's self-image. The contrast is worked out in touching detail in 'Balla' (Sligo) and London in Yeats's early fiction *John Sherman* (1891), though here we meet a *biedermeier* intimacy rather than the astringency of Connemara fishermen. To see Ireland, or even parts of Ireland, as 'primitive' was a task greatly eased by the success of Protestant Ascendancy. For a start, the middle classes were evidently dismissed from the discussion by the polarized sectarianism of nineteenth-century Ireland. Second, the antique dignities and guilts which the myth of Protestant Ascendancy laid upon the landowning class rendered the invocation of medieval and feudal sources all the more plausible – one of Yeats's more ridiculous fictions was that in which he converted Augusta Persse's evangelical upbringing into a feudal apprenticeship. Finally, the de-Christianized 'Protestantism' of John Butler Yeats on the one hand, and of various Ulster Unionists on the other, rendered the presentation of a Catholic peasantry as *ur*-native, pagan, all the more convincing to a public denied any reliable historical discussion.

In the sixteenth section of *Autumn Journal* (1938) Louis MacNeice considers retrospectively some of the reasons why 'we ... like being Irish'. They include membership of a 'world that never was', the territorial smallness of which allows one to think of the place 'with a family feeling', and so forth. The passage ends, unconvincingly, 'It is self-deception of course.'[2] Since the days of Spenser, it had been policy to present Ireland as reprehensibly backward by comparison with England; only with the operations of Protestant Ascendancy, and the attendant moulding of a new image of Ireland in the nineteenth century, was it possible to regard Ireland as desirably primitive. In particular, the west

---

[2] Louis MacNeice, 'Autumn Journal', *Collected Poems*, 2nd ed., ed. E. R. Dodds (London: Faber, 1966), pp. 132-3.

of Ireland accumulated in the course of the century a reputation as the repository of all that was venerable, primitive, and undeveloped in Irish culture. The Famine accelerated that process by drawing attention to the linguistic distinctiveness of the region, and the movement to restore the Irish language (the Gaelic League was founded in 1893 but it had several precursors) gave prominence to the idea of the west as the *real* Ireland, compared with which Belfast or Kildare were but regrettable aberrations, were indeed somehow to be treated as if they were less than real. For Yeats, the west was first and foremost the landscape of Sligo, its mountains and lakes, though *John Sherman* is there to remind us just how clearly he saw the provincial town and its limitations. Turning his back upon these evidences of a *petit bourgeoisie* and related actualities, he concentrated upon the possible intimacy of peasant and nobleman, cabin and Big House in the landscape of post-Famine Ireland. Intimacy, the experience of a bond which is not rationalized or qualified by external pressures, lent to notable scenes of western landscape a distinctiveness which the world of factories and timetables had allegedly lost. Yeats's poetry abounds in these concrete allusions to the real world of the west — Inisfree, Dromahair, Lissadell, the Seven Woods, Páirc-na-Lee, Knocknarea, etc., etc. But we underestimate the subtle reservations of Yeats's poetic perception if we mistake the *possibility* of intimacy for the thing itself, if we mistake the accessibility of those place-names on the map for the integration of a poet in a known and comprehensive culture. One feature of Yeats's position *vis à vis* this actual world, which advises caution, is the role of linguistic juncture, the extent to which place-names radiated meaning for the very reason that their language was no longer an acknowledged vernacular.

We approach Yeats, therefore, warned against a too easy acceptance of him as local celebrant. Yet the kind of foreground which topographical allusion enjoys in his poetry may alert us to a more subversive and concealed aspect of the poetry generally. Yeats was deeply indebted to French Symbolism; he wrote an essay on 'The Symbolism of Poetry' as well as one on 'The Philosophy of Shelley's Poetry'. As

against this prominent evidence of Yeats's commitment to
symbolism generally, we should also note his interest in
Spenser, his edition of Blake, and other activities in which a
recognition of a different mode of writing and of interpretation is present. Spenser's allegorical method is decisively
lodged in the period of the English Renaissance, but Blake's
elaborate system is at once romatic and allegoric. The work
of David Erdman and others has rescued Blake from the
starry metaphysics of romantic symbolism, and related his
poems directly (though not simplistically) to the social and
political world in which he wrote and worked. Blake's
vigorous rejection of duality rendered that rescue always
possible, whereas in Yeats the possibility of such a reading is
more complicated. Nevertheless, we should note what may at
first seem an unremarkable yet covert element in the work —
its deployment of emblems in a manner which is close to
allegory. The Big House, Standish O'Grady, September 1913,
Coole Park, Parnell, the Municipal Gallery — any reader's
response to these elements surely includes attention to their
social and historical contexts. It is wrong to see Cuchulain
as allegorical of Charles Stewart Parnell; but wrong too to
forget that Parnell, in other poems, is a historical figure who
should not be promoted to mythological glory without
attention to that historical dimension.

Perhaps two movements in Yeats's work can now be
identified: (i) a movement towards rendering concrete certain vestigial or marginal aspects of social experience in a
manner which lends (rather than confers) a distinctive
integrity and wholeness to them; (ii) a movement towards
assimilating certain prominent, recognizable, and immediate
aspects of social experience in a manner which absorbs and
accommodates them. The first of these can be related to
allegory, the second to symbolism. The danger inherent in
an emphasis on the first is the reduction of Yeats to dexterous celebrant of Irish 'realities'; with the second we run
the risk of Platonizing him out of existence. What is of
genuine interest is the historical conjuncture of these rival
possibilities and the access they give us to an insight into the
discrete activities of modernism. Yeats is more revealing of
the values of Modernism than Eliot is, precisely because he

is less 'pure' a Modernist. He is of course also a great deal
more prolific not only as poet and dramatist, but as critic,
philosopher, and propagandist. This, together with the
length of his active career as poet, renders a comprehensive
account of his *œuvre* impossible except in the artificial and
distorting context of that *œuvre* alone. What follows, therefore, is an investigation which adopts two approaches to the
question of Yeats and his historical position, and beyond
that a concentration upon 'Purgatory' as the classic text of
the later period.

Why should the *œuvre* itself be regarded as an inadequate
context in which to judge the poet? There is little need
nowadays to argue against the more extreme hermeticism
of the New Critics, and yet in the case of Yeats particularly
a warning against the dangers of an isolated criticism is
timely. Firstly, we should remind ourselves that when we
speak of Yeats we do not mean the biographical individual
(even if the individual subject were still a viable concept in
the late twentieth century) but rather the *summum* of texts
bearing his name; and that these texts, properly and fully
treated, are a web of relationships and not a monadic thing-
in-itself. Beyond this theoretical point, there are distinct
tactical advantages to be gained by some implicitly comparative method by which contrasting perspectives may be cast
upon the principal area of attention. Above all such considerations however, in the case of Yeats there is the paramount
responsibility to resist his prescription of the history, let
alone *œuvre*, in which we might see him. Not only is Yeats's
work a multifarious act of self-making and autobiography but
the ramifications of that endeavour aspire to create a new
history in which that undertaking appears exemplary, necessary, and accomplished. Thus Yeats, in his treatment of the
eighteenth century just as in his adopting of Nōh conventions, rewrites the terms upon which he would be interpreted. This is not simply a matter of invention or distortion:
it involves the suppression and silencing of those avenues by
which he gains access to his material. In the case of the Irish
Augustans, he is obliged to suppress much of the intervening
history of both Ireland and Britain; in the case of the Nōh —
not our principal concern here but still relevant in the context

of Celticism — he silences those Orientalist modes of European thought about Japan through which his 'unmediated'
Nōh conventions are made available.

There is a thematic and critical point to be observed here,
and it reintroduces the notion of modern allegory. Yeatsian
emblemism does not employ the stone in the midst of all,
the nettles waving on a shapeless mound to indicate the
actualities of history: instead what is posited is a substitution
of myth for history, an interpretation of history which veers
into the cyclical movements of the ahistorical. And yet in
Yeats's work — whether considered in the particularities of
a poem such as 'Nineteen Hundred and Nineteen' or in the
larger conceptual debate on Tradition — there is constantly
evident the stresses and tensions of that divergence.

1.   PUBLIC OPINION, FROM W. E. H. LECKY TO 'NINETEEN HUNDRED
AND NINETEEN'

'Nineteen Hundred and Nineteen' is characteristic of one
important element in Yeats's work in that we are regularly
tempted to hear the poet in his own voice, to hear the poem
as expressive of attitudes directly attributable to a specific,
biographical author. The seductive intimacy of Anglo-Irish
literature, its adoption of the coterie as symbolic of all its
transactions, has deluded us into thinking ourselves initiate
to those mysteries. In more rigorous moments of thought,
when the allure of cultural advertisement is resisted, we
concede that poems are read and not heard, and that the
expressive notion of poetry is crudely inadequate to that
aspect of poetic meaning which one might describe as all that
the poems significantly exclude. Curtis Bradford, who has
provided us with transcripts of the early drafts of 'Nineteen
Hundred and Nineteen', speaks of Yeats's slow accumulation
of the images he needed 'to express the idea contained in
his subject', and proceeds to place the poem among those
which 'use variations of the I-persona'.[3] This is at least more
cautious than Donald Torchiana's insistence that Yeats opens

---

[3]   Curtis B. Bradford, *Yeats at Work* (Carbondale: Southern Illinois University
Press, 1965), pp. 12, 17.

the poem by establishing 'the wisdom of the high-minded few among the Protestant rulers of the Anglo-Irish eighteenth-century', as the modern counterpart of ancient classical sanctities.[4] T. R. Henn, with even greater precision, *locates* the drunken soldiery of 'Nineteen Hundred and Nineteen' in Galway and Clare.[5] In contrast, when Harold Bloom compares the poem to work by Wallace Stevens, we are almost relieved at his ignorance of Irish history, his neglect of the Onomasticon Godelicon.[6]

On the whole the historians have been more sensitive to the literature than the critics have been sensitive to history, its materials and its methodology. Yet if the critics have scattered historical solecisms to left and right while the historians quote poetry with fond precision, is not the greater responsibility still lying with the historians? F. S. L. Lyons has recently acknowledged the neglect by his Irish colleagues of the whole area of *Kulturgeschichte*.[7] Such an omission is not to be justified or even awkwardly apologized for on the grounds of its subject being merely a superstructural aspect of a social reality more concretely analysable in, say, export figures for the port of Dublin. Far from being secondary to such economic realities as Cattle and Shipbuilding, culture is a central concern of the historians, being a highly specific area not only of production but of consumption also. It is much to the point, both critically and politically, to insist on the problematic nature of literature in the productions we call Anglo-Irish relations and to emphasize the extent to which the metropolitan colony within the United Kingdom of Great Britain and Ireland was devoted to the manufacture of ideology.

It would follow from these observations that what is called for here is not simply a renewed attentiveness on the part of critics to the data of historical research nor a more subtle

[4] Donald T. Torchiana, *W. B. Yeats and Georgian Ireland* (Evanston: Northwestern University Press, 1966), p. 316.

[5] T. R. Henn, *The Lonely Tower: Studies in the Poetry of W. B. Yeats* (London: Methuen, 1965), 2nd ed., rev., p. 229.

[6] Harold Bloom *Yeats* (New York: Oxford University Press, 1970), p. 357.

[7] F. S. Lyons, 'T. W. M.', in *Ireland Under the Union: Varieties of Tensions. Essays in Honour of T. W. Moody*, edd. F. S. L. Lyons and R. A. Hawkins (Oxford: Clarendon Press, 1980), p. 24.

reading of texts as symbolic structures. On the contrary, such objectives consolidate the merely tangential figuration of literature's relation *to* history or history's *to* literature. It is salutary to remember from time to time that history and literature are themselves conceptual formations, operating within that larger social totality which relates them. These are, however, uncomfortably large matters to handle in the present confined circumstances. The social relatedness of literature and history may be approached through a study of smaller conceptual areas. Public opinion is just such an area, with a specific historical development, and a complex but articulate set of relations with other, contiguous areas. In the Irish context, we shall be concerned with W. E. H. Lecky's *The Leaders of Public Opinion in Ireland* and with Yeats's poem 'Nineteen Hundred and Nineteen'. In their inter-relatedness we will note the significance of that pre-eminent ideological formation, the Protestant Ascendancy.

However, it is with Public Opinion that we should now proceed. Though the words public and opinion are venerable, their collocation has only come into general use (with the meaning we now associate with it) in comparatively recent times. In *Felix Holt*, George Eliot has her hero address 'a man in dirty fustian' in the following terms:

'I'll tell you what's the greatest power under heaven,' said Felix, 'and that is public opinion — the ruling belief in society about what is right and what is wrong, what is honourable and what is shameful. That's the steam that is to work the engines. How can political freedom make us better ... if people laugh and wink when they see men abuse and defile it?'[8]

This is Felix's moral argument against the formal liberty promised in an extension of the franchise. It is akin to Edmund Burke's advice to Irish Catholics that they should 'aim at other rescourses [*sic*] to make themselves independent in fact before they aim at a nominal independence.'[9] In George Eliot we note the combination of moral subject (what

---

[8] George Eliot, *Felix Holt, the Radical*, ed. Fred C. Thomson (Oxford: Clarendon Press, 1980), p. 250.

[9] Edmund Burke, 'To the Rev. Thomas Hussey' [*post* 9 December 1796], *Correspondence*, vol. ix, edd. R. B. Mc Dowell and John A. Woods (Cambridge: Cambridge University Press, 1970), p. 172.

is right and what is wrong) and mechanical imagery (the steam that is to work the engines) in Public Opinion. In both Eliot and Burke we note a direction against sumptuary excess — expensive modes of living and dissipation modelled on a higher social class, in the case of Burke; drunkenness in the case of George Eliot's artisans. In both cases, moral restraint is channelled powerfully to suggest a middle-class consolidation, the legitimization of which will be the special function of Public Opinion.

Of course, opinion has cropped up often in English literature long before Eliot's day. In *1 Henry IV*, the King extols the power of opinion, but the difference between the Tudor and Victorian usages is marked. Broadly speaking, one might say that the Tudors could not speak of *public* opinion, because the distinction between private and public had not yet rigidified as it was to rigidify in succeeding centuries. To be sure, the early stages of that distinction are discernible in *Henry IV* and elsewhere in Shakespeare. But it is perhaps only in Shakespeare's closest approach to domestic tragedy, *Othello*, that the distinction as a frontier of complex emotional and social significance has a structural role to play in the drama. More particularly, however, *I Henry IV* and *Felix Holt* are literary works which are (in the popular sense) historical: that is, they are set at a date significantly earlier than that of their composition. *Henry IV* is a late sixteenth-century play ostensibly about the early fifteenth century; *Felix Holt* was written shortly before the second Reform Act (1867) and is set in the period of the first (1832). Moreover, opinion and public opinion are invoked in each as an agency by which historical continuity across division and turbulence is effected on behalf of a specific social class.

The date of *Felix Holt* (1866) is sufficiently close to that of Lecky's book (1861) to encourage some further exploration of that period. On the topic of Public Opinion, the first volume of Henry Thomas Buckle's *History of Civilisation in England* (1857-1861) offers a panorama which relentlessly yokes Tudor and Victorian under a positivist teleology. Starting from a hypothetical division of citizens into lay and military occupations, Buckle proceeds to tabulate the advance of civilization in England:

In each successive generation this tendency towards a separate organization was more marked; the utility of a division of labour became
clearly recognized; and as by this means knowledge itself advanced,
the authority of this middle or intellectual class correspondingly
increased. Each addition to its power lessened the weight of the other
two classes ... At present, it is enough to say, that, taking a general
view, this third, or intellectual, class, first displayed an independent,
though still a vague, activity, in the fourteenth and fifteenth centuries;
that in the sixteenth century, this activity, assuming a distinct form,
showed itself in religious outbreaks; that in the seventeenth century,
its energy, becoming more practical, was turned against the abuses of
government, and caused a series of rebellions, from which hardly any
part of Europe escaped; and finally, that in the eighteenth and nineteenth centuries, it has extended its aim to every department of public
and private life, diffusing education, teaching legislators, controlling
kings, and, above all, settling on a sure foundation that supremacy of
Public Opinion, to which not only constitutional princes, but even the
most despotic sovereigns, are now rendered strictly amenable.[10]

The grand gesture by which the alleged laying-down of
medieval arms leads to 'that supremacy of Public Opinion'
in the Victorian period is of course but the appearance of
historical process. Far from analysing the genealogy of Public
Opinion, Buckle quite simply exemplifies its ideological
function, the legitimization in terms of the past of a middle-
class present. As an illustration of the operations of Public
Opinion he significantly chooses the repeal of the Corn Laws
in the eighteen-forties:

whoever will minutely trace the different stages through which this
great question successively passed, will find, that the Government, the
Legislature, and the [Anti-Corn-Law] League, were the unwitting
instruments of a power far greater than all other powers put together.
They were simply the exponents of that march of public opinion . . .[11]

Of course, Buckle's sweeping narrative raises the question
of *when* the English bourgeoisie did emerge — under the
Tudors, or the Stuarts or the Hanoverian Georges. Such a
question has a relevance for any Irish inquiry if we remember
the extent to which Irish land and Irish titles became rewards

---

[10] H. T. Buckle, *History of Civilization in England*, vol. i (London, 1857),
pp. 189-90.
[11] Ibid., p. 251.

for English adventurers from the seventeenth century onwards. Yet, the historical concept of Public Opinion cannot
be shuttled backwards and forwards from one stage of
development to another without vitiating its historical
nature. For Flaubert in the eighteen-fifties, it was already a
cliché: in the *Dictionnaire des idées reçues* he defined the
stock exchange as 'thermometre de l'opinion publique'.[12]
French intellectual cynicism at the stupidity of the average
bourgeois casts a light upon Buckle's happy identification of
these two factors in the advance of civilization in England.
Such displacements help to highlight the crucial importance
of uneven development in the transition from one mode of
production to another. The repeal of the Corn Laws, hailed
in England as a triumph of Public Opinion and the harbinger
of increased agricultural prosperity, in Ireland was seen as
something less universally positive. Buckle is obliged to speak
of the history of civilization *in England* as distinct from the
United Kingdom of Great Britain and Ireland, for Public
Opinion assumes unanimity in order to impose it. One effect
of Victorian Public Opinion, still powerfully evident today,
was the notion that England remained intact and unaltered
amid the global consequences of its colonial and imperial
activity.

The psychological structure of Public Opinion is perhaps a
topic too abstract and large to be investigated here. It may be
sufficient to say that it operates within a strictly delimited
social space (not necessarily a small one but certainly one
possessing a *sense* of homogeneity), and that such spaces tend
to be urban. This of course is in keeping with the strong
affiliation of Public Opinion with the legitimization of a
middle-class consensus which we have noted in Burke,
Buckle, and Eliot. If we anticipate briefly our discussion of
Lecky's four leaders of Public Opinion in Ireland, this
delimited arena is immediately evident. Swift's success in
the Wood's Halfpence controversy is founded on the intense
exploitation of the Dublin publishing industry; furthermore,
a controversy over the issue of coinage as such 'naturally'

[12] See Gustave Flaubert, *Dictionary of Accepted Ideas*, trans. etc. Jacques
Barzun (New York: New Directions, 1968), p. 83.

focuses itself on that area of society in which the cash economy is most articulate. In the cases of Henry Flood and
Henry Grattan, the struggle for legislative independence and
restored civil rights for Catholics is effectively transformed
into the creation of a Public Opinion within the little
universe of the Dublin parliament. The qualified reality of
that institution measures the limits to which these achievements were really held. With Daniel O'Connell, the area of
operation seems at first to be a great deal larger than that
chosen by Swift or Grattan. But, by the nineteenth century
the increased sophistication of the Press and (in this instance)
the reorganization of the priesthood provided the conditions
in which Public Opinion is capable of formulation on a
national scale. Of the nineteenth-century newspaper and the
Maynooth-trained priest one could argue with equal validity
in either case that their influence was felt as something at
once pervasive and remote. The newspaper, no longer something encountered in the coffee-shop but entering the home
and read by the family generally, brought together reflections
of the private and public domains in their most polar distinction. Similarly, the social origins of the Maynooth priest
drew him towards the localized social experience of the mass
of his lower-middle-class congregation, while the highly ultra-
montane loyalties of at least a significant sector of the priesthood counteracted that sense of integration between clergy
and laity. Public Opinion, which assumes unanimity in order
to impose it, is necessarily contradictory, and the priesthood
as an agency of it is not exempt in this respect. Psychologically, therefore, one can say that Public Opinion operates
precisely upon the tension engendered by the increasingly
rigidified distinction between the private and public domains.
At the risk of paradox, it could be asserted that the significant experience of Public Opinion is essentially private and
often unconscious. The laughter which Felix Holt anticipates
will greet any presumptuous insistence on explicit, formal
liberties is that laughter which implies that it knows more
than its victim knows. According to Buckle, parliament is the
unwitting instrument 'of a power far greater than all other
powers put together'.[13] In this respect, we distinguish sharply

[13] Buckle, op. cit., p. 251.

between Public Opinion as cited by Eliot and Buckle and the statistics gathered today by opinion polls; or, to be more precise, we should observe that what the gallup-polls do is not to register and measure public opinion but rather to disseminate certain issues whose validity Public Opinion requires. Public Opinion has little to do with the head-counting of Social Democrats in this constituency or that; it has everything to do with the insistence on parties and constituencies as the delimitations of political action.

A similar attention to the categories inserted in the argument, rather than a simple assessing of the validity of the contents of the argument, may help us as we approach William Edward Hartpole Lecky's *Leaders of Public Opinion*. First published in 1861, and reissued at least ten times between then and 1903, the book originally contained five essays — on Jonathan Swift, Henry Flood, Henry Grattan, Daniel O'Connell, and 'Clerical Influences'. Two important changes occur in the course of this publication history; first, the four essays on individual figures are expanded and revised for the Longmans edition of 1871; second, and more significant, the last essay on clerical influence is dropped. The effect of this latter revision is of course to steer the work towards that character-istic Victorian tendency to see history as biography writ large, but more drastically also to cast the work decisively as *history*. If we take the title of the 1903 edition at face value, we might expect to find Charles Stewart Parnell or Michael Davitt; at no point does Lecky (after the removal of 'Clerical Influence') assume that his area of inquiry is other than the past. It is tempting to see his objective as yet another exercise in envisioning the Irish past as a Golden Age, but there is in fact a more complex undertaking in progress. Given his inclusion of Swift, Flood, and Grattan, he quite deliberately associates these three distinctively eighteenth-century figures with the emergent Victorian concept of Public Opinion. O'Connell is there as a bridgehead to the contemporary world, and none too sound a bridgehead in Lecky's ultimate estimate. Yet the implication of this linking of past and present is cancelled, or rather reversed, by the elision of the essay on clerical influence. As with Buckle, what is enacted here is not simply an account of Public Opinion but an exemplification of its central concern with the legitimization of 'the intellectual class' as a line of historical continuity.

If we consider Swift's success in the matter of Wood's Halfpence, Flood's in relation to Irish Free Trade, and Grattan's apostrophe to legislative independence, these issues in isolation constitute impressive achievements for their authors. The broader perspective insists, however, that Walpole remained Prime Minister, that Irish Free Trade remained lodged in the structures of British capitalist development, and that the Dublin parliament was internally anomalous. Had Lecky extended his list to include Edmund Burke the implications of this pattern might have been immediately evident. For Burke's great success in turning the opinion of his party, and of the British public generally, against the principles of the French Revolution, acknowledges the irreversible changes which have come to France. The dominant metaphor of the Great House which informs Burke's *Reflections* points both to the sublimity and redundancy of that architectural symbol. Furthermore, Burke's success in awakening British opinion to the dangers of revolution stands in painful contrast to his embittered failure in attempting to persuade it that Irish Catholics were reliable allies deserving generous respect in the counter-revolutionary struggle. In Burke we would find, explicitly, that demarcation between Britain and England, England and Ireland which it is the function of Public Opinion to repress. Burke could not be accommodated in *Leaders of Public Opinion in Ireland* first because he shatters the deliminations of social space within which Public Opinion can operate; and second because, *considered in itself*, his work scorns unanimity as simple-minded, inadequate, and partial.

Drawing together, therefore, the evidence of those figures whom Lecky includes (Swift, Flood, and Grattan especially) with the evidence of his significant exclusions (especially Burke, Parnell, and Davitt), we can see the underlying assumption of his notion of Public Opinion is the value of consensus. Swift, Flood, and Grattan are presented in terms of their success in creating a shared social effect. Seen within the delimited social space which Public Opinion requires, success may indeed be ascribed to them, but then Public Opinion has no place in the 1720s or even the 1780s. What is possible, however, is to inquire into the extent to which Antonio Gramsci's notion of hegemony, and his concept of the intellectual as an emergent social formation, might illuminate these contradictions.[14] Such an inquiry would inevitably open up other issues which have been largely ignored by historian and critic alike — the material origins in the eighteenth century of the families, institutions, and other social agencies which constellate as the Anglo-Irish Literary Renaissance, and the prominence of cultural production in the broader area of Anglo-Irish relations within the United Kingdom.

Some conclusions about Public Opinion might now be hazarded. First, it points towards and consolidates a middle-class perspective, in which moral integrity in the individual and moderate conduct in disadvantaged groups is approved. Second, it is dependent on the bourgeois emphasis on a strict demarcation between private and public domains. Third, and virtually as a reformulation of these points, its moment of emergence is mid-Victorian. There are, however, equally important contradictions to be noted; of these we are most concerned with the retrospective insertion of the concept of Public Opinion in accounts of the past. This may strike some people as a harmless anachronism, as when one refers to Burke as a conservative or *Gulliver's Travels* as a best-seller. Walter Benjamin's 'Theses on the Philosophy of History' concludes with an intense appeal for the practice of history in a manner at once Messianic and materialist — 'Thinking involves not only the flow of thoughts, but their arrest as well.'[15] This arrest of thought through the construction and deconstruction of concepts allows the inquirer to draw together aspects of history which narrative holds apart.

[14] See 'Problems of History and Culture', in *Selections from the Prison Notebooks of Antonio Gramsci*, ed. and trans. Quintin Hoare and Geoffrey Nowell Smith (London: Lawrence and Wishart, 1971), pp. 3-120, esp. pp. 3-23.

[15] Walter Benjamin, 'Theses on the Philosophy of History', *Illuminations*, ed. Hannah Arendt, trans. Harry Zohn [n.p.]: Fontana/Collins, 1973), p. 264 (thesis 17).

Public Opinion calls out to Protestant Ascendancy, and in two senses. The belief that Irish society reaches its summit in 'the Anglo-Irish landed ascendancy', 'a numerically small Protestant landed ascendancy', 'the influence and authority of the Protestant ascendancy' is sufficiently widespread to deserve acknowledgement as a tenet of Public Opinion.[16] More than that, from the Williamite Settlement 'until the impact of the French Revolution . . . the "protestant ascendancy" was to rule unchallenged.'[17] More specifically, Swift is recognized as having articulated in *The Drapier Letters* (1724–1725) 'the watchword of the protestant ascendancy'.[18] Yet a close scrutiny of Protestant Ascendancy reveals a second sense in which its affinities to Public Opinion takes on added significance. This is not the place to rehearse all the evidence available to plot the trajectory of the term Protestant Ascendancy; it is sufficient to say that, far from dating from the reign of William and Mary, or the pages of *The Drapier Letters*, we do not find the phrase occurring before January 1792 when the Corporation of Dublin adopted it as an anti-reform slogan. Despite its emergence in the revolutionary 1790s, and sponsored by the guild members of a city corporation, Protestant Ascendancy is destined to become the title of a venerable, veritably aristocratic, rural and landed élite.[19] This back-dating of Protestant Ascendancy is probably not under way until the middle decades of the nineteenth century when O'Connellite democracy is forcing a reassessment of the eighteenth century. A version of this revisionism may be detected in Lecky's essay on Swift and the Wood's Halfpence incident:

[16] See for such examples Kevin B. Nowlan, *The Politics of Repeal: A Study in the Relations between Great Britain and Ireland, 1841–1850* (London: Routledge and Kegan Paul, 1965), p. 3, etc. I should stress, however, that Professor Nowlan also attends in detail to the role of a Protestant middle class in the politics of the 1840s.

[17] J. C. Beckett, *The Making of Modern Ireland 1603–1923* (London: Faber, 1966), p. 146. I am grateful to Professor Beckett for his most helpful and generous discussion of this question at the Conference of Irish Historians in Britain (March 1982, in the University of Sussex.)

[18] Ibid., p. 166.

[19] The *glissade* from ascendancy to aristocracy as a description of the Anglo-Irish background is more evident among literary scholars than historians; see e.g. p. 12 above.

There is no more momentous epoch in the history of a nation than that in which the voice of the people has first spoken, and spoken with success. It marks the transition from an age of semi-barbarism to an age of civilisation — from the government of force to the government of opinion. Before this time rebellion was the natural issue of every patriotic effort in Ireland. Since then rebellion has been an anachronism and a mistake. The age of Desmond and of O'Neil [sic] had passed. The age of Grattan and of O'Connell had begun.[20]

The succeeding paragraph begins, 'Swift was admirably calculated to be the leader of public opinion in Ireland . . .'.[21]

If we turn now to Yeats's poem 'Nineteen Hundred and Nineteen' it is not to give an exhaustive formal analysis of its imagery and structure, as to suggest how the interrogation of a concept (even so unpoetic a concept as Public Opinion) can point to the full feasibility of exhaustive analysis both historically and critically. John Holloway has written of such poems of Yeats's that they 'produce the poetic effect of being, by the totality of what is in them, not a mere reflection of some external reality, but an independent reality with a nature of its own.'[22] It is just such praise of Yeats which excites the literary historian to suspect Yeats, without checking to see if this praise in any adequate sense is based upon a reading of the poem, and not upon an *a priori* preference for poetic autonomy.

It would be folly to concede that analysis *per se* now supersedes historical and conceptual investigations, as if the latter were only a framework for the former. A comprehensive reading of the poem is comprehensive to the extent that it establishes the mediations between literature and history, language and form, draft and text, and so forth. Perhaps Pierre Macherey is guilty of French extremism when he writes that 'the critic, employing a different language, brings

[20] W. E. H. Lecky, *Leaders of Public Opinion in Ireland*, new ed. (London, 1871), p. 49.
[21] Idem.
[22] John Holloway, 'Style and World in *The Tower*', *An Honoured Guest: New Essays on W. B. Yeats*, edd. Denis Donoghue and J. R. Mulryne (London: Edward Arnold, 1965), p. 97.

out a *difference* within the work by demonstrating that it is *other than it is.*'[23] Critics following T. R. Henn certainly jeopardize any such distance; Donald Torchiana's reading of the poem's content as the poem's meaning is in this sense undifferentiating:

> The so-called world of that poem has been nearly altogether missed. However, all I would draw attention to is the relevance of the exalted Protestant ideal from eighteenth-century Ireland to the world of revolution in 1919 ... Yeats opens [the poem] by pointing to those sacred and ornamental classical safeguards (for the multitude) whose modern counterparts — impartial law, humane habits, enlightened public opinion — have vanished. The wisdom of the high-minded few among the Protestant rulers of the Anglo-Irish eighteenth century also had its unpopular counterpart here in the continuing ideal of public service that had marked Irish, English, and European governments before the revolutions now come to a head in the year after the Great War's end.[24]

This is not so much criticism as paraphrase, and paraphrase based on the assumption that the speaker of the poem may be identified with Yeats himself. Moreover, such commentary has its allegiance to a specific reading of the history of the Protestant Ascendancy, as we shall see. As against such interpretations, I would prefer Daniel Harris's view of the speaker as possessed by inexpiable guilt while the poem itself shows Yeats's gradual recovery of constructive imaginative power. Harris insists, 'Reiterating the public pronoun "we", the speaker makes himself the scapegoat of an entire coterie.'[25] Though we may want to extend some of these terms, and indeed question the nature of Yeats's recovered power, this discriminating formal analysis is useful.

Let us consider the most fundamental linguistic aspect of the poem, its title. Nineteen Hundred and Nineteen not only names the poem it implicitly places it in relation to history. Lest this point should be lost, the poem — like very few of Yeats's — is dated after its closure with the numerals 1919.

[23] Pierre Macherey, *A Theory of Literary Production*, trans. Geoffrey Wall (London: Routledge and Kegan Paul, 1978), p. 7 (original emphasis).

[24] Torchiana, op. cit., p. 316.

[25] Daniel Harris, *Yeats, Coole Park and Ballylee* (Baltimore, London: Johns Hopkins University Press, 1974), p. 156.

This post-scriptum date at once helps to confirm the title as a placing in history, and to draw attention to the particular form adopted in the title. The title employs words, not numerals, but it employs one of several possible verbal formulations. It prevents us from particularizing the year as One Thousand, Nine Hundred and Nineteen; it prevents us from slurring it to a loose Nineteen Nineteen. Thus, the element Nineteen is repeated but not emptily so, for we are directed to the middle term, indicative of the completed nineteenth century and its nineteen year excess. The post-scriptum date, on the other hand, is unpronounceable or at best variously pronounceable.

All this may seem tangential to the poem itself, but is not so. First of all, the signatory date is false for the poem was not finished until 1921, and underwent modifications for the collection *The Tower* in 1928. It is thus more a ratifying pre-scriptum date, repeating in mocking conclusive miniature the title at the head of the poem. Second, the poem's title as originally published in *The Dial* and *London Mercury* in 1921 was 'Thoughts Upon the Present State of the World'. Thus the evolution of title and signatory date is an admission of historical focus combined with a falsification of compositional history. Within the poem there are two particular moments when this attention to dating is articulated: Section IV reads *in toto*:

> We, who seven years ago
> Talked of honour and of truth,
> Shriek with pleasure if we show
> The weasel's twist, the weasel's tooth.[26]

What is crucial here is not so much the fixing of a 'setting' in time for the poem, as it is the acknowledgement of time passing with man's alteration as its measure. For, in Section II we have read:

> So the Platonic Year
> Whirls out new right and wrong,
> Whirls in the old instead;[27]

---

[26] W. B. Yeats, 'Nineteen Hundred and Nineteen', *Collected Poems* (London: Macmillan, 1963), pp. 235-6.
[27] Ibid., p. 234.

the Platonic Year being a cycle of about 25,000 years in
which the heavenly bodies were supposed to move through
all their possible positions and return to their original relative
positions. With this vast cycle offering at once perfect opti-
mum movement and the absence of ultimate change, the
changes of seven years are powerfully contrasted. If these
suggest that only deterioration results from time-passing, the
image of the weasel leads us back to the first section of the
poem:

> The night can sweat with terror as before
> We pieced our thoughts into philosophy,
> And planned to bring the world under a rule,
> Who are but weasels fighting in a hole.[28]

Such an echo manifestly is not to be read as symbolic pat-
terning. Repetition proliferates in the poem; the lines just
quoted reach back to

> Public opinion ripening for so long
> We thought it would outlast all future days.
> O what fine thought we had because we thought
> That the worst rogues and rascals had died out.[29]

The repetition of thought discredits thought. It is as if Yeats
were aware of the American usage 'weasel-word', that word
in a sentence which drains it of significance as weasels drain
eggs. Repetition, like the vast planetary monotony of the
Platonic Year, implodes throughout 'Nineteen Hundred and
Nineteen'. 'Weasels fighting in a hole' just fails to evoke
Swift's letter to Bolingbroke of 21 March 1730 in which he
expressed the wish not to 'die here in a rage, like a poisoned
rat in a hole'.[30] Later, Thomas Kinsella's 'Nightwalker' will
also use the weasel as allegorical of Ernest Blythe, sometime
Free State minister for finance and inheritor of Yeats's
Abbey Theatre.[31] To an even greater degree, Kinsella exactly

[28] Ibid., p. 233.
[29] Ibid.
[30] Jonathan Swift, *Correspondence*, ed. Harold Williams (Oxford: Clarendon
Press, 1963), vol. iii, p. 383.
[31] In the debates of Dáil Éireann for 1922 (vol. ii, cols. 71-3) Kevin O'Higgins,
the minister for defence, was interrupted in his speech on the government's illegal
execution of Rory O'Connor and others, by the interjection of 'The weasel must

reflects his subject by a poetics of inadequacy, for 'Night-walker' sees its locus as the Sea of Disappointment. The distance between Yeats and the speaker of his poem transforms potential disillusion into something different from the satire of Kinsella and the vituperation of Swift.

It was Harold Bloom who remarked that the circumstances in which the poem arose had a cleaner bitterness than the civil war and its poems. Yet the evolving title of the poem, and the retained counterfeit date, indicate that the perception of that contrast was necessarily gradual. That title minimally avoids the sterile repetition of Nineteen Nineteen, just as the Platonic Year is juxtaposed with the seven years of palpable alteration. The poem is felt to shift in history, but hardly to move with it. Yet that grudging miniature is perhaps closer to a real historical understanding of the poem than T. R. Henn's autobiographical paraphrase:

The great age of that society had, I suppose, been the eighteenth and early nineteenth centuries; from the 1850s onwards it seems to have turned its eyes too much towards England, too conscious of its lost influence in its hereditary role of The Ascendancy. By 1912 it was growing a little tired, a little purposeless, but the world still seemed secure.[32]

Stanza 2 then follows as the most natural thing in the world.

Far from embodying this attitude Yeats, by the ironic means of his speaker, exposes it. We may say that the Ascendancy, far from having its great age in the eighteenth century, is conceived in its last decade, and conceived in very different circumstances from the landed culture evoked here and elsewhere by Henn and critics who adopt his history. And, far from losing its grip from the 1850s onwards, it is from mid-century onwards that Protestant Ascendancy acquires its identification with a rural, landed élite of long-established Protestant families. 'Lost influence in its hereditary role' is precisely the motivation of that retrospection. When the speaker points to

---

spit' — the interrupter was D. J. Gorey, TD for Carlow/Kilkenny. For Thomas Kinsella's poem see Selected Poems 1956-1968 (Dublin: Dolmen Press, 1973), pp. 85-98.
[32] T. R. Henn, op. cit., p. 4.

> Public opinion ripening so long
> We thought it would outlast all future days[33]

the organic metaphor points to the false consciousness of a
class, or class fraction, projecting itself into the past and
erecting a contradictory and illusory delimitation of social
space within the effective economy of the United Kingdom
of Great Britain and Ireland. Returning to Daniel Harris's
useful formulation, we can agree that through the public
pronoun 'we' the speaker makes himself scapegoat of a
coterie. But it is necessary to add that the speaker does not
limit his confessions to aesthetic self-indulgence. On the
contrary, he is a man

> lost amid the labyrinth that he has made
> In art or politics;[34]

And the public pronoun 'we' is better regarded as the collective pronoun, the pronoun of a social speaker who transcends
the single generation to allude to Swift, Phidias, Loie Fuller,
Shelley. To read the poem solely in terms of the year 1919 is
simple-minded historicism, to read it in eighteenth-century
terms an exercise in myth.

Drafts of the poem indicate the difficulties Yeats experienced in formulating its multivocal levels. Curtis Bradford
has substantially printed three manuscripts, all late (i.e.
1920–1), which document the poem's evolution. Yet in the
first manuscript of the first section, the line ultimately
referring to Public Opinion still reads:

> No swaggering soldier on the public ways
> Who weighed a man's life lighter than a song;[35]

Here 'public' is still used in a pre-nineteenth-century sense —
there are no private ways. In the third manuscript this has
altered momentarily to a half-line 'A public conscience'
which is immediately cancelled and followed by the line
virtually as it is published in *The Dial* for September 1921.
What is significant here is that Public Opinion gradually

---

[33] W. B. Yeats, 'Nineteen Hundred and Nineteen', op. cit., p. 233.
[34] Ibid., p. 235.
[35] See Curtis Bradford, op. cit., p. 66.

emerges to crystallize a consensus of long-ripening habit, faith in the future, and 'knowledge' of the past which is evoked mockingly in the first two stanzas. In so far as the speaker evokes an eighteenth-century hegemony — and it strikes me as *not* far — public opinion is relevantly anachronistic, given its relentless retrospective self-justification. In so far as the speaker looks behind the late Victorian and Edwardian traces to the nineteenth century, then Public Opinion is central to that entire first section of the poem and the consensus it displays and explodes. Indeed it is not too much to say that from the insertion of the phrase into the poem much else takes its new bearings. However, the mediations between draft and canonical text continue to be active in the totality which the literary historian looks for. For the speaker public opinion acts in the poem; for the reader — or as Macherey would have it, the critic — the genealogy of Public Opinion is reactivated and exposed.

The speaker is multivocal, historical as well as contemporary, despairing in his deterministic view of the Platonic Year as well as dreading the freedom seven years uncover. So much seems certain, unshakeable, included throughout the poem. Numerological methods tempt us to see the iterated nineteens of the title and the signatory date as indicating a nineteenth-century preoccupation which the text itself never articulates; thus, the nineteenth century becomes the significantly excluded meaning of the poem. This view is attractive and, within its limitations, valid. It does however bypass a more obvious and subtle omission or exclusion, and that is the elimination in the final section of 'Nineteen Hundred and Nineteen' of the speaker, the I-persona in any variation whatsoever. Nowhere in Section VI is there a discernible first-person singular or plural; instead the cumulative imagery builds upon wearisome circling and the return of evil, to conclude:

> But now wind drops, dust settles thereupon
> There lurches past, his great eyes without thought
> Under the shadow of stupid straw-pale locks,
> That insolent fiend Robert Artisson

> To whom the love-lorn Lady Kyteler brought
> Bronzed peacock feathers, red combs of her cocks.[36]

It is concretely *this* fourteenth-century witchcraft which is followed by the resilient dating '1919' in the poem's printings. But with the tense juxtaposition of remote and ostentatious history with a (doctored) contemporaneity, there goes hand in hand the elimination of the public 'we' and the private 'I' of the previous sections. The abolition of the speaker enacts the central contradiction of Public Opinion, its valorization of the privatized Ego and the elimination of the contextualized Self. The result is a subject-less narcissism, which the sequence of sections in 'Nineteen Hundred and Nineteen' rationalizes.

This eclipse of the bourgeois individual voice, with his colonizing interest in a multivalent claim upon the past, raises an issue in specifically Irish terms which has already been touched upon in relation to the emergence of Public Opinion in Great Britain. The function of Public Opinion was to legitimize a family tree for middle-class hegemony, at last asserting itself in the middle decades of the nineteenth century. Of course, the notion of a middle class had been viable in Britain centuries earlier, but the issue of its hegemony in Ireland had (perhaps tactically, and in the manner of rugby scrums) been retained in the maul of a different political vocabulary. The various levels of historical allusion in Yeats's poem posit a choice of historical moments at which bourgeoise politics might be seen as emerging in Ireland — plantation in the seventeenth century, merchant prosperity in the eighteenth, Catholic democracy in the Victorian period, Sinn Fein protectionism in the early twentieth century. None of these can be chosen, for the poem is poised between the disguise of one bourgeois element as Protestant Ascendancy (in 1919 virtually redundant) and the adoption of populist nationalism by another bourgeois element not yet fully emergent in institutional terms.

Beyond this one may point to a larger issue, which Public Opinion encapsulates and does not answer, and that is the

---

[36]   W. B. Yeats, op. cit., p. 237.

real nature of the differing modes of production coexisting within the United Kingdom of Great Britain. Lecky's work points to the divergent definitions of Public Opinion in Ireland and Britain, while Yeats's ultimately demonstrates the centrality of cultural production in those relations.

2. SONS AND FATHERS

In 1893, when he was fifty-five years of age, Henry James published a short story called 'The Middle Years' dealing with a middle-aged novelist who had just published a novel called *The Middle Years*.[37] Such meta-formalism, of course, has a long and noble ancestry in, for example, Shakespeare's use of the masque within his plays. More recently, 'Hamlet' has itself been incorporated into many works of literature; to consider only the novel, one may point to Fielding's *Tom Jones*, Goethe's *Wilhelm Meister*, Dickens's *Great Expectations*, and Joyce's *Ulysses*. In such recent literature the allusion to an earlier work of art may serve two purposes — the elaboration of an internal thematic coherence which is felt (for whatever reason) to lack resonance, and the implication of a universalizing validity for the novel itself. In this latter instance, the argument apparently runs that, if art is illusion, then art-within-art is an illusory illusion — akin to reality. Such a chemistry of internal and external objectives is bound to be an anxious undertaking.

The tension between these needs is not dissimilar to another tension in modern literature. If we look towards the area of characterization, a tension between primary relations is increasingly evident. Again, 'Hamlet' is exemplary, for the Oedipal conflict which we now see as unavoidable in reading the play is more explicitly at work in *Ulysses* and *Sons and Lovers*. If we are seeking a more complex — if not more concentrated — instance of the meta-formalist device coinciding with the father/son conflict, then *Under Western Eyes* surely fits our requirements. There Conrad, with a delicately modulated crudeness, engineers a scene in which

---

[37] *The Novels and Tales of Henry James* (Clifton NJ: A. M. Kelley, [c.1974]), The New York Edition, vol. xvi, pp. 75-106.

a parcel containing the journal that is the narrator's source is
handed by one character to the narrator. And in the same
novel, Razumov's parentage remains obscure though it is his
shadowy and influential father who determines much of the
hero's fate.

The notion of determinism is central to the tense characterization of this modern fiction. It obsesses Razumov for
whom the Czarist bureaucracy is some intimate and ghastly
extension of his own bodily existence, controlling his consciousness and bending him to its service even when he
perceives his own separate existence. That his acknowledged
father links him to this mechanism is Conrad's irony, for the
Father is supremely the necessary cause which the Son may
identify as having made him as he is. Freud's explication of
the Oedipal base of western psychology is no timeless statement of eternal fact, but a symbolism of the determinist
science which characterized so much nineteenth-century
historical and philosophical thought. The condition, it might
be said, was capable of formulation only in the interrogative
mood. Or perhaps we should suggest that the very different
answers provided by James, Yeats, and Freud address themselves to a central inquiry.

The connection between characterization (understood in
this larger sense) and the device of meta-form is explicit in
Henry James. A recent critic has summarized a recurring preoccupation of the novelist's in terms of recurring images:

The central symbol in James's work is thus the cage, trap, box, mold,
cadre in which the free soul is *fixed* or *placed*, compelled to sit motion-
less, like a still life, a work of art. And the symbolism evolves from the
antithesis of freedom and slavery, motion and immobility, life and
automatism or mechanism, nature and art.[38]

The idea that a man or woman should feel outraged, threatened or on the verge of annihilation by the possibility of
reduction to a mere thing is neither new nor profound. What
is perhaps missing from this peculiarly modernist account of
such feelings is the near-total absence of that *positive* awareness of the creative implications of such a sea-change, the

[38] Daniel J. Schneider, *Symbolism: The Manichean Vision* (Lincoln: University of Nebraska Press, 1975), p. 63.

absence of Keats's confident vision of a new world of poten-
tiality lying ahead of the mere self. If the Jamesian character
resents the aptness of 'still life' as an account of his existence,
it is because such meta-formal images insist that he is not a
human personality but only the depiction of such a personality, the depiction indeed of the appearance only of a
human being. In 'The Middle Years' the intimacy between
character and art-within-art is very close, close but inverse.
As Dencombe's health diminishes, so the reader gradually
comes to appreciate the quality of what is now evidently
Dencombe's last novel. It is not too much to say that *The
Middle Years* grows in achievement and stature as its author
approaches dissolution and death. In keeping with this, a
further adjustment, change, revelation is at work in the story,
the recognition by Dencombe and Dr Hugh that each fulfils
some essential, symbolic role in the life of the other. This too
is available in dual form, either as master-artist and sympathetic reader, or as (quite simply) father and son. I advance
these as alternative views, alternative hypotheses, for James's
irony operates subtlely to suggest that certain imprecisions in
the one interpretation render the other necessary if tentative
also.

Yet behind this duality there is an implied reading of the
relationship as constituting James's account of the relationship between art and artist. Just as the Father is author of the
Son, so the writer or painter creates the novel, play or
portrait. This relationship takes on greater complexity when,
by virtue of the Chinese box of artifice-within-aritifice, the
writer draws attention to a heightened reality to which access
is, however, formally remote. There is a body of work which
I associate with a characteristic modernist anxiety in which
endangered, or obscured, or decomposed relations between
father and son reveal the anxious relation of the artist to his
world and to his work. In so far as the artist looks to his
world, to exterior reality, he is a son, created and made
(perhaps determined) by all that he is not. In so far as he
looks to his work, he is the father, creator at will. In *Ulysses*
and *Under Western Eyes* the fillial relation is biological and
estranged: in 'The Middle Years' its psychological reality
tends towards the symbolical. As we return to Yeats's *œuvre*,

we realize the potency with which these tensions operate for him as for James.

It is, however, Yeats's drama which most immediately reveals its affinity to this modernist condition: from the Cuchulain of 'On Baile's Strand' (1904) to the Old Man of 'Purgatory' (1938) Oedipal conflict takes its inverted place in the plays. In both cases the apparent cancellation of Oedipal rebellion against the father is allied to the father's despairing encounter with his own elusive doom; in this, perhaps, sons take a satisfactory revenge. If Yeats's poetry declines to accept such elemental forms, we should not conclude that it differs in essence from the drama. In so achieved a poem as 'Ancestral Houses' we should admire the skill with which residual Carlylean notions of the hero as a model of cultural transmission, and Darwinian acceptance of biology as a science of causation, are deployed in their own transvaluation:

> Some violent bitter man, some powerful man
> Called architect and artist in, that they,
> Bitter and violent men, might rear in stone
> The sweetness that all longed for night and day,
> The gentleness none there had ever known;
> But when the master's buried mice can play,
> And maybe the great-grandson of that house,
> For all its bronze and marble, 's but a mouse.[39]

Yeats, despising science and rationalism, chose to acknowledge nineteenth-century biology under the name of heredity. The social nuances of that choice may be petty — 'Is not all charm inherited?' — but it is for the same reason irreducible. We are mistaken if we think that he had some privileged access to Castiglione, or even to Lord Chesterfield.[40] There is a temptation, on the other hand, to mock at what appears to be day-excursions to the Italian Renaissance. With so dialectical a mind as Yeats's neither position is either entirely true or false. Having heard all the evidence, we cannot doubt that he did in truth labour to obtain the past, to re-*present* it

---

[39] W. B. Yeats, 'Meditations in Time of Civil War — (i) Ancestral Houses', *Collected Poems*, pp. 225-6.
[40] W. B. Yeats [Journal, 2 January 1909], *Memoirs*, transcr. and ed. Denis Donoghue (London: Macmillan, 1972), p. 140.

in his own day. In middle age he composed *A Vision* as his own personal philosophy of history, according to which great spiritual figures throughout the ages might be seen congruently, as it were, at the round table of the moon's phases. But *A Vision* has more the appearance of dealing with history; in essence it is a tabulation of humours, a psychology elaborated in terms of certain timeless attitudes or forms.

Duality in Henry James's fiction is expressed in the polarities of character and symbol, nature and art, garden and home. In Yeats's work the *gemini* are history and symbol, process and permanence. Denis Donoghue sees the last stanza of 'Among School Children' as the acme of these unions, 'Life assumes the freedom of art, art the fullness of life . . . Symbolism has become secret history, and history is transfigured.'[41] The role of history in the *œuvre* has been discussed by Thomas Whitaker and by Daniel B. Harris; as with so many other dialogues in which Yeats participated, it is not so much a matter of participation as of contradiction, more argument than dialogue. 'Meru', a poem of 1934, looks back to a *Journal* entry of February 1909. The retrospect is not complacent; having pronounced upon the Incarnation, Yeats had concluded:

All civilisation is held together by a series of suggestions made by an invisible hypnotist, artificially created illusions. The knowledge of reality is always by some means or other a secret knowledge. It is a kind of death.[42]

Secret history, secret knowledge . . . What is the secret? Given the material symbolism of Yeats's work, we can see that the heart of the matter is myth, for in myth history and symbol, character and symbol presume to unity. Because it is non-rational and non-individual, the experience of myth is never conscious. In the work of Yeats's contemporary, Freud, it is made clear that the most potent myth of the age is that of which the conscious mind knows nothing — innocent guilty Oedipus. A decade earlier, and attending to the literary and philosophical aspects of Greek myth, Nietzsche

---

[41] Denis Donoghue, *Yeats*, Fontana Modern Masters series ([n.p.] : Fontana/ Collins, 1971), p. 89.
[42] W. B. Yeats [Journal, 12 February 1909], *Memoirs*, p. 166.

had frankly declared that 'the chances are that almost every one of us, upon close examination, will have to admit that he is able to approach the once-living experience of myth only by means of intellectual constructs'.[43] Nor is it enough to bemoan industry and education as destructive of the old acceptance of myth. The chasm runs much deeper into human history than the circulating libraries and factories which Yeats disliked. It is a discrepancy which Nietzsche located in the very survival of the Greek drama, 'the myth, we might say, never finds an adequate objective correlative in the spoken word.'[44] Indeed, the possibility of such a correlation is often rejected or ignored in modernist fiction: Lawrence, in an essay on Edgar Allan Poe, fulminates against the craving to *know*: 'Keep KNOWLEDGE for the world of matter, force and function. It has got nothing to do with being'.[45] In Joyce's *Ulysses*, the proliferation of styles emphasizes the absence of any central style, any purely matter-of-fact manner, and this is in keeping with the unconsciousness of Bloom that he is Odysseus, Stephen that he is Telemachus.[46]

This hostility between myth and the word — the word, that is, as the microcosm of all intellection and formal organization — is the greatest of the many obstacles Yeats confronted in his career. Despite the apparatus of the Great Memory, he initially faces his world through the medium of intellectual constructs, and the method of poetic composition which he developed to overcome the chasm, by advancing from prose summary towards a numinous ideal, relies upon that from which it would escape:

> I must lie down where all the ladders start
> In the foul rag and bone shop of the heart.[47]

---

[43] Friedrich Nietzsche, *The Birth of Tragedy* and *The Genealogy of Morals*, trans. Francis Golffing (New York: Doubleday, 1956), p. 136.

[44] Ibid., p. 103.

[45] D. H. Lawrence, *Studies in Classic American Literature* (Harmondsworth: Penguin, 1977), p. 76.

[46] See Hugh Kenner, *Joyce's Voices* (London: Faber, 1978), pp. 40-1.

[47] W. B. Yeats, 'The Circus Animals' Desertion', *Collected Poems*, p. 392. In relation to Yeats's method of composition see Jon Stallworthy's two studies *Between the Lines* (1963) and *Vision and Revision in Yeats's Last Poems* (1969) (both published by the Clarendon Press).

Numen, from *nuere,* the Latin verb 'to nod (assent)', is an objective which by definition lies beyond words. The encounters with reality which such poems posit may yield a secret knowledge, but the contradictions of that term remain crucial. The Yeatsian heroes, Oisin, Cuchulain, the Old Man of 'Purgatory' dramatize such encounters by inhabiting a 'kind of death'. In formal terms we may see them as having reached Lukács's great door — through which there is no passage. And in terms of the plays' *dramatis personae,* the Yeatsian hero achieves definition through a problematic relationship with 'primary relations', most frequently, fathers and sons. These relationships, I suggest, are the equivalent in modernist literature to the attenuated relations between the artist and his world, the artist and his creation.

It may seem that I am deliberately accepting a modernist insistence on the autonomy of the literary text in distinguishing so particularly between the artist, his world, and his creation. Nevertheless, any distinction between text and society — for that is the issue at stake — is, willy-nilly, a relationship however reluctant or coy. The hypostasized text is only possible in a society conceived in hypostasized terms, whether biological or mechanistic.[48] The continuum of language in which poetic form may achieve unique effects alerts us to the fact that to pose the problem exclusively as a dichotomy between text and society is to frustrate its solution. Just as the architectonics of eighteenth-century antithesis contributed much to the *content* of political thought, indicating the range and limitation of possibility so to speak, so dichotomy in the modernist period characterizes an inability or unwillingness to conceive of literature in positive relationship with social and political energies. In historical terms, of course, the experience of society *as* hypostasis necessarily obliges the reader of modernist literature to grant a relative validity to the distinction.

With so many themes invoked — the self-conscious artefact

---

[48] The OED's notion of the verb 'to hypostasize' — to make into or treat as a substance — refers back to its definition of 'hypochondria' as 'morbid depression of spirits'. The *abnormality* of conceiving relations and continuing processes in static and individualized terms is here regarded as resulting in hypostasis.

of modernism, the relation of myth to history, German romanticism, and Anglo-Irish poetry — it is as well to choose some single, central area for a more detailed examination. That area will inevitably lie at the crossing of two paths, and it is wise to take our bearings carefully. That Yeats was the contemporary of Freud, his early work coinciding with the maturity of James and the eclipse of Nietzsche, is a legitimate statement of a comparative analysis. Many who prefer what they regard as the dynamics of literary history — often no more than a calendar of literary events — choose to see Yeats the Anglo-Irish poet as J. J. Callanan writ large. It is true that he wished to be accounted one of a company including 'Davis, Mangan, Ferguson', and no less true that Lecky and Le Fanu helped him towards the form which that allegiance took — there is no closed shop in the matter of poetic influence, prosemen have their part to play also. However, in looking at Yeats's place at the head of a nineteenth-century tradition of Irish writing we do not place him back in that tradition. Nothing in nineteenth-century Irish writing predicts Yeats, and nothing in Yeats requires that body of work; without him it has no more claim to validity as tradition than a wallet of expired cheques. Karl Marx, in the 'Eighteenth Brumaire', emphasizes that while men do make their own history they make it 'under the given and inherited circumstances with which they are directly confronted'.[49] Yeats's recourse to the Irish past is not the effect of some magnetism in that past but of the historical conditions of his own day, conditions which cannot be defined in purely local terms.

A few examples may suffice to demonstrate the principle, the first taken from *The Wanderings of Oisin*. At the close of Book II, the daemon Niamh murmured to Oisin:

> 'Love, we go
> To the Island of Forgetfulness, for lo!
> The Islands of Dancing and of Victories
> Are empty of all power.'
>   'And which of these

---

[49] Karl Marx, 'The Eighteenth Brumaire of Louis Bonaparte', *Surveys from Exile* ed. and introd. by David Fernbach (London: Allen Lane/New Left Review, 1973), p. 146.

Is the Island of Content?'
         'None know,' she said;
And on my bosom laid her weeping head.[50]

Yeats had built his poem on a nineteenth-century English translation of Michael Comyn's eighteenth-century Gaelic rendering of an older, legendary poem. The third island which Oisin will visit before returning to Ireland represents the principal innovation which Yeats introduced into his inherited material. Before Yeats's hero returns to an Ireland in which the Fenians are superseded by the Christian dispensation, he has need to seek a further transcendence, a third island in which memory of 'intellectual constructs' is dissolved. If the introduction of the third island marks Yeats's transformation of his inheritance from the nineteenth century, it does so by assimilating the poem as a whole to the wider anxiety of European modernist literature. Though Niamh may take Oisin to the Island of Forgetfulness, his desire to know which of these realms may reconcile knowledge and action — for that is what content must mean for Oisin — calls forth a comprehensive denial of knowledge, 'none know'. Though the first island has offered 'always more anxious sleep', the vision ends with an admission that even here 'the kingfisher turns to a ball of dust' — an evolutionary obsolescence in poetic speed-up worthy of Wells's *Time Machine*. At the end of each voyage Oisin indeed confronts a kind of death, but he nevertheless is destined to return to Patrician Ireland and saintly rebuke. For there is a dialectical interplay between these figures which establishes them as more intimately connected than the spokesmen of rival ideologies. The conclusion of the Fenian hero's long account of the Island of Forgetfulness — an account riddled by poignant memory — takes the argument to Patrick, who is pressed

Speak, you too are old with your memories, an old
         man surrounded with dreams.[51]

Oisin had been preserved in the mythic youth of the Islands:

[50] W. B. Yeats, *Collected Poems*, p. 431.
[51] Ibid., p. 445.

he only succumbed to his three hundred earthly years when he fell from the saddle to the ground. In the dialogue he has been both the elder and the younger of the two participants: as Fenian hero he looks down on Patrick's age-obsessed evocations of Hell; as fallen revenant he recognizes the younger faith's present reality. For Oisin, modern Ireland is a kind of death.

If we see Patrick merely preaching Hell-fire and Oisin fondly declaring his allegiance to the long-dead Fenian heroes, the debate in 'The Wanderings' cannot be resolved. The irresolvability is not irresolution: rather it is a narrative attempt to give form to a more complex dilemma.

Through his investigation of myth, drawn from Irish sources and from the work of anthropologists such as Sir James Frazer and Andrew Lang, Yeats came to present this heroic condition in more specifically dramatic terms. 'On Baile's Strand' opens with a repeated evocation of Cuchulain's state of being as it was prior to the action of the play: the Blind Man and Conchubar both testify to the fact that Cuchulain is preoccupied by the question of his having a son. The king knows Cuchulain to the bone:

> I have heard you cry, aye in your very sleep,
> 'I have no son', and with such bitterness
> That I have gone upon my knees and prayed
> That it might be amended.[52]

As the Blind Man *knows*, Cuchulain does have a son, the Young Man who has at this moment landed from the sea to challenge the hero to mortal combat. The 'wildness' Cuchulain must abjure by his oath of allegiance to his king is precisely a state of unknowing: he is to be drawn into that 'secret knowledge' which is civilization, rule of law, rule of illusion. Against the weight of the king's polity, the hero repeatedly invokes the image of a hawk. The intimacy with which the hawk is conjured up justifies its recognition as Cuchulain's totem, that is, the species in nature with which he is identified. Yeats had encountered totemism in Lang's

---

[52] W. B. Yeats, 'On Baile's Strand', *Collected Plays* (London: Macmillan, 1963), p. 257.

Custom and Myth and, crucially, in Frazer's four-volume *Totemism and Exogamy*.[53] The central principle of totemism should have prohibited Cuchulain from killing the Young Man because the latter has, at the outset, announced the hawk to be his totem also:

> I will give no other proof than the hawk gives
> That it's no sparrow.[54]

Read even superficially, the play reveals a greater subtlety of conflict than the dispute in 'The Wanderings'. Cuchulain is caught between two obligations – to kill the challenger of Conchubar's authority, and to respect his own totemic identity as announced in the challenger's imagery. The dilemma might be formulated as the rival claims of civilization and nature, obligation and affinity; it meets, perhaps, the minimal requirements of A. C. Bradley's contemporary discussion of tragedy in that it presents a conflict of good with good.[55] This depth of conflict is rendered possible by Yeats's introduction of the totemic convention into Irish source material for which the totem was an exotic borrowing from Frazer's researches on aboriginal religion in Australia. As with the third island of 'The Wanderings of Oisin', the innovation has the effect of drawing the local and the historical into participation with a broader aspect of European cultural inquiry.

Cuchulain's position, however, is more comprehensively tragic than the Bradleyan parallel suggests. As he dimly begins to recognize – unknowing having been abjured – the Young Man is his son, born to Aoife, 'one of those cross queens that live in hungry Scotland'.[56] Aoife too has as her totem the hawk – 'At the Hawk's Well' subsequently

[53] Andrew Lang, *Custom and Myth* (London, 1885); J. G. Frazer, *Totemism and Exogamy* (London: Macmillan, 1910, 4 vols.). Freud, in *Totem and Taboo* (London: Routledge and Kegan Paul, 1950), emphasizes the importance of the female line (p. 107) as the means of totemic inheritance, thus indicating the logic of exogamy as a taboo against mating within the identity group.
[54] W. B. Yeats, 'On Baile's Strand', *Collected Plays*, p. 265. See also Appendix G.
[55] See A. C. Bradley, *Oxford Lectures on Poetry*, with intro. by M. R. Ridley (London: Macmillan, 1965); esp. the chapter 'Hegel's Theory of Tragedy' (pp. 69–92) which is dated 1901, the volume being first published in 1909.
[56] W. B. Yeats, 'On Baile's Strand', *Collected Plays*, p. 252.

provides this proto-drama to 'On Baile's Strand'. And totemism is closely related to exogamy, the obligation to mate outside the tribe and outside its totemic imagery. We see therefore that, prior to the action of the play, Cuchulain has broken
the prohibition forbidding sexual union within the totemic
group, and that as a consequence he is obliged to kill his own
son. In these two vital offences we see Cuchulain enact precisely the same offences which characterize Oedipus — that is
the overvaluing of blood (or totemic) relationship in sexual
union, and the undervaluing of such relationship in killing the
father (or son). It is true that by killing his son Cuchulain appears to deviate most significantly from the Oedipal pattern,
but the binary system of overvaluing and undervaluing a
primary relationship is strictly maintained. Cuchulain's oath
of allegiance to Conchubar, signally his acceptance of civilization in the place of totemic identity, does not liberate him
from his original offence but rather brings with it knowledge
of that offence extended and intensified by the complementary offence of killing his son. The schematism of this underlying structure is most effectively transformed by Yeats into
a dramatic tension of great poignancy: Cuchulain's near-
knowledge is confirmed by the Fool and the Blind Man, as
the hero sits on the bench with them after the fight:

Cuchulain.   I had rather he had been some other woman's son. What
   father had he? A soldier out of Alba? She was an amorous woman —
   a proud, pale amorous woman.
Blind Man.   None knew whose son he was.
Cuchulain.   None knew! Did you know, old listener at doors?
Blind Man.   No, no; I knew nothing.
Fool.   He said a while ago that he heard Aoife boast that she'd never
   but the one lover, and he the only man that had overcome her in
   battle. (*Pause.*)
Blind Man.   Somebody is trembling, Fool! The bench is shaking. Why
   are you trembling? Is Cuchulain going to hurt us? It was not I who
   told you, Cuchulain.
Fool.   It is Cuchulain who is trembling. It is Cuchulain who is shaking
   the bench.
Blind Man.   It is his own son he has slain.
Cuchulain.   'Twas they that did it, the pale windy people. Where?
   where? where? My sword against the thunder![57]

[57] Ibid., p. 276.

This initiation into knowledge and the price paid for civilization finds its dramatic conclusion when Cuchulain, killer
of his own son, attacks his symbolic father, Conchubar:

Blind Man. What is he doing now?
Fool. O! he is fighting the waves!
Blind Man. He sees King Conchubar's crown on every one of them.

.....

Fool. The waves have mastered him.[58]

Here, of course, we find a version albeit indirect and oblique
of the classic Oedipal patricide. And it is a kind of death for
Cuchulain also. The dramatic character, having annihilated
his son, his longed-for form and permanence, turns upon the
author of his offence, the authority to whom he has sworn
himself in abjuring totemic identity. Yet it is significant that
inhibitions and censorings are evident here. The act of self-
annihilation (as the Fool reports it naturalistically) cannot be
made specific, cannot be brought directly into the drama.
Its sources so deeply embedded in Cuchulain's existence, his
death may only be reported to the audience. And, as 'The
Death of Cuchulain' will reveal, the report is in any case
premature, incomplete, indirect. But there is a more significant cause of this off-stage 'kind of death' which Cuchulain
rushes towards, and that is its coincidence (so to speak)
with his attack, as he believes, upon the heads of Conchubar.
This more explicit form of Oedipal undervaluing of relationship is admittedly symbolic — Conchubar is not the hero's
'real' father — but for this reason it participates in the symbolism by which we see the hero as hero/artist tragically
placed between the hostilities of that which makes him as he
is and that he has made (and destroyed). Such effective
dramatic identity of divergent perspectives — the Fool's
and Cuchulain's — should not disguise the manner in which
Cuchulain hypostasizes separate worlds of the determinant
and the created.

Yeats's innovation in introducing the third island into his
inherited schema for 'The Wanderings of Oisin', like his elaboration of tragic conflict in 'On Baile's Strand', exemplifies

[58] Ibid., pp. 277-8.

his transcendence of literary history as mere debt and of tragic genre as a timeless category. In this early work he maintains a distinctive perspective on the problematical nature of modernism, while demonstrating that this perspective, by taking its material from his experience of nineteenth-century Irish culture, is not an isolated or eccentric one. At the end of his career we shall find a counter-truth to 'On Baile's Strand' filling out its play; the Old Man of 'Purgatory', having killed his father, futilely seeks to end consequence by annihilating his son. And in one of the last letters which Yeats wrote, he emphasized once again the dichotomy of knowledge and being, 'Man can embody truth but he cannot know it.'[59]

These two approaches to Yeats can now be related to each other more explicitly, and the pressure leading to their initial separation identified as one existing within Yeats's work itself. In analysing 'Nineteen Hundred and Nineteen', we found that the meaning of the poem lay close to its excluded subject, nineteenth-century Public Opinion, and the consolidation of bourgeois hegemony, complicated in Ireland by the ideology of Protestant Ascendancy. Ostensibly lamenting the passing of an uncommon civilization, the poem in practice exposes its merely ornamental evidences of culture. The ironic, guilt-wracked speaker invokes surrogate-aristocracy and medieval chaos, but the poem advances other historical placings of itself. In analysing 'On Baile's Strand' and 'The Wanderings of Oisin', we found that the modernist preoccupation with the primitive — the crucial alliance of myth, pre-historical setting, and primary relations — can be obliged to manifest more up-to-date themes such as biological entropy. Yeatsian Augustanism and Yeatsian primitivism are the two sides of a more recent coin. The importance of this interdependence, or mutual definition, can be gauged by the extent to which Yeats's critics strive to keep the two apart, either through the periodization of his career, or through the autonomy imposed upon texts.

But here, as elsewhere, Yeats out-manœuvres his foes and

[59] W. B. Yeats to Elizabeth Pelham, 4 January 1939, *The Letters of W. B. Yeats*, ed. Allan Wade (London: Rupert Hart-Davis, 1954), p. 922.

in 'Purgatory' we find the ultimate coming-together of that surrogate aristocracy and those primary relations. True the aristocratic evidences will be shown in ruins, and the primary relations even more centrally inverted, but the late dramatic poem brings together elements which have been held apart previously. Eighteenth-century primitivism, a Cuchulain who murmurs 'Hush-a-bye, baby' — these are Yeats's conclusive images. In these two preliminary approaches, however, no such synthesis is yet possible. 'Nineteen Hundred and Nineteen' required especial attention to its content, the historical language which it variously rearranges round the concept of 'public opinion'. 'On Baile's Strand', in contrast, demanded attention to its tragic form and to the contribution of a primary genealogy to its tragic climax. Those rigid categories have their validity of course, but the ultimate analysis of 'Purgatory' is intended to counterbalance them. For it is a persistent theme of *Ascendancy and Tradition* that the modernist symbolism of primary relations, of Oedipal and anti-Oedipal tension, and the modernists' preoccupation with political racism, needs to be unmasked historically. In place of the genealogy which is valorized so often in Yeats, we need to locate the historical genesis of such texts. 'Purgatory' can be persuaded to give up a more comprehensive view of Yeats's modernism but that view will involve both quintessentially literary concepts such as Tradition and extra-literary concerns such as fascism and eugenics. It remains to be seen how Anglo-Irish modernism provides a suitable context in which the interaction of these forces can be measured in the second last decade of the twentieth century.

9. THE INVENTION OF TRADITION

1. THE ANXIETY OF TRADITION

The crime of Tradition was a new one . . .

(J. H. Blunt)[1]

The term *tradition* has today an honoured place in literary criticism, thanks largely to its deployment by T. S. Eliot and F. R. Leavis. Its status has been enhanced by the manner in which some critics have discerned behind the great tradition of modern English literature a neo-Platonic tradition. In the figure of W. B. Yeats these two senses of tradition converge, together with the added vibrancy of that traditional lore which the poet absorbed from his study of Irish folk culture. 'Traditional sanctity',[2] consequently, carries with it a rich synthesis of implications. Yeatsian critics have been assiduous in assimilating these qualities to their own work, and one recent commentator on Anglo-Irish literature manages in the course of just sixteen pages to invoke tradition twenty-three times, a frequency only rivalled by the first-person singular pronoun. This nervous insistence is perhaps timely in that the values which tradition is often thought to ratify are un-doubtedly under pressure in Ireland. But beyond this local anxiety there is the wider concern for the future of literary criticism itself, besieged as it is by such new disciplines as the sociology of culture, structuralism of various kinds, and a radical philosophy of literary history. In that wider struggle for the hearts and minds of Arts Faculties, tradition is a highly contentious term in which the indebtedness to continental (especially German) thought of the various challengers provides them with a drastically different perspec-tive on tradition than that available through Eliot's essay on 'Tradition and the Individual Talent' or Leavis's *Great Tra-dition*. If tradition is frequently identified with a conservative

[1] John Henry Blunt, *Dictionary of Sects* (London, 1874), p. 128.
[2] W. B. Yeats, 'Coole Park and Ballylee, 1931', *Collected Poems* (London: Macmillan, 1963), p. 276.

literary history we should remind ourselves that *traditional societies* are those which have no sense of their own historicity.

In short, behind the literary critics' valorization of tradition, the word and the social practices surrounding it carry the most varied implications. If for a moment we follow the example of Eamon de Valera and consult the Oxford Dictionary, tradition is revealed to have a series of usages we should not neglect.[3] The first meaning is a legal one — 'handing over'. *Traditio* 'was a mode of transferring the ownership of private property in Roman law.'[4] Here, it is worth noting the distinction between the handing over of an object or a property, and the handing over of ownership or rights to such an object or property. For while the latter possesses a normative element, in that it was *thus* ownership was handed over, the physical handing over of an object might well be in conflict with legal requirements. In this way tradition came to mean 'a giving up, surrender, betrayal' in which rights or responsibilities are subordinate to other considerations or motivations. Judas's betrayal of his leader was 'cryste ys tradicion and passion', while tradition was also used to mean the 'surrender of sacred books in times of persecution' — as for example in the reign of Diocletian. This non-normative sense of tradition (a sense generally connoting moral offence) may be secondary now to the valorized sense of tradition as legitimate 'handing down', but we should be alert to the precise historical conditions in which the matter is given its prominence in British literary criticism.

Etymologically entailing a 'handing down', tradition is too often taken as synonymous with what is handed down rather than with the social and cultural dynamics of the process of handing down, the place of this in the modes of production of the period and the historical character of that period. This tendency to identify tradition with its objects can be traced in Eliot's subsequent reflection on his own essay. But its reassessment as a concept close to the heart of the Yeatsian aesthetic is in keeping with a scrutiny of the intensification

---

[3] Except where otherwise stated all citations in this paragraph may be found in the *Oxford English Dictionary*, s.v. 'tradition'.

[4] Edward Shils, *Tradition* (London: Faber, 1981), p. 16.

of class as group or category (rather than as social formation) in the term ascendancy. Yeats's encounter with it comes first by way of folk tradition, and it is fitting that our subsequent inquiry into his most (idiosyncratically) neo-Platonic play, 'Purgatory', will involve a demonstration of the element of historical process in the timeless material he collected as amateur folklorist.

That late nineteenth-century emergence of Anglo-Irish literature requires synchronization with continental developments as well as with the changing perceptions of class inside the United Kingdom. Perhaps the most telling divergence between British and European intellectual developments was the growth of sociology in Germany, Italy, and France as the intellectual meeting-ground of urgent political, cultural, and philosophical concerns.[5] British sociology remained indebted to the positivism of Comte and J. S. Mill, and on the islands grand schematization was reserved for the development of a British school of anthropology. It is significant that the study of primitive society became prominent in the intellectual superstructure of the greatest imperial economy the world had known, and that at a time when High Capitalism was entering its crisis. Sir James Frazer's *Golden Bough* (1890–1914) and Max Weber's *The Protestant Ethic and the Spirit of Capitalism* (1904–5) are emblems of these contrasting preoccupations.

Weber is important not solely for his attempt to correlate changes in Christian theology with economic development, but for the broader differentiation between such rationalization in industrial and developed societies and the organization of traditional societies.[6] Traditional here signified a mode of continuity and cohesion drastically different from the pattern of climaxes and changes which progressively revolutionized post-medieval western Europe. Within the larger sense of Europe, traditional societies existed though for the most part as residual elements within political units already well advanced in their industrialization — southern

---

[5] See for this background H. Stuart Hughes, *Consciousness and Society: The Reorientation of European Social Thought 1890–1930* (Brighton: Harvester Press, 1979), 2nd ed.

[6] See Edward Shils, op. cit., *passim*.

Italy, for example. Given Weber's highly ambiguous attitude
to the most recent rationalization to be reached in Europe —
that of imminent proletarian revolution — traditional societies had for him something of that double sense present
in the Latin usages of the term. Tradition was the means of
transmission and succession in societies which were economically outmoded and politically subordinate: tradition also
was the alternative to crisis and revolution. The first of these
senses of tradition relates to a diachronic order in society,
albeit a vestigial and threatened one: the second relates to
an internalized apprehension of order conceived in synchronic resistance to history and its changes.

The publication of Weber's work in 1904-5 is a marker in
that European nexus of which Anglo-Irish literature forms a
sizeable and influential aspect. The 'protestantism' of its title
serves also as a reminder of the disjunction occurring between
the acquisitive ethic and reformed theology in the Irish
circumstances of Protestant Ascendancy. One further area
linking this marginality and the centre of European politics
in the twentieth century is marked by G. B. Shaw's interest
in the 'New Protestantism' of Houston Stewart Chamberlain,
British apologist for Hitler and politicized racism.[7] Yet for
all that Shaw's family embody the bourgeois element in
Dublin's Protestant Ascendancy, and for all his interest in
the strong man theory of politics, he remains tangential to
the real line of action uniting nineteenth-century Irish culture
and the trauma of twentieth-century politics on the Continent. Shavian politics was by no means hostile to theory, but
its preference was for practice. Notoriously, Shaw regarded
traditional reputations as the material for modern satire, his
treatment of Shakespeare being only the most blatant. Yet,
through his ·exploitation of Caesar, Shakespeare, and
Napoleon, Shaw held his version of left-wing naturalism and
positivism in touch with a historical dynamic. In Germany,

[7] 'You have only to compare a great Protestant Manifesto like Houston
Chamberlain's Foundations of the Nineteenth Century with the panics of Sir
Edward Carson and Lord Londonderry to realize how completely Ireland has
been kept out of the mighty stream of modern Protestantism by her preoccupation with her unnatural political condition.' G. B. Shaw, *The Matter with
Ireland*. (London: Cape, 1962), pp. 68-9. Chamberlain's book had been published
in 1911.

Nietzsche represented one particular form of historical scepticism, strongly laced as always with Nietzschean irony. It is however with the work of Martin Heidegger that anti-historicism, combined with a thoroughgoing metaphysical abstraction, that German thought made its most penetrating analysis of tradition.

Yeats's lack of interest in German culture was fairly comprehensive. Apart from Goethe and Nietzsche (whose theories of the *daemonic* appealed to him) no German figure earned more than his passing acknowledgement. Yet, in his last essays, *On the Boiler* (1939), he went out of his way to praise Edmund Husserl whose *Ideas* he considered a modern restatement of Berkeleyan immaterialism.[8] That brief gesture towards the domestication of German phenomenology is characteristic of Yeatsian procedures in the construction of Irish Augustan tradition: analogy permits Husserl to be accommodated in a schema whose coherence is determined by the intensity of such gestures: analogically, Parnell becomes Cuchulain, or Swift is resurrected to reprimand the epigones of the Irish Free State. In 1909 he wrote,

Every day I notice some new analogy between [the] long-established life of the well-born and the artist's life. We come from the permanent things and create them, and instead of old blood we have old emotions and we carry in our head that form of society which aristocracies create now and then for some brief moment at Urbino or Versailles.[9]

The very term 'Anglo-Irish literature' is valid solely by virtue of the intensity of need which underwrites the analogies upon which it is constructed. In calling it a tradition, however, we do more to highlight those needs than to confirm those analogies. Yeatsian landscape, for example, or the construction of Yeats's Goldsmith, are intellectual endeavours *at interpretation,* interpretation shot through with specific anxieties and ambitions. Through such details as these — landscape, Goldsmith's biography, etc. — I hope to unmask the Yeatsian tradition; in the words of Heidegger 'this

[8]   See W. B. Yeats, *Explorations* (London: Macmillan, 1962), p. 435 n.
[9]   W. B. Yeats, 'Journal', *Memoirs*, ed. Denis Donoghue (London: Macmillan, 1972), p. 156.

hardened tradition must be loosened up, and the concealments which it has brought about must be dissolved.'[10]

Tradition, for Heidegger, is the entire tradition of ontology which has dominated philosophy since the days of the Greeks. It is, therefore, the most general and comprehensive sense of the term, under which the particularities of recent literary criticism may be considered separately:

When tradition thus becomes master, it does so in such a way that what it 'transmits' is made so inaccessible, proximally and for the most part, that it rather becomes concealed. Tradition takes what has come down to us and delivers it over to self-evidence; it blocks our access to those primordial 'sources' from which the categories and concepts handed down to us have been in part quite genuinely drawn. Indeed it makes us forget that they have had such an origin, and makes us suppose that the necessity of going back to these sources is something which we need not even understand . . .[11]

But for all his insistence that Being possesses 'historiological interests' and zeal for an interpretation which is philologically objective, Heidegger's inquiry into the operations of tradition does not lead in the direction of history. While the political implications of Heideggerian ontology became clear after the accession of Hitler, the unmasking of tradition as cousin-german to ideology can contribute to the reorientation of Anglo-Irish literature within the broader context of twentieth-century European culture.

The Yeatsian synthesis of tradition, in which folklore, Platonism, and the Irish Augustans join forces, is badly in need of such an analysis. Yet it must not be thought that Yeats and Heidegger are at loggerheads totally: in their different ways each exemplifies an attitude to human society which is characteristic of the modernist crisis. According to Heidegger, modern man lives in a fallen world of inauthenticity; according to Yeats, man has lost that Unity of Being of which Dante spoke. But whereas Marx sought to analyse that situation with the intention of bringing about its transformation in an active and actual future, Yeats and Heidegger

---

[10] Martin Heidegger, *Being and Time*, trans. John Macquarrie and Edward Robinson (Oxford: Blackwell, 1980), p. 44.

[11] Ibid., p. 43.

saw no such solution, imminent or remote. Wrenching
ontology out of its Platonic timelessness, Heidegger delivered
it over to no historical process. His passive acceptance of
National Socialist rule in Germany is entirely consistent with
his philosophical rejection of history and his search for a
primordial 'presence'. Yeats's intermittent and yet reiterated
approval of Mussolini and Hitler may have been punctuated
with specific reservations and specific commendations:
nevertheless, it saw the past as more authentically *real* than
any mundane political programme. In such attitudes Hitlerian
power found a convenient source of authority.

2. 'POETRY AND TRADITION' (1907)

> Someone lacking a tradition who would
> like to have one is like a man unhappily
> in love.
>
> (Ludwig Wittgenstein)[12]

Discussing the several versions of phenomenology which have
affected literary debate, Frank Lentricchia singles out the
early Yeats to illustrate the affinity between Husserl's *Ideas*
of 1913 and emergent modernism. In 'The Autumn of the
Body' (1898) Yeats had declared that writers all over Europe
were struggling against 'that "externality" which a time of
scientific and political thought has brought into literature'.[13]
The essay concludes with an enthusiastic summary of
Mallarmé's manifesto in favour of a poetry dedicated to
making 'an entire word hitherto unknown to the language';
the arts will deal with 'the essences of things, and not with
things'.[14] If the sources of this search for poetic autonomy
lie deep in nineteenth-century French culture, with Flaubert
as well as Mallarmé, the affinity to German phenomenology
can be traced clearly along three crucial lines — a vigorous

[12] Ludwig Wittgenstein, *Culture and Value*, trans. Peter Winch (Oxford:
Blackwell, 1980), p. 76e.
[13] W. B. Yeats, 'The Autumn of the Body', *Essays and Introductions* (London:
Macmillan, 1961), p. 189; see Frank Lentricchia, *After the New Criticism* (London:
Athlone Press, 1980), pp. 67–8.
[14] W. B. Yeats, 'The Autumn of the Body', p. 193.

anti-psychologism, the abstention from any natural standpoint in relation to perception, and the concentration instead upon 'the eidetic reduction'. By this last procedure, the phenomenologist discards those phenomena which are inessential to the idea in question and is left with 'a specification of the essential ones'.[15] Thus, while Yeats was fond of recommending forms and transmissions of knowledge peculiar to folk-culture, or elaborated more systematically in neo-Platonic theory, there was simultaneously available a philosophy propounding a broadly similar doctrine.

Yeats's essay 'Poetry and Tradition' is a curious illustration of his phenomenologist tendencies. Like so much of his prose, it is stuffed with opinions on matters about which he felt poets should not concern themselves. One topic upon which it has remarkably little to say is tradition, and in this the essay demonstrates both the phenomenological procedure and the problematic history of Yeatsian aesthetics. It is divided into four numbered parts, and these might be given headings such as 'Irish History from Henry Grattan to John O'Leary', 'Style', 'Breeding and Freedom', and 'John O'Leary and Class'. Such headings of course would crudely distort Yeats's argument which is effective precisely because it is *not* signposted — in this way the evasiveness of tradition is itself masked from the reader. Those who consider the early Yeats indecisive by comparison with the single-minded rhetoric of *On the Boiler* should note the following passage from the first part:

New from the influence, mainly the personal influence, of William Morris, I dreamed of enlarging Irish hate, till we had come to hate with a passion of patriotism what Morris and Ruskin hated.[16]

That commitment to positive hate will be echoed in the 'General Introduction for my Work' but here in the essay of 1907 its role is more puzzling. Why should patriotism provide a model for the passion of Morris and Ruskin or their Irish disciples? One answer lies in the fact that Yeats originally

[15] Roger Waterhouse, *A Heidegger Critique* (Brighton: Harvester Press, 1981), p. 30.
[16] W. B. Yeats, 'Poetry and Tradition', *Essays and Introductions* (London: Macmillan, 1961), p. 248.

published his essay under the title 'Poetry and Patriotism', and that the amended title fails to reflect upon what had previously been an echo of the title. Yet the essay found the poetry of the Young Ireland school inadequate in that it was merely patriotic, and praised John O'Leary precisely because he never accepted patriotism as an end in itself.

The second part of the essay is briefer and less discursive. In it, Yeats defines style 'which is but high breeding in words and in argument'.[17] This association of literary style with pedigree and manners is expanded into a more explicit sociological prejudice: the writer 'has at all times the freedom of the wellbred, and being bred to the tact of words can take what theme he pleases, unlike the linen-drapers, who are rightly compelled to be very strict in their conversation.'[18] 'Breeding' of course is a species of portmanteau word in which two related but distinct ideas converge: breeding may mean the deliberate genetic planning and selection of — say — pets or domestic animals; breeding may also mean refined or approved behaviour fostered by training and education. 'Born and bred' distinguishes between the two meanings. In his *Journal* Yeats spoke of the *analogy* between the 'long-established life of the well-born and the artist's life', and the analogical procedure is one step along the way towards abolishing that distinction. Yeats's commitment to spiritualism and theosophy, doctrines that deny or minimize the body, is accompanied by his constant recourse to metaphors drawn from the body and its 'breeding'.

'Poetry and Tradition' succeeds in introducing the topic of tradition by reference to the 'spiritism' of Irish country people as an element in the final conflict which will re-establish lost Unity of Being:

Perhaps, too, it would be possible to find in that new philosophy of spiritism coming to a seeming climax in the work of Frederic Myers, and in the investigations of uncounted obscure persons, what could change the country spiritism into a reasoned belief that would put its might into all the rest . . . We were to forge in Ireland a new sword on

---

[17] Ibid., p. 253.
[18] Ibid.

our old traditional anvil for that great battle that must in the end re-establish the old, confident, joyous world.[19]

This is as near to a prediction as Yeats allows himself, and significantly he predicts the old world, speaks of *re*-establishing the past rather than of establishing a future. Lionel Johnson is praised for his ability to relate Irish tradition to a greater tradition and 'he was in all a traditionalist, gathering out of the past phrases, moods, attitudes . . .'.[20] Yet these constitute virtually all the references to tradition in the course of the entire essay, the opening and closing sections of which might be more properly published under the original title, 'Poetry and Patriotism'.

Nevertheless, the order of the four sections, like the alteration of the title, has its particular significance. Having muffled William Morris's socialism, and shifted from a discussion of O'Leary's approval of artistic integrity to the definition of style as breeding, Yeats returns in the final section to deliver a more extended judgement on O'Leary and his times:

I could not foresee that a new class, which had begun to rise into power under the shadow of Parnell, would change the nature of the Irish movement, which, needing no longer great sacrifices, nor bringing any great risk to individuals could do without exceptional men, and those activities of the mind that are founded on the exceptional moment. John O'Leary had spent much of his thought in an unavailing war with the agrarian party, believing it the root of change, but the fox that crept into the badger's hole did not come from there. Power passed to small shopkeepers, to clerks, to that very class who had seemed to John O'Leary so ready to bend to the power of others, to men who had risen above the traditions of the countryman, without learning those of cultivated life or even educating themselves, and who because of their poverty, their ignorance, their superstitious piety, are much subject to all kinds of fear.[21]

If this sounds like 'épater les bourgeois' one should remember

---

[19] Ibid., p. 249.
[20] Ibid., p. 253.
[21] Ibid., pp. 259–60. It is worth noting here that the essay appeared first in December 1908 in a Cuala Press limited edition under the title 'Poetry and Patriotism'; by the time it was collected in *The Cutting of an Agate* (1912), its familiar title was well established.

the difference between French and Irish social life — Ireland, despite well-publicized rake-hellish elements, had no bohemianism on which to base an assault on public opinion. Yeats's analysis is a mixture of unconscious Protestant Ascendancy views on history and class, and a conscious but unconfessed anti-Catholicism. What is more important, of course, is the manifest unoriginality of the complaint — which is rather more amusingly presented in Maria Edgeworth's *Absentee*.

The strategies of 'Poetry and Tradition' are now more evident. A historical statement about the nature of change in Irish society between the time of Grattan and the death of Parnell is interrupted by two briefer, more intense statements on style and artistic freedom. Style is breeding, the artist is an aristocrat by vocation. The blatancy of historical interpretation is modified by the positioning of the two sections dealing with style: indeed, the insertion of these suggests a breakdown of historical continuity which is reproduced in the alienation of the poet from a new bourgeois and philistine public. That this new element is not so new is disguised by the sectional divisions of the essay, and the result is to emphasize that qualitative break which characterizes all readings of Anglo-Irish modernism. Style is breeding — this is Yeats's own highly distinctive way of dealing with the embarrassment of literary inheritance. Officially, the argument might have been more aptly titled 'Poetry *or* Patriotism' but unofficially Yeats is unwilling to relinquish all rights to the impurities of politics. 'Poetry and Tradition', however, is an apparent misnomer also, for there is little on the subject of tradition *per se*. 'Poetry *from* Tradition' would be more accurate both in the implication that poetry derives much of its power from that source, and for the more important suggestion that poetry results from an experience of separation from that source, that apparent unity of belief and action which Yeats refers to as 'the traditions of the countryman'. By positing a historical continuity from the late eighteenth century to the era of O'Leary and Parnell, and by then intruding into that continuity with the claims of style and aristocratic freedom, Yeats at once takes the first steps towards the enunciation of his Irish Augustan tradition and concedes the less than unproblematic nature of this identification of history and that tradition. Yet his final choice of title, and the preceding decisions and eliminations, enact that process of eidetic reduction which confers upon tradition that hypnotic intensity which it has long possessed for literary critics.

There is no one canonical statement of Yeats's Anglo-Irish tradition. It may be clearly traced in a variety of texts, poems such as 'The Seven Sages', the play 'The Words Upon the Window-Pane', and the introduction to that play, 'Pages from a Diary in 1930', etc., etc. The sources I have named are all relatively late, and there is a certain logic in seeing Yeats's Augustanism as part of his reaction to developments in the Irish Free State — that is, his eighteenth century was conceived as a counter-truth to a new semi-independent Ireland. As we have seen, however, elements of the theory may be found certainly as early as 1907, and the basic 'aristocratic' assumptions on which it depends stem from his campaigns in favour of Lady Gregory and John M. Synge as inheritors of Parnell's tragic mantle. The poem 'Upon a House Shaken by the Land Agitation' (1910) is a turning-point, a recognition of altered economic relations and modes of production, and of impending modifications of relation between the elements of the United Kingdom.

Given this diffused statement of Yeats's tradition, it may be useful precisely to indicate my own approach to the problem here. In the first section of this chapter, I have stressed the problematic nature of the concept of tradition in the modernist generation. In the second I have dealt with Yeats's own attempt to relate poetry to tradition in his essay of 1907. The next section will deal briefly with the Victorian treatment of Swift, Berkeley, and Burke, and this introduced by a consideration of Yeatsian landscape as a form of urgent memory. The fourth section will follow on this by demonstrating in more detail how Goldsmith's biography was constructed in the nineteenth century, and how the figure of that name in Yeats's poems is part of a dramatic strategy based on a repressed sectarian psychology. Finally, we come to a broader discussion of that much-postponed topic, the nature of Anglo-Irish literature itself. Only by such preparation can we hope to do justice to the complex issues raised by the play 'Purgatory' which I take to be Yeats's ultimate interrogation of tradition.

3. CONSTRUCTING THE EIGHTEENTH CENTURY

> I wish someone would one day attempt a *tragic history of literature* showing how the various nations, which now take their highest pride in the great writers and artists they can show, treated them while they were alive.
>
> (Arthur Schopenhauer)[32]

As literary hero, Jonathan Swift possesses two complementary but contrasting qualities. He is himself immovably a man of integrity though one frequently moved in his emotional response to human folly. He acts as catalyst upon those whom he meets, changing their lives and accelerating their proper advance, yet he remains sequestered in his own obscurity, a darkness not of his own making though it mirrors the Christian humility his public mask too often fails to express. Among Irish authors, Sheridan Le Fanu, Thomas Caulfield Irwin, W. B. Yeats, Denis Johnston, Austin Clarke, and Sybil Le Brocquy have responded to the mystique of Swift as fictional hero. In essence, Swift is a shorthand term for crucial romantic themes, and the historical reasons why a writer born in the seventeenth century should take on this romantic role from the 1840s to the 1960s undoubtedly involve Swift's tangential relation to Augustanism, a relation which is itself an aspect of the entire political nexus of Anglo-Irish relations to which Swift devoted so much of his energies after his fall from grace in London.[23] In *The Sense of an Ending*, Frank Kermode has provided a cautionary account of how 'fictions can degenerate into myths whenever

---

[22] Arthur Schopenhauer, *Essays and Aphorisms*, sel. and trans. R. J. Hollingdale (Harmondsworth: Penguin, 1970), pp. 210-11.
[23] For an authoritative but succinct account of this complex area see J. A. Downie's new biography of Swift (London: Routledge and Kegan Paul, 1984).

they are not consciously held to be fictive' — and the case of
Swift (not to mention the notoriously elusive and omni-
present Goldsmith) illustrates the extent to which Anglo-
Irish culture is haunted by ghostly fictions who still pack
considerable mythic punch.[24] That such revenants do not
always take the form of the individual human figure is
evident if we consider the fond attention lavished on so-
called eighteenth-century architecture. The deeper exchanges
between architecture and human society lie, however,
beyond the horizons of this present study.

Nevertheless landscape mediates between these terms, and
in a way which can be rendered historically vital once more.
Between the abolition of the Irish parliament in 1800 and the
Treaty of 1921, Ireland had become an anomaly in which a
heightened consciousness of distinguishing features flourished.
Allegedly, at one end of the social scale (or rather, somewhere just below the middle), insurgent claims to social and
political authority emphasized certain interpretations of the
past as the facts of an argument; near the other, a super-
annuated élite stressed their perceptions of time and landscape as evidence of their survival. (The analysis of class
implied in these observations is far from adequate, yet it
serves to underline a common attachment to 'fact'.) Joyce's
Ulysses is not only a celebration, by way of parody, of the
encyclopaedic method: it is the initiation rite accorded to
certain social 'facts' — the arrival of the urban *petite bourgeoisie*, the impact of consumerism, etc. etc. The landscape
of Yeats's early poetry — and of much that he wrote later
also — is a synthesis of geographical, linguistic, historical, and
mythological reference to 'facts'. All such facts, whether
Joycean or Yeatsian, exist in a state of perpetual challenge
or permanent change, for they are part of an undefined
culture, subject to the (seemingly) arbitrary manipulations
which the colonial system requires. This effect is not restricted to the physical territory of Ireland, it pervades the social
fabric of the United Kingdom as a whole. In *Reveries Over
Childhood & Youth,* the young Yeats's experience of London
topography is recorded:

[24] Frank Kermode, *The Sense of an Ending* (London: Oxford University
Press, 1968), p. 39.

No matter how charming the place (and there is a little stream in a hollow where Wimbledon Common flows into Coombe Wood that is pleasant to the memory), I knew that those other boys saw something I did not see. I was a stranger there. There was something in their way of saying the names of places that made me feel this.[25]

To contrast this simply to the landscape of home is to miss all the subtleties of Yeats's implication of class and history in such passages. There is a passage in Yeats's introduction to Lady Gregory's *Cuchulain of Muirthemne* which reveals the sense of urgent mediation in such readings of the landscape:

We Irish should keep these personages much in our hearts, they lived in the places where we ride and go marketing, and sometimes they have met one another on the hills that cast their shadow upon our doors at evening. If we will but tell these stories to our children the Land will begin again to be a Holy Land, as it was before men gave their hearts to Greece and Rome and Judea. When I was a child I had only to climb the hill behind the house to see long, blue, ragged hills flowing along the southern horizon. What beauty was lost to me, what depth of emotion is still perhaps lacking in me, because nobody told me, not even the merchant captains who knew everything, that Cruachan of the Enchantments lay behind those long, blue, ragged hills.[26]

It is not difficult to see that the true significance of these words is all but the precise opposite of their literal meaning. For those for whom the hills *automatically* had mythological references, those who needed no dictionary to decode place-names, there was little sense of any creative discovery in the landscape. The obvious requires no statement. But to Yeats it was precisely the barrier, which he came to recognize between his childhood experience and those obvious meanings, which generated a poetic significance. To accomplish this transformation by which a knowledge of ignorance becomes art Yeats performs certain adjustments to the facts of his own life — 'the house', posing as the family (perhaps, ancestral) home, was in reality a place of holiday resort owned by relatives: 'the merchant captains', demythologized, were

[25] W. B. Yeats, 'Reveries Over Childhood and Youth', *Autobiographies* (London: Macmillan, 1955), p. 49.
[26] W. B. Yeats, *Explorations* (London: Macmillan, 1962), pp. 12-13.

those relatives. Any reassessment of Yeats must acknowledge the primal authority for him of his belief that such facts are subject to the transformation of art. In acknowledging this, we go no further than the orthodoxies of romanticism. But the adjustments to Yeats's place in Irish society, to what is conveniently if inadequately called *class*, should advise us that the specifically Anglo-Irish manifestation of romanticism-becoming-modernism will involve political matters of the greatest weight. For the argument rests precisely on that fatal line distinguishing between Kermode's fictions and his myths. It is one thing for Yeats to fudge his history for artistic purposes: it is another for critics, tourists, and other politicians to accept those fictions as effective myths.

Central to any such re-assessment is Yeats's own historical position *vis-à-vis* the eighteenth century. The impression that the tradition of Swift and Burke was his discovery is of course part of a dramatic technique pervasive in Yeats's mythologizing. Neither Swift, Berkeley, Goldsmith nor Burke required resuscitation as individual reputations, though undoubtedly Yeats's association of the four added a new dimension to each. As a corollary, his lack of interest in Henry Brooke, Edward Malone, and R. B. Sheridan is a further conditioning factor in the isolation of those who will come to exemplify the traditional role. Even more drastically, Yeats was prone to identify his own comparative ignorance of Gaelic culture with objective judgement, and his lack of curiosity on this question left him open to an uncritical inheritance of Victorian views of the Irish past, especially in the case of Goldsmith. Finally, while we should recall that Yeats's attitude between 1890 and 1930 swung from a rejection of the Irish Augustans as irrelevant to the Celtic Revival to a veritable establishment of Swift and Burke as the unofficial opposition in the politics of the Irish Free State, it is also true that association, lack of interest, rejection, and veneration proceed in a historical continuum.

Although Swift disturbed the Victorians, a decidedly sympathetic account of his life appeared in Lecky's *Leaders of Public Opinion in Ireland*.[27] Lecky saw his subjects as

[27] See Donal MacCartney, 'Lecky's *Leaders of Public Opinion in Ireland*', *Irish Historical Studies*, vol. 14 (1964–5), pp. 119–41.

mediators between the imposed order of colonial government
and the impotent politics of Jacobite resentment. Yeats in
the course of time came to accept Swift and with him a neo-
Jacobitism of his own. In the 1890s, however, he had no use
for a mediator with the people of Ireland; they were accessible, he felt sure, through folklore and a literature based on
folk tradition. Yeats's respect for Swift is not without
precedent in Lecky's early work, and indeed the same author's
monumental study of the Irish eighteenth century is an
integral part of the historical readjustment which Yeats
dramatizes in his work.

Turning to Burke we are of course returning to the origins
of this inquiry into Anglo-Irish literature and its political
connotations. Burke's Victorian reputation is too well known
to need repetition here; half a dozen biographies testify to
his position in British thought, and Disraeli's choice of title
(Earl of Beaconsfield) was a visible appropriation of Burke's
place in political history. By 1882, however, a new reading
is emerging: in *Irish Essays and Others* Matthew Arnold had
taken as his chief witness to Irish conditions and the Irish
psyche the author of the *Reflections*. We have seen that there
is little paradox in the principal ideologue of the new
imperialism — for it was thus the Victorians read Burke — becoming a key figure in Arnold's investment in Celtic culture.
Was it not Burke himself who taught us to love the little
platoon we belong to as our first duty towards humanity?
The particularism of *Lyrical Ballads* was not absent from the
Reflections, it was simply stated in universal terms. With
Arnold, it is stated more explicitly in global terms.

With Berkeley the altering terms of debate are less publicly
accessible. In 1824 Maria Edgeworth had corresponded with
an American lady on literary matters, and recommended
'that most amiable man and bishop' whose *Querist* inquiries
'are all or almost all applicable at the present day to the state
of Ireland'.[28] Two points should be noted, the less important

[28] *The Education of the Heart: The Correspondence of Rachel Mordecai Lazarus and Maria Edgeworth*, ed. Edgar E. MacDonald (Chapel Hill: University of North Carolina Press, 1977), p. 58. Maria Edgeworth's copy of the 2-vol. edition of Berkeley's *Works* (Dublin, 1784) is in the library of King's College, Cambridge.

being that the American had read nothing of Berkeley. More importantly, Maria Edgeworth considered Berkeley's contribution to be a fundamentally utilitarian one, an analysis of economic and social questions affecting the well-being of Ireland. Later, in 1865, we find Isaac Butt — who was shortly to initiate the Home Government Association which affected the development of cultural tradition in a far wider sphere than the strictly economic — choosing Berkeley as the subject of a prestigious afternoon lecture in Dublin.[29] There is perhaps nothing entirely original in Butt's assessment of the Bishop of Cloyne, yet in contrast to Maria Edgeworth he sees Berkeley's work as a unified view of reality in which economics, optics, and metaphysics are aspects of one central argument. Furthermore, he links this idealism to Wordsworth's 'Immortality Ode'. Butt is echoing on the one hand certain contemporary philosophers who had resurrected some of Berkeley's views on sense-perception and, on the other, a distinctly Victorian and pious interpretation of romanticism. Nevertheless, the projected solipsism of Berkeley's philosophy and the protectionism which Butt read into his economics are welded into a kind of comprehensive account of Berkeley. A more determinedly objective view of the philosopher resulted in the publication in 1871 of an edition of his works, including for the first time the *Commentaries* from which Yeats culled the anti-Lockean tag. 'We Irish do not hold with this.'[30]

Discussing Berkeley then, we can trace a specifically Irish

[29] Isaac Butt, 'Berkeley', *Afternoon Readings in the Museum, St. Stephen's Green, Dublin* (London: [1866]), pp. 185–224.

[30] W. B. Yeats, *Explorations*, p. 333. Yeats's insistence on the anti-English direction of Berkeley's argument is a fine example of analysis by way of predisposed need. The four entries (392, 393, 394, 398) in Notebook B where Berkeley refers to 'we Irish men' etc. appear in the context of an argument against 'the Philosophers', 'the Mathematicians', 'Materialists & Nihilarians', etc. His use of 'we Irish' is simply a recourse to the view of ordinary people, the people of the place he lived and worked in. Indeed, entry 406 speaks scathingly of 'hypothetical Gentlemen' and in the *Three Dialogues* Berkeley prefers butchers to professional philosophers, 'I have quitted several of the sublime notions I had got in their schools for vulgar opinions.' These latter citations might as easily suggest a class bias in Berkeley's deliberately argumentative method: A. A. Luce, in the notes to the standard edition of the *Philosophical Commentaries*, discounts any notion of aggressive nationalism. (*Works of George Berkeley*, vol. i (London: Nelson, 1943), p. 124.)

prologue to Yeats's enthusiasm; stages of which are Maria
Edgeworth's strictly practical reading, Butt's more comprehensive account marked by strictly *period* emphases on piety
and poetry, and finally Yeats's own early discounting of
Berkeley (with Swift) as a significant exemplar for the Celtic
Revival. Closely following this last declaration, there is the
second Fraser edition of 1901. However, a broader background immediately presents itself. The polar extremes of
Berkeley's reputation as either ultra-empiricist or supreme
idealist were observed by Coleridge even within the pages of
one work, *Siris*, which is 'announced as an Essay on Tar-
water, which beginning with Tar ends with the Trinity'.[31]
Donald Davie, writing in 1955, claimed that Berkeley 'until
twenty or thirty years ago, was regarded as a proto-Romantic
philosopher, one of the fathers of subjective idealism; and
Yeats became interested in him at just about the time when
Berkeleyans began to challenge this reading of him ....'.[32]
But the challenge to Berkeley as subjective idealist was part
of a larger revision of British intellectual history, the reassertion by Bertrand Russell, G. E. Moore, and others of the
empiricist tradition eclipsed in the latter half of the nineteenth century by neo-Hegelian idealism. Fraser's editions of
Berkeley in 1871 and 1901 virtually delimit the period of
idealist dominance in Cambridge. That later date of course
takes us close to a further change in the history of philosophy to which we have already alluded, the origins of
phenomenology and the general crisis of European culture
known as modernism. One is tempted to seize on A. D.
Nuttall's advice to the reader approaching Berkeley — 'do not
allow yourself to be elevated by the dexterous, liberating
thought you are about to watch; only remember that you
will end exactly where you began.'[33]

[31] S. T. Coleridge, *Biographia Literaria*, ed. George Watson (London: Dent, 1960), p. 166.
[32] Donald Davie, 'Yeats, Berkeley, and Romanticism', in S. P. Rosenbaum, ed., *English Literature and British Philosophy* (Chicago, London: University of Chicago Press, 1971), pp. 278-9. This essay was first published in *Irish Writing*, vol. 31 (summer, 1955), pp. 36-41. A further development of these influences is discussed in A. P. Swarbrick, 'Donald Davie, Berkeley, and "Common Sense"', *Long Room*, nos. 20/21 (1980), pp. 29-35.
[33] A. D. Nuttall, *A Common Sky: Philosophy and the Literary Imagination* (London: Chatto and Windus, 1974), p. 30.

4. OLIVER GOLDSMITH: TRADITIONAL BIOGRAPHY

> And yet when I arrived at page two of
> the narrative I saw the extreme putridity
> of the social system out of which
> Goldsmith had reared his flower.
>
> (James Joyce)[34]

In dealing with Goldsmith's biography there are two crucial historical moments. The first of these is the collection of documents preserved in Trinity College Dublin, and known as the 1641 Depositions. In due course, we shall exhume material from The Reverend John Goldsmith's account of his sufferings during the Irish rebellion of that year, and relate the suppression of such genealogical traces to the question of the construction of a Goldsmith biography. The other historical moment is likewise textual, the following lines of Yeats's:

> Oliver Goldsmith sang what he had seen,
> Roads full of beggars, cattle in the fields,
> But never saw the trefoil stained with blood,
> The avenging leaf those fields raised up against it.[35]

The historical Goldsmith stands midway between these two moments, but the ideological nature of the biographical enterprise is not best revealed by strict adherence to chronology. Instead let us turn to John Forster's Victorian life of the poet.

Forster published *The Life and Times of Oliver Goldsmith* in 1871. When he had earlier ventured into the field, he had been attacked by a rival biographer, James Prior, essentially on a charge of plagiarism. Returning to the question in 1871, Forster declared that the attack had been on Prior's part 'nothing less than the claim to an absolute property in facts'.[36] As to his own work, he continued: 'Not only are

---

[34] *Letters of James Joyce*, vol. ii, ed. Richard Ellmann (London: Faber, 1966), p. 99 (JJ to Stanislaus J, 19 July 1905.)

[35] W. B. Yeats, 'The Seven Sages', *Collected Poems* (London: Macmillan, 1963), p. 272.

[36] John Forster, *Life and Times of Oliver Goldsmith* (London: Chapman and Hall, 1875), 6th ed., p. vii.

very numerous corrections to every former publication
relating to Goldsmith here made, and a great many new facts
brought forward, but each fact, whether old or new, is given
from its first authority.'[37] This talismanic addiction to facts
(and to the word 'fact') permits Forster to ignore entirely
the question of Goldsmith's origins and the larger perspective
of his place in the formation of Anglo-Irish society. Given the
date at which he is writing, Forster does not have to concern
himself with the issue of Anglo-Irish literature or the Irish
Augustan tradition. And yet the Victorian Goldsmith (like
the Victorian Swift) is one source for the Yeatsian model of
the same name.

The lines I have quoted from 'The Seven Sages', in common with Yeats's usual placing of Goldsmith, are explicitly
dramatic. Goldsmith is seen or accounted for in dramatic
relation to Swift or Burke. He represents the happy imperception of imminent revolution which is counterbalanced
by Swift's involuntary witnessing of 'the ruin to come' in
'The Words Upon the Window-Pane'. Each figure acts in
complementary relation to others, and Goldsmith is con-
sistently seen 'sipping at the honey-pot of his mind'.[38] The
Yeatsian universe is always a matter of antinomies, and
Goldsmith's permanent, partial function is to embody a
transitory unity between antinomies. Thus he unites expression and perception, sings what he sees, and his vision
specifies the beggars as well as the noblemen. Goldsmith,
in Yeats's system, contributes permanence with inadequate
acknowledgement of that process inherent in permanence;
Swift, one might say, stands for the reverse — an excessive
awareness of the process of imminent 'ruin' unchecked by
the actual. Unable to see the bloodstained trefoil (shamrock
and gibbet?), Goldsmith embodies a state of pre-lapsarian
harmony, pristine innocence, the perfect conjunction of
word and object, signifier and signified. As against this, we
see Swift as fallen, knowing, self-divided, ironic, savage.

It is worth emphasizing at this point the degree to which
this Yeatsian view of the Irish eighteenth century is a

37 Ibid., p. ix.
38 W. B. Yeats, *Collected Poems*, p. 268.

Romantic construct, in which a Victorian positivism and a Nietzschean opposition of knowledge to power are all but explicit. That Yeats celebrates the age as 'that one Irish century that escaped from darkness and confusion' is no abdication from such a dualism.[39] Swift and Berkeley, Goldsmith and Burke may be recruited as *dramatis personae* in an enactment of this play, yet it is admitted (tacitly) that they too were a reversal of the age, that Swift was evicted from court circles, Berkeley sequestered in remote Cork, Goldsmith jeered into eccentricity, and Burke held in continued opposition. Thus, while the eighteenth century shows up the 'darkness' of the nineteenth, Swift and Goldsmith by their knowledge and innocence show up the tawdry mechanical achievements of the Augustan hegemony. As Swift rarely ceased from saying, pre-eminent among these mechanical achievements was the administration of Ireland whose land was largely owned by those Berkeley characterized .as 'vultures with iron bowels'.[40] Properly indifferent to questions of localized setting and the preoccupation with naturalism, Joyce could read a few pages of *The Vicar of Wakefield* and diagnose the kind of culture in which Goldsmith worked — but in 1905 Joyce was also unaffected by the imminent Yeatsian myth of the Anglo-Irish Augustans. Looking at the symmetry of Swiftian knowledge and Goldsmithian innocence, we come finally to recognize the intensity of ideological investment in this myth.

The Protestant tradition which Yeats thus creates is to be seen in the historical moment of its articulation and not of its alleged setting alone. That is to say, it follows upon the dead Parnell, and the exertions of Augusta Gregory and Horace Plunkett after the turn of the century. By extending these values as exemplary to the new Free State, it contributes a family tree to that version of Victorian philanthropy which Yeats disguises as aristocratic service. This 'non-political' service may be elevated into a tradition by the invocation of a sequence of such figures — from Swift to Burke. The

---

[39] Yeats, 'Introduction to "The Words Upon the Window-Pane"', *Explorations*, p. 345.
[40] 'A Word to the Wise' *The Works of George Berkeley*, edd. A. A. Luce and T. E. Jessop (London: Nelson, 1953), vol. iii, p. 243.

contradiction at the centre of this formulation is precisely this, that its sequence is not historical but mythic, and its order dramatic rather than diachronic. Add to this, the by now self-evidently oppositional nature of this service and Yeats's tragic aesthetic is seen as the vehicle by which a specifically *fin de siècle* social dichotomy is provided with a resonant history, an Edenic past from which it is a falling-away nobly transformed.

Here we may resume contact with the issue of Goldsmith's biography and its metamorphosis. Yeats's categorization of Irish society, like his periodization of its history, required polar terms, and these he found in the Catholic/Protestant antagonism. From the 1790s onwards, these terms had gradually shifted from a relationship of mutual hostility (i.e. rival versions of the same creed) to one of mutual exclusivity. In this the deployment of sectarian feeling contributed to the perception of a rigidly stratified class system in Ireland, in which class is intensively perceived as a group rather than as the complex relations of a social formation. Goldsmith, within the Yeatsian schema, while embodying an innocent harmony of the 'seen' and the 'sung', is required to remain within a back-dated eighteenth-century reflection of this essentially post-revolutionary sociology.

It is at this point that the first of our historical moments should be considered, the 1641 Depositions:

John Goldsmith, parson of Burrishoole, in the county of Mayo, sworn and examined, says that between three and four years before the last rebellion in Ireland began, Francis Goldsmith, the deponents brother, who is a Romish priest of good account, living at and being Captain Maior of the castle of Antwerp in Brabant, wrote and sent a letter to this deponent ... which was delivered to him, this deponent, by one Father Richard Barret, a Jesuit and Spanish preacher ... This letter, as this deponent has heard, was first delivered at Antwerp aforesaid to Malone, the arch-Jesuit that dwelt in Dublin ... he is hereby persuaded that the said Malone had forewardly revealed the intended plot of rebellion to this deponents said brother which induced him so earnestly to write for this deponent, his wife and children to leave the kingdom and so escape the danger thereof which this deponent did not suspect, nor in any way understand, until the latter end of July next ... [41]

[41] Trinity College, Dublin, MS 831, fo. 145 etc. Some of this material was

Even as historical evidence of the rebellion, this document contains serious defects — as legal testimony it is and was less than worthless. Nevertheless, together with the subsequent confession of 'having been formerly a romish priest and converted to the protestant religion by the light of God', it establishes our poet's family's origins as including active Catholics. More surprisingly, the resemblance of The Reverend John Goldsmith's experiences in 1641 to the conventional view of poor Nol has not been noted. (To have had three-and-a-half years' notice — on good authority! — of a rebellion universally execrated for its precipitative treachery, and yet to have been pathetically embroiled as victim, this indeed is worthy of Oliver Goldsmith's reputation for thriftless vulnerability.) One reason for this failure to note Goldsmith's Catholic pedigree may be identified in Sir John Temple's omission of such associations in reporting the case of The Reverend John Goldsmith — though he was not averse to using them in other instances.[42] That the document was known to biographers almost from the outset cannot be denied: James Prior cited it at some length in the opening pages of his 1837 *Life*.[43] Prior, however, was also the biographer of Burke (1824) and was well aware of Burke's contemptuous dismissal of the Depositions as propaganda.[44]

Prior uncritically cites the Depositions in 1837, but John Forster has entirely eliminated them by the time his *Life* first appeared in 1848. Forster's laundering of Goldsmith's ancestry, while it superficially appears to remove crude

included in Mary Hickson, *Ireland in the Seventeenth Century,* 2 vols. (London, 1884).

[42] Sir John Temple, *The Irish Rebellion; or, an History of the beginnings and first progress of the general rebellion raised within the kingdom of Ireland, upon the three and twentieth day of October, in the year 1641. Together with the barbarous cruelties and bloody massacres which ensued thereupon* (London, 1646), pp. 67, 116–18. The most dispassionate analysis of Temple's unreliability, and of the Depositions generally, is still W. E. H. Lecky in his *History of Ireland in the Eighteenth Century* (London, 1896), vol. i, pp. 72–6.

[43] James Prior, *The Life of Oliver Goldsmith* (London, 1837), vol. i, pp. 2–3. Prior's source may well have been Temple's highly influential and grossly prejudicial *History* of events in which he personally had lost a great deal of money.

[44] 'the rascally collection in the College relative to the pretended Massacre in 1641', Burke to Richard Burke Jnr., 20 March 1792, *The Correspondence of Edmund Burke*, vol. vii, edd. P. J. Marshall and John A. Woods (Cambridge: Cambridge University Press, 1968), p. 104.

innuendo and self-contradictory evidence of a bygone
controversy, is a far more damaging blow to genuine historical veracity than Prior's unanalytical citations of the
Depositions. However, the onward march of a sectarian
sociology of Ireland (together with a romanticizing of the
eighteenth century in retrospect) required the elimination
of the admission that Goldsmith's ancestor had been a
Catholic priest, and that in the 1630s there had been affable
correspondence between the Goldsmith brothers, one
Catholic, one Protestant. It is true of course that the poet
and his brother told Thomas Percy about a forebear called
Juan Romeiro, a Spanish tutor who settled and married a
good Protestant Miss Goldsmith.[45] That 'tradition' of course
is a conveniently narrative explanation (John the Swordfish)
of a more significant social transformation occurring between
the early seventeenth and late eighteenth century. The late
Gerald Simms observed in this connection that 'Oliver
Goldsmith's Irish background was very different from that of
Jonathan Swift . . .'.[46] and we might add that these differences amount to a demolition of the ironically *nationalistic*
model which Yeats imposed on Goldsmith and Swift as a
rebuke to De Valera and Cosgrave. However, such exercises
as these are meaningless if they do not also establish the
historical continuity which led to the Yeatsian model.
Instead of Yeats's Goldsmith, we substitute no seemingly
pristine Goldsmith's Goldsmith, but instead seek to recover
every stage of the process by which Johnson, Percy, Prior,
Forster, and others contribute to the neo-romantic Goldsmith
of 'The Seven Sages'. Our reading of the poet does not itself
recover that figure, rather it contributes a further element to
the object of its own attention. In this way, tradition successively ratifies and condemns itself.

[45] See Katherine C. Balderston, *The History and Sources of Percy's Memoir
of Goldsmith* (Cambridge: Cambridge University Press, 1926), p. 13. Patrick
Murray has surveyed the factual problems of the Goldsmith biography, though
he is not concerned to draw interpretive conclusions, 'Goldsmith's Ancestry:
Fact and Tradition', in Harman Murtagh, ed., *Irish Midland Studies* (Athlone:
Old Athlone Society, 1980), pp. 147–58.
[46] I am grateful to Dr Hugh Shields who provided me with a copy of an unpublished paper (from which I quote here) delivered by his father-in-law, the
late Professor J. G. Simms, at a Goldsmith centenary celebration in 1974.

5. THE ANGLO-IRISH LITERARY TRADITION

> The tradition of the dead generations
> weighs like a nightmare on the minds of
> the living. And, just when they appear
> to be engaged in the revolutionary
> transformation of themselves and their
> material surroundings, in the creation of
> something which does not yet exist,
> precisely in such epochs of revolutionary
> crisis they timidly conjure up the spirits
> of the past to help them . . .
>
> (Karl Marx)[47]

Can we therefore come at last to a conclusion, lay the ghost
of Yeats's tradition, define the limits of Anglo-Irish literature
within newly ratified frontiers, and . . . so to bed? It is not
so easy. For one thing, we have yet to confront the ultimate
Yeatsian working out of tradition (in 'Purgatory'), the
moment at which the local politics of Catholic Nationalism
and Protestant Ascendancy throw vast shadows cast by the
ghastly light of Europe. For another, revisionism which
unmasks one system in the pretence of establishing none
leads either to densely annotated scepticism or simply to a
rearranged schedule of events. Literary history requires more,
because more is required of it in the peculiar circumstances
of Irish culture.

A literature which includes Yeats and Joyce is in no imminent danger of neglect; they, together with Synge, Shaw,
O'Casey, Wilde, and Moore, ensure the viability of Anglo-
Irish literature as an academic industry. And, though there
are difficulties attaching to the term 'Anglo-Irish literature',
it is too late to purge it from our critical vocabulary. There
is of course a general linguistic ambiguity lying behind the
specifically Anglo-Irish problems — there are the multiple
ways in which the word 'literature' is used. Though the sense
of 'imaginatively composed and formally organized written
works' predominates, there is also the looser (or larger)

[47] Karl Marx, 'The Eighteenth Brumaire of Louis Bonaparte', *Surveys from Exile*, ed. David Fernbach (London: Allen Lane, 1973), p. 146.

sense of 'written works about, or commentaries upon, a subject or topic' — thus there is the literature of industrial disputes, of parapsychology, and so forth. This ambiguity is
a radical one for it brings together in the one term the rival
claims of form and content, manner and matter, style and
theme. But there is another dimension: by English literature
we mean at times the literature produced by the English
people or the English nation, and the moment of English
literature's emergence can be related to specific developments
in English politics and social institutions; at other times, however, English literature is the sum of texts (wherever written)
in the English language. Anglo-Irish literature, therefore, is
not so much a description or a definition, but an eclectic
convenience. We must take care that we do not attempt false
analogies on the basis of the term's outward resemblance to
'English literature'. For to do so would be to disclose a
curious instability in the noun 'Anglo-Ireland' and its adjectival derivative, an instability which might suggest a route
to discovering contradictions in our implicit notions of
Ireland, England, Britain, etc.

One previous attempt at a theory of Anglo-Irish literature
deserves notice here. For Daniel Corkery, literature was
national in so far as it dealt with the experience of the Irish
people. His concept of the Irish people, their experience, and
the way that literature 'deals with' experience, was fundamentally crude — exile, non-Catholicism, a neglect of local
setting were sufficient to disqualify a Shaw or a Moore. But
to see that Corkery was not without distinguished predecessors in this approach, one has only to consider Yeats's
early quarrel with Edward Dowden and his rejection of Swift
and Berkeley (in the 1880s) as irrelevant to the new rural
consciousness, the new nationalism. And yet there is something curiously abstract about the notion of an Augustan
tradition in Ireland. Even if we leave aside the question of
Yeats's debt to the Victorians in his construction of the
Goldsmith of 'The Seven Sages', it remains true that the common identity which the Irish Augustans possess is the paradoxical sharing of isolation. (This becomes evident at a
further level if one considers the relationship of Gaelic literature to Berkeley, say, or Grattan.) We should be careful that

we do not replace nationalist or Yeatsian myths with a museum curator's display model of history. The idea that research can reconstruct a miraculously untarnished and un- changing work of art, the 'ding-an-sich', is ludicrous. Every act of criticism and interpretation is an attempt to bring together past and present, and we should be cheated if we were to accept literature simply as the graph of history. Robert Weimann has suggested that 'it is surely no idealism to assume that the work of art is not merely a product, but a "producer" of its age; not merely a mirror of the past, but a lamp to the future', and he associates this approach with Marx's 'special forms of production – as in the sense that the work of art can produce its audience, and influence their attitudes and values'.[48] This is sensible as far as it goes; it is perhaps advisable to emphasize that literature is not only a form of knowledge which might be translated into others – into statistical data, social analysis, or political history. Literature is a special form of knowledge in that it not only knows but *informs*; it both longs for and imposes order. It is simultaneously a form of knowledge and a knowledge of form. The idea of Corkery and Marx in cahoots is perhaps fanciful, and yet neither gave sufficient attention to the special forms of production which might operate in an advanced colonial society in which the manufacture of liter- ary ideology in the modernist period became pre-eminent.

T. S. Eliot's famous essay 'Tradition and the Individual Talent' appeared in 1919 and leads directly into the post- war phase of English-language modernism. At work on 'The Waste Land', Eliot is concerned in the essay to relate the modernism and traditionalism of his values:

What happens when a new work of art is created is something that happens simultaneously to all the works of art which preceded it. The existing monuments form an ideal order among themselves, which is modified by the introduction of the new (the really new) work of art among them. The existing order is complete before the new work arrives, for order to persist after the supervention of novelty, the *whole*

---

[48] Robert Weimann, *Structure and Society in Literary History: Studies in the History and Theory of Historical Criticism* (London: Lawrence and Wishart, 1977), p. 48.

existing order must be, if ever so slightly, altered; and so the relations, proportions, values of each work of art toward the whole are re-adjusted; and this is conformity between the old and the new.[49]

Here we have the declarative heart of an essay which began tentatively enough, 'In English writing we seldom speak of tradition, though we occasionally apply its name in deploring its absence.' From this cautious opening Eliot proceeds in a way which has been inadequately noted to deal with litera-ture through the metaphor of *works*, that is mental objects rather than the relations or processes conveniently sum-marized and concentrated in the metaphor of their being separate things. Wishing to establish relations between con-temporary literature and that of the past, he is prepared to minimize the relational existence of literature *per se*. Here, the valorization of the past as more real than the present and the increased autonomy of the modernist work of art are shown to be hand in hand. In a later essay, Eliot reformulates his fundamental point but significantly conceives a series of great artists whose genius is apparently quantifiable: 'When-ever a Virgil, a Dante, a Shakespeare, a Goethe is born, the whole future of European poetry is altered.'[50] By 1948, the modernist emphasis on the ability of the present to change the past has dwindled to this less exciting announce-ment. The truth is that every event in literary history is potentially a present event, and the past cannot simply be inherited; as Eliot rightly observed in 1919, 'if you want it you must obtain it by great labour.'[51]

The continuing process of representing the past, of achieving a re-vision of it, is indeed asserted by Yeats himself, thus sanctioning the eclipse of his own assertion:

> Civilisation is hooped together, brought
> Under a rule, under the semblance of peace
> By manifold illusion; but man's life is thought,
> And he, despite his terror, cannot cease

[49] T. S. Eliot, 'Tradition and the Individual Talent', *Selected Prose*, ed. Frank Kermode (London: Faber, 1975), pp. 38-9.
[50] T. S. Eliot, *Notes towards the Definition of Culture* (London: Faber, 1948), p. 114.
[51] Eliot, 'Tradition', p. 38.

Ravening through century after century,
Ravening, raging, and uprooting that he may come
Into the desolation of reality.[52]

To refer these lines to Nietzsche, to a modernist aesthetic, to Yeats's interest in a secret or symbolist history, is in each case possible. Possible also is it to demonstrate that, with these lines available to us, we can now re-read that splendid, nervous passage from Burke's *Reflections on the Revolution in France* opening with the assertion that 'society is indeed a contract', proceeding to elevate that contract into a universal, moral imperative, and concluding with a staccato evocation of the 'antagonistic world of madness, discord, vice, confusion and unavailing sorrow which must follow any violation of the contract'.[53] In other words, we could now come at last to the conclusion that the Anglo-Irish tradition begins with Burke rather than Swift, Burke rather even than Maria Edgeworth. Yet to do so would be to abdicate from the business of identifying the operative historical points of focus through which literary history becomes effective, in favour of yet another chronology.

Leaving aside, then the question of Burke and Yeats, we can concentrate more profitably on the method rather than the material. Three historical points of focus are involved, the first revolving round the reader's specific responsibilities. In *Truth and Method* Hans-Georg Gadamer has provided guidance in this connection:

The reader does not exist before whose eyes the great book of world history lies open. But nor does the reader exist who, when he has his text before him, simply reads what is there. Rather, all reading involves application, so that a person reading a text is himself part of the meaning he apprehends. He belongs to the text that he is reading.[54]

The term which Gadamer provocatively uses for the charac-

---

[52] W. B. Yeats, 'Meru' (Supernatural Songs), *Collected Poems*, p. 333.

[53] Edmund Burke, *Reflections on the Revolution in France* (Harmondsworth: Penguin, 1969), pp. 194-5. See Patrick J. Keane's 'Revolutions French and Russian: Burke, Wordsworth, and the Genesis of Yeats's "The Second Coming"', *Bulletin of Research in the Humanities*, vol. 82, No. 1 (Spring 1979), pp. 18-52.

[54] Hans-Georg Gadamer, *Truth and Method*, trans. and ed. Garrett Barden and John Cumming (London: Sheed and Ward, 1975), p. 304.

teristic which the reader brings to his text is *prejudice*: there can be no view of past literature which is not positively affected by the prejudices of the reader. Because, for Gadamer, all experience is experience of human finitude it follows that the reader is obliged to be aware of his own position in the historical process: by prejudice he means a consciousness of all those attitudes, needs, abilities, and inadequacies which characterize the reader as he confirms his relationship with the past by the act of reading. And the term which Gadamer uses for this relationship is properly *dialectic*, that is, question and answer, dramatic conversation. 'Tradition is not simply a process that we learn to know and be in command of through experience; it is language, i.e. it expresses itself like a "Thou". A "Thou" is not an object, but stands in relationship with us.'[55] Only through such a revised concept of reading itself can we begin to discover a new tradition, a tradition in which the future is acknowledged as real. In my final chapter I hope to say something about the condition in which the reader of Anglo-Irish literature finds himself, about the prejudices he must recognize as he applies himself to the 'handing down' which is tradition.

The second historical point of focus through which literary history can become effective centres on the question of the nature of the literary text. One can see that the tacit assumption of Eliot's modernist aesthetic was that literature consists of artefacts, objects or works which possess a degree of autonomy criticism has no need to challenge. Now that the moment of the New Critics has passed this concept of the work of literature probably has few serious advocates. With the renovation of psychoanalysis in France and elsewhere, and with other related practices emphasizing other forms of repression as active within and around the official contours of an artwork, it is more profitable now to consider if significant absences do not constitute a meaning of literature and art. The genesis of a text is a function of the text's meaning, just as the reader too contributes his application in the act of reading. It is not enough, however, simply to regard all texts from the canon as equally susceptible to these altered

[55] Ibid., p. 321.

procedures: in order to identify the text which forms an *operative* historical point of focus one needs to draw upon a historical materialism which reads history as possessing more than a determined past. In other words, the entire political unconscious which underlies the extensive cultural production we have called Anglo-Irish literature must be articulatable through the reading of this text, if the text is effectively an operative focus. In the following chapter I take Yeats's play 'Purgatory' to be such a text, and in analysing it I hope to show that its significant absences also throw light on the repressed history of Yeats's tradition, the history which has been betrayed by the ideological operations of Protestant Ascendancy. Using Edmund Burke and W. B. Yeats as the poles of an argument, and concluding with an examination of 'Purgatory' seen as the ablation of this tradition, I read the play as the supreme statement of Yeats's tradition, but I require the term 'ablation' to convey the play's complexity in both defining and destroying the tradition it brings to completion. Far from employing such terminology to divert attention from an inquiry into the social base of Irish culture, and the modes of production therein, I hope to ground my argument very solidly on the evidence of the author's social experience. Perhaps one might say that this experience influenced the play. It is preferable to speak of the text's genesis through this experience and through the broader medium of the language in which it finds itself. There is a *pensée* of Pascal's which can summarize the position for us:

Since everything then is cause and effect, dependent and supporting, mediate and intermediate, and all is held together by a natural though imperceptible chain, which binds together things most distant and most different, I hold it equally impossible to know the parts without knowing the whole, and to know the whole without knowing the parts in detail.[56]

But there is a third historical point of focus, larger than reader or effective text. It is not simply the epoch, as Hippolyte Taine argued, though 'Purgatory's' place in the era

---

[56] Blaise Pascal, *Pensées* (London: Dent, 1931), p. 20.

of fascism can hardly be passed over without comment. It is rather the suppressed history of such crises, the business of the literary historian being the identification of that suppression as it turns the larger historical sequence towards a particular ideological purpose. In charting the Victorian construction of a Goldsmith biography, we have already observed the obverse of this suppression. In examining 'Purgatory' we will encounter a particularly pure form of this suppressed Victorian history. A full account of Yeats's place in the history of Victorian thought remains to be written: here in looking briefly at Lecky, Arnold, Forster, or even Dowden as precursors we are not bound to seek for verbal echoes or to document loans and borrowings. Yeats is the culmination of a mid- and late-Victorian rereading of the Irish eighteenth century, a rereading which can be conveniently dated from Arnold's Oxford lectures *On the Study of Celtic Literature* given in the year of the Irish poet's birth.

However, there is silence in Yeats's rhetoric also: hand in hand with the invocation of Swift and Burke there are elisions and lacunae. Take, for example, a passage where he seeks a universal metaphysic which yet retains the appearance of the concrete world, one of those visions of the disembodied and yet muscular world to which his phenomenological tendencies led him:

It was indeed Swedenborg who . . . discovered a world of spirits where there was a scenery like that of earth, human forms, grotesque or beautiful, senses that knew pleasure and pain, marriage and war, all that could be painted upon canvas, or put into stories to make one's hair stand up.[57]

The probability exists here that Yeats has the fiction of Sheridan Le Fanu in mind, for in *Uncle Silas* and in the short stories of *In a Glass Darkly* Le Fanu explicitly used Swedenborgian doctrines in his sensational plots. Nevertheless, Yeats's prose remains inscrutable, refusing to divulge a name. Now, Liam Miller has revealed that the earliest draft of 'The Words Upon the Window-Pane' connects the theme of the play to Le Fanu's fiction, especially the tales of *In a*

Glass Darkly.[58] The point is not simply that Yeats suppressed the nineteenth-century avenue by which he sought to approach Jonathan Swift, the central (and absent) character of the play. Le Fanu had indeed family links with Swift (through the Sheridans) and had inherited a number of relics of the Dean's. More significantly however, the specific function of Swedenborgianism in Le Fanu's fiction was to provide a symbolism through which neurosis was analysed; and while the characters of the stories seem discrete and private when considered individually, the over-all structure of *In a Glass Darkly* transforms their personal symptoms into a cultural malaise explicitly related to the French Revolution and 'the ruin to come'. The suppression of the Le Fanu reference and its attendant apparatus is dramatically effective; more specifically, its effect is of a consciously tragic kind. Without the intervention of Le Fanu's bourgeois neurosis, the image of Swift is projected directly on to the audience's imagination with the minimum of historical or narrative mediation. That is, the dean is caught in the truth of his own prophecy.

The elimination of the Le Fanu reference from the early stages of the play's genesis is not just a negative feature of the play, something we know by virtue of our scholarly prurience. In 'The Words Upon the Window-Pane' Swift's tragic vision of civilization's end is prefaced and produced by the vulgarity of table-rapping and a distinctly *petit-bourgeois* cast of spiritualists. As they discuss their contributions to the séance, practise their lines for the longed-for encounter with departed spirits, and criticize their fellows, the figures constitute a play-within-the-play. They may also be regarded as an audience awaiting Swift's performance, though ironically they will have departed before his spirit speaks through Mrs Henderson. Their departure, the elimination of the play-within, the obliteration of Mrs Henderson's voice by that of Swift, enacts the suppression of those historical connections by which Yeats reaches Swift. The discarding of Le Fanu's *In a Glass Darkly* is an integral part of the structure and meaning of the play.

[58] Liam Miller, *The Noble Drama of W. B. Yeats* (Dublin: Dolmen Press, 1977), p. 287.

What then is the significance of this suppressed history?
What particular value has 'The Words Upon the Window-
Pane' as a demonstration of this suppression? Despite (or
perhaps because of) the immaturity and unevenness of his
work, Le Fanu was the literary spokesman of the Irish
Victorian middle classes, a formation uniquely affected by
the notions of Protestant Ascendancy. In Marx's terms one
might see Le Fanu's colleagues timidly conjuring up the
spirits of the past to help them. What Yeats's play achieves —
and with a vengeance! — is to take that metaphor of spirit-
conjuring seriously *and* to eliminate the timid bourgeois who
foolishly have recourse to such theatrical props. The redundancy of the so-called Ascendancy, the prevalence of exile
settings, the location of identity solely in guilt — these are
the hallmarks of Le Fanu's fiction. Swedenborg's solipsistic
cosmology allowed him to reveal the purposelessness of the
Great House in *Uncle Silas,* while in *In a Glass Darkly* the
same doctrines provided an analysis of individual neurosis.
What Le Fanu and his characters find unacceptable, unin-
telligible, is their merely contingent existence, their bourgeois
condition. Yeats's exclusion of all this stems from his recognition of the *validity* of Le Fanu's diagnosis, validity that
is within the circumstances (the prejudices as Gadamer would
have it) of Yeats's own historical position as reader. In order
that Yeats may artistically acknowledge his own origins in
the self-destructive world of Le Fanu — and to transform
those origins artistically — he must expunge them from his
work. They form a negative mould, an antithetical shape
from which Yeats's imagination releases itself. To be specific,
one can see the sequence of events in 'The Words Upon
the Window-Pane' as an implied or desired causation: the
departure/suppression of the *petit-bourgeois* cast will allow
unmediated access to aristocratic tradition in Swift, but that
revelation is necessarily tragic in itself, and admonitory to
us.

And the notion of tradition is peculiarly relevant here,
especially if we note Freud's radical reinterpretation of the
artistic urge. Connecting individual neurosis and civilization
(*Kultur*) he argues that 'neuroses ultimately reveal themselves
as attempts to solve on an individual basis the problems of

wish compensation that ought to be solved socially by institutions.'[59] For Freud, *Kultur* only shows the ways men have attempted 'to bind their unsatisfied wishes under the varying conditions of fulfilment and denial by reality . . .'.[60] I have already suggested how reality in Ireland underwent a continuous process of obfuscation, or was atomized into a scintillation of facticity. Thus, it is doubly true that in colonial Ireland tradition offered a publicly sanctioned compensation for necessary cultural renunciations.[61]

Marx . . . Eliot . . . Gadamer . . . all three perspectives cited here are called into being, called into question, by the concentration and purity of 'Purgatory'. The sight of conjured spirits dramatizes once again the tragedy of Protestant Ascendancy, but not in the aesthetic self-congratulation of 'The Words Upon the Window-Pane' — there is no Swift to bolster the pretence that this drama is remediable history. As Eliot astutely observed, after the supervention of this novelty the whole pre-existing order is modified, however slightly, modified and changed by the apparent dramatization of unchanging process. Finally, we read this text applying ourselves to its meaning, finding our meaning there in murderous consequence of endogamous pride.

---

[59] Sigmund Freud, 'The Claims of Psychoanalysis to Scientific Interest', quoted by Jurgen Habermas, *Knowledge and Human Interests*, trans. Jeremy J. Shapiro (Boston: Beacon Press, 1971), p. 276.

[60] Idem.

[61] This sentence is in part a rephrasing of Habermas on Freud (Habermas, p. 276). The later chapters of *Knowledge and Human Interests* suggest the broad application of the method of psychoanalysis as a literary hermeneutic, because 'Freud always patterned the interpretation of dreams after the hermeneutic model of philological research' (p. 214).

10.   ON 'PURGATORY'

A second chance — that's the delusion.
There never was to be but one. We work
in the dark — we do what we can — we
give what we have. Our doubt is our
passion and our passion is our task. The
rest is the madness of art.

(Henry James)[1]

1.   SOURCES AND FORMS

What is 'Purgatory'? Its successful stage-career proves that
it is effectively a play. On the other hand, the text itself
resembles those dialogue poems which Yeats wrote at various
stages of his life. For a play, it seems limited in its presentation of setting; for a poem, it seems overloaded with action.
These generic uncertainties should be read positively as
evidence of Yeats's full engagement in 'Purgatory', Yeats the
dramatist, Yeats the poet. But the uncertainties also mark a
crisis in modernist aesthetic categories, a railing against form
or the persistent erection of one form as a bulwark against
another.

This unease — the term is too bland, but let it pass — in
'Purgatory' has local and global implications. For, while we
can show that the play draws extensively on Yeats's experience of Irish social history, we can also point to parallels in,
say, German culture. Some of these German parallels may
have their own prior association in Irish literary history;
others — that involving Wagner, notably — suddenly open up
the entire horizon of twentieth-century European cultural
crisis. With this perspective in mind, the shadowy setting of
'Purgatory' may stimulate once again that sense of embarrassment at the confluence of mighty reputations and marginal
references which has already been discussed. Of course,

---

[1] Henry James, 'The Middle Years', *Novels and Tales* (Clifton, NJ: A. M.
Kelley, [*c*.1974], The New York Edition, vol. xvi, p. 105.

followers of Lucien Goldmann's genetic structuralism may
find in all these parallels material for an analysis of the
homologies between the deep consciousness of a specific
period and the structures of certain crucial works of literature. Such works are then seen to possess a 'world-historical
view'.[2] In *Le Dieu caché*, Goldmann had elaborated this theory in analysing Pascal's *Pensées* and Racine's tragic drama
and relating the structures of these works to the theological
and social structures of Jansenism — he was, it should be
noted, less successful in applying the method to twentieth-
century literature. The relatively marginal position of Jansenism in France, as opposed to official Catholicism, should
encourage those who are dismayed by the marginality of
Ireland in relation to European affairs: not only did Yeats
reproduce the proportions of marginality/centrality which
Goldmann encountered in Pascal, but Yeats shared with
Racine a specifically *tragic* outlook. It is worth noting these
effective horizons within which Goldmann's original research
was conducted before accepting the fashionable dismissal of
genetic structuralism and its homologies. In the Anglo-Irish
field marginality is *de rigueur*, and in that sub-set of the field
known as Yeats tragedy is pervasive. 'Purgatory' brings together these characteristics, together with the generic tensions outlined above.

It is crucial to Goldmann's argument, of course, that the
correlation of historical period or epoch and specific literary
works is based on the form of the latter and not on their
contents. It is only in inferior writing that one finds simple
relations between content and context, and in such novels
or plays one can only encounter an *'unachieved* consciousness
of the time'.[3] The resemblance between 'Purgatory' and
an obscure German romantic play neatly illustrates this
distinction. Zacharias Werner's 'Vierundzwanzig Februar'
(1809) certainly resembles the plot of Yeats's play in several striking respects — recurrent murder within the family,
the tyranny of Fate or a determined destiny, coincidence,

---

[2] Raymond Williams, 'Marxism, Structuralism and Literary Analysis', *New Left Review*, 129 (September–October 1981), pp. 51-66 (p. 58).
[3] Ibid., p. 58.

etc.[4] The appeal of German romanticism in Ireland, and especially in what has been termed 'Anglo-Ireland', was very great indeed — the notorious weakness of the German middle class and the undeveloped condition of the German state offered parallels to the Protestant Ascendancy. If the land-owners of Davitt's day gave the impression of possessing a heritage as venerable as that of pre-Bismarckian Junkers in Prussia, there is plenty of literary evidence as to where this belief originated. 'Purgatory' does not derive its world-historical view from its resemblance to degenerate versions of Sturm und Drang: — indeed, one significant divergence between the two plays is particularly important. Werner's play makes specific the sectarian divisions of Swiss mountain society in which it is set, whereas Yeats's final version of 'Purgatory' is silent on the Protestant/Catholic antagonism. In a manuscript scenario prepared in advance of the text, however, Yeats had specified as a crucial aspect of the *mésalliance* at the heart of the play that the marriage be-tween the Lady and the Groom had taken place in a Catholic church — the lady had demeaned herself not simply by marrying her stablegroom but by marrying outside the sectarian 'tribe'.[5] Bearing this proto-history of the canonical text in mind, we confront the casual but heartfelt condem-nation of 'Purgatory's' ritual of aesthetized murder as fascist. But it is not simply the manifest content of the play which relates it to epochal catastrophe; its sources and forms are far more eloquent. Evidence of the play's genesis, in the manu-script scenario and in earlier utterances of Yeats's, specifies its assumption of the Protestant/Catholic antagonism as tribal if not racial, as the operational field of taboo and totem. One crucial structural aspect of the play becomes therefore the suppression of this specified ideology in the canonical text.

'Purgatory' occupies a special place in the Yeatsian canon, yet its significance depends not on its uniqueness but on its centrality. Written virtually at the close of the poet's life

---

[4] See James Clarence Mangan's translation of Werner's play under the title 'The Twenty-fourth of February', in *The Dublin University Magazine*, vol. 10 No. 55 (July 1837), pp. 26–53.

[5] Cited by Donald Torchiana in *Yeats and Georgian Ireland* (Evanston: Northwestern University Press, 1966), pp. 220 and 361.

it illuminates a great deal of his drama which, without 'Purgatory', might seem merely experimental. And while achieving a very distinctive language at once poetic and dramatic, it succeeds also in integrating much that had appeared casual in Yeats's prose. It is in such terms that we view the centrality of the play to Yeats's career, and beyond that perspective it is 'Purgatory' above all else which reveals the nature of that modernism which Yeats did so much to render possible in English.

From the outset, heroism was at the heart of the Yeatsian aesthetic. As a consequence, dramatic technique (if not always dramatic form) closely engaged the poet's attention. From the Cuchulain of 'On Baile's Strand' (1904) to 'The Death of Cuchulain' (1939) the encounter which defines Yeatsian heroism is the potentially evasive nature of death itself — the hero fights the ungovernable tide, the Old Man pleads for an end to process and consequence. That death should not be frankly confrontable is the essence of the tragic hero's dilemma: doomed, he is yet uncertain if he can trust to his own doom. Yeats's tragedies revolve around what Fredric Jameson has described in another context as 'heroic cynicism'.[6] In 'Purgatory' Yeats finally confronts that cynicism of form which modernism depended upon.

Like 'The Words Upon the Window-Pane' and 'The Death of Cuchulain', 'Purgatory' deals with the burden of the past. Much of it can be seen as — *inter alia* — Yeats's meditation on his own previous meditation: it is a self-scrutiny, and in this it has its affinities with 'The Dead'. Yet in its historical concern Joyce's short story adopts what may appear to be a naïve transparency in its anatomy of nineteenth-century Ireland while the play is frequently taken to evoke the famous Yeatsian eighteenth century, 'that one Irish century that escaped from darkness and confusion'.[7] Like Burke's *Reflections*, the play adopts as its style and form a dominant metaphor which it reveals as virtually redundant. In 'Purgatory' the dominant metaphor is pollution, especially hereditary pollution; the characters on stage appear to suffer

[6] Fredric Jameson, 'The Vanishing Mediator: Narrative Structure in Max Weber', *New German Critique*, vol. 1 (Winter 1973), pp. 52–89.
[7] W. B. Yeats, *Explorations* (London: Macmillan, 1962), p. 365.

the consequences of ancestral offence. The stratagem of bringing pollution to an end by killing the boy is pathetic self-deception. As with Burke's Great House, the dominant metaphor of the play turns sardonically upon itself.

Donald Torchiana concluded *Yeats and Georgian Ireland* with an analysis of 'Purgatory' in the context of its appearance in the poet's handbook of violent diatribe *On the Boiler*. As his title suggests, Torchiana is concerned to see the play as 'the symbolic tragedy of the eighteenth century and its consequence for modern Ireland.'[8] While his documentation of Yeats's current interest in eugenics and Nazi legislation tactfully reminds us of the modern context in which the play was written, the acceptance of Yeats's superficial allusions to the eighteenth century successfully conceals the real logic of Yeats's relationship with fascism. Source and style, in the case of 'Purgatory', combine most effectively to point to the nineteenth-century origins of that historical movement which reached its apotheosis in European fascism.

The most frequently cited source for the play is *The Celtic Twilight* (the expanded edition of 1902). Here Yeats recorded many West of Ireland tales about the Devil, purgatory, the dead, and their ghosts. An informant from County Galway had confided: 'And another time I saw Purgatory. It seemed to be in a level place, and no walls around it, but it all one bright blaze, and the souls standing in it.'[9] Undoubtedly, this is a source for the play — if one wishes to take a fairly simplistic view of the relationship between source and art. The immediately previous paragraph of Yeats's account of the Galway seer offers an observation in which a more reciprocal kind of source is at work:

I have seen Hell myself. I had a sight of it one time in a vision. It had a very high wall around it — all of metal, and an archway, and a straight walk into it, just like what'ud be leading into a gentleman's orchard, but the edges were not trimmed with box, but with red-hot metal.[10]

[8] Torchiana, op. cit., p. 351.
[9] W. B. Yeats, *The Celtic Twilight*, rev. and enlarged ed. (London: Bullen, 1902), p. 77.
[10] Idem. A further amusing element of folklore's reflection of bourgeois Ireland's interest occurs in Yeats's account of a Mayo woman whose demon-lover manifested himself in a strange manner; she was waiting by the roadside 'when

That Hell should be described in the terminology of a gentleman's residence would have appealed politically to Yeats in
1902 to a degree inconceivable in 1938. Peasants' accounts
of the Devil tend to see him in the garb of their social
superiors, which in turn suggests that he looks very much like
a folklore collector. In 1902, however, Yeats was determined
to exploit folklore as a direct communication with 'Ireland',
and to do so he suspended attention to his own social
position in Ireland. The period of his activities as a collector
of lore is significant in that it coincides with the collapse of
the landlord system and the eclipse of the resident gentry.
We recognize 'Upon a House Shaken by the Land Agitation'
(1910) as a turning-point in Yeats's career, the point after
which he resumes attention to his own position in Irish
society. It has been customary to identify 'land agitation' as
the culminating activity of tenants and propagandists; this is
sentimental. Yeats was sufficiently shrewd to know that
Wyndham's Act of 1903 did more than merely codify the
agitation of half a century. It signalled *Government's* abandonment of the Irish Great House. *The Celtic Twilight*, in
recording the gentleman's orchard in Hell's fire, records a
specifically nineteenth-century folk-imagination.

   In the course of this argument I shall be concerned to
show how the sources Yeats drew upon in 1938 for 'Purgatory' have a concentration in time which is revealing; their
period is, roughly speaking, very late Victorian and Edwardian. That is to say they are located in the years when
Irish politics was more evidently and palpably concerned
with social issues rather than nationalist principles. Writing
his *Reveries Over Childhood & Youth* in 1914, Yeats recalled
his childhood excursions to Castle Dargan in County Sligo.
Again, to capture the reciprocal quality of the poet's involvement with his material, we must look beyond the familiar
sentences and quote *in extenso*:

---

something came flapping and rolling along the road up to her feet. It had the
likeness of a newspaper, and presently it flapped up into her face, and she knew
by the size of it that it was the *Irish Times*' (ibid., p. 69). The *Irish Times*, at this
time, was a liberal unionist paper closely identified with the Protestant Ascendancy.

Sometimes I would ride to Castle Dargan, where lived a brawling
squireen, married to one of my Middleton cousins, and once I went
thither on a visit with my cousin George Middleton. It was, I dare say,
the last household where I could have found the reckless Ireland of a
hundred years ago in final degradation. But I liked the place for the
romance of its two ruined castles facing one another across a little lake,
Castle Dargan and Castle Fury. The squireen lived in a small house
whither his family had moved from their castle some time in the
eighteenth century, and two old Miss Furys, who let lodgings in Sligo,
were the last remnants of the breed of the other ruin. Once in every
year he drove to Sligo for the two old women, that they might look
upon the ancestral stones and remember their gentility, and he would
put his wildest horses into the shafts to enjoy their terror.

He himself, with a reeling imagination, knew not what he could be
at to find a spur for the heavy hours. The first day I came there, he gave
my cousin a revolver, (we were upon the high road), and to show it
off, or his own shooting, he shot a passing chicken; and half an hour
later, when he had brought us to the lake's edge under his castle, now
but the broken corner of a tower with a winding stair, he fired at or
over an old countryman who was walking on the far edge of the lake.
The next day I heard him settling the matter with the old countryman
over a bottle of whiskey, and both were in good humour . . . At last he
quarrelled with my great-uncle William Middleton, and to avenge himself gathered a rabble of wild country lads and mounted them and himself upon the most broken-down rascally horses he could lay hands on
and marched them through Sligo under a land-league banner. After
that, having now neither friends nor money, he made off to Australia
or to Canada.

I fished for pike at Castle Dargan and shot at birds with a muzzle-
loading pistol until somebody shot a rabbit and I heard it squeal. From
that on I would kill nothing but the dumb fish.

XI

We left Bedford Park for a long thatched house at Howth, Co.
Dublin. The land war was now at its height and our Kildare land, that
had been in the family for many generations, was slipping from us.
Rents had fallen more and more, we had to sell to pay some charge or
mortgage . . .[11]

There is much material for drama here. If the practical jokes
and extraneous violence look back to Buck Whaley and the

[11] W. B. Yeats, *Reveries Over Childhood and Youth* (London: Macmillan,
1916), pp. 99-103.

rake-hellish life of regency days, they also confirm that the
Old Man in 'Purgatory' in asking 'Where are the jokes and
stories of a house/It's threshold gone to patch a pig-sty?' may
not be referring to any remoter history than that of the
1870s. Here, in autobiographical form, we have the Great
House deserted, the debauched master, the shameful mediation of whiskey between the classes — all features of the
play of 1938. The passage also implicates Yeats himself,
not only in the damage done by Land League agitation to the
Yeats's rents in Kildare, but also in the surrogate huntin'
and shootin', soon rejected for the more discreet killing of
'dumb fish'. Once again, a source for 'Purgatory' is revealed
to contain a dialectical presence of the author himself; it is
no mere raw material for reflection.

In his biography of the poet, J. M. Hone records a ghost
story which Yeats told at a Friday evening gathering in
Charles Ricketts's house. Hone's commentary dates the
occasion to the years immediately preceding the Great War,
and connects it to the essay 'Swedenborg, Mediums and the
Desolate Places' which subsequently appeared as an epilogue
to Lady Gregory's *Visions and Beliefs of the West of Ireland.*
Though Hone's version, supplied by Thomas Lowinsky, an
artist who had been present for Yeats's performance, retains
marks of its transmission, there are clear suggestions of
'Purgatory':

Centuries ago there lived in a castle in Ireland a man and wife. To their
abounding sorrow they remained childless despite prayers and pilgrim-
ages. At last, when they had long given up all hope, the woman, to her
joy, found herself pregnant. Her husband, who till then had been
tender and trusting, became sullen and suspicious, often giving himself
up to lonely bouts of drinking. Barely had the child been born when
the man, roaring drunk, rushed into the upper chamber where his wife
lay. With cries of 'Bastard, bastard' he wrested the baby from her
breast, and with the screaming infant in his arms strode raging from the
room. Down the winding wooden stairs he ran into the hall, where, all
reason fled, he beat and beat the tiny thing against anything he could.
From her bed the mother rose and followed . . . to arrive too late. Her
son was dead. Picking him up from where had had been flung, she
turned and slowly climbed the spiral stairs that led to the threshold
of her room. She moved as in a trance till, through the open door,
the sight of the bed brought her to earth with a spasm of despair.

Vehemently clasping the child, in a flash she bent beneath the bar
which fenced the stairs, and dropped, like a singed moth, to the stone
floor below. The man, his frenzy spent, was overwhelmed with grief. He
sought consolation in taking another wife by whom he had other sons.
Thus a family was founded and generation followed generation, each
living much the same uneventful bucolic lives as those whom they
succeeded. Although they cared for their castle and husbanded its
land, each in turn from time to time abandoned himself to the same
solitary bouts. The house as a rule was a happy place but, during those
spells, when its master was saturated with drink, an ashen woman
would drift past him, ascending the curved stairs. Transfixed, he would
wait the tragedy that he knew he was doomed only to see when he was
drunk. Always with the same simple gesture she would reach the top-
most step; always in the same way, pause, then bend, to drop a flutter-
ing mass. Yet when he peered down he could see nothing. With the
years the family vice grew like a cancer until it ate away their entire
fortune and they were reduced to poverty. To crown their misery fire
gutted the castle. The descendant to whom it belonged was without
the money or the desire to re-build. Indolent and inane, he left with
few regrets to live in far-distant Dublin. Thenceforth the family and its
fount seemed after countless years to have severed every bond. But
destinies and traditions are hard to break and one day the grandson
of this deserter was drawn to the very spot. His boon companion, killed
by the kick of a horse, was to be buried within sight of the crumbling
towers. Moved partly by affection for his friend, partly by curiosity
to see the place whence his stock had sprung, the survivor of this long
line had journeyed to attend the funeral. He met many friends and
tippled with them all and, drunk, he found himself at dusk before the
sombre shell of a stronghold. There being no door, he walked straight
into the empty well up the wall of which had twined the oaken stairs.
As he gazed he saw a fragile dishevelled form glide past him up and
round the walls as though the steps were still there. Almost at the top
she stopped, then with a burst of emotion dived, to disappear. The man
knew no surprise. He felt that he had watched this melancholy scene
innumerable times before — and for an instant he dimly understood
that neither his children nor yet his children's children could ever purge
themselves of a crime that they had inherited with their blood.[12]

Many of the sparse details of the play can be found here in
narrative form — the drunken husband, the woman seen in
repetition of her trauma, the returned grandson, the notion

[12] J. M. Hone, *W. B. Yeats 1865–1939* (London: Macmillan, 1962), 2nd ed.,
pp. 283–4.

of hereditary suffering. Even if we admit that this last source only reaches us at third hand, it shares with *The Celtic Twilight* and *Reveries* the tone and structure of late Victorian and Edwardian recollection. To seize upon 'centuries ago' as sanctioning an eighteenth-century provenance for the tale is to travesty the basic conventions of oral narrative, especially of the supernatural tale. The central and significant feature of the events at Ricketts's house is that, in 1914 or thereabouts, Yeats found a tale of recurring and hereditary suffering a satisfactory narrative; he found it to have *form*. When we come to 'Purgatory', utter dissatisfaction, a railing against form within form, is the dominant tone.

In connection with these sources we have to ask how Yeats transforms the raw material of ghost story and childhood recollection into the tight structure of 'Purgatory'. It might be more precise to say that it is Yeats's recollection of this material in 1938 which can be properly regarded as the play's source. And while this refinement would involve a further consideration of Yeats's newspaper interview on the subject of Nazi respect for the ancient sanctities, it may be more critically profitable to concentrate on the texts in hand. A major distinction between the play and its source is that the drama specifically spurns narrative. In relation to the story told at Ricketts's, we can see that this process is achieved by the deliberate elimination of the psychological rationale of the father's drunken fury — his suspicion that the child is not his — in favour of class hatred. The logic of the ghost story identifies violent fury (for which no adequate justification is provided) as the cause of hereditary suffering; that the origin of this fury may be a suspicion of *mésalliance* is secondary. In 'Purgatory' of course fury and *mésalliance* are placed in immediate conjunction in a manner approved by (at least) the Old Man. At a structural level we can describe this transformation of the material as the elimination of all notions of linear time in favour of 'other events that lie side by side in space [,] complements one of another',[13] as Yeats puts it in *On the Boiler*. For the agony of the different

[13] W. B. Yeats, *On the Boiler* (Churchtown: Cuala Press, 1939), p. 36. It is perhaps worth noting that this astringent analysis of Irish life was written 'here in Monte Carlo' (p. 37).

generations in 'Purgatory' has only the appearance of sequence; dramatically, the Old Man and the Boy go through
their violent ritual simultaneously with the Bride and Groom.
In the idiom of Saussurean linguistics, the play prefers the
synchronic to the diachronic axis. That preference, of course,
has been pervasive in modernist literature, and even more so
in the practical criticism it has begotten, being the basis of
an aesthetic justifying the text as autonomous and 'self-
delighting'.

Despite Practical Criticism and the New Criticism, that
sense of autonomy was of course never absolute. Novelists
such as Joyce and Thomas Mann employed an irony which
is directed as much at the pretensions of artistic form as at an
intractable world. Irony in Yeats, however, enjoys a less
official status, and the problem is doubly sensitive in the case
of 'Purgatory', requiring some method of responding critically to those explicit avowals of Nazi attitude which are
concentrated in the interview printed in the *Irish Independent* after the first performance of the play in August 1938.
In advance of that encounter with German legislation some
further traces of the play's origin may still prove valuable.

2. 'ASCENDENCY WITH ITS SENSE OF RESPONSIBILITY...'

The Celtic Twilight, Reveries, and the story told at Ricketts's
offer comparisons which only approximate to something in
'Purgatory'. Each in isolation would fail to prove itself the
seed from which the play grew. Nevertheless, the collocations
of house, ghost, and returning degenerate heir impose themselves as evidence of a prima-facie quality. There is a plaus-
ibly insidious process by which *The Tower* and the many
allusions to Great Houses in the poems of that period are
read as a personal hallmark of Yeats, a process which leads
critics to an autobiographical reading of 'Purgatory'.
Torchiana confidently identifies the lines 'to kill a house/
Where great men grew up, married, died, / I here declare a
capital offence' as spoken 'in what is certainly Yeats's own
voice'.[14] Harold Bloom has reservations about the play, and

---

[14] Torchiana, op. cit., p. 362.

concludes: 'Yeats is not separate enough from the old man's rage to render the play's conclusion coherent. That hardly makes the play less powerful, but perhaps we ought to resent a work that has so palpable a design upon us.'[15] Now my position is delicate, and I must try to formulate it with some precision. I am pointing to the immediacy of Yeats's historical experience of nineteenth-century social change in those tales which resemble 'Purgatory' — here the squireen relative and his Land League antics are especially relevant. I resist, however, the idea of the Old Man's speech as a statement verbatim from the poet. I wish to show that, prior to the last despairing lines, the play, *read as a dramatic text*, establishes real relations with the world it comes from. Those final lines are seen as a cry of despair from within the self-regulating modernist art-work, an appeal for release from the sovereignty of the text. If the source material for 'Purgatory' can be shown to have its roots in the disturbed soil of nineteenth- (and early twentieth-) century social change, we may turn to an examination of style in search of Yeats's transformative method.

A central passage from the Old Man's exposition reads:

> Great people lived and died in this house;
> Magistrates, colonels, members of Parliament,
> Captains and Governors, and long ago
> Men that had fought at Aughrim and the Boyne.
> Some that had gone on Government work
> To London or to India came home to die,
> Or came from London every spring
> To look at the may-blossom in the park.[16]

The Old Man commends these great people and their relationship with the house; the offence he condemns most eloquently in his father is that 'he killed the house . . .'. For this passage we can find remarkable parallels in two sources. The first is in Yeats's own voice, his 'Commentary on "A Parnellite at Parnell's Funeral"':

The influence of the French Revolution woke the peasantry from the medieval sleep, gave them ideas of social justice and equality, but

[15] Harold Bloom, *Yeats* (New York: Oxford University Press, 1970), p. 429.
[16] W. B. Yeats, *Collected Plays* (London: Macmillan, 1963), p. 683.

prepared for a century disastrous to the national intellect. Instead of the Protestant Ascendency with its sense of responsibility, we had the Garrison, a political party of Protestant and Catholic landowners, merchants and officials. They loved the soil of Ireland; the returned Colonial Governor crossed the Channel to see the May flowers in his park, the merchant loved with an ardour, I have not met elsewhere, some sea-board town where he had made his money, or spent his youth, but they could give to a people they thought unfit for self-government, nothing but a condescending affection. They preferred frieze-coated humanists, dare-devils upon horseback, to ordinary men and women.[17]

Edmund Burke was our starting-point, and let us now briefly return to Burke. No passage from Yeats echoes the author of the *Reflections* more clearly than that quoted above; its rhythm integrates the particular and the abstract in a manner Burke would have approved. And the vocabulary of social distinction derives from Burke's writings on Irish history. Yet here we must scrutinize Yeats closely: the terms are Burkean but their meanings have undergone a process of interchange which acknowledges (at least) the intervening century. Ascendancy and Garrison are, then, terms common to Burke and Yeats. In his letter of 1792 to Sir Hercules Langrishe, Burke employs 'garrison' to describe the role of the Protestant settlers prior to the constitutional reform of 1782; Britain, he claims,

saw that the disposition of the *leading part* of the nation would not permit them to act any longer the part of a *garrison*. She saw that true policy did not require that they ever should have appeared in that character; or if it had done so formerly, the reasons had now ceased to operate. She saw that the Irish of her race were resolved to build their constitution and their politics upon another bottom.[18]

The garrison, for Burke was the means by which Ireland was held to the crown, before the reforms of 1782 granted a measure of equity in trade and liberty in law-making. At another level the garrison was the condition in which Ireland existed within the king's dominions.

---

[17] W. B. Yeats, *The Variorum Edition of the Poems*, edd. Peter Allt and Russell Alspach (New York: Macmillan, 1957), pp. 833–4.

[18] Edmund Burke, 'A Letter to Sir Hercules Langrishe', *Works* (London: Bohn, 1856), vol. iii, p. 322.

Burke's garrison resented their condition: Yeats's, however, clung to theirs as the only means by which they might
attach themselves to their lands. For Burke, garrison is
Ireland before 1782; for Yeats it is Ireland after 1800. But
if garrison is an older term than Yeats admitted, 'ascendancy'
has the more exciting history. Coined in the 1790s, it was for
Burke virtually the equivalent of junto or clique, and denomi-
nated the arrogant political undertakers of the College Green
parliament:

New *ascendancy* is the old mastership. It is neither more nor less than
the resolution of one set of people in Ireland to consider themselves as
the sole citizens in the commonwealth; and to keep a dominion over
the rest by reducing them to absolute slavery under a military power.[19]

For Burke, ascendancy is jobs, for Yeats responsibility.
    In the 'Commentary on "A Parnellite at Parnell's Funeral"'
Yeats is not writing history; so much is clear. He is perhaps
engaged with one more of those antinomies which run
through his imagination, wisdom against power, the wisdom
of the old 'national intellect' at war with the new power of
O'Connellite democracy. But the commentary, ostensibly
upon 'Parnell's Funeral', more explicitly is echoed in 'Purgatory' — 'the returned Colonial Governor [who] crossed
the Channel to see the May flowers in his park' becoming
'Some . . . came from London every spring/ To look at the
may-blossom in the park', while the Governor retains his
place in the play alongside magistrates, colonels, Members
of Parliament. The most zealous literary metaphysician,
whether sceptic or structuralist, could hardly deny the congruity of the two passages. And the tone of the commentary
is as evidently not commending as the Old Man's speech is
commending. Here we have congruity and contradiction at
once. It seems that if the speech is 'certainly Yeats's own
voice', we must find some higher authority for the prose
commentary, or — better still — find some larger notion of
the author's relationship with his drama.
    If we pass by 'the Protestant Ascendancy with its sense of
responsibility' we come to Yeats's garrison, the political

[19] Edmund Burke, 'Letter to Richard Burke', *Works,* vol. vi, p. 65.

party of landowners, merchants, and officials. The tone here
does not seem to hide any reserve of ambiguity. It is true that
there is an element of wistful regret that the Ascendancy
should have declined to such a condition; it is appreciated
also that, unable to offer more than condescending affection
to the population of Ireland, the merchants and governors
loved its soil. And yet having taken these subordinate issues
into account, we still find that Yeats sees these figures as
smaller imaginations, diminished presences.

This transvaluation, occurring between the commentary
and the play, is all the more remarkable when considered in
the light of their common source. In her journal on 3 June
1922 Lady Gregory had written: 'I have been out till after
9 o'c. Everything is beautiful, one must stand to look at
blossoming tree after tree; the thorns in the Park that W. used
to come over from London to see at this time of year best of
all'.[20] Yeats, who visited Coole two days later, saw and
remembered the entry. Donald Torchiana notes that Mrs
Yeats felt sure the poet thought such trips of Sir William
Gregory's all too typical of Garrison irresponsibility and
sentiment. The career of Sir William, some time governor of
Ceylon and MP for Galway, is also that of the succession of
proprietors invoked in 'Purgatory'; his father having been
permanent head of the Irish civil service in the 1820s, the
contribution of officials is accommodated also. Yet the
careers of these Gregorys lie exclusively within the nineteenth century, after the Union, after the Ascendancy had
given way to the Garrison. 'Purgatory' may well have been
written with Coole Park in mind, but Yeats did not entirely
transform his notion of Garrison irresponsibility into Ascendancy celebration. The text, approached carefully, can reveal
its own mordant perspective upon the Great House.

Let us look closely at the play, in particular its recital of
previous proprietors in the Great House — 'magistrates,
colonels, members of Parliament,/Captains and Governors'.
Does Yeats have in mind here the Resident Magistrate of
Somerville and Ross's stories, the well-meaning and vaguely

[20] Augusta, Lady Gregory, *Journals*, ed. D. J. Murphy, vol. i (Gerrards Cross: Smythe, 1978), p. 362.

ON 'PURGATORY' 383

comprehending Major Yeates? Almost certainly not. And yet the R.M. stories can serve to remind us that the magistracy was an institution of less than absolute dignity. Until the Whig reforms of the 1830s, it carried no salary, and its patronage was restricted to the resident gentlemen of a county. Through them, rights of property and a simplified jurisprudence were administered to the tenantry. Magistrates were not necessarily men of great substance, intellect or learning; William Le Fanu recalled a 'stirring' magistrate of the 1820s whose utter devotion to authority and partial grasp of literacy led him to begin all his reports 'Dear Government . . .'. With the introduction of a stipendiary magistracy, the social base of the office was broadened and a less thoroughly Williamite interpretation of law admitted. Needless to say, the Garrison resented this development.

And so to the colonels. Defined by the dictionary as the superior officer of a regiment, the colonel was traditionally a man most immediately regarded as a soldier's leader, generals being unconnected to any one regiment. However, in the large number of civilians who retained the rank as an honorific, many were not the retired commanders of regular army regiments, but of county militias or yeomanry corps. Colonel Henry Bruen, the long serving MP for Carlow in the first half of the nineteenth century, was of this latter kind. Colonels, then, may be either the heroes of foreign battlefields or takers of the salute at local coat-trailing reviews.

This disrespectful analysis should be kept in perspective. It is not to the point to prove that Yeats's pantheon consisted simply of well-dressed rogues or impostors. What is significant, however, is that the magistrates and colonels are not necessarily 'great people' in any open, social sense. Being succeeded by

> Some that had gone on Government work
> To London or to India came home to die
> Or came from London every spring
> To look at the may-blossom in the park . . .[21]

they are not excluded from Yeats's prosaic contempt for Garrison sentiment. Loving the land and condescending to

[21] W. B. Yeats, *Collected Plays*, p. 683.

the tenantry, nineteenth-century estate owners enacted in
their emotions the precarious social relationships underlying
property. Latter-day absentees, they were too marginally in
possession to risk the open ridicule of Ireland which had
characterized Maria Edgeworth's Clonbronys. In so far as
'Purgatory' is amenable to historical analysis — and we are
certainly not restricted to such an approach — it reveals
evidence of specifically *nineteenth-century* social patterns.
Because Yeats has elsewhere spoken warmly of the eighteenth century, and because the Old Man of the play is taken
literally as Yeats's oracle, the lines above are read as an
objective (and yet Yeatsian!) eulogy of the 'one Irish century
that escaped from darkness and confusion'. Indeed darkness
and confusion is the condition of 'Purgatory' as understood
by the Old Man.

3.   METALANGUAGE, METADRAMA

If we turn for a moment to the structure of the play, some
illustration of the nature of its modernist anxiety may
emerge. I have said that, formally, the play employs Platonic
and Swedenborgian concepts of 'dreaming back' or phantasmagoria to describe the experience of the dead. But 'Purgatory', far from serving to make accessible some 'radical
innocence', actually reveals ineradicable guilt; there can be
no end to the consequence upon themselves of the Bride and
Groom's *mésalliance*. This late admission of Yeats's is central
to the problematic nature of modernism with its enthusiasm
for the self-delighting integrity of the literary text. However,
aspirations to Renaissance completeness — the same enthusiasm in thematic guise — may be the best evidence of its
unavailability. 'Purgatory' abandons such assumptions of
integrity and self-completeness in the final lines where Plato
and Swedenborg are cast aside:

> O God,
> Release my mother's soul from its dream!
> Mankind can do no more. Appease
> The misery of the living and the remorse of the dead.[22]

----

[22]   Ibid., p. 689.

The appeal to God is neither Yeats's acceptance of theism nor the character's surrender to established values. In these last lines 'Purgatory' is forced to appeal beyond itself for some order which will bring to an end, to completion, its intolerable self-generation. The modernist aesthetic finally reaches out in supplication from the isolation of the work of art to a world it had thought to apply itself to. The God of 'Purgatory' is blatantly not that of the churches, though it may have some affinity to Blake's divinity. Maybe the appeal is directed to *us*, the audience to whom Prospero needs appeal at the conclusion of 'The Tempest' for release and meaning, the audience to whom Timon bequeathed his own wild and contradictory epitaphs. Such a self-consciously metadramatic device is in keeping with much of the play's structure.

To suggest that the dominant metaphor of a work turns in upon itself may be to do nothing more than point to a pervasive irony. And irony is no exclusive property of modernism. But the particular manner in which 'Purgatory' implodes is not simply ironic: it employs devices closely identified with modernist technique — metalinguistic and metadramatic reference. To take metalinguistics first, we can begin by noting how the play draws attention to the verbal nature of its settings, implied and explicit. The Old Man's speech gradually transforms the House into a human metaphor:

> . . . he killed the house; to kill a house
> Where great men grew up, married, died,
> I here declare a capital offence.[23]

This speech is the culminating focus of a movement away from larger perspectives (the theory of phantasmagoria, the social background of Bride and Groom), and the ruined house is directly available to the audience as man's condition. However, within the speech, a further interiorization is already at work. 'All / The intricate passages of the house' refers immediately to the complex architecture of the building *known from within*; it also posits a metaphorical

---

[23] Ibid., p. 683.

interpretation according to which the house is a difficult text, its intricate passages obscure to our understanding. This metaphor is supported throughout the play not only by the Old Man's initial command 'Study that house, / I think about its jokes and stories . . .' but also by the recurring references to his own incomplete education, his own limited ability to decipher what is before him. As the one who burnt the house he is the 'author' of its ruined condition. We call this de-lineation of the house metalinguistic because, within the verbal ordering of the play, it is further identified with other verbal constructs — 'what the butler said', and

> old books and books made fine
> By eighteenth-century French binding, books
> Modern and ancient, books by the ton.[24]

This metalinguistic aspect of the play is — most people will agree — unobtrusive. It is part of the deception to which Harold Bloom ascribes the play's success. Certainly 'Purga-tory's' concentrated unity is in part due to the manner in which the setting and the text act mutually as tenor and vehicle one for the other. Yet this unity is also a form of radical division, for being so hermetically complete the play distinguishes itself drastically from all that it is not. As the Old Man creates the Great House by his speech, the play presents him as achieving Coriolanus' vain wish that a man be author of himself. Yet the House and the Tree stand radically apart from him and apart from each other. These, the primary elements of the setting, are at one and the same time static and mutually repelling. This congruence of unity and disunity can be traced in the texture of the play's style. A passage such as

> It's louder now because he rides
> Upon a gravelled avenue
> All grass to-day.[25]

achieves its effect of drawing past and present, event and re-enactment, into a single image by the elision of the con-nective — 'a gravelled avenue [that is] all grass to-day'.

---

[24] Ibid., p. 684.
[25] Ibid., p. 685.

Placing the two nouns together Yeats suggests their identity, and it would seem that style and content are at one. However, the conclusion of the play will reveal that this effect is appearance merely, and so we notice in addition that, though the two nouns are indeed brought together, they are held in tension, held reservedly apart by the line division:

> Upon a gravelled avenue
> All grass to-day.

A refined tense exploitation of line-division indicates the poetic (as distinct from dramatic) text, and the use with it of what amounts to a dual syntax recurs in 'Purgatory'; a further striking example is the elision of 'should' from the lines

> And if he [should] touch he must beget
> And you must bear his murderer . . .[26]

to create the *appearance* of a present tense in 'touch'. The corollary applies a few lines later:

> If I should throw
> A stick or a stone they would not hear . . .[27]

where the 'should' draws attention specifically to the subordinate role which the Old Man believes himself to have in the drama he is watching.

If, instead of looking within the Old Man's speeches, we look at the relationship between them and the Boy's contribution to the dialogue a very different aspect of 'Purgatory' comes to light. On several occasions early in the play, the Old Man continues his exposition across the interjection of the Boy's lines, as if the Boy did not exist. For example,

> Old Man The souls in Purgatory that come back
>   To habitations and familiar spots.
> Boy   Your wits are out again.
> Old Man   Re-live
>   Their transgressions, and that not once
>   But many times . . .[28]

[26] Ibid., p. 686.
[27] Ibid.
[28] Ibid., p. 682.

Here, the commencement of the Old Man's second speech
with a finite verb draws attention to the first and its grammatical incompleteness as a sentence. And yet the maintenance of a poetic line (rhythmically thus, 'Your wits are out
again. Re-live') makes a formal acknowledgement of the
Boy's perspective. We find a dichotomy between speech and
action which is gradually both exposed and resolved by the
murder of the Boy. Yet the killing only achieves a state of
affairs which, in one stylistic respect, the Old Man had
initially assumed. The circularity of 'Purgatory' is evident
in its minutest stylistic details.

These features of the play take on a greater significance
if we move on to its metadramatic dimensions. Just as the
Old Man creates the setting by establishing its verbal nature,
so he is involved in establishing the original sin of social
mésalliance as a drama whose performance he now perforce
witnesses:

> He has gone to the other side of the house,
> Gone to the stable, put the horse up.
> She has gone down to open the door.
> This night she is no better than her man
> And does not mind that he is half drunk,
> She is mad about him. They mount the stairs.
> She brings him into her own chamber.
> And that is the marriage-chamber now.
> The window is dimly lit again.

And later

> The window is lit up because my father
> Has come to find a glass for his whiskey.
> He leans there like some tired beast.[29]

For us, the Old Man makes accessible areas we cannot see; or,
if we see certain scenes we cannot, without his commentary,
interpret them. There are two levels of this original drama, or
drama of origins. First, there is the historical marriage and
mating of Bride and Groom, which reaches us through the
Old Man's exposition. Second, there is the re-enactment in
the soul of the Bride of her offence as she 'dreams back'

[29] Ibid., pp. 685–7.

through the events of her life in search of peace or 'radical innocence'; this reaches us by virtue of the Old Man's attendance as audience. By such elision of verbs as we have noted, the play places these two levels side by side: the Old Man watches *at once* the bridal night, his own conception, and the endless repetition of these offences in the dreaming back. The result is of course that he is more than the audience at the drama, he is an absent character in it:

> Go fetch Tertullian: he and I
> Will ravel all that problem out
> Whilst those two lie upon the mattress
> Begetting me.[30]

The Old Man exists in a multiple dramatic relation. He is a character in the play we are watching; he is audience to Bride and Groom in their re-enactment, and he is also a character in the original drama. But further, he is the dramatizer of these *ur*-events; it is he who renders them drama by transmitting them to us in speech synchronized to their performance. He is, on this level, both dramatist and audience. His attendance before the Great House and the Tree is not accidental, but part of the script to which he repeatedly draws our attention, the House as 'intricate passages', as 'Purgatory'.

4.   THE FASCIST CHARGE

> *The stage shows the middle of a room.*
> *A great ash-tree thrusts its branches*
> *through the roof. Downstage right is*
> *the hearth with, behind it, a store room.*
> *Back centre the great entrance door . . .*

This is not the set for some avant-garde production of 'Purgatory' in which the familiar elements of the play's sparse design have been juggled about to achieve exciting notices in the theatrical press. It is the opening scene of *Die Walküre*, the second opera of Richard Wagner's mythological cycle *Der*

---

[30]   Ibid., p. 686.

Ring des Nibelungen. The elements are indeed similar —
house and tree are crucial in each scene. But Wagner's tree
merges with the roof, and its trunk is in effect the pillar upon
which the house rests. Yeats, in stark contrast, separates the
two elements, and places his characters between, as it were,
the polar antagonism of Nature and Artefact.

I invoke Wagner because the issue of Yeats's compact with
fascism should be kept in perspective. As early as 1898 Shaw
had elaborated an anti-capitalist interpretation of *The Ring*
which, if it does nothing else, demonstrates the common
idiom of German romanticism in Marx and Wagner.[31] And it
was Nietzsche, arch-romantic and bitter opponent of German
militarism, who recognized Wagner as the author of the origin
myths at the heart of the Second and (later) the Third Reich.
These German allusions are not exotic: the movement in
European culture which gives meaning to Gaelic revivalism,
to the Victorian Irish gentry's interest in philology, *is*
German romanticism. (Synge's predecessors include Zeuss
and Windisch as well as O'Grady and O'Donovan.) We are
mistaken if we accept nineteenth-century notions of history
as biological science, and, as a consequence, literature as un-
reflective truth: this way lies the *Volk* and the burning of
Ulysses. If interpretation is truly a critical relation between
text and reader, we should acknowledge that, just as the
text is a specific form of a social production (language), so
the reader is a particular member and expression of a known
culture. In the case of 'Purgatory' our reappraisal of the
play's historical nature is not some positivistic rebuke to
Yeats. Far more important than any adjustments of our
estimate of the poet as historian is a revitalized consciousness
of our own historical predicament. The nadir of the Anglo-
Irish élite in the Irish Free State found many expressions, the
burnt-out house being the most celebrated. In that period it
was appropriate to see 'Purgatory' in terms of that élite's
eighteenth-century heyday. In critical terms the play was
read as a neo-classical elegy for neo-classicism. The philistine
Victorian bourgeoisie excoriated by Yeats in his early

---

[31] See G. B. Shaw, *The Perfect Wagnerite: A Commentary on the Ring of the
Nibelings* (London, 1898).

journalism was, by its own aesthetic, entitled to think of its past as aristocratic, noble, proud. But this should be distinguished from the habit of some present-day commentators of seeing pre-independent Ireland as the playground of belted earls and 'droit de seigneur'. The need of senescent nationalism to conjure up an aristocratic past is rooted in its own bourgeois condition, a condition it shares with its alleged historical foe. 'Purgatory' therefore is now the focus of a critique directed at the romantic reading of history. Modernism as the culmination of romantic philosophy is its proper context.

In conclusion, some examination of key structures in 'Purgatory' may take place in the arena between philosophy and literary technique. 'Dreaming back', the phantasmagoria of Plato and Swedenborg, is symbolically integrated in the play because it is Yeats's account of history. While the surface of 'Purgatory' emphasizes causality almost to the point of obsession, the result is not an unambiguous view of history as process: the metadramatic complexity of the Old Man ensures that the successive events of history are also accessible simultaneously, as events that lie side by side, complements one of another. In this view of history we find an idealism fraught with solipsistic anxiety; in this simultaneity we find a preference for synchronic order at the expense of diachronic logic. The Old Man of the play (not unlike figures in Tennyson's dramatic monologues) is poised tensely upon a penultimate moment. The play is eschatological in that it attends to 'the last things', but its attendance can never quite be transformed into presence, because in the presence of those last things, speech, especially dramatic speech, is inconceivable. The Old Man approaches the condition of Cuchulain, but if tragedy is a joy to the dying hero, there is neither joy nor death. In so far as he articulates a cynical acceptance of his doom the Old Man retains a vestigial heroism; however, if we permit ourselves to anticipate 'The Death of Cuchulain' we are made aware of the drastic distinction between Hero and Old Man which Yeats resorts to; in his last play, the complexities of the Old Man's role, as director of the play he announces, amount to formal cynicism. The Yeatsian hero is finally permitted to die, but the price paid is acknowledged in terms of the text's cynical rejection of its own form.

T. R. Henn has complained, mildly enough, that 'Purgatory' suffers perhaps 'from the disadvantage that we must accept Yeats's theory that past actions are re-created by the dead in time'.[32] But the phantasmagoria is more closely associated with Yeats's idealistic notion of history than this would suggest. Furthermore, the doctrine of purgatory is no theological *donnée* upon which the playwright may perform strictly limited variations. The soul in purgatorial fire experiences precisely the same frustration as the hero to whom death is elusive: both possess consciousness without vision, both must recoil from that which is longed for. If one were to translate this terminology into secular or classical allusion, one would see Yeats as concerned essentially with the *daemonic*. Romantic literature, Shelley as much as Goethe, has seen in the mediate condition of the daemon an image of the artist's attempt to transform material into method, and method into action.

Yeats's place in that tradition has long been recognized. Yet if we look more locally at the materials of his work as poet and playwright, we will find in the history of the Victorian Anglo-Irish élite a daemonic reading of their experience which is relevant to all those sources of 'Purgatory' we have examined. Before he discovered the method of art to be virtually the nature of language itself, J. M. Synge struggled to express this history in a play which he called 'When the Moon Has Set'. Like the temporal dimension of 'Purgatory', the title of Synge's play acknowledges two potential movements neither of which is endorsed: neither greater darkness nor greater light. In one version of the play, Synge's *alter ego* comments: 'I suppose it is a good thing that this aristocracy is dying out. They were neither human nor divine.'[33] It is a strictly inartistic line. Nevertheless it concentrates a historical reality with which Yeats had to struggle over many years. Only in 'Purgatory' did he exploit the daemonic as a metaphor for the distinctive sociology from

---

[32] T. R. Henn, *The Harvest of Tragedy* (London: Methuen, 1956), p. 209.

[33] J. M. Synge, *Collected Works*, vol. iii, *Plays* (II) (London: Oxford University Press, 1968), p. 162.

which his work rose in an act of self-identification and reflection.

If, then, we distinguish sharply between Yeats's attention to the decline of Ireland's landed gentry and Wagner's role as celebrant of Teutonic assertiveness, may the accusation of fascism brought against the poet be at last dismissed? Certainly, since Conor Cruise O'Brien published his essay 'Passion and Cunning' in 1965, no account of Yeats's ideas has been able to avoid the topic.[34] Unlike his friend Ezra Pound, Yeats's association with fascism was exclusively located in the pre-war period, and no spectacular trial or incarceration concentrates the issues for us. An interest in Yeats's fascism, one might say, has its own historical locus and is not unrelated to the altering politics of Ireland from the mid-sixties onwards. The trouble has been that most accounts rely almost exclusively on Yeats's utterances about Mussolini, 'modern heterogeneity', and so on, without reference to questions of history and form. Yet history and form cannot be ignored as we turn to look at his own reported commentary on 'Purgatory'.

The play was first performed at the Abbey Theatre on 10 August 1938 in the course of a Festival during which the directors of the theatre, speaking through Lennox Robinson, were anxious to stress the Abbey's *national* status and *national* preoccupations. Yeats participated in a discussion of his new play, and his comments to an interviewer were published in the *Irish Independent* of 13 August. Donald Torchiana has very valuably drawn attention to the importance of these comments for an interpretation of the play, though his re-publishing of the heart of the interview has not led many others to take it into consideration in assessing Yeats's politics. As reported by the paper Yeats declared:

There is no allegory in 'Purgatory', nor, so far as I can remember, in anything I have written . . . William Blake said that allegory is made, not by inspiration, but by the daughters of memory. I agree, and have avoided it.

---

[34] Conor Cruise O'Brien, 'Passion and Cunning: An Essay on the Politics of W. B. Yeats', *In Excited Reverie*, edd. A. Norman Jeffares and K. G. W. Cross (London: Macmillan, 1965), p. 278 n.

Symbolism is another matter. There is symbolism in every work of art. A work of art moves us because it expresses or symbolizes something in ourselves or in the general life of men.

Father Connolly said that my plot is perfectly clear but that he does not understand my meaning. My plot is my meaning. I think the dead suffer remorse and re-create their old lives just as I have described. There are mediaeval Japanese plays about it, and much in the folklore of all countries.

In my play, a spirit suffers because of its share, when alive, in the destruction of an honoured house; that destruction is taking place all over Ireland today. Sometimes it is the result of poverty, but more often because a new individualistic generation has lost interest in the ancient sanctities.

I know of old houses, old pictures, old furniture that have been sold without apparent regret. In some few cases a house has been destroyed by a mésalliance. I have founded my play on this exceptional case, partly because of my interest in certain problems of eugenics, partly because it enables me to depict more vividly than would otherwise be possible the tragedy of the house.

In Germany there is special legislation to enable old families to go on living where their fathers lived. The problem is not Irish, but European, though it is perhaps more acute here than elsewhere.[35]

Yeats postulates three means by which houses have been destroyed. The first of these is poverty, upon which he has nothing further to say, not even to the effect that this poverty must inevitably have constituted a reverse of fortune in a family possessing such a house. The second, perhaps incorporating the first, is public sale, or sale at least conducted without apparent regret or reservation. 'Old' is now repeatedly emphasized as if to achieve an antiquity which is otherwise unreliable. When we recall the uncertain scale of the Irish 'Big House', the recent emergence of 'the Protestant Ascendancy', and the essentially Victorian sub-text of allusion in the play, this emphasis is noteworthy. It may be that Yeats had in mind the destruction of Coole Park after Lady Gregory's death: if this was so, then the house's origins

---

[35] Torchiana, op. cit., pp. 357–8, was the first to publish this material, which is also included in A. Norman Jeffares and A. S. Knowland, *A Commentary on the Collected Plays of W. B. Yeats* (London: Macmillan, 1975), p. 275. For the original interview and some related material see *Irish Independent*, 13 August 1938, p. 9.

in mercantile profits from the East India Company should be noted also. But if sale — whether reluctant or otherwise — unquestionably results in destruction of the house — whether old or not so old — we should note Yeats's assumption that the house and the family are virtually identical, are metaphor one of the other. The transmission of the house by sale, even if it is to another family or another owner, does not count. This assumption is all the more significant when we come to the third means of destruction — *mésalliance* — for the second has already been infused with the notion of house and family as one flesh, as sacramentally a blessed union. It is not enough to say, as Dr Cullingford proposes as a general thesis, that in such matters Yeats follows Burke rather than Mussolini or Hitler — between 1791 and 1938 the whole ideology of a bonding between blood and place (*Lebensraum*) had taken on different overtones.[36] *Mésalliance* is a prejudicial term which fails to announce precisely what it is prejudiced against — class inferiority, 'racial' difference, sectarian difference. To see that the term has ambiguous force even today in Irish affairs one has only to consult Brian Friel's significantly titled play, *Translations*:

Do you know the Greek word *endogamein*? It means to marry within the tribe. And the word *exogamein* means to marry outside the tribe. And you don't cross those borders casually — both sides get very angry. Now, the problem is this: Is Athene sufficiently mortal or am I sufficiently godlike for the marriage to be acceptable to her people and to my people?[37]

To a degree which he has perhaps not recognized the speaker is an endogamist, and the entire cultural tension between Synge's 'When the Moon Has Set' and Yeats's 'Purgatory' is the tension between an exposition of exogamy within a sectarian culture and a dramatization of the consequences of such exogamy in a setting which has masked its sectarian ideology.

Mésalliance is a prejudicial term then, and no universal equation of *mésalliance* and destruction can stand without

---

[36] Elizabeth Cullingford, *Yeats, Ireland, and Fascism* (London: Macmillan, 1981), p. 154 *et passim*.
[37] Brian Friel, *Translations* (London: Faber, 1981), p. 68.

the vigorous implementation of that prejudicial element. In the play the *mésalliance* is ostensibly one of class, allied to moral habits (drunkenness etc.) not unknown among all classes. But in the draft of the play, sectarian *mésalliance* had been admitted: vestigially it survives in the Old Man's reference to learning Latin from the Catholic curate. The suppression of that sectarian reference leads in the *Irish Independent* commentary to Yeats's decision to found his play on the exceptional case, partly because of his interest in eugenics. The biological concept of race, of selective breeding, replaces that of sectarianism, while at the same time retaining a strong element of class-hatred. The *mésalliance* of 'Purgatory' can never be specified purely in terms of race or class, because the repressed ideology of sectarianism vitiates these alternatives. And if the parentage of the Boy accidentally recalls the parentage attributed to John Giffard, the Dog-in-Office, then we can posit Protestant Ascendancy as an absent meaning of 'Purgatory', and acknowledge too that nothing is accidental in Yeats's philosophy of history. Yeats's own marriage to an Englishwoman provided him with the material for a passionate concentration on his own alienation from the Irish linguistic past.

Elizabeth Cullingford finds Yeats not guilty of fascism, but her neglect of all discussion of what fascism is and was renders the acquittal doubtful. Grattan Freyer disagrees and significantly describes Yeats's political place in 'the anti-democratic *tradition*'.[38] Both Cullingford and Freyer are silent on 'Purgatory' and ignore the *Irish Independent* interview which Torchiana had made available fifteen years earlier. The essays in *On the Boiler* which were excluded from *Explorations* when Mrs Yeats was overseeing the publication of an interim collected works certainly provide additional evidence of Yeats's strongly authoritarian opinions — and 'Purgatory' was first published in *On the Boiler*.[39] There

[38] Grattan Freyer, *W. B. Yeats and the Anti-Democratic Tradition* (Dublin; Gill and Macmillan 1981). The other notable contribution to the debate was Patrick Cosgrove's reply to Conor Cruise O'Brien, 'Yeats, Fascism, and Conor O'Brien', *London Magazine*, July 1967.

[39] Torchiana discusses the place of 'Purgatory' in the context of *On the Boiler*, op. cit., pp. 344–52.

is, however, a far more accessible statement of Yeats's
political position in the late 1930s, in the final paragraph of
'A General Introduction for my Work':

When I stand upon O'Connell Bridge in the half-light and notice that
discordant architecture, all those electric signs, where modern heterogeneity has taken physical form, a vague hatred comes upon out of my
own dark and I am certain that wherever in Europe there are minds
strong enough to lead others the same vague hatred rises. In four or five
or in less generations this hatred will have issued in violence and
imposed some kind of rule of kindred. I cannot know the nature of
that rule, for its opposite fills the light; all I can do to bring it nearer
is to intensify my hatred.[40]

The passage deserves comparison to the interview: in both
Yeats shifts his ground. To the *Irish Independent*, he said
that 'the problem is not Irish, but European, though it is
perhaps more acute here than elsewhere.'[41] In the introduction, he identifies his hatred with that of European strong
minds whose ultimate rule he cannot know because its
opposite now fills the light, or half-light, in Ireland, now. If
Yeats approved fascism because he disliked de Valera, fascism
is not thereby abated in its 'vague hatred'. But it is pointless
to seek explicit endorsements of Mussolini or the Nazis in
the manner of Ezra Pound: Yeats's involvement in fascism is
a projection of certain latent developments in his inheritance
of Protestant Ascendancy, a projection which is necessarily
distorted and contradictory, but also for those reasons, valid.
That is, his political judgements contain a revelation of the
objective of their subject, even at the expense of consistency.
This is not to say that Protestant Ascendancy was proto-
fascist, but rather to identify the manner in which Yeats
imaginatively enacts the connections and disconnections between that Irish ideology within the United Kingdom and
the broader European movement of fascism.

The shifts of ground are therefore symptomatic. We
concentrate on style here for a variety of reasons. (It is
13 August 1938, Germany mobilized for the invasion of

[40] Edward Callan, ed., *Yeats on Yeats: The Last Introductions and the
"Dublin" Edition* (Mountrath: Dolmen Press, 1981), pp. 72-3.
[41] *Irish Independent*, 13 August 1938, p. 9; see n. 35, above.

Czechoslovakia on 12 August, Yeats is interested in eugenics
and Nazi legislation.) We have found a revealing intimacy between style and substance in Yeats, even when that intimacy
was violent. The sentence concerning old families in Germany
certainly approved the Nazi attitude to inheritance and blood
continuity in the sense that it proves its presence in Yeats's
mind. And a great deal of Yeats went further than such strict
approving. Yet the style of the sentence is helpful: 'to go on
living' is one of those club-footed phrases we find in Yeats
when he is shuffling round uncertain topics. The Yeatsian
'ancient sanctitites' cannot be legislated into the future,
nor can Cuchulain be 'enabled' to survive. This rhythmical
betrayal of the cause is not to be taken as the poet's innocence, evidence that he never really knew what he was doing
in his fascism. On the contrary it is proof of his perception
of the spurious nature of fascist aristocracy, Hitlerian authority. Thus, it is not enough to say that he saw through
fascism: there is the permanent suspicion that he would have
been prepared to see it through, had he lived. His point of
perspective, however, was O'Connell Bridge, rather than
the bridge of sighs.

The editor of 'A General Introduction' annotates the final
paragraph with a quotation from the 1930 'Pages from a
Diary' — 'tradition is kindred.'[42] The modernist valorization
of tradition is part and parcel of the susceptibility to extreme
right-wing politics which affected Yeats, Eliot, and Pound. As
a barrier between history and the Now, tradition facilitated
the rewriting of literature in terms of order and the transmission of power. In 'Pages from a Diary' the guts of the
matter are displayed without affectation; that preference
of genealogy over historical genesis, of biology and over-
determined blood-relationship over social dynamics, is one
statement of the fascist longing to resolve all contradictions
in a single conflagration. The intellectual sources of Yeats's
fascist loyalties may be various, but the ideology of Protestant Ascendancy anticipated in certain restricted circumstances several of these preferences.

The noble past invoked in 'Purgatory' is revealed by the

---

[42] Callan, ed., *Yeats on Yeats*, p. 73.

play to be in part bogus. The manner in which sources for the play may be traced in Yeats's prose allows the reader to document the poet's stylistic transformation of an unclear Irish bourgeois history into the permanence of aristocratic value. Yet the play insists on permanence as process, process as permanence, and it sends its audience once more in quest of release to history — the text's dramatic context, its theatrical occasion (together with the internal emphasis on metadrama), is in this respect crucial in liberating 'Purgatory' from the charge of aesthetizing ritual murder. That Yeats's prose, drama, and poetry incorporate such evidence is a mark of his artistic greatness, of his integrity. No one who has ignored the authentic dramatization of his inauthentic tradition in 'Purgatory' may easily point the finger at Yeats as fascist. Just as Joyce's therapeutic fictions establish him as a critical modernist, in that his work contains a critique of modernist aesthetics, so we may say of Yeats's political dramas that they constitute a critical fascism. Beyond that, of course, it is necessary to add that the active reader's reception contributes to and modifies and (potentially) transforms any such essentialist definition of the work's meaning.

POSTSCRIPT

> The artist takes sides so little that he
> sides with the lies of tradition against
> the truth of deceit.
>
> (Karl Kraus)[1]

Ascendancy and Tradition was written over a period of more
than six years, in changing circumstances personal, intellectual, and political. For the most part, it consists of detailed
and extensive critiques of central texts and concepts in Anglo-
Irish literature. The broader implications for the study of
Anglo-Irish relations in economic, social, and political terms
cannot be dealt with here. Nevertheless, it might now be acknowledged that culture (and literature, specifically) can no
longer be regarded as an innocent party to the age-old — and
the present — disputes. 'There is no document of civilization
which is not at the same time a document of barbarism' —
Walter Benjamin's dictum, hitherto read all but exclusively in
continental terms, might be taken to heart in Britain and
Ireland.[2]

It should not be assumed that the author has gone over
to the view that all literature is ideology and no more. He
believes that the foregoing pages exonerate him from any
such charge of fundamentalism. Nevertheless, he sees the
position of the artist well emblemized in the following
passage from Thomas Mann's *Doktor Faustus*:

The impression was painful and, intentional or not, it wounded. But I
quickly forgave him as he went on, and I heard the moving musical
diction given to the parable in the *Purgatorio* of the man who carries

---

[1] Karl Kraus, 'Nestroy und die Nachwelt' (May 1912), *Untergang der Welt
durch schwarze Magie*, ed. H. Fischer (Munich, 1960), p. 238; quoted in translation by C. E. Williams, *The Broken Eagle: The Politics of Austrian Literature
from Empire to Anschluss* (New York: Barnes and Noble, 1974), p. 193.

[2] Walter Benjamin, 'Theses on the Philosophy of History', *Illuminations*, ed.
and intro. Hannah Arendt, trans. Harry Zohn ([n.p.]: Fontana/Collins, 1973),
p. 258.

a light on his back at night, which does not light him but lights up the path of those coming after.[3]

In the context of a tradition much indebted to German romanticism and shot through with the iron categories of Protestant Ascendancy and its resultant sociology, this image is apt. Only through such a critique of our culture can we hope to recognize Benjamin's 'revolutionary chance in the fight for the oppressed past'.[4]

[3] Thomas Mann, *Doctor Faustus*, trans. H. T. Lowe-Porter (Harmondsworth: Penguin, 1968), p. 158.
[4] Walter Benjamin, op. cit., p. 265.

APPENDICES

A. *Reflections* and the Politics of Editing

Note the role of the terms 'British Tradition' and 'French Enlightenment' in the fifteen innovatory chapter headings introduced by our
recent American editor:

1. The British Friends of the Revolution in France
2. The True Constitutional Principles of Kingship in Britain
3. The Errors of the French Revolution
4. The True Meaning of the Rights of Men — Dr. Price Answered
5. A Critical Analysis of the French Revolution
6. British Tradition versus French Enlightenment
7. The Church is One of the Foundations of the British Commonwealth
8. The Confiscatory Policy of the National Assembly
9. A Defense of the French Monarchy and Aristocracy
10. The Church in the New Order in France

Part Two

1. The National Assembly
2. The New Constitution of the Legislature
3. France Considered as a Confederacy, and the Common Interests of the Members
4. The Executive Power in the New Order
5. The Fiscal Policy

Although these are *not* Burke's subdivisions but have been 'inserted
in the text to facilitate classwork and reading assignments', we can
chart in the headings the accumulating attention to the existing regime
in France, its policy and structure. While the polemic is hostile to these
developments and arguments are deployed against them, the weight of
the narrative (thus summarized) increasingly falls on the actuality of
the Revolution. Moreover, this summary represents only one narrative
of the *Reflections*, and there are others which contribute further to
the richly contradictory meaning of the work.

B. 'The Dog-in-Office'

Information on Giffard — known in his time as 'the Dog in Office' — is
limited. He is believed to be the author of some doggerel, including a

piece called *The Orange*, and is the subject of several equally scurrilous pamphlet attacks. One of these, *The Life and Surprising Adventures of a Dog* (Anon. publ. in Dublin early in the 19th C.), provides him with a colourful biography in which some fact is probably admixed:

> The Dog, alias John Giffard, is the illegitimate son of a travelling tinker, who had our hero by a farmer's servant some time in the summer of 1741. The tinker's name was Foy, and our Dog was known in Wexford by the name of Johnny Foy, until it was determined by a loyal protestant gentleman to put Johnny into the yellow-legged College in Oxmantown (p. 10).

Prior to this advance, Foy attended a Catholic hedge school, from which the pamphleteer alleges he stole the bell used at the elevation at Mass. The occasion of the death of his mother may have prompted the transfer from one school (and denomination) to the other. She had a habit of stealing washing as she strolled; one day 'the old lady had fallen in with a few uninhabited shirts, trembling on a hawthorn', and in reaching for them had fallen also into a stream and drowned (p. 12).

R. R. Madden, in the second series of *The United Irishmen; their Lives and Times* (Dublin, 1858) devotes six pages (pp. 291–6) to Giffard and the *Dublin Journal*. He records Henry Grattan's extempore (!) reply to an insult received from Giffard's lips at a by-election in 1803:

> Mr. Sheriff, when I observe the quarter from whence the objection comes, I am not surprised at its being made. It proceeds from the hired traducer of his country, the excommunicated of his fellow-citizens, the regal rebel, the unpunished ruffian, the bigoted agitator. In the city a firebrand; the court a liar; in the street a bully; in the field a coward[.] And so obnoxious is he to the very party he wishes to espouse, that he is only supportable by doing these dirty acts the less vile refuse to execute (p. 293).

According to Sir Jonah Barrington (who was a candidate in the by-election) Giffard's reply was 'I would spit upon him in a desert.'

Giffard's promotion in society was effected through the strictly Protestant guild of apothecaries, which gave him access to a seat in the Corporation of Dublin. He enjoyed the protection of John Fitzgibbon, the Lord Chancellor, and was employed by Dublin Castle as an intermediary with Collins the spy inside the United Irishmen. Though it is probably pointless to seek for a single individual to whom the phrase 'Protestant Ascendancy' can be attributed, Giffard's claim is at least prima facie plausible. Frank MacDermott, in *Theobald Wolfe Tone and his Times* (1939), refers in passing to Giffard 'alleged to have been the inventor of the term Protestant Ascendancy' (Dublin: Anvil Press, 1980, p. 75) — his source is Jonah Barrington.

R. B. McDowell's 'Proceedings of the Dublin Society of United Irishmen', *Analecta Hibernica*, no. 17 (1949), pp. 1–143, consists of a series of letters from Thomas Collins, principally to Giffard. For Giffard's financial plight in 1795 see Edward Cooke to the Earl of Westmorland, 2 February 1795 (Westmorland Corresp., No. 120).

C.   Nugents and Edgeworths

The theme of the past as an ideology of survival is relevant not only in *Castle Rackrent* but also in *The Absentee* where the name Nugent is numinously employed. It may be helpful to extend briefly an account of Edgeworth vicissitudes in the seventeenth century.

In 1689 Sir John was dispossessed of his lands in Ireland as a Protestant proprietor, and outlawed and attainted by King James. While he was seeking redress in England, Lady Edgeworth was caught up in the manœuvres preliminary to the dynastic wars between James and William soon to be decided on Irish battlefields. She and her younger children were forced to become camp-followers of a Williamite platoon *en route* for Belmullet, where they were deserted by their protectors. Now prisoners of the Jacobites, the Edgeworths marched on foot towards Derry. *The Black Book* continues:

> A few miles from the besieged town they were deposited in the custody of a Mr. Nugent, who treated them with great humanity. There they remained till the raising of the siege, when they were set at liberty. They had, however, no home to go to. Sir John with Francis and Ambrose [his sons] was in England. Robert [another son] was a prisoner in Longford Gaol, having been arrested by Colonel Nugent of Coolamber, who was Governor of Longford in the interests of King James (pp. 26–7).

The Nugent who took Lady Edgeworth into custody was presumably one of the travelling party of Jacobites passing from the midlands towards Derry, and as such was very probably a neighbour in Longford. The colonel who imprisoned Robert was of course one of the family celebrated in O'Carolan's music.

Richard Edgeworth, son of the Francis who had been in England in 1689, was brought up virtually as an orphan, under the protection of a Pakenham relative. But when Pakenham died in 1719, the young man was friendless. In *The Black Book* he described how, after a period of despair, he at last 'thought of Mr. Walter Nugent of Carpenterstown in the County of West Meath, a gentleman of fortune and family, who had been bred an attorney'. The editors of *The Black Book* add to this tribute:

Mr. Nugent had been intimate with Mr. Pakenham and cheerfully accepted the position of guardian. Under his guidance and with the ready help of his Uncle Henry and his wife, and above all by his own indomitable energy and by the sound legal knowledge which he eventually acquired, Richard gradually set his tangled affairs in order, freed his estates of all encumbrances, recovered what had been lost through the malpractices of Robert and Ambrose [his uncles], paid off the debts of his father and grandfather (which amounted to more than £7,000) and settled down at Edgeworthstown in the house which he built for himself and which still stands as his memorial (pp. 64–5).

D.   Captain Rock in 1821

From a variety of sources it is possible to piece together the following summary of events:

Courtenay's agent, Edward Carte, resigned in 1818 when the fall in agricultural prosperity after the Napoleonic wars threatened a deterioration of conditions at Newcastle. His successor, Alexander Hoskins, was an Englishman unfamiliar with Irish customs and habits. He bought up the arrears of rent in the estate, that is, he paid a sum considerably lower than the actual arrears to the Trustees, and proceeded to levy the arrears with the current rent. He also refused a reduction of rents at a time when reductions were common. 'The discontents were fomented by persons of a much higher class, who being themselves in arrear, perhaps from bad management and extravagant housekeeping, were apprehensive of being called on peremptorily to discharge them [i.e. the arrears]' (*Quarterly Journal of Agriculture* 1838, pp. 390–411, 'On the Agriculture and General Condition of the County of Limerick'). An attack was made on the castle, a relatively small but ancient building on the edge of the town, but Hoskins repelled the assailants. However, they then intercepted his son, who was returning from a coursing expedition, and murdered him. (There is an alternative account which stresses a deliberate plan to ambush the boy who may have lured abroad for the purpose.) The date of the attack on Thomas Hoskins was 27 July 1821, and he died on 1 August. His father resigned on 10 October 1821. (*Begley Scrapbook*, in Limerick City Library.)

I am grateful to Arthur Harwood Grayson for information from local sources, and to the Librarian for permission to quote from the scrapbook. Quite apart from the nation-wide notoriety of Captain Rock, there was a particular reason why Sheridan Le Fanu was well informed of the Courtenay estate and its tribulations; when his father was appointed rector of Abington, Co. Limerick, in 1823, he employed as his agent Edward Dartnell, a clerk in the Courtenay agent's office.

E.   *Ulysses'* Halls and Windows

Though it is noted by Clive Hart and Leo Knuth (*Topographical Guide To James Joyce's* Ulysses, Colchester: A Wake Newslitter Press, 1975), to the best of my knowledge no one has previously commented critically on the displacement of the Merrion Hall by the Metropolitan Hall in this passage. Kenner (*Ulysses*, p. 65) introduces the notion of Clare Street's vanishing in the 1916 Rising, thus seeking to explain the absence of Bloom the dentist in 1922 when readers bought Joyce's novel. Thom's *Directory* indicates that there may have been two dental Blooms (father and son?) practising at No. 2 Clare Street between 1904 and 1916. In 1917, however, a surgeon dentist named Peter Dunne is listed at that address: thus, the dental windows survived the Rising though the inscription on the glass may well have been altered. Considered in terms of criticism rather than socio-biography, the allusion to 'Mr Bloom's dental windows' should be contrasted with 'Mr Lewis Werner's cheerful windows' 10 lines further up the page — the bearing of the adjective upon the noun being in the one case *literally* objective (Bloom's windows are dental because they say so) and in the other *reflectively* subjective (Werner's windows are cheerful because, for whatever reason, Leopold B. thinks they are so).

As to the Metropolitan Hall, which on the map is in Lower Abbey Street and not round the corner from Clare Street, it was in an area heavily damaged by shelling during the 1916 Rising. However, Thom's lists the building (Metropolitan Building) as standing in 1917 without any mention of damage; strangely, there is no entry in Thom's for it in 1922.

F.   Moore's *A Drama in Muslin* as a source for *Finnegans Wake*

I quote below from four consecutive paragraphs of George Moore, *A Drama in Muslin* (London: Walter Scott, 1886), pp. 158-9, to convey the texture of Moore's prose and its bearing upon this aspect of *Finnegans Wake*:

The weary, the woebegone, the threadbare streets — yes, threadbare conveys the moral idea of Dublin in 1882 . . . how infinitely pitiful.

Look at the houses! Like crones in borrowed bonnets some are fashionable with flowers in the rotting window frames.

We are in a land of echoes and shadows. Lying, mincing, grimacing . . . Catholic in name, they curse the Pope for not helping them in their affliction; moralists by tradition, they accept at their parties women who parade their lovers to the town from the top of a tram-car. In Dublin there is baptism in tea and communion in a cutlet.

We are in a land of echoes and shadows. Smirking, pretending, grimacing, the poor shades go by, waving a mock English banner over a waxwork show. . . . Shadows, echoes, and nothing more. See the girls! How their London fashions sit upon them.

There is no satisfactory account of Moore's work as a whole, but some aspects of the fiction set in Ireland are discussed in Robert Welch, ed., *The Way Back: George Moore's The Untilled Field & The Lake* (Gerrards Cross: Smythe, 1982).

G. W. B. Yeats, Lady Gregory, and Geoffrey Keating

In Lady Gregory's *Cuchulain of Muirthemne* — a primary source for Yeats's 'On Baile's Strand' — there is no evidence of totemism. Instead the names of Cuchulain and Conlaoch (the Young Man) indicate etymologically the bond between them, thus emphasizing the import-ance of the Young Man's oath to his mother that he would not reveal his name. It is significant therefore that Yeats, while introducing the totemic device, declines to name the Young Man. A three-stage comparison between Yeats, Gregory, and Geoffrey Keating (one of her sources) indicates further important discrepancies:

(a)   Keating has the Young Man's oath (that he shall not reveal his name, and that he shall visit his father in Ireland) as descend-ing from *geasa* imposed by Cuchulain through Aoife on their son. That is, the hero's inability to recognize his own son derives ironically from his own injunctions.

(b)   Lady Gregory emphasizes Aiofe's jealousy of Emer, Cuchulain's wife, as the motive which drives her to send their warrior son to confront Cuchulain. In this attempt at revenge she succeeds ironically in that, although Cuchulain survives her stratagem, he does so by slaying his own son.

(c)   It is in Yeats that the tensest variation upon the theme is enacted. Cuchulain is placed between obligation to Conchubar and affinity with the Young Man, while Aoife is relegated to the background. Though she is an absent character in the drama the totemic allusions powerfully intensify the Oedipal elements of the dramatized conflict.

See Augusta Gregory, *Cuchulain of Muirthemne: The Story of the Men of the Red Branch of Ulster Arranged and Put into English*, with a preface by W. B. Yeats (London: John Murray, 1902); and Seathrun Ceitinn, *Foras Feasa ar Eirinn* (The History of Ireland by Geoffrey Keating, ed. with trans. and notes by Patrick S. Dinneen), vol. ii (London: Irish Texts Society, 1908).

INDEX

An italic page reference indicates the inclusion of significant bibliographical information. Some variant spellings of place-names, etc., have been conflated in this index, and mnemonic citations of names such as Burke are selectively indexed.